A

TREATISE

ON THE

PRINCIPLES OF PLEADING,

IN CIVIL ACTIONS.

BY JAMES GOULD.

'It is one of the most honourable, laudable, and profitable (useful) things in our law, to have the science of well *Pleading*, in actions, real and personal.' *Littleton.*

Ordine placitandi servato, servatur et Jus. *Coke.*

'The *Law* itself *speaketh* by good *pleading*'—'as if pleading were the *living voice* of the Law itself.' *Ib.*

THE LAWBOOK EXCHANGE, LTD.
Union, New Jersey
2002

ISBN 1-58477-158-5

Second printing 2004

Printed in the United States of America on acid-free paper

THE LAWBOOK EXCHANGE, LTD.
33 Terminal Avenue
Clark, New Jersey 07066-1321

Please see our website for a selection of our other publications and fine facsimile reprints of classic works of legal history:
www.lawbookexchange.com

Library of Congress Cataloging-in-Publication Data

Gould, James, 1770-1838.
A treatise on the principles of pleading, in civil actions / by James Gould.
p. cm.
Originally published: Boston : Lilly and Wait, 1832.
Includes bibliographical references and index.
ISBN 1-58477-158-5 (alk. paper)
1. Pleading—United States. 2. Civil procedure—United States. I. Title.

KF8870 .G6 2001
347.73'72—dc21 00-059549

A

TREATISE

ON THE

PRINCIPLES OF PLEADING,

IN CIVIL ACTIONS.

BY JAMES GOULD.

'It is one of the most honourable, laudable, and profitable (useful) things in our law, to have the science of well *Pleading*, in actions, real and personal.' *Littleton.*

Ordine placitandi servato, servatur et Jus. *Coke.*

'The *Law* itself *speaketh* by good *pleading*'—'as if pleading were the *living voice* of the Law itself.' *Ib.*

BOSTON:
PUBLISHED BY LILLY AND WAIT.
1832.

TO THE

HON. ROGER MINOT SHERMAN, LL.D.

THE FOLLOWING TREATISE IS INSCRIBED,

AS A TESTIMONIAL OF THE GREAT RESPECT,

AND SINCERE AFFECTION,

OF HIS FRIEND AND BROTHER,

THE AUTHOR.

PREFACE.

It is probably known to most of those, into whose hands the following Treatise is most likely to fall, that I have, for many years, been employed in the instruction of Law-Students, by a course of Lectures, embracing all the principal titles of the common law. The work, here presented, contains, with some additions, the substance of my lectures on *Pleading*. This, and the several other titles, I have digested, upon one uniform plan, with a view, originally, to the possible future publication of some, or most of them. But the further prosecution of this purpose will probably depend, in a great measure, upon the degree of countenance, which may be shown, by the Profession, to the present publication. It may be proper, however, to suggest, in this connexion, that though my digests of all the other titles have been formed upon precisely the same *general plan*, as that of *pleading*; yet the latter far exceeds, in *length*, any of the others. No other single title, in the whole number, will probably extend to more than half the length of the present; and most of them will not occupy, singly, even one third of the space devoted to the present work.

The limits of the present Treatise have been thus extended, chiefly by the frequent and copious reasonings and illustrations, which have been deemed necessary to the elucidation and vindication of rules of pleading, and which that title more eminently requires, than almost any other in the law. To those of the Profession, who are already well versed in the science of pleading, many of these reasonings and illustrations may probably appear superfluous: But such are requested to consider, that the digest, from which the work, in its present form, has been prepared, was originally made for the instruction of *Students at Law*, to whose use the Treatise is meant to be especially adapted; and that the entire work is intended to be as *elementary*, as if it had been designed exclusively for that class of readers.

The title of *Pleading* has been selected for present publication, for several reasons, not necessary to be detailed; but principally, because it is deemed to be the most instructive, and therefore the most important *single* title in the law, and yet is less thoroughly understood, in general, than almost any other. The relative importance of *pleading*, among the several titles of the common law, has been fully attested, by the most distinguished and authoritative names, which adorn the list of common-law jurists. Lord *Coke*, in particular, among his other and frequent commendations of the science of pleading, has characterized it, as 'the *truest guide* to the knowledge of the common law'—as 'the KEY, that opens its inmost recesses, and an EXPOSITOR, that discloses and explains the most abstruse parts of it.' This pre-eminence it owes, not solely to the intrinsic value of its own exact and logical principles, but also, and in no small degree, to the fact, that the principles of pleading are necessarily and closely *interwoven*, both in theory and practice, *with those of every other title of the law.* I say, 'necessarily' interwoven, because even the most simple of the judicial remedies, which the law affords, and without which it would be, practically, a dead letter, cannot be obtained, without the aid of *pleading*. And it has been well remarked by an intelligent Judge, that if the practice of *special pleading* were entirely banished from courts of justice; the science of pleading would still be the most instructive branch of the common law.

The question will, however, naturally present itself — What can be the probable utility of a new original work on Pleading, while so many others, on the same subject, are already in the hands of the Profession? On this point I cannot, perhaps, better explain my own views, than by merely stating the OBJECT of the present Treatise, which — to express it in few words — is simply to render the doctrines of Pleading more *intelligible, and more easy of attainment*, than many have supposed them to be, by showing them to be *reasonable:* In other words, by exhibiting them, not as a compilation of *positive rules*; but as a system of *consistent and rational principles*, adapted, with the utmost precision, to the administration of justice, according to uniform rules, or, (which is the same thing), according to law. How far I may have advanced towards the attainment of this object, it is for others to decide. But I shall not, I trust, be deemed invidious or presumptuous, in venturing to remark, that most of our digests and treatises, on the title of pleading, are useful, rather as *manuals, or books of reference*, for the practitioner, than as works of *instruction in the science of pleading*. The same remark may, indeed, be extended to almost all our modern and most popular treatises, upon the various other titles of the common law. For while every other science is taught, by a detailed explication of its *principles*, the doctrines of the common law are usually exhibited, in our legal treatises, as if they were the insulated enactments of *positive* law — without reference to the *reasons* on which they rest. And thus the common law is presented, in most of our books, rather as an *art*, than a *science;* and the acquisition of it made to depend, more upon the mechanical strength of the reader's *memory*, than upon the exercise of his *understanding*. But it has been left on record, by the highest legal authority, that 'the law is unknown to him, who knoweth not the REASON thereof.' An axiom, which cannot fail to command the assent of every intelligent mind.

As the *English* system of pleading is, in general, the basis of that of our country; the former has, in the following Treatise, been followed exclusively, without regard to any peculiarities in the latter, excepting a very few references to those, which exist in the law of my native State.

Knowing well the fate, which usually and justly attends the *apologies* of authors, for the imperfections of their published works, I abstain from offering any, for those of the following Treatise. That it will be found, in many respects, imperfect, I have not the vanity to doubt. But with all its defects and errors — whatever they may be — I submit it to the judgment of the Profession.

JAMES GOULD.

LITCHFIELD, (CONN.) JAN. 1832.

CONTENTS.

ERRATUM.

The reader is requested to expunge the last sentence of note (14 *a*) on page 287., (as it does not express the author's meaning) and substitute the following —

Upon the same supposition, an allegation of *jurisdiction* in the inferior court would seem to make the plea effectual.

CHAPTER I.

OF PLEADING IN GENERAL.

CHAP. I.

Nature of Pleading.

SECTION 1. PLEADINGS are the mutual altercations of the parties to a suit, expressed in legal form, and in civil actions reduced to writing (*a*). In a more limited sense, however, 'the pleadings' (in the *plural*) comprehend only those allegations, or altercations, which are *subsequent* to the count, or declaration (*b*). In England, these altercations were anciently *oral;* having been offered, *vivâ voce*, by the respective parties or their counsel, in open court; as is still, generally done, in the pleadings on the part of the defendant, or prisoner in *criminal* prosecutions. And hence it is, that in the *Norman* language, in which most of the ancient books of the English law are written, the pleadings are frequently denominated the *parol* (*c*): Though for centuries past, all pleadings, in civil actions, have been required to be *written*. In some instances, however, the term *parol* is still used to denote the entire pleadings in a cause: As when in an action, brought against an *infant heir*, on an obligation of his ancestor's, he prays that the *parol may demur;*

(*a*) Com. Dig. *Pleader*, A. 3 Black. Com. 293.

(*b*) Com. Dig. *Pleader*, A. Reg. Pl. 2. 54. Lawes' Pl. 1.

(*c*) Ibid. Lawes' Pl. App. 80-4 Bac. Abr. *Amendment*, &c. A.

CHAP. I.

i. e. that the pleadings may be stayed, till he shall attain full age *(d)*.

Nature of Pleading.

§ 2. The mutual altercations, which constitute the pleadings in civil actions, consist of those formal allegations and denials, which are offered, on one side, for the purpose of maintaining the suit, and on the other, for the purpose of defeating it; and which, generally speaking, are predicated only of matters of *fact*.

§ 3. For pleading is, practically, nothing more than affirming or denying, in a formal and orderly manner, those *facts*, which constitute the ground of the plaintiff's demand, and of the defendant's defence *(e)*. Pleading, therefore, consists merely in alleging matter of *fact*, or in denying what is alleged as such by the adverse party.

§ 4. But in the theory, or *science* of pleading, the averment of facts, on either side, always presupposes some principle, or rule of *law*, applicable to the facts alleged; and which, when taken in connexion with those facts, is claimed, by the party pleading them, to operate in his own favour. For all rights of action, and all special defences, result from matter of fact and matter of law combined. And hence, in every declaration, and in all special pleading, some *legal* proposition (i. e. some proposition consisting of matter of *law*), though not in general *expressed* in

(d) 3 Black. Com. 300. 4 East, 485.

(e) Bac. Abr. *Pleas*, &c. *Introd.* 3 T. R. 159. Doug. 159.

CHAP. I.

Nature of Pleading.

terms, by the pleader, (because the court is supposed judicially to know it), is always, and necessarily, *implied*, or — to use the language of grammarians — *understood.*

§ 5. For it would be obviously to no purpose, for either party to state facts, of which no principle of *law* could be predicated in his favour. Indeed, all that a party submits to the *court*, by alleging facts, is their *legal* operation: And for the purpose of deciding what their operation in law is, the rule of law, in virtue of which the pleader claims the matter of fact alleged by himself, to be in his favour, must always be *tacitly supplied*, or understood.

Pleading, *a logical* process.

§ 6. By contemplating the subject in this point of view, we are enabled to apprehend the striking propriety and full import of Lord Mansfield's remark, that 'the substantial rules of pleading are founded in strong sense, and the soundest and closest *logic*' (*f*). For those rules, when considered in their proper connexions and dependencies, will be found to involve a connected, methodized body of PRINCIPLES, constituting a complete and coherent system of *legal logic:* A system, artificial indeed in its form and structure; but admirably adapted to the important ends of *simplicity, uniformity and certainty*, in the modes of administering justice.

§ 7. For the purpose of explaining and illustrating this view of the subject, we may observe, that

(*f*) 1 Burr. 319.

CHAP. I.

Nature of Pleading.

all pleading is essentially a *logical process.* And by analyzing a good declaration, or any good special pleading, if we take into view, with what is expressed, what is necessarily supposed or implied; we shall find in it the elements of a good *syllogism:* All good pleading being in substance a *syllogistic* process; though abridged in form, like some of the syllogisms of the schools: So that not only every good declaration, but all good special pleading on either side, in each successive stage of the pleadings, is essentially a good *syllogism.*

§ 8. Thus, in an action, brought for a trespass committed upon land, the declaration may be presented in the following form: 'Against him, who has forcibly entered upon my land, I have a right, by law, to recover damages: The defendant has forcibly entered upon my land: Therefore, against him I have a right, by law, to recover damages.' In the example here given, the first, or major proposition asserts the *legal* principle, on which the plaintiff founds his claim: The second, or minor, alleges the matter of *fact,* to which that principle is to be applied, in the particular case: The conclusion is the legal inference, resulting from the law and fact *together,* as they appear in the premises. And the judgment of the court, (if for the plaintiff), is a *re-affirmance of this conclusion* (g), together with an award, or sentence of *recovery* in pursuance of it.

(g) 3 Black. Com. 396.

CHAP. I.

Nature of Pleading.

§ 9. In the case now stated, the plaintiff's alleged right of recovery may be contested, by a denial of either of the three propositions, which constitute his declaration. And as the denial of either of them is, in effect, a complete denial of the plaintiff's whole claim, the defendant is not allowed, (by the rules of the common law,) to deny more than one of them. For if he can successfully deny any one of them; he will, by so doing, attain every object, which he could have proposed in denying them all.

§ 10. If, then, the defendant would deny the major, or first proposition above stated, which consists of matter of *law*, he must do it, by tendering what is called an *issue in law* — which is merely a technical denial of some *legal* proposition, or supposed rule of law. The minor or second proposition in the declaration — as it consists only of matter of *fact* — must be denied, if at all, by what the law denominates an issue *in fact;* or, more strictly speaking, by *tendering* an issue *in fact* — which is the legal mode of denying by plea, what has been alleged, as matter of fact, on the other side (*h*). But assuming the major to be correct in principle, and the minor true in point of fact, (upon which supposition, neither of them can be successfully denied); the conclusion must inevitably follow, unless the defendant can repel it, by alleging some *new* matter, (i. e. some distinct collateral fact) which is inconsistent with it, and which therefore *by consequence* implies a

(*h*) 3 Black. Com. 396.

CHAP. I.

Nature of Pleading.

denial of it: There being no form of *direct negation*, in which the conclusion can be distinctly answered.

§ 11. Let it be supposed then ,that in the case just stated by way of example, the plaintiff's premises are both undeniable; but that he has released his cause of action to the defendant, and that the release is the particular fact, or new matter, upon which the defendant relies, for defeating the suit. Under these circumstances, the defendant's plea, or defence, if reduced to a syllogistic form, will stand thus:—'If he, upon whose land I have forcibly entered, releases to me his right of action for such entry; he has thenceforth no right by law to recover damages for it, against me: But the plaintiff has released to me his right of action, for my entry upon his land: Therefore he has, by law, no right to recover damages for that cause, against me.'

§ 12. To this defence the plaintiff has now, in his turn, a right to reply, by denying either of the three propositions, advanced by the defendant. But if he admits both of the defendant's premises; or if, as we are now assuming, he cannot successfully deny either of them; his suit must of course fail, unless he can destroy the defendant's *conclusion*, by some new matter of fact, which will be, in legal effect, a denial of it.

§ 13. For the purpose then of carrying this process one stage further, let us suppose that the release, pleaded by the defendant, was extorted from

Nature of Pleading.

the plaintiff, by *duress;* and that this fact is the *new* matter, by which the plaintiff proposes to overthrow the defendant's conclusion. The plaintiff's reply may, upon this state of facts, be resolved into the following syllogism:—'A release extorted from me, by *duress*, does not in law destroy any pre-existing right of mine, to recover damages: But the release, pleaded by the defendant, was extorted from me by duress: Therefore, that release does not destroy my right by law to recover damages against him.'

§ 14. It is now necessary for the defendant, if he persists in denying the plaintiff's claim, to contest this reply; and this he may do, by denying either of the three propositions, of which it consists. But assuming, as in the preceding stages of this illustration, that neither of the *premises* can be safely denied, the consequence must be, that the plaintiff will prevail, unless the defendant can, on his part, allege some further new matter, which may destroy the plaintiff's *conclusion*. And the pleading of such new matter, of whatever facts it may consist, will contain the elements of another syllogism—which the plaintiff will be at liberty to answer, by another still; and the same syllogistic process may be repeated, by the parties, alternately as long as there remains new matter to be alleged on either side.

Post, ch. 2, § 23.

§ 15. For, that both parties may respectively have the full benefit of pleading whatever the nature and exigencies of the case, on their respective sides, may require, it is obvious that each must be

CHAP. I.

Nature of Pleading.

at liberty to answer the allegations made against himself, by denying, at his election, *either* of the three propositions contained in those allegations: In other words, each party must be at liberty to deny whatever he considers as false, either in law, fact, or inference, in his adversary's pleading. Each party, therefore, has a right to allege *new* matter, in any stage of the pleadings, as long as he has occasion to answer new matter—i. e. as long as *such* matter is alleged against him. And thus the right of *electing* between the three regular modes of meeting his adversary's allegations, is continued to each party, until one of the *premises* in the pleading on one side, is directly denied on the other; or (to substitute legal, for scholastic language,) until the pleadings terminate in the tender of a proper *issue*, in law or in fact.

§ 16. An *issue*, of either kind, precludes the allegation of further new matter on either side, and thus regularly closes the pleadings (*i*). For before any issue can be tendered, both parties will necessarily have an opportunity to allege whatever the nature of the case, on either side, may require. And as the whole controversy, which is the subject-matter of the pleadings, is, by the issue, reduced to some one point of fact or law; no necessary or useful purpose can be attained, by carrying the pleadings further. For the question, upon which the contest depends, is now distinctly presented by the issue, and ripe for determination. And it only re-

(*i*) Co. Litt. 126. a. 3 Black. Com. 314.

mains for the court, or the jury, to decide the point in issue, and for the former to render judgment. If the issue be taken upon matter of *law*, it is to be determined by the court—if upon matter of fact, it is, in general, though not universally, to be tried by the jury: It being the province of the former to decide questions of *law*, and of the latter, ordinarily, to ascertain matters of *fact* (*k*). And the issue, whether in law or fact, being decided, the judgment of the court, which is merely the sentence of the law (*l*), deduced from the facts ascertained, must follow in favour of that party who appears, from the whole record, entitled to it.

Nature of Pleading.

§ 17. From this very general outline, it will be apparent that all pleading is a *logical* process. And the great object of the process is to facilitate the administration of justice, by simplifying the grounds of controversy, and ultimately narrowing down the contest to a single and direct affirmative and negative—i. e. to some definite point of law or fact, affirmed on one side, and denied on the other.

Special pleading.

§ 18. By *special* pleading, is meant the allegation of *special* or *new* matter, as distinguished from a direct *denial* of matter previously alleged on the opposite side.

§ 19. The matter of *fact*, which, in the preceding illustration, constitutes the subject of the minor proposition, is, in the established forms of pleading,

(*k*) 3 Black. Com. 315.

(*l*) Ib. 396.

4

CHAP. I.

Nature of Pleading.

always expressly alleged: Since the *facts*, upon which the complaint or defence is founded, is supposed to be unknown to the judges. The conclusion, or third proposition, in the syllogistic process, is also expressed, in the existing mode of pleading, either by the *demand*, which the plaintiff makes of damages, debt, or other thing, on the one hand, or by defendant's *prayer of judgment* against the plaintiff, on the other. For it cannot appear, from facts stated *alone*, what benefit the pleader proposes to claim from them; and he can, therefore, derive from them no advantage which he does not claim from them, in his pleading.

§ 20. But as has been already suggested (*m*), the *principle*, or rule of *law*, of which we have represented the major proposition to consist, (and which, according to ancient usage, was, in certain cases, always recited, or formally alleged by the pleader) (*n*), is now, in general, not actually *expressed* in the pleadings, in any form. For the judges, whose province it is to decide upon the legal sufficiency of all pleadings, are presumed to *know judicially*, what the law, upon any given or alleged state of facts, is: And the nature of the *facts*, actually alleged on either side, taken in connexion with the *demand* laid in the declaration, and with the *prayer of judgment*, in the subsequent pleadings, will, in every case, and with perfect certainty, indicate the supposed rule of law upon which the pleader relies, as his major proposition. And in this

(*m*) Ante, § 4. (*n*) Post. Chap. 2.

Nature of Pleading.

manner, that proposition, though not expressed in terms, is necessarily understood and tacitly supplied.

§ 21. Thus, in the example already given, of a declaration in trespass, the plaintiff, in alleging that the defendant has forcibly entered upon his land, and demanding damages for that cause, assumes and tacitly asserts the general principle, that he, upon whose land such an entry has been made, has a right by law to recover damages against him who made it. For unless that principle of law were tacitly supplied, or presupposed, the averment of the defendant's entry, and the demand of damages, which follows it in the declaration, would be altogether unmeaning and nugatory: Since no right of action could result from the defendant's act, if no such legal principle existed.—And this principle, or the proposition which would express it, is as clearly indicated by the matter of fact alleged, and the demand made in the declaration, and may therefore be as easily apprehended and applied, as if it had been expressly and formally stated.

§ 22. The object, thus far proposed, has been to exhibit a general analysis of the law of pleading, considered as a *science*, or *system* of *principles*. And though the scholastic terms and forms, which have been introduced for this purpose, are unknown in the established language and practice of pleading; yet the essential properties and the results of the preceding syllogistic process, though differently ex-

CHAP. I.

Nature of Pleading.

pressed, are in effect the same as those of the less scholastic modes of pleading, adopted by the common law.

§ 23. Thus, an issue in law which, in the foregoing analysis is called a *denial of the major proposition* of the adverse party, is described in legal language, as an *admission of the facts* alleged by that party, but a *denial of their legal operation* in his favour. These different terms however express, in effect, one and the same thing—or rather, the operation thus differently described, is essentially one and the same.

§ 24. Thus also, the *new*, or *special* matter, which in the foregoing analysis is called a denial of the adverse party's *conclusion*, is, in legal language, denominated matter of *avoidance*—i. e. matter which, admitting both of the other party's premises, avoids or repels, in the particular case in question, the *consequence*, or *inference*, which would otherwise result from them. And that inference is, universally, the *syllogistic* conclusion in the adverse party's pleading, if his pleading be reduced to a syllogism. It is therefore manifest, that matter of *avoidance*, and matter which, in the syllogistic formula, goes in denial of the adverse party's *conclusion*, are in substance one and the same thing.

§ 25. In concluding this introductory chapter, it may be proper to observe, that the forms of scholastic logic, employed in the preceding pages, have

CHAP. I.

Nature of Pleading.

been introduced for the purpose of resolving the law of pleading into its constituent principles: A process which has been deemed conducive to a correct and systematic exhibition of the original and essential nature of all pleading. And as those forms are more simple, and exact, than any other mode of analysis, of which the subject would admit; they have been, of course, thought better adapted than any other to the end proposed.

CHAPTER II.

OF THE GENERAL DIVISIONS OF PLEADING.

CHAP. II.

The writ.

SECTION 1. UNDER this head it may be premised, that the *original writ*, which forms the first stage of a suit at law, and is the foundation of all the subsequent proceedings in it, is no part of the *pleadings;* since it does not consist of the allegations, and is not the act, of either party; but is a mandatory *precept* (1), issued by the authority, and in the name of the sovereign or the state, for the purpose of compelling the appearance of the defendant before the court, to which it is returnable, that he may there make answer to the plaintiff's complaint (*a*). The general nature of the plaintiff's demand is, indeed, mentioned in the writ—that the defendant may know, before he appears in court, to what *kind* of complaint he is required to answer; but the *particular* cause of action—the specific wrong or breach of contract complained of—does

(*a*) 3 Black. Com. 273. 1 Tidd, 93.

(1) In England, the writ is directed only to the *sheriff* of the county, in which the cause of action is alleged to have arisen: In the practice of some of the American states, it is directed to either of several ministers of the law—as the sheriff, his deputy, or a constable.

not appear, until the declaration is filed (*b*) (2). But though the writ is no part of the pleadings, it may, for various causes, be excepted to and destroyed, by pleading: As for the want of any legal requisite, or in general, for any irregularity, informality or mistake. The writ.

§ 2. The suit commences, from the *issuing* of the original writ; and if the writ bears a fictitious date; the true time of its issuing may be proved, whenever the time is material, and the ends of justice require that the time of its actually issuing be shown (*c*). Post. ch. 4.

§ 3. The *pleadings*, in a civil suit, commence with the *declaration*, or *count* (*a*): The word *plea*, (*placitum*) being a generic, or collective term, comprehending all the allegations, made on either side, in the various stages of pleading (*d*); though, in a more limited and appropriate sense, the term *plea*, in the singular, is used to denote the *first* plea, or First stage of the pleadings. The count.

(*b*) Bac. Abr. *Actions in Gen.* C. 1 Tidd, 96.
(*c*) 2 Burr. 962–6. Cowp. 454. 3 Black. Com. 273. 285. 7 T. R. 4. 1 Wils. 147.
(*a*) 3 Black. Com. 393.
(*d*) Carth. 334. Skinn. 554. 1 Saund. 338, n. 6.

(2) It will be perceived that all civil suits are supposed, in the text, to be commenced by *original writ*. In the modern practice of the courts of Westminster, however, there are modes of commencing actions *without* an original writ. But a delineation of the different means of instituting suits belongs to the title of *Practice*.

CHAP. II.

answer made by the defendant, to the declaration or the writ (*e*).

The count.

§ 4. The *declaration* is a statement at large of the cause of action, (of which the writ gives only a *general* description); or — as it is usually denominated — an amplification, or exposition, of the original writ, with the addition of the time when, and the place where, the cause of action arose, and of all necessary circumstances (*f*).

Defendant's plea.

§ 5. The pleadings, which *succeed* the declaration, begin with the defendant's *plea:* For the writ being returned, and the plaintiff's complaint being presented in full; it is incumbent on the defendant, within a reasonable time, to make defence, and put in an answer or plea; as judgment must otherwise go against him, by *default* or *nil dicit* (*g*). For if he fails to make answer, within the time required by the rules of practice; he impliedly confesses the truth of the complaint (*h*).

Defence, and kinds of.

§ 6. But as introductory to the plea, the defendant must, in general, make *defence;* which is of two kinds, called *full* defence, and *half* defence. The term 'defence' signifies, in the language of pleading, not a *justification*, but *resistance* or *denial;* as is very manifest from the established form, in which defence

(*e*) 3 Black. Com. 299. 301.

(*f*) Co. Litt. 303, b. 3 Black. Com. 293. Bac. Abr. *Pleas*, &c. B. 1.

(*g*) 3 Black. Com. 296.

(*h*) 1 Stra. 612.

CHAP. II. Defence.

is made. That form — when the defence is *full*, and expressed in full — is the following; — 'And the said C. D.' (the defendant), 'by E. F. his attorney, comes, and defends the wrong and injury, (or force and injury), when and where it shall behove him, and the damages, and whatsoever else he ought to defend' (*i*). Now it would be absurd to suppose that the defendant, in saying that he 'defends' the wrong and injury, is to be understood, as *justifying* them — not only because a wrong cannot, in the nature of the thing, admit of justification; but also, because the defendant may, with legal consistency, as he frequently does, subjoin at the close of his defence, a *denial* of what the plaintiff complains of as a wrong (*j*).

§ 7. In writs of *entry* also, when no injury is alleged, and when of course none can be denied (as the demandant states only his own *right*, and the defective title of the tenant, or defendant, without complaining of any *wrong*), the tenant *defends* the *demandant's right*. And in writs of *right*, the tenant, for the same reason, always *defends* the *right* and *seisin* of the demandant (*k*): Examples, which decisively show that the meaning of the word *defence*, in pleading, is that which has now been assigned to it.

(*i*) Bac. Abr. *Pleas*, &c, D. Co. Litt. 127, b. Lawes' Pl. 89. 2 Chitt. Pl. 409. 2 Saund. 209, c.

(*j*) 3 Black. Com. 297.

(*k*) Ibid.

CHAP. II.

Defence.

§ 8. It is obvious then, that to make *defence* is to *resist* the plaintiff's suit; the reasons or grounds of which resistance must appear in the plea, which follows the defence.

§ 9. *Half* defence, in the form in which it was anciently distinguished from *full*, is thus expressed: 'And the said C. D. by E. F. his attorney' (or 'in his own proper person), comes, and defends the force (or wrong) and injury'—omitting the sequel in the above form of full defence (*l*).

§ 10. *Half* defence is adapted to pleas, which deny the jurisdiction of the court, or the *legal competency* of the plaintiff to prosecute. *Full* defence is an implied *waiver* of these two preliminary exceptions; because, by defending '*when and where* it shall behove him', the defendant is considered as impliedly acknowledging the *jurisdiction* of the court; and by defending 'the *damages*, and *whatsoever else* he ought to defend,' he is deemed virtually to admit the plaintiff's *competency* to sue (*m*).

•§ 11. *Full* defence, however, is adapted, it seems, to *all other* pleas than those last mentioned. But to any other pleas than those, half-defence is not apposite; and consequently, *half* defence, when coupled with a plea of any other kind, is fatal to

(*l*) Co. Litt. 127. 2 Saund. 209, c. n. Bac. Abr. *Pleas*, &c, D. 2 Chitt. Pl. 409.

(*m*) Com. Dig. *Abatement*, I. 16.

it (*n*). For such defence impliedly *waves* all exceptions, other than those, to which the two pleas above mentioned are adapted; and is therefore inconsistent with all others.

Defence, effects of.

§ 12. As to the difference, between the effect of *full* and of *half* defence, there is, however, some contradiction and confusion, in the books. According to some, full defence would seem to be improper for, a dilatory plea, of *any* kind (*o*). The distinction above expressed appears, however, to be the established one.

§ 13. Much importance was formerly attached to these different modes of making defence; and any deviation from that form, which the nature of the plea required, gave occasion to many critical and subtle exceptions. These exceptions, however, being merely technical, were, at a subsequent period, much discountenanced, and now seldom or never occur. For though the distinction between full and half defence still exists theoretically; yet the *forms*, by which they were originally distinguished, and which have already been recited, have lost their practical importance, by becoming obsolete: Since, according to modern usage, neither of those precise forms is employed; but the defendant, by adding to the ancient form of *half*-defence, as before recited,

(*n*) Co. Litt. 127, b. Bac. Abr. *Pleas*, &c, D. Lawes' Pl. 90. 3 Lev. 240.

(*o*) Com. Dig. *Abatement*, I. 16.

CHAP. II.

Defence.

merely the words 'when, &c,' is at liberty to connect it with either species of plea: The '&c,' being construed to imply either *full* or *half* defence, as the subject matter of the plea may require (*p*).

§ 14. It must be acknowledged, however, that the rules, relating to the forms of *defence* in pleading, are very artificial, not to say arbitrary. It is, at least, very difficult to discover on what original *principle*, defence of either kind is, or ever was, necessary: Since it amounts only to an *indefinite* introductory suggestion of what must, afterwards, appear distinctly in the plea. Indeed, in certain actions, in which force and injury are, and must be, alleged, viz, in trespass for an assault, or for breaking the plaintiff's close, *no* defence is required, merely because the ancient precedents contain none, in either of those two classes of cases (*q*). Yet, if the *essential principles* of pleading required defence to be made, in any case, it would seem as necessary in those particular actions, as in any other.—But however this may be, want of defence, when required by the foregoing rules, is still regarded as a defect, though only as a defect in form (*r*).

§ 15. It is almost unnecessary to observe, that in a less technical sense, the word 'defence' is used, as well in legal as in popular language, to signify —not a clause or form, in pleading—but the *sub-*

(*p*) 8 T. R. 633. Willes, 40. 2 Saund. 209, c. (n). Lawes' Pl. 92. 2 Chitt. Pl. 409, (n. o.)—*Cont.* Sty. 273. 3 Black. Com. 298.

(*q*) Bac. Abr. *Pleas*, &c, D. Lawes' Pl. 90–91.

(*r*) 3 Salk. 271. Lawes' Pl. 92.

ject of the plea. Thus, if to an action on contract, the defendant pleads infancy, or to an action of trespass, a license; infancy, in the one case, and a license, in the other, is called the defence.

Imparlance.

§ 16. But before the defendant is required to plead, he is, according to ancient practice, regularly entitled, on his prayer for that purpose, to an *imparlance*, or *licentia loquendi*: A term which, in its primitive sense, (being derived from the French word *parler*, to speak) signifies an allowance, to the defendant, of time to *talk* or *confer* with the plaintiff, for the purpose of bringing the controversy, if the parties can agree, to an amicable termination (*s*). But an allowance to either party, of time to answer his adversary, (as, to *reply*, *rejoin*, &c,) is, in the more comprehensive sense of the word, called an *imparlance* (*t*). In its present more usual signification, 'imparlance' is an allowance, to the *defendant*, of time to *plead* (*u*). Though at this day, time for pleading is, in most cases, allowed according to certain established rules of practice, without the formality of an *imparlance* (*v*).

Kinds, and effects of.

§ 17. *Imparlances* are of three kinds, of which the first is called *general*—the second, *special*—and the third, *general-special*, or (according to Sir William

(*s*) 3 Black. Com. 299. Id. App. III, s. 6.
(*t*) Com. Dig. *Pleader*, D. 1. 1 Tidd, 417.
(*u*) 1 Tidd, 417. 2 Mod. 62.
(*v*) 1 Tidd. 417, 420–1. 1 Wils. 154.

CHAP. II.

Imparlance; kinds, and effects of.

Blackstone), *more special* (*w*). A *general* imparlance is one, granted upon a prayer, in which the defendant reserves to himself *no exceptions;* and imparlances of this kind are always from one term to another (*x*): Whereas *special*, and *general-special* imparlances may extend only to a future day, in the *same* term, in which they are granted (*y*). After a *general* imparlance, the defendant can plead only to the *merits*, or, in legal phrase, to *the action;* and is, of course, precluded from pleading to the jurisdiction of the court, the disability of the plaintiff to sue, or the form of the writ (*z*). For by asking leave to imparl, without reserving any right of exception, in any of these particulars, he tacitly *acknowledges* the jurisdiction of the court, and waves all objections, which do not go to the *right* of *action*.

§ 18. An imparlance is said to be *special*, when the prayer, upon which it is granted, contains the clause, 'saving to himself all advantages and exceptions, as well to the *writ*, as to the *declaration* aforesaid' (*a*) (3). After an imparlance of this kind, the defendant is at liberty to plead, as well in *abate-*

(*w*) 1 Tidd, 417. 3 Black. Com. 301. Lawes' Pl. 94.
(*x*) 1 Tidd, 417. 6 Mod. 28. Lawes' Pl. 94.
(*y*) Com. Dig. *Pleader*, D. 1. 1 Tidd, 417.
(*z*) 3 Black. Com. 301. 1 Tidd, 418. 1 Mass. R. 347.
(*a*) 2 Chitt. Pl. 407-8. 2 Saund. 2. (n. 2.) Lawes' Pl. 94.

(3) If the suit was commenced by *bill*, the saving should be 'of all advantages and exceptions to the said bill.'

ment as to the *action;* i. e. to offer, in his plea, exceptions either to the *writ* or the *count* (*b*). For the benefit of all such exceptions is reserved to him, by the granting of his prayer, in which there is an express reservation of them. But he cannot, after a special imparlance, plead to the *jurisdiction of the court.* (*c*) For exceptions to the jurisdiction are not, in this case, among those reserved in the defendant's prayer for leave to imparl; and the act of praying such leave, without saving exceptions to the *jurisdiction*, is an implied admission of it.

Imparlance; kinds, and effects of.

§ 19. A *general-special* imparlance is one in which the defendant reserves '*all* advantages and exceptions *whatsoever*' (*d*). This kind of imparlance not only leaves the defendant at liberty to plead whatever he might have pleaded, under a *special* imparlance, but does not preclude him from pleading to the *jurisdiction* of the court (*e*). For as the prayer for leave to imparl expressly reserves *all* exceptions; such as go to the jurisdiction are of course reserved, as well as others. He cannot, however, after an imparlance of either kind, plead a *tender*, with a *touts temps prist*, (an averment that he was *always ready* to pay): For by asking *delay* — as he does, by praying for leave to imparl, he practically admits that he is *not then* ready to pay what the plaintiff demands; and thus his prayer for leave to imparl would falsify the plea (*f*).

(*b*) 1 Tidd, 418. Lawes' Pl. 94. (*c*) Id.
(*d*) 2 Chitt. Pl. 408 (*e*) 1 Tidd, 418. 1 Lev. 54.
(*f*) 1 Tidd, 418. 2 Salk. 622. 2 Mod. 62. Reg. Pl. 56.

CHAP. II.

Imparlance, kinds, and effect of.

§ 20. If the defendant, after an imparlance, pleads any thing, which the imparlance *waves* or *falsifies;* the plaintiff may sign judgment against him, as for *want* of a plea (*g*). For a plea, pleaded out of the regular course or order of pleading, may be treated as a *nullity*. Or, instead of signing judgment, the plaintiff may, in such a case, move the court to set aside the plea as being irregular (*h*); or he may *demur* to it (*i*); for the matter pleaded, whatever it may be, appears upon the face of the record to be *ill* pleaded: Or finally, he may *specially reply* the imparlance, by way of *estoppel* (*j*); i. e. by showing in his replication, that the defendant is *precluded*, by his own act apparent upon the record, from availing himself of the matter alleged in his plea. For whenever a party, in pleading, *contradicts* what he has before alleged or admitted upon the record, his previous allegation or admission, may be pleaded, *as conclusive* against him. But if the plaintiff, instead of taking any of these advantages, *answers the matter* of the plea; it will stand as if pleaded without an imparlance (*k*). For by omitting to object to it as irregular, or out of course, he *waves* all exceptions to it, in these particulars; or in other words, all exceptions to its *admissibility*.

(*g*) 1 Tidd, 419. 4 T. R. 520. 7 Id. 447, *note (d)*.

(*h*) 6 T. R. 373.

(*i*) 1 Wils. 261. 1 Black. R. 51. 6 T. R. 369. 2 Bos. & Pul. 384. 2 M. & S. 484.

(*j*) 1 Tidd, 419.

(*k*) 1 Vent. 236.

CHAP. II.

§ 21. When an action is founded upon a *deed*, pleaded with a *profert in curiâ*, (an averment that the plaintiff brings the deed into court), the defendant, before he can be required to plead, is entitled, (upon demanding it,) to *oyer* of the instrument; i. e. according to the original meaning of the word, to *hear* it read (*l*): Though the immediate object, now proposed in demanding *oyer* of a deed, is to obtain a copy of it, to which the defendant is entitled of course (*m*). But as the subject of *oyer* must be distinctly examined hereafter, all further explanation of it is for the present omitted.

Oyer.

Post. ch. 8.

§ 22. These preliminary proceedings on the part of the defendant, being had, it is incumbent on him to put in his *plea* (*n*); in which, if he has waved no legal exception, he may either contest the *merits* of the plaintiff's demand, or except to the *jurisdiction* of the court; or take advantage of any legal defect, incongruity or informality in the *mode*, in which the suit has been commenced or pursued. And hence arises the division of pleas, on the part of the defendant, into two kinds, viz. *dilatory* pleas, and pleas to *the action* (*o*); the different characters and uses of which are to be explained hereafter.

Defendant's plea.

§ 23. If the plea — of whichsoever of the two foregoing kinds it may be — advances *new* matter,

(*l*) 3 Black. Com. 299. Lawes' Pl. 96.
(*m*) 2 Salk. 497. Lawes' Pl. 96. 1 Tidd, 526-7.
(*n*) 3 Black. Com. 301.
(*o*) Id. Bac. Abr. *Pleas*, &c. A.

CHAP. II.

it may of course be met by the plaintiff, in either of the three modes, in which (as has been shown already) new matter, advanced on either side, may always be contested (*p*).

Replication, rejoinder, &c.

§ 24. The plaintiff's answer to the plea is called the *replication;* and the regular stages or parts of the pleading, which succeed the replication, are the *rejoinder*, which is the defendant's answer to it — the *surrejoinder*, which is the plaintiff's answer to the rejoinder — the *rebutter*, which answers the plaintiff's surrejoinder — and the *surrebutter*, which is in answer to the defendant's rebutter (*q*)

§ 25. No train of pleading has ever been carried, it seems, beyond a *surrebutter;* which has, therefore, been regarded as the ultimate attainable stage of special pleading: Though in the nature of the process, there would seem to be no inherent impossibility of extending the series still further.

§ 26. The orderly parts of pleading then, when carried to the utmost limit, which has ever been attained in practice, are, (to recapitulate them), the *declaration*, or *count* — the *plea* — the *replication* — the *rejoinder* — the *surrejoinder* — the *rebutter* — and the *surrebutter*.

§ 27. In relation to the *offices* of these several divisions of pleading, it is to be observed, that in

(*p*) Ante, chap. I. 3 Black. Com. 309, 310.

(*q*) Reg. Pl. 57–61. 3 Black. Com. 310. Lawes' Pl. 34.

Replication, rejoinder, &c.

each successive stage of the process, subsequent to the defendant's *plea*, the new matter, advanced by each party, must be not only such as will form a sufficient *answer* in law, to what is last before alleged against him, but such also as will *fortify* what he himself has before pleaded.

§ 28. And therefore, if matter pleaded (after the defendant's plea), by either party, does not go in *support* of what has been before alleged by *himself;* the pleading is ill, even though it might, in itself, be a good *answer to the adverse allegations*, which immediately precede it. For however extended the train of pleading, in any given cause, may be, he, who ultimately prevails, must prevail upon the grounds *first* assumed, on his own part; which grounds, however, he can maintain in his subsequent pleading, only by repelling what has been advanced against him, in the intermediate allegations of his adversary. The plaintiff must therefore prevail, if at all, upon the facts stated in the *declaration;* the defendant, upon those stated in the *plea*. And whatever the parties may respectively allege in their subsequent pleadings, must all go to *fortify the declaration* on the one side, and the *plea* on the other. If it were otherwise, the foundation of the action, and of the defence, might be entirely *changed*, in each successive stage of the pleadings; and the great objects of all pleadings might thus be defeated. (Vid. *post*, ch. 8, pt. 3, § 65.)

CHAP. II.

§ 29. The replication must, therefore, *so* answer the plea, as to support the *declaration*—the rejoinder, in answering the replication, must support the *plea;* and in the same manner, the surrejoinder must support the *replication;* the rebutter, the *rejoinder*, and the surrebutter, the *surrejoinder* (*r*). The process being thus conducted, that which is *last* pleaded, on either side, necessarily goes in support of what was *first* pleaded, on the same side. Thus, a good *surrebutter* virtually supports the *declaration;* inasmuch as it directly supports the surrejoinder, *which* directly supports the replication, and which last directly supports the declaration (4). In the same manner, a good *rebutter* consequentially fortifies the *plea:* Since it goes directly in support of the rejoinder, *which* directly supports the plea.

Departure.

§ 30. The dereliction of a prior ground of complaint or defence, and the substitution of another, in violation of these principles, constitute what is called a *departure* in pleading; for a particular explanation of which, and of its consequences, the reader is referred to a subsequent chapter.

Ch. 8, Part 3.

(*r*) Co. Litt. 303. b. 304. a. Reg. Pl. 112. 167. 3 Black. Com. 310.

---

(4) In these illustrations, the defendant's plea is supposed to be in answer to the *declaration*. If, however, the plea attacks the *writ*, instead of the declaration; the replication, and of course all the subsequent pleadings, on the plaintiff's part, must go in support of the *writ*, and not of the *declaration*.

Pleas on the defendant's part, kinds of.

§ 31. Pleas on the part of the defendant, as has been already suggested, are of two kinds: First, *Dilatory* pleas; Secondly, Pleas to the *action* (*s*). The latter are usually called pleas in *bar;* though sometimes, and especially in the older books of the law, they are denominated *perpetual* or *peremptory* pleas, or pleas *in chief* (*t*).

Dilatory pleas.

§ 32. I. *Dilatory* pleas are such as delay the plaintiff's remedy, by questioning, not the cause of action, but the *propriety* of the suit, or the *mode* in which the remedy is sought. And hence they derive the denomination of *dilatory* pleas (*u*).

§ 33. Sir William Blackstone defines dilatory pleas to be 'such, as tend merely to delay, or put off, *the suit*' (*v*). It would, perhaps, be more correct to say, that they tend to delay the plaintiff's *eventual remedy*. For though pleas of this kind were, formerly, often used for the mere purpose of delay, without any foundation in truth; and though the interlocutory questions, raised by such a plea, may still incidentally have the mere effect of *delaying* the termination of the suit; yet the proper and direct effect of a plea of this kind, when it prevails, is in general, and with a very few exceptions, to *defeat* forever *the* particular suit, in which it is used (*w*): Though it leaves the *merits*, or right of action, un-

(*s*) 3 Black. Com. 301. Bac. Abr. *Pleas*, &c, A.
(*t*) Co. Litt. 304. a. Lawes' Pl. 36. Com. Dig. *Abatement*, B.
(*u*) Reg. Pl. 76. 3 Black. Com. 301.
(*v*) 3 Black. Com. 301.
(*w*) Bac. Abr. *Pleas*, &c, F. 14. 3 Black. Com. 303.

CHAP. II.

determined; so that the plaintiff is still at liberty to seek his remedy, by a new suit. The peculiar office of a dilatory plea is, therefore, in general, to *defeat* the individual suit, in which it is pleaded, without affecting the *right of action.*

§ 34. Dilatory pleas are, by Sir William Blackstone, divided into three kinds: — 1. Pleas to the *jurisdiction* of the court: As that the defendant is privileged to be sued, exclusively, in some other court; or in some cases, that the cause of action arose without the limits of the court's jurisdiction, &c, (*x*): 2. Pleas to the *disability* of the plaintiff, or as they are frequently termed, to the *person* of the plaintiff: As, that he is an alien enemy, an outlaw, or under some other legal incapacity to maintain a suit (*y*): 3. Pleas in *abatement* of the writ, or count. Pleas of this last class are founded upon some defect or mistake, either in the *writ* itself — (as that it is deficient in some legal requisite, or that the defendant is *misnamed* in it, &c,) — or in the mode, in which the count *pursues* it: As that there is some *variance*, or *repugnancy* between the count and the writ; in which case, the fault in the *count* furnishes a cause for abating the writ (*z*). But any mistake or insufficiency, apparent upon the face of the *declaration*, (or count) *without reference* to the writ — i. e. any mistake or insufficiency, in the

(*x*) Bac. Abr. *Pleas*, &c, E. Ib. *Courts*, D. Gilb. H. C. P. 188. 189. 3 Black. Com. 301.

(*y*) Bac. Abr. *Pleas*, &c, F. 1. Co. Litt. 128, a. 129, b.

(*z*) 3 Black. Com. 301. Com. Dig. *Abatement*, G. 1. 8. Ib, *Pleader*, C. 14, 15. Bac. Abr. *Pleas*, &c, F. 7.

statement of the cause of action, is in itself no ground of abatement, though a good cause of demurrer (*a*) (5). CHAP. II.

§ 35. *All* dilatory pleas are sometimes called pleas in *abatement*, as contradistinguished from pleas to the action (*b*). This, however, is a vague use of the term, and never proper when strict accuracy is required.

§ 36. If no dilatory plea is offered — or if any, or all of those, which the law allows, have been pleaded and overruled as insufficient; the defendant is still at liberty to plead,

II. To *the action* (*c*). For it would be unreasonable to render a final judgment against him, until he has been required to answer, and has had opportunity to contest, the *merits* or *grounds* of the suit: And these he is not bound to answer, until he has exhausted, or *waved* his right to interpose dilatory exceptions. Pleas to the action.

(*a*) Willes, 410. 1 Show. 91. 1 Salk. 212. 1 Mass. R. 500.
(*b*) 3 Black. Com. 302. *Notis Chr.* Lawes' Pl. 37.
(*c*) Co. Litt. 303. a. Bac. Abr. *Pleas*, &c, A. 3 Black. Com. 303.

---

(5) Most writers on pleading have treated of dilatory pleas, under a more minute and complex division, which will be presented in a subsequent chapter. But the *threefold* division, mentioned above, will here be pursued, as being not only more simple, and more easily understood; but sufficiently minute for the ends proposed in this Treatise. Post. ch. 5, § 1. 10. 11.

CHAP. II.

Pleas to the action.

§ 37. On the other hand, the defendant, by pleading to the action, *waves* all dilatory pleas, except those, the matter of which has *afterwards* accrued (*d*). For by denying the *cause* of *action* itself, he tacitly admits the *mode*, in which the remedy is pursued, to be correct.

§ 38. Pleas *to the action* (or *in bar*), are usually divided into two kinds: 1. The *general issue*: 2. A *special* plea in bar (*e*). There is however a plea to the action, which does not strictly fall under either of these two denominations, and which is called a *special issue* (*f*);—a plea termed *special*, as distinguished from the *general* issue; but which differs also from what is appropriately denominated a '*special* plea in bar,' in this—that the latter is, universally, a plea *advancing new matter*: Whereas the plea, called a *special issue*, never advances such matter; but merely *denies* some particular *material* allegation, the denial of which is in effect a denial of the entire right of action. These several pleas are called, indifferently, pleas *to the action*, pleas *in bar*, or pleas *in chief*.

§ 39. A plea to *the action*, being an answer to the *merits* of the complaint, always goes in denial of the alleged *right of action*. And this the defendant may deny, either 1, by *denying*, in whole or in

(*d*) Co. Litt. 303. a. Bac. Abr. *Pleas*, &c, 2. 1 Tidd, 572.

(*e*) 3 Black. Com. 303. 305. Bac. Abr. *Pleas*, &c, G. 1. 3.

(*f*) Bac. Abr. *Pleas*, &c, G. 3. Com. Dig. *Pleader*, R. 1. 2. Lawes' Pl. 110. 112.

part, the allegations in the declaration; or, 2, by alleging new matter, which *admits* the truth of the plaintiff's allegations, but goes *in avoidance* of them; or, 3, by pleading matter of *estoppel* (*g*): A defence which, neither admitting nor denying any of the facts alleged by the plaintiff, denies his *legal right to allege* them.

§ 40. 1. When the defendant proposes to deny *all* the material allegations in the declaration, his proper plea is the *general issue*. But if the cause of action consists of several distinct, but connected facts, capable of being separated in pleading; the defendant, instead of denying them all, by the general issue, may deny singly, any one of them, which is *essential* to the plaintiff's right of recovery, without taking notice of the others: And such denial is a sufficient answer to the whole declaration (*h*). For where each of several concurring facts is necessary to one entire cause of action, the denial of *either* of them is, necessarily, a denial of the *whole* cause of action. The plea, in this case, is a *special issue* (*i*).

§ 41. When the defence, upon which the defendant is to rely, does not involve a *denial* of any of the material allegations in the declaration, he may still deny the right of action by pleading,

(*g*) 3 Black. Com. 303. 308. Lawes' Pl. 37-8. 115-6. 130. 3 East, 346. 365. Willes, 13.

(*h*) Bac. Abr. *Pleas*, &c, G. 3. Lawes' Pl. 112. 113. 135. Com. Dig. *Pleader*, R. 1. 2.

(*i*) *Iidem.*

CHAP. II.

§ 42. 2. Matter of *avoidance;* i. e. *new* matter, which admits the delaration to be true, but shows, nevertheless, either that the defendant was *never* liable to the recovery claimed against him, or that he has been *discharged* from his original liability, by something supervenient (*l*). In either case, the plea is a *special* plea in bar—as is also,

3. A plea in *estoppel*, when pleaded to the declaration. A plea of this kind, like a plea in *avoidance* of the declaration, always advances new matter; but it differs from the latter, in this—that instead of confessing and avoiding the plaintiff's *allegations*, it neither admits nor denies them; but alleges some matter of *estoppel* (as a record, or deed, to which he is a party, or privy), and which, being inconsistent with his allegations, *precludes* him from availing himself of them (*m*). Such are the different kinds of pleas *to the action*.

Demurrer to the declaration.

§ 43. There is still, however, another mode, in which the defendant may deny the plaintiff's right of action; viz. by *demurring* to the declaration—i. e. by confessing the facts alleged in it, but denying, that they constitute, in law, a cause of action (*n*). But a demurrer to the declaration is not classed among *pleas* to the action—not only because it may be taken, as well to any other part of the pleadings, as to the declaration; but also because it neither

(*l*) 1 Tidd, 590. Lawes' Pl. 115.

(*m*) 3 Black. Com. 308. Willes, 13. 3 East, 346. 365.

(*n*) Bac. Abr. *Pleas*, &c, N. 1. 3 Black. Com. 314.

CHAP. II.

affirms nor denies any matter of *fact*, and is, therefore, not regarded as strictly a *plea*, of any class; but rather as an excuse for *not* pleading (*o*) (6). As, however, a demurrer to the declaration is one of the modes of contesting the right of action; there seems to be a propriety in adverting to it, in connexion with *pleas to the action*—although all demurrers are, in their nature, as well as structure, essentially different from all *pleas*, properly so called.

Post. ch. 9, part 1, s. 2.

(*o*) Bac. Abr. *Pleas*, &c, N. 1.

(6) The proposition, that a demurrer is not strictly a *plea*, is warranted, as well by its form, as its essential nature. For the party demurring, after having averred that the adverse pleading, and the matter contained in it, are 'in no wise sufficient in law,' &c, proceeds to say, that 'he hath no necessity, neither is he obliged, by the law of the land, in any manner to *answer* the same,' i. e. to *plead* to it. (3 Black. Com. App. No. III, § 6. 3 Wils. 292. 2 Chitt. Pl. 678.) *Vide* ch. 9, s. 2.

CHAPTER III.

OF THE GENERAL RULES OF PLEADING.

CHAP. III.

BEFORE we enter upon a separate examination of the several divisions of Pleading, enumerated in the preceding chapter, it will be proper to premise certain miscellaneous rules, applicable to pleading in general.

Requisites of pleading.

Post. ch. 9, s. 13.

§ 1. There are two indispensable requisites to all good pleading: 1, That the *matter* pleaded (i. e. the *facts* alleged,) be sufficient in law to avail the party who pleads it; and 2, That it be deduced and alleged, according to the *forms of law*. And if either of these requisites be omitted, the pleading is ill (*p*). For all pleading is required to be sufficient, not only in substance, but in *form* also: By which latter term, we are here to understand those technical or artificial *modes* of introducing and detailing the subject-matter pleaded, which have been established by usage, and which cannot be dispensed with, without

(*p*) Hob. 164. Bac. Abr. *Pleas*, &c. *Introduction*. Cowp. 683.

impairing that *certainty*, *regularity* and *uniformity*, which are essential in all judicial proceedings (1). CHAP. III.

§ 2. It is regularly essential then to all good pleading, that the party, offering new matter, allege every *substantive* fact, which is necessary in law to the maintenance of his suit or defence (*q*). For if any such fact be omitted, the claim or defence, as disclosed by the pleader, must of necessity be defective. All necessary facts.

§ 3. But that which already appears sufficiently, in the pleading of either party, without a formal allegation, need not be expressly averred (*r*). For it would be obviously nugatory and absurd, to require a distinct and substantive averment of that which, by the supposition, already appears with sufficient certainty. What already appears need not be averred.

§ 4. Thus, in pleading a covenant to *stand seized to uses*, (which is a species of conveyance founded only upon the consideration of *kindred* or *marriage*,) if it is expressly shown that the deed is from a

(*q*) Bac. Abr. *Pleas*, &c, A. Com. Dig. *Pleader*, C. 76. Lawes' Pl. 46.

(*r*) Co. Litt. 303. Yelv. 176, *note*. 7 Co. 40 b. 9 Ib. 54. a. b. 11 Ib. 25. a. 2 N. Rep. 77.

---

(1) This consideration may account, in a great measure, for the importance which courts of justice attach—and which they are, sometimes, charged with attaching, unnecessarily—to matters of mere *form*, in pleading.

CHAP. III.

father to his *son*, or other *near relative*, there is no need of averring distinctly that the conveyance was made in *consideration* of kindred (*s*): For that such was the consideration, (there being no other alleged,) is apparent from the relationship, which is expressly stated. And upon the same principle it is, that though, in trespass or trover, for the taking or conversion of goods, or specific chattels, the *value* of the property must regularly be alleged; yet if the action is brought for taking or converting *current money* (as one hundred dollars, current coin of the United States), it is unnecssary to make a distinct averment of its value (*t*): Since that fully appears from the number of dollars stated.

§ 5. Thus also, in an action upon a covenant for quiet enjoyment, (in which the eviction of the plaintiff must be shown to have been under *elder* title) if it *appears* clearly, from facts stated in the declaration, that the evictor's title *is* the elder, there is no need of formally and distinctly averring that it is so (*u*).

Circumstances implied.

§ 6. Upon a similar principle, circumstances, however material, if *necessarily implied* in any fact expressly stated, need not themselves be substantively alleged (*v*). And therefore, if one pleads a

(*s*) Iid.
(*t*) 11 Co. 54. b.
(*u*) 4 T. R. 617. 2 Lev. 37.
(*v*) Bac. Abr. *Pleas*, &c, I. 3. Co. Litt. 303. b. 1 Salk. 91. 8 Co. 82. b.

CHAP. III.

feoffment, without expressly averring livery of seisin, this omission does not vitiate the pleading (*w*): Since livery of seisin, being of the essence of every feoffment, a feoffment, *ex vi termini*, implies such livery. And therefore, to allege a feoffment, is by necessary implication to allege livery of seisin. Again: If the plaintiff in ejectment describes the land in question as lying in the parish of A, it is not necessary, in laying the *ouster*, to allege that it was *committed* in the same parish: For that fact sufficiently appears from the local description before given of the land (*x*).

Gist of the action, &c.

§ 7. All facts alleged in good pleading, consist either, 1, of the *gist* or *substance* of the complaint, or defence—or, 2, of matter of *inducement*, or as it is sometimes termed, *conveyance*—or, 3, of matter of *aggravation*. Whatever else is stated, in any part of the pleadings, is but *surplusage*. For what is termed *form* in pleading, constitutes no distinct *matter*, but simply the *manner*, in which the matter pleaded is stated.

§ 8. The *gist* of the complaint or defence is the *essential ground*, or *principal* subject-matter of it; or that, without which no legal cause of complaint can appear, on the one hand, or no legal ground of defence, on the other; however perfect, in point of

(*w*) Iid. 2 Saund. 305, n. 13. Com. Dig. *Pleader*, E. 9. Cro. Jac. 411. Cro. Eliz. 401. See ch. 10.

(*x*) Com. Dig. *Pleader*, C. 20. Cro. Jac. 555, 557. 2 Mod. 304. 2 Black. R. 706.

CHAP. III.

form, the pleading may be. Of this nature is the *consideration* of the defendant's promise, in assumpsit—the performance of a *condition precedent*, in an action on a contract, containing such a condition—the *conversion* in trover, &c.

Inducement.

§ 9. Matter of *inducement* is that which is merely *introductory* to the essential ground or substance of the complaint, or defence—or in some respect *explanatory* of it. or of the manner in which it originated or took place. Thus in trover, the *loss* and *finding* of the plaintiff's goods (*y*)—and in an action for a nuisance to a house or land, the plaintiff's *possession* of the subject injured—are respectively matters of inducement.

Aggravation.

§ 10. Matter of *aggravation* is that which, in actions for forcible injuries, is intended to show the circumstances of *enormity*, under which the principal wrong complained of was committed. Thus if the plaintiff, in trespass for breaking and entering his house, superadds to his statement of the breaking and entry, that the defendant at the same time made an affray, beat his servants, scattered his goods, and committed other enormities, these superadded facts are only matters of *aggravation*, which require neither proof nor answer: The breaking and entering of the house being alone the *gist* of the action (*z*)—and whatever sufficiently answers *these*, is

(*y*) Bull. N. P. 33. Lawes' Pl. 66.
(*z*) 3 Wils. 294. 3 T. R. 292. 1 H. Black. 555. Lawes' Pl. 70.

of course a sufficient answer to the whole complaint, including all matters of aggravation (*a*).

CHAP. III.

§ 11. The last observation is equally true of matter of *inducement*; which, from its nature as already explained, does not in general admit of a distinct denial or precise answer of any kind (*b*). For any sufficient answer to the *material* facts, alleged in the pleading of the adverse party, covers all that he has alleged — including as well matter of inducement as matter of aggravation. — *Surplusage* is that which is *impertinent* or entirely *superfluous*, as not being necessary either to the substance or the form of pleading (*bb*).

Surplusage.

§ 12. It is regularly necessary in pleading to state nothing except *facts*, and as the case may be, *conclusions* from them (*c*); or in other words, nothing except facts as they really exist, or are, by legal fiction or presumption, deemed to exist. It is of course unnecessary, generally speaking, to allege matter of *law* (*d*). For the judges are always presumed — as has been suggested in a former chapter — to know judicially what the *law* is; and have therefore no occasion to be informed of it by the pleadings.

Facts only necessary to be pleaded.

§ 13. In some few instances, however, it was formerly thought necessary, and was therefore cus-

Matters of law not necessary to be pleaded.

(*a*) Iid. Lawes' Pl. 70.

(*b*) Lawes' Pl. 118. Bull. N. P. 33.

(*bb*) Com. Dig. *Pleader*, C. 28. 29. E. 12. Lawes' Pl. 63.

(*c*) Doug. 159. 278. Lawes' Pl. 46. (*d*) Iid. 8 Co. 155.

CHAP. III.

tomary, in declaring, to state the *law* as well as the facts upon which the action was founded. Such was the practice in declaring in actions *ex delicto*, against *common carriers* for goods lost or damaged by their negligence or breach of trust; and in similar actions against *innkeepers*, for the effects of their guests, when lost or injured *infra hospitium* (*e*): In both of which cases, the plaintiff, according to the ancient form of pleading, recited in his declaration the custom of the realm, i. e. the rule of *law*, in virtue of which he claimed a recovery (*f*) (2). But 'the custom of the realm' being, in all cases, no other than the *common* or *general unwritten* law of the realm, there was never, on principle, any need of reciting it. And of late, that practice has in a great measure fallen into disuse (*g*): Though in actions sounding in tort against innkeepers, it appears still to be usually, though unnecessarily, followed (*h*).

§ 14. In the same manner, it was formerly usual in declarations on *bills of exchange*, to recite the *custom of merchants* (i. e. the rule of mercantile law) upon which the action was founded (*i*). But in this instance also, as in the two former, such a recital

(*e*) Hob. 18. 3 Mod. 227. 1 Wils. 281. 2 Chitt. Pl. 273. Bac. Abr. *Carriers*, A. Id. *Inns*, C. 6. (n).

(*f*) 1 Sid. 245. Com. Dig. *Action on case for neg.* C. 2. Bac. Abr. *Inns*, C. 6. 3 Co. 32. a. F. N. B. 94.

(*g*) 3 Wils. 429. 2 Chitt. Pl. 271–2. 274.

(*h*) 2 Chitt. Pl. 274.

(*i*) Pl. Assist. 40. Kyd on Bills, 177. 180. Chitt. on Bills, 184–5. 233–4.

(2) In some few other instances also, the same mode of pleading formerly prevailed. (Vid. 1 Lill. Ent. 67. 68. 69. 80. 81).

was, upon the *principles* of pleading, clearly unnecessary: Since the 'custom of merchants,' or which is the same thing — the law-merchant, is a branch of the *common* law (*k*). In the modern precedents, therefore, the *recital* of the custom is in general omitted (*l*). And even the practice, which still prevails (*m*), of *counting* upon the custom (i. e. of making an express *reference* to it in the declaration, without reciting it), appears for the same reason to be an unnecessary formality, and has been so adjudged (*n*).

Inferences of law when stated.

§ 15. In some instances, however, inferences of law are advanced in pleading, for the purpose of showing the intended *application of the facts* pleaded, or for the sake of mere form. — Thus in declaring on bills of exchange, after the statement of the *res gesta*, or material facts, the plaintiff adds, 'by means whereof, &c, the defendant became *liable*,' i. e. in law, 'to pay,' &c (*o*). It is also usual for the defendant, in a plea of justification — after stating the special matter which constitutes his defence — to accompany his confession of the facts alleged against him with a *prout ei bene licuit;* i. e. to aver that he did the acts complained of, 'as by *law* he well might' (*p*). In this instance also, the proposition

(*k*) 1 Ld Ray. 88. 175. 2 Ib. 1542. Carth. 288.

(*l*) Iid. Pl. Assist. 80. 81. 241. Chitt. on Bills, 184. 234.

(*m*) Chitt. on Bills, 233-4. Pl. Assist. 241.

(*n*) 1 Ld Ray. 88. 175. 234. Carth. 83. 269. Chitt. on Bills, 234, (n. c).

(*o*) Chitt. on Bills, 235-244. Pl. Assist. 241.

(*p*) 8 T. R. 79. 2 Chitt. Pl. 503-506. 524-530.

CHAP. III.

involved in the clause just quoted, is only an *inference* of law from the facts which constitute the justification, and therefore is not of the substance of the plea.

Particular customs.

§ 16. In pleading *particular customs* (q), or *private statutes*, not only must the *facts* which bring the case within the custom or statute be pleaded; but the custom or statute *itself* — or at least so much of it as is material to the case — must be *recited* by the party complaining or defending under it (r) (3). But the recital, in these cases, is not to be deemed matter of *law*. For such customs and statutes — although they may respectively furnish the *rule of decision* in cases falling within them — are no part of the general law of the land; but, like private records, prescriptions, deeds, &c, are regarded and treated in pleading as matters of *fact*, of which the

(q) 1 Black. Com. 76. Co. L. 175. Litt. § 265. Dr. & St. 18.

(r) 1 Black. Com. 86. Cro. Jac. 139. 4 Co. 76. 2 East, 341. Bac. Abr. *Statute*, L. 2. 1 Saund. 193.

---

(3) There is a material distinction, not always observed by writers on pleading — and the non-observance of which has sometimes occasioned confusion — between *pleading*, *counting upon*, and *reciting* a statute. *Pleading* a statute, is merely *stating the facts* which bring a case within it, without making mention or taking any notice of the statute itself. *Counting upon* a statute, consists in making *express reference* to it — as, by the words, 'against the form of the statute' (or, 'by force of the statute'), 'in such case made and provided.' *Reciting* a statute, is *quoting* or stating its *contents*. A statute may, therefore, be *pleaded* without either reciting or *counting* upon it; and may be *counted upon* without being *recited*.

courts of justice cannot judicially take notice (*s*). Hence it is, that the existence of any such custom or statute may be *denied* by plea (*t*); and that when so denied, it must be proved as a *fact*, and can be tried only on an issue in fact. Whereas matter of *law*, properly so called, can never be denied in pleading (*u*).

Fictions in pleading.

§ 17. But under the rule requiring all material *facts* to be pleaded, it is sometimes necessary to allege not only those which really exist; but also certain *conclusions*, or *fictions*, which the law founds upon, or connects with them, and which it regards as *facts*, though they exist only in legal intendment.

§ 18. *Fictions* in pleading were devised for the sole purpose of advancing *justice* (*v*) (4); and having been sanctioned for this purpose, they require, on the one hand, no proof, and on the other, they cannot be traversed (*w*): Since to require the one, or permit the other, would defeat the end for which they were designed. The fictions employed in pleading are numerous; but their general nature and ope-

(*s*) 1 Black. Com. 86. 4 Co. 76. a. b. 1 Stra. 187. Doug. 378. 380. *n.*

(*t*) Bac. Abr. *Statute*, L. 2.

(*u*) 8 Co. 28.

(*v*) 3 Black. Com. 43. 107.

(*w*) Id. Cowp. 177–8.

---

(4) Fictions in pleading are seldom employed, except in the *declaration;* but are not, however, *universally* confined to that part of the pleadings.

CHAP. III.

ration may be sufficiently illustrated, for the present purpose, by two or three familiar examples: —

Fictions.

§ 19. In the action of *indebitatus assumpsit*, if there is an actual *debt*, or *legal liability*, (by simple contract), on the part of the defendant, but, as is frequently the case, no *express* undertaking to pay the debt; the plaintiff, in his declaration, must regularly allege a *promise* (*x*) (5). For as the action of assumpsit is, in its form and structure, adapted to no other demands than those arising upon *promises;* the law, — when no promise has actually been made — *implies* or *presumes* one, from the fact of the defendant's being indebted; for the purpose of en-

(*x*) Cro. Eliz. 913. 1 Lev. 164. 2 Ld. Ray. 1517. 2 Stra. 793.

(5) It is held, however, that in declaring, in assumpsit, on a *bill of exchange*, against the drawer, or on a *promissory note*, against the maker, a statement of the facts, which render the defendant liable to pay, is sufficient, without expressly alleging a *promise* on his part. (1 Salk. 128. 1 Stra. 224. Ld Ray. 538. 2 New Rep. 63. n.) The reason, assigned for the rule, is, that the drawing of the bill, or making of the note, is of itself an *actual* promise: So that alleging the act of *drawing*, &c, is virtually alleging a *promise*, by the drawer, &c, to pay. — Whether this rule, so far as it regards the declaration on a *bill of exchange*, (in which the drawer makes no *express* promise), is agreeable to the analogies and principles of pleading, appears at least questionable. For in all other cases of *indebitatus assumpsit*, the facts, stated in the declaration, as the ground of the defendant's liability, are regarded, upon the face of the record, only as the *consideration* of the promise, which the declaration alleges, and must allege. But whether the rule is, on principle, correct or not, the universal practice is, to allege a *substantive promise*, by the drawer of the bill.

Fictions.

titling the plaintiff to this beneficial action, instead of the precarious and less remedial action of debt, which was anciently his only remedy in such a case. But whenever the promise is thus implied, it is declared upon as an *express* one, and upon the face of the record is always taken to be express. There is, indeed, no such thing as an implied promise *in pleading;* or rather, the fact of its being implied appears only in *evidence*, and never upon the record (*y*).

§ 20. In trover also, the goods, for the conversion of which the action is brought, are, according to the precedents, alleged to have been *lost*, and to have come to the defendant's hands by *finding* (*z*). For as trover originally lay only for the conversion of goods *actually* lost and found (*a*); the averment of a *loss* by the plaintiff, and a *finding* by the defendant — which, in most cases, is a mere fiction — was, at a later period, introduced for the purpose of extending this liberal action to cases, in which there was anciently no other remedy, than that afforded by the more narrow and inconvenient action of *detinue* (*b*). And thus, by the aid of this fictitious averment, which is not traversable, the action of trover now lies in all cases, in general, in which he who is, by *any* means, in possession of another's

(*y*) 6 Mod. 131. Cowp. 289. 7 T. R. 351. *n.* 1 Ld. Ray. 538.

(*z*) 1 Lill. Ent. 70. 3 Black. Com. 153. 2 Chitt. Pl. 223-231.

(*a*) 3 Black. Com. 152. Bac. Abr. *Trover. Introd.*

(*b*) 3 Reeve H. E. L. 385-6. 526. 3 Black. Com. 153. 3 Woodes. 212.

CHAP. III.

personal chattels, converts them to his own use (*c*) (6).

Fictions.

§ 21. So also in the modern English *ejectment*, which lies nominally only for a *term of years*, the lease to the nominal plaintiff, his *entry* under it, and the *ouster* charged upon the casual ejector, (all which were originally material *facts*, and are still stated as facts in the declaration), are in reality mere fictions, devised for the purpose of escaping from the inconvenient forms of real actions, and facilitating the determination of questions of title to *real* property (*d*). And by these fictions, aided by corresponding rules of practice, this convenient remedy is accommodated practically to the trial of *freehold* titles (*e*).

Fee-simple, how to be pleaded.

§ 22. Whenever it is necessary for a party, in any stage of the pleadings, to show an estate in *fee-simple*, it is sufficient, in general, to allege the estate in *general* terms, (as that he, or another, was 'seised in his demesne as of fee'), without stating when or how the estate commenced, or was created (*f*).

(*c*) Bac. Abr. *Trover*. *Introd.* Cro. Eliz. 781. Bull. N. P. 33.

(*d*) 3 Black. Com. 199. 201. 206. 2 Burr. 667-8.

(*e*) 1 Wils. 220. 7 T. R. 327. 334. 1 Bos. & P. 573.

(*f*) 1 Ld Ray. 333. 2 Salk. 562. Comb. 476. Carth. 444. 3 Wils. 70. 72. 12 Mod. 191.

---

(6) Since the action has been thus extended, it is held, that the averment of *finding* is not indispensable (5 Bac. Abr. *Trover*, F. 1. Bull. N. P. 33.) It is still retained, however, in the approved precedents.

CHAP. III.

Particular estates, how pleaded.

But when title to any *particular* estate — as an estate in tail, for life, or for years — is necessary to be shown in a *plea in bar*, *avowry*, *replication*, or any of the pleadings *subsequent* to the declaration, the *commencement* of the estate, and the mode of its derivation, must be specially stated (*g*).

§ 23. The principal reason of this diversity appears to be, that an estate in *fee simple* may be, and frequently is acquired by means, consisting of sheer matter of *fact*, (as by a continued disseisin of the rightful owner, or by long possession), of which the jury is competent to judge (*h*); and which need not, therefore, be *specially* shown to the court upon the record: And hence a *general* allegation of a seisin in fee simple is traversable (*i*). Whereas *particular* estates, which must always be derived out of the fee simple, can regularly be created only by legal conveyance, or by operation of law (*k*); both of which modes of acquisition necessarily involve matter of *law*; of which the jury are not competent judges: And therefore, a *general* allegation of a seisin or possession of *such* an estate is ill; because it improperly blends law and fact, and therefore is not traversable (*l*).

§ 24. It is hence necessary — when title to estates of the latter kind is to be averred in a *plea*,

(*g*) Iid.

(*h*) 2 Salk. 562. 3 Wils. 72. Co. Lit. 297. a.

(*i*) Comb. 476. 12 Mod. 191.

(*k*) 3 Wils. 72. 12 Mod. 191. 2 Salk. 562.

(*l*) Comb. 476. Carth. 445. 12 Mod. 191. 2 Salk. 562.

CHAP. III.

Particular estates, how pleaded.

avowry, &c, — that the time and manner of their derivation be specially shown in the pleading; that the plaintiff may be able to traverse distinctly any particular point in the title. For as there is no *general issue* to pleas, avowries, replications, &c; no traverse can, in general, be taken upon them, otherwise than by denying *precisely* some or all of the *specific* allegations contained in them (*m*).

§ 25. But in *personal* actions, this latter rule holds, in general, only of those parts of the pleadings, which are *subsequent* to the declaration. And therefore if a tenant in tail, for life, or for years, brings a suit for an injury to his possession, (as in trespass *quare clausum fregit*, trespass on the case for obstructing a way, &c); it is not necessary for him to state the commencement of his title in his *declaration* (*n*). For the action is not founded on *title*, but on *possession*. It is not necessary, therefore, in such a case, to state his *title* in any manner whatever: It being sufficient to allege merely his *possession*. For, as against a *wrong doer*, possession alone, in the plaintiff, is sufficient (*o*); and in actions of this kind, the defendant is always charged as such.

§ 26. And in general, when, as in the preceding cases, a particular estate is only matter of *induce-*

(*m*) 2 Salk. 562.

(*n*) 2 Salk. 562. Comb. 476. Cro. Car. 571. Carth. 444.

(*o*) 1 Ld Ray. 333. 266. Com. Dig. *Pleader*, C. 39. Sayer, 32. 1 Wils. 327. 1 Vent. 319.

ment, it is unnecessary, in *any* stage of the pleadings, to state when or how it commenced (*p*) : The reason of which is apparent, from the principles, (already stated), which regulate the pleading of matter of inducement, in general. Indeed the single consideration, that such matter is never contested in *the pleadings*, furnishes a sufficient reason for the rule.

Ante, § 11.

§ 27. And therefore, in an action of trespass for an assault and battery, if the defendant, being a tenant for years of a house or land, justifies the acts complained of, as having been done in resisting the plaintiff's unlawful entry into the one, or upon the other; it is sufficient for the defendant to aver in his plea, that he was '*possessed* of a certain dwelling-house' (or 'a certain close') &c, without stating the time at which, or the manner in which, his possession commenced (*q*). For his estate or possession is but matter of *inducement*.

§ 28. As a general rule, all *material* facts, (7) pleaded on either side, must be stated in *positive and direct* terms, and not *argumentatively*, (i. e. in a manner which leaves them to be collected by *in-*

Material averments must be direct and positive.

(*p*) 3 Wils. 72. 1 Ld Ray. 334. 8 T. R. 79. 299. 2 Chitt. Pl. 529-531. Com. Dig. *Pleader*, C. 43. E. 19. Carth. 444.

(*q*) Ibid.

(7) *Material* facts are such as are *essential* to the right of action, or defence, and are therefore of the *substance* of the one, or the other.

CHAP. III.

Material averments. Post. § 42, et seq.

ference); nor by way of *recital*, as under a 'whereas' (*r*). This requisite is prescribed, not only for the sake of *precision;* but also that the adverse party may be enabled to traverse the matter alleged, *directly* and *distinctly*. And therefore, if in an action of covenant broken, the defendant — instead of pleading *performance* generally, or specially, as the nature and terms of the contract may require — pleads that he has *not broken* his covenant; the plea is ill (*s*). For it leaves the fact of *performance* to be *inferred* from that of the covenant's not being broken (8), so that the former fact, (the only one, on which such a plea can be supposed to be founded), cannot be *directly put in issue* by a traverse of the plea.

§ 29. Upon the same principle, if in trespass for tearing the seal from a deed, alleged to have been made by A. to B., and to have conveyed to B. a certain manor, the defendant pleads that A. did *not convey* the manor to B.; the plea is argumentative, and of course ill (*t*): Since it denies the trespass only by *inference* — i. e. only by denying the existence of such a deed as that described — instead of putting the wrongful *act* alleged directly in issue.

(*r*) Co. Litt. 303. a. Bac. Abr. *Pleas*, &c, B. 5. (4.) I. 5. *Trespass*, I. 2.

(*s*) 8 T. R. 278. 2 Black. R. 1312. 2 Vent. 156.

(*t*) Yelv. 223. Com. Dig. *Pleader*, E. 3.

---

(8) The plea stated in the text would also be ill, as improperly blending law and fact.

The proper plea, for the defence pleaded, in the case here stated, would be the general issue.

Material averments.

§ 30. Argumentative pleading is aided, however, by verdict, or on general demurrer (*u*). For the defectiveness of such pleading is not in the *matter* pleaded, but in the *manner* of pleading it; and is therefore only a fault in *form*.

§ 31. It is for a similar reason, that the general rule disallows the allegation of material facts by way of *recital;* as under a 'whereas.' For as this form of averment does not *directly assert* the fact recited, a traverse of the averment would not put the fact *directly* in issue. If therefore, in an action of trespass for an assault and battery, the plaintiff should complain, by saying in his declaration, '*whereas* the defendant with force and arms assaulted,' &c; or if in trespass *quare clausum fregit,* he should declare '*whereas* the defendant with force, &c, broke and entered his close;' the declaration would, in both cases, be ill (*v*) (9). For this mode

(*u*) Com. Dig. *Pleader,* E. 3. 1 Saund. 274. (n. 1.) Aleyn, 48. 9 Johns. R. 314. *Cont.* Bac. Abr. *Pleas,* B. 5. (4.)

(*v*) Bac. Abr. *Pleas,* &c, B. Tresp. I. 2. 5. 4. Co. Litt. 303. a. 2 Salk. 636. 1 Stra. 621. Com. Dig. *Pleader,* C. 86.

---

(9) When the suit is by *original writ,* (as in the English court of Com. Pleas,) such an averment in the declaration is good — being aided by the *recital of the writ,* in the declaration. (Com. Dig. *Pleader,* C. 86. 1 Wils. 99. 2 Ib. 203. Fort. 376. Bac. Abr. *Trespass,* I. 2.

CHAP. III.

Material averments.

of stating the injury would not constitute a positive allegation of the trespass in either case; and the plea of *not guilty* would be tantamount only to saying, in the one case, '*whereas* the defendant did not with force and arms assault,' &c, and in the other, '*whereas* he did not with force, &c, break and enter the plaintiff's close.'—A principal reason therefore, why the averment of material facts by way of recital is inadmissible is, that as such averments do not admit of a *direct* negative, no proper *precise* issue can be taken upon them.

§ 32. But in debt on bond, the allegation that '*whereas* the defendant, by his writing obligatory, sealed,' &c, 'acknowledged himself held and bound,' &c, 'yet he has not paid,' has always been held a sufficient averment of the execution of the bond; though that fact, which is the gist of the action, is stated only by way of recital: And in this form are all the common precedents of declarations on bonds, covenants, and specialties of every kind (*w*). The reason of this apparent deviation from the general rule is said to be, that as the statement under the 'whereas' is part of an entire sentence, of which the *latter* clause is a positive averment, the *former* part is in construction also positive, and therefore capable of being directly traversed (*x*). However this construction may appear, in a grammatical view, it has always prevailed in the forms of pleading.

(*w*) Bac. Abr. *Pleas*, &c, B. 5. (4.)—1 Lill. Ent. 144—187. 2 Chitt. Pl. 151—178. 191—9.

(*x*) Bac. Abr. *Pleas*, &c, B. 5. (4.)

§ 33. But in a declaration, the whole of which may be denied by the general issue, a material averment, under a 'whereas,' though formerly held incurable, is now amendable, and is ill only on *special* demurrer (*y*): The defect being not in the *matter* alleged, but in the *manner* of alleging it.

Material averments.

§ 34. The words *pro eo quod*, (for this that)—*quia* (because)—and *licet* (although,) are respectively sufficiently direct and positive for introducing a material averment (*z*); as they are all considered as terms of *affirmation*. But the word '*quare*' (wherefore), though used in the *writ* in certain actions, is inadmissible in a material averment in the *pleadings* (*a*): For it is merely *interrogatory*. And therefore a declaration which begins with complaining of the defendant, '*wherefore* with force, &c, he broke and entered' the plaintiff's close, is ill.

Pro eo quod.

Quare.

§ 35. A material averment may also be introduced by a *videlicit*, or *scilicit* (*to wit*); in which case, if the averment immediately preceding the '*viz.*' is direct and positive, that which immediately follows it is so (*b*). Thus if the plaintiff in trespass declares that the defendant took and carried away his '*goods, viz.*' such and such articles specifically

Videlicit.

(*y*) 2 Salk. 636. 1 Stra. 621. Com. Dig. *Pleader*, C. 86. 2 Stra. 1151. 1162. 1 Chitt. Pl. 375. 1 Wils. 99. 2 Mass. R. 358. 7 Johns. R. 109.

(*z*) 1 Saund. 117. (n. 4.) Com. Dig. *Pleader*, C. 77. 1 Lev. 194. 2 Lill. Ent. 429. 431. 435. 2 Chitt. Pl. 369—393.

(*a*) 2 Salk. 636. Bac. Abr. *Pleas*, &c, B. 5. (4.)

(*b*) Hob. 172. Com. Dig. *Parols*, A. 8.

CHAP. III.

Material averments.

mentioned, the specification under the '*viz.*' is a positive and traversable averment (*c*). So also in debt on bond, for the penal sum of £1000, if the defendant pleads that there is due on the bond 'a much less sum than £1000, *viz.* £500, and *no more*,' this last averment under the '*viz.*' is regarded as a *direct* allegation, and is traversable, as it would have been, if the *viz.* and the quoted words immediately preceding it, had been omitted (*d*).

§ 36. The proper office of a '*scilicit*,' or '*videlicit*,' is to *particularize* what is *general* in the words preceding it, or in some other manner to explain what goes before it (*e*). A '*viz.*' may therefore restrain the generality of preceding *words*, but cannot enlarge or diminish the preceding *subject-matter* (*f*). For in the former case, the '*viz.*' is merely an *explanation* of the language which precedes it; but in the latter, it is *repugnant to*, or *variant from*, the preceding matter. Thus if a grant is made to 'A. and his heirs, *viz.* heirs of his body,' the interest granted is an estate tail (*g*): For here the '*viz.*' is only explanatory of the sense in which the word 'heirs' is first used, and not inconsistent with it. But if one having *three* acres of land in the parish of A., grants '*all* his land in A., *viz. two acres*,' the *three* acres will pass (*h*): Or if he grants 'all his land' in the parish

(*c*) 2 Chitt. Pl. 99. 272. 379. 385.

(*d*) 2 Saund. 291. b. (n. 1.) 6 T. R. 460. 2 Wils. 332. 335.

(*e*) Hob. 175. 2 Saund. 291. b. (n. 1.) 2 Wils. 332. 335.

(*f*) Hob. 172. Com. Dig. *Parols*, A. 8.

(*g*) Iid.

(*h*) Iid. 2 Saund. 291. a. (n. 1.)

of *A.*, *viz. black-acre*, which lies *out* of that parish; black-acre will not pass by the grant *(i)*. For in both these cases the 'viz.' is *repugnant* to that which precedes it. The same distinction applies to the use of a 'viz.' in *pleading*.

§ 37. Yet in the application of this general distinction to the rules of pleading, there is one important difference to be observed, (as regards the use and effect of a 'viz.') between the averment of *material* and *immaterial* facts. When a *viz.* is followed by what is *material*, and *necessary* to be alleged, and preceded by words of direct averment, the *videlicit*, being regarded as a positive and direct allegation, is therefore traversable *(k)*: In other words, a material averment under a *viz.* is traversable, whenever it would have been so, if it had been made *without* a *viz.* Thus, when in debt on bond for a certain penal sum, conditioned for the payment of a less sum, the defendant pleaded that he was indebted to the plaintiff, 'in a large sum of money, *to wit*, *the said* sum in the said condition mentioned,' and then alleged special matter in avoidance—an exception was taken to the plea, as not containing any statement, in an *issuable* form, of the sum due on the bond: But the court overruled the objection, and held the statement under the '*to wit.*' to be travers-

(i) Iid. Hob. 170.

(k) 3 Burr. 1730. 1 Saund. 169. 170. (n. 2.) 2 Ib. 291. b. (n. 1.) 1 Black. R. 495. Yelv. 94, *note.* 4 Johns. R. 450. 2 Pick. 222.

CHAP. III.

able (*l*). And the rule appears to be universal, that *any* fact, which is in its nature traversable, may be traversed, though pleaded under a *videlicit* (*m*).

§ 38. It is apparent from what has been said, that a material fact cannot be made *immaterial*, by being pleaded under a '*viz.*' (*n*). Therefore, if an averment under a 'viz.' contains matter in itself material, but which is *repugnant* to what goes before; the pleading is ill (10). Thus where to an action against a sheriff for an escape, he pleaded a recaption of the prisoner, on fresh suit, '*before* the exhibition of the bill, *viz. on the* 8*th of May*' (which was in fact *after* the bill was exhibited), the court held the plea ill (*o*). For the time of retaking was material; inasmuch as a recaption, *after* the exhibition of the bill, is no defence in law to such an action.

§ 39. As material facts averred under a *videlicit* are traversable; it follows that they must, if traversed, be proved: For nothing is legally traversable by either party, except what the adverse party may be required to prove. If therefore in pleading

(*l*) 2 Wils. 332. 335.

(*m*) 5 T. R. 71. 1 Ib. 656. 4 Johns. R. 450. 1 Stra. 233. 2 Saund. 291. a. c. (n. 1.) 6 T. R. 460. 463. 1 Saund. 169. 170. (n. 2.)

(*n*) Iid.

(*o*) Latch, 200. 201. 2 Saund. 291. c. (n. 1). 1 Black. R. 495.

(10) On this point, however, there have formerly been some contradiction and confusion. Latch, 200. 201. Cro. Jac. 135. 154. 662. 12 Mod 579. 580.

a *record*, or *written instrument* of any kind, the pleader misstates the date of it, or otherwise misdescribes it in any material particular, though under a *videlicit*, he must fail in his proof: For the record or instrument, when produced in evidence, will, by its *variance* from the description of it in the pleading, appear to be a *different* record or instrument from that pleaded *(p)* (11).

§ 40. But if that which comes under a *videlicit* is *immaterial*, or matter of mere *form*; its repugnancy to what goes before does not *vitiate*, nor in any way affect, the pleading. In such a case, the *videlicit* is regarded as wholly nugatory and void, and is therefore rejected as *surplusage* *(q)* (12). For as it contradicts nothing that is *material* in what precedes it, (if it did, it could not be strictly *immaterial*), it falls within the legal maxim, '*utile per inutile non vitiatur.*' And the pleading will be good or ill, precisely

(p) 4 T. R. 590. *et vide* 1 Ib. 656. 6 Ib. 463. 2 Saund. 291. b. (n. 1).

(q) 1 Lev. 195. 1 Saund. 116. 287. 2 Ib. 291. (n. 1). Com. Dig. *Pleader*, C. 19.

---

(11) The term 'variance' signifies, in law, a discrepancy between the statement or description of a record, written instrument, or express contract *in pleading*, and the record, instrument, &c, itself, as shown in evidence.

(12) In most of the numerous cases, usually cited to this point, the question has arisen *after verdict*. It was directly decided, however, in the case cited above from 1 Lev. 194–5, and 1 Saund. 116, (which was determined upon great deliberation, and after several arguments), that the rule holds as well before, as after verdict.

CHAP. III.

as it would have been, if the 'videlicit', including the averment under it, had been omitted or struck out. Thus, if in trover the plaintiff declares that he was possessed of the goods in question, on the *tenth* day of May, in such a year, and that the defendant, 'postea' (*afterwards*) '*to wit*, on the *first* day' of the same month, converted them, the 'videlicit' will be rejected as surplusage (*r*). For the particular day of the conversion being *immaterial*, and that stated under the '*videlicit*' being repugnant to the preceding 'postea,' the 'videlicit' is held to be void. The consequence is, that the declaration will stand, in regard to its legal sufficiency, as if the plaintiff had alleged that he lost the goods on the 10th day of May, and that the defendant '*afterwards* converted them,' (omitting the *videlicit*, and stating no particular day); in which case, the declaration would be good, unless *specially* demurred to (*s*). So also, if the plaintiff in ejectment declares on a lease dated the *tenth* day of May, by virtue of which he entered, and alleges that the defendant '*afterwards*, to wit, on the *first* day' of the same month, ejected him; the 'videlicit' will be rejected, as in the last case; and the effect will be the same (*t*), and for the same reason. It is hardly necessary perhaps to add, that an *immaterial* 'videlicit' cannot be traversed, and need not be *proved* (*u*).

(*r*) Com. Dig. *Pleader*, C. 19. Cro. Jac. 428. 135. 1 Lev. 195. 12 Mod. 579. Stra. 232. 1095.

(*s*) 1 Lev. 195. 1 Saund. 286. 287, a. Com. Dig. *Pleader*, C. 19. *vide* Cro. Jac. 96. 429.

(*t*) Cro. Jac. 96. Com. Dig. *Pleader*, C. 19.

(*u*) 1 Black. Rep. 495. *per Blackstone, arg.* 2 Saund. 291. c. (n. 1). 3 T. R 68. *Vid.* 3 M. & S. 175.

CHAP. III.

§ 41. But a *videlicit* can never be rejected, *unless repugnant* to what goes before it (*v*). For when *consistent* with what precedes it, there can be no more propriety in rejecting it, than there would be in rejecting and treating as surplusage any, and every other averment, which the pleader may find to operate against himself.

Material averments, by way of recital, are in some cases good.

§ 42. The general rule, (*ante*, § 28), requiring material facts to be alleged in terms of *direct and positive* averment, is itself by no means universal. For in *declarations*, facts which are material, and even of the *gist* of the action, may in some instances be stated under a 'whereas.' And the distinction, collectible from the precedents, appears to be, that all those facts which are *directly denied by the terms of the general issue*, or which may, by the established usage of pleading, be *specially traversed*, must be averred in *direct and positive* terms: But that facts, however material, which are *not directly denied by the terms* of the general issue, though liable to be contested under it, and which, according to the usage of pleading, *cannot be specially traversed*, may be alleged in the declaration by way of recital.

§ 43. The reason of this distinction appears to be, that as facts of the former class are *directly* traversable, either by the general or a special issue; they ought to be *so* alleged, that the issue which may be taken upon them shall consist, (as all issues

(*v*) 5 East, 244. 1 Saund. 169.

CHAP. III.

regularly must), of a *direct affirmative* on one side, and a *direct negative* on the other — which could not be the case, if they were alleged by way of recital: Whereas, facts of the latter class — i. e. all material facts, which, though not in terms denied by the general issue, are yet liable to be contested under it, and which cannot be made the subject of a special traverse — may as well be alleged by way of recital, as in direct and positive terms; because all such facts may always be controverted, *without* being *directly* and *in terms put in* issue. And as it can never be necessary, in pleading, to answer the averment of any such fact, by a *direct negative;* it can, of course, never be necessary to make the averment in terms of *direct affirmation.*

§ 44. To illustrate this distinction: — In trespass *quare clausum fregit,* or for taking and carrying away the plaintiff's goods, the forcible breaking and entering of the plaintiff's close, in the one case, and the forcible taking and carrying away of his goods, in the other, must be *directly and* positively alleged in the declaration (*w*). In trespass for an assault and battery, the act of assaulting and beating must be averred in the same manner (*x*). In the same manner also must be alleged the *conversion* in trover (*y*) — the *ouster* in ejectment (*z*) — the erection of the nuisance, in an action for that injury (*a*) — and the

(*w*) 1 Lil. Ent. 431. 453. 2 Chitt. Pl. 382. 391. 393. 377.
(*x*) 1 Lil. Ent. 429. 436. 455. 2 Salk. 636. 2 Chitt. Pl. 367-8.
(*y*) 1 Lil. Ent. 70. 2 Chitt. Pl. 323, *et ult.*
(*z*) 2 Chitt. Pl. 395. 402.
(*a*) 2 Chitt. Pl. 240-1. 331-8.

taking of the cattle or goods, in replevin (*b*) — the *neglect* of a bailee, in a special action on the case, by the bailor, for damage occasioned by such neglect (*c*) — the *being indebted*, in debt on simple contract (*d*) — the *permitting of the escape*, in an action against a sheriff for an escape, &c. (*e*). For the acts, or facts, specified in these examples (to which many others, falling within the same rule, might be added) are such as the general issue, in the several cases supposed, would *directly and necessarily* deny. This will be very obvious, when it is considered that in no one of these examples, can the fact specified be *admitted* by the defendant *consistently* with the general issue. And as the particular fact, mentioned in each of these examples, is liable to be thus *directly* denied by the general issue; it must be *directly and positively* alleged. In assumpsit also, the *promise* must be stated, in terms direct and positive (*f*); because the general issue (*non assumpsit*) purports to be a *direct* denial of the promise (13).

§ 45. So also in declaring on specialties — as in covenant broken, debt on a covenant, or a special

(*b*) 2 Lil. Ent. 356. 369. 2 Chitt. Pl. 364—368.
(*c*) 2 Chitt. Pl. 103-125. 274-5.
(*d*) 2 Chitt. Pl. 141. 237.
(*e*) 1 Lil. Ent. 60. 2 Chitt. Pl. 147-151. 299-302.
(*f*) Chitt. on Bills, tit. *Precedents*, passim.

---

(13) The application of the general rule to the action of *assumpsit* requires a distinct explanation; (for which *vide post.* § 47, and note 15).

CHAP. III.

declaration on a bond (14) — if the right of action depends on a condition *precedent; performance* of the condition must be alleged, in terms of direct averment (*g*). For as the fact of performance, on the plaintiff's part, is of the *gist* of his action; the defendant must be at liberty in some way to contest it. But as he cannot do this under the plea of *non est factum* — inasmuch as that plea is not adapted to such a defence; he must of course be at liberty to take a special issue upon the plaintiff's allegation of performance, by a *traverse*. That allegation must, therefore, be *so* made, that an issue, thus taken upon it, may consist of a *direct* affirmative on one side, and a *direct* negative on the other. The same rule holds, as to all *material* facts alleged in the declaration, and which cannot be controverted under the general issue.

§ 46. And even in assumpsit, in which, (for reasons peculiar to that action) advantage *may* be taken of a condition precedent, under the general issue; performance of such a condition must, nevertheless, be averred in *direct* terms (*h*): Because the defendant may, if he so elects, take a special issue upon the fact of performance. Thus, if A. promises to pay money to B., in consideration of B.'s *hereafter*

(*g*) 2 Chitt. Pl. 197. 485-6.
(*h*) Hob. 106. Cro. Eliz. 201. Com. Dig. *Pleader*, G. 11. C. 69.

(14) A special declaration on a bond is one, which counts as well on the *condition*, as the penal part, and assigns a breach. (Bac. Abr. *Pleas*, &c. B. 1. Doct. Pl. 84.)

delivering certain goods to A., and B. brings assumpsit for the money; he must *directly* allege the delivery of the goods, according to the agreement. For the delivery of the goods is a condition precedent, and therefore *specially traversable.* So also, if one is bound by his promise to pay the debt of a stranger upon *request*, or upon *notice* given of its amount; a request or notice must, for the same reason, be specially and *directly* alleged in the declaration (*i*).

§ 47. But the *consideration in assumpsit,* though of the *gist* of the action, may, when *executed*, (as in the case of a liability *existing at the time* of the promise), be stated under a 'whereas'. And in this form is the consideration in such cases laid, in the precedents (*k*). For the consideration is not directly denied by the *terms* of the plea of *non assumpsit;* and cannot be made the subject of a *special traverse* (*l*) — because such a traverse would be, in effect, the *general issue informally pleaded*, and therefore inadmissible. There is, consequently, according to the foregoing principles, no need of a direct averment, in stating the consideration. As, however, it is of the substance of the cause of action, the defendant

(*i*) Iid. I Saund. 32. Com. Dig. *Condition*, L. 11. *Pleader*, 73. 3 Salk. 308. Doug. 21.

(*k*) 1 Lill. Ent. *in assumpsit, passim.* Chitt. on Bills, tit. *Precedents, passim.*

(*l*) Com. Dig. *Pleader*, G. 11. 14. Cro. Eliz. 201. Hob. 106. Hetl. 50. Doug. 21. Bac. Abr. *Pleas*, &c. H. 5.

CHAP. III. is, of course, at liberty to deny it: But he must do this, if at all, under the general issue (15).

§ 48. Thus also, and for the same reason, the plaintiff's *property* (or his *lawful possession*, which implies a property), in the goods for which trover is brought — his *possession* of, or *interest* in the house or land, alleged to be injured, in an action for a nuisance — his *lease*, in ejectment — his *delivery* of the goods to the defendant, in a special action on the case, for negligence, against the latter as bailee — (to which various other examples, of a similar kind, might be added) — may respectively be stated in the declaration, under a 'whereas' (*m*). For none of these particular facts are *directly* denied, in any of the several cases mentioned, by the plea of *not guilty;* indeed they may respectively be *admitted* by the defendant, *consistently* with that plea. And

(*m*) *Vide References*, Ante, § 44, from (*y*) to (*e*). Bac. Abr. *Pleas*, &c. B. 4.

---

(15) It is true that in special assumpsit (i. e. assumpsit upon an *express* promise), the defendant may, under the general issue, *admit* the promise, without destroying the plea; and still deny or impeach the consideration; or show that the promise has been performed, released, or in any way extinguished. But this appears to be in consequence of an anomaly in the pleadings, in this particular action; or rather, of a *deviation* from the strict original principles of pleading — occasioned by confounding the pleadings, on the part of the defendant, in *special* assumpsit, with those in *general* or *indebitatus* assumpsit, and thus giving the same meaning and effect to the general issue, in the former as in the latter. (Vid. 1 Mod. 210; and *post.* chap. vi, §§ 46. 47. 48. 49.)

as a *special* traverse of either of them would be improper, as being an informal *general issue;* it is apparent, from what has been said before, that there can be no necessity for stating any of them, by way of *direct* averment. They are severally liable, however, to be contested (16); but this can be done only in evidence, under the general issue: And if so contested, they must respectively be *proved;* or the plaintiff must fail in his action. It is therefore manifest, that all the facts just specified are in strictness *material,* in the several cases supposed, though usually classed with matters of *inducement.*

Material averments in the plea, &c. must always be direct.

§ 49. This distinction, however, is applicable only to the *declaration.* In all the subsequent pleadings, as the plea in bar, replication, &c, the general rule, requiring material facts to be alleged directly and positively, admits of no exception (*n*): For as there is no *general issue* to any of these subsequent pleadings (17); the only mode, in general, of denying any of them, is by precisely traversing some or all of the particular issuable facts alleged in them.

(*n*) Lawes' Pl. 134.

---

(16) In the modern English ejectment, the real defendant is not indeed permitted, under the *common rule,* to deny the fictitious lease, counted upon in the declaration. But this is merely a positive regulation, by *rule of Court;* and does not affect the correctness of the position in the text, so far as regards the *original principles* of the action.

(17) A replication, containing a *new assignment,* may indeed be answered by the general issue. But a new assignment is in the nature of a new declaration. (*Post.* ch. 6. Part 2.)

CHAP. III.

Hence, the allegation of every such fact must be so framed, as to admit of a *direct* negative answer.

Inducement, how pleadable.

§ 50. It is apparent from the preceding rules, that matter of *mere inducement*, in the declaration, may always be stated by way of *recital*. For as such matter neither requires nor admits of a *direct answer* of any kind, in pleading; it can never require a *direct* allegation. This rule, however, must not be understood to apply, without exception, to what is termed the *inducement* to a *traverse*, in the subsequent pleadings.

Certainty.

§ 51. An important requisite, in all pleading, is *certainty* (*o*). This requisite implies, that the matter pleaded must be clearly and distinctly stated; so that it may be fully understood by the adverse party, the counsel, the jury, and the judges; and especially, (as regards the *declaration*), that the defendant may be enabled to plead the judgment, which may be rendered in the cause, in bar of any subsequent action for the same cause (*p*). For if a vague or partial description of the matter in controversy, in a given case, were allowed; and in a subsequent suit for the same thing, the declaration should contain a full and precise description of it; the cause of action, though actually the same in both cases, would not *appear*, from a comparison of the two records, to be so.

(*o*) Bac. Abr. *Pleas*, &c. B. 1. Hob. 295. 5 Co. 34-5.

(*p*) 2 Ld Ray. 1411. 4 Burr. 2456. 5 Co. 34. 1 Day, 315. Bac. Abr. *Trover*, F. 1. Reg. Pl. 4.

Degrees of certainty.

§ 52. Certainty in pleading is, according to Lord Coke, of three sorts or degrees: viz. 'Certainty to a *common* intent' — '*certainty to a certain intent in general*' — and 'certainty to a *certain* intent in *every particular*' (q). These degrees, which it would be difficult to distinguish by exact logical definitions, have been sometimes treated as idle and unintelligible refinements. It seems agreed, however, by all common-law jurists, that there are different degrees of certainty, (however they may be denominated), required for different kinds or classes of pleas: And the objection to Lord Coke's denominations of them is not, that the law does not recognize *any* distinction, in respect to the requisite degree of certainty in different branches of pleading; but that the language, in which he has endeavoured to express the distinction, is not sufficiently precise and intelligible, to convey any very definite notion of it. The objection thus understood, is undoubtedly well founded; but we are not, for this reason, to discard all distinction between different degrees of certainty in pleading (r): Since such degrees are not only recognized in legal theory; but practically observed, to a certain extent at least, in all the authoritative precedents. Without attempting, however, to frame exact legal definitions of these different degrees of certainty, (which — as they are merely *relative*, and referrible to no fixed standard — would seem impossible) — it may suffice, perhaps, to present the following general explanation of them:

(q) Co. Litt. 303. a. Com. Dig. *Pleader*, C. 17.
(r) *Per* Buller, J. 2 H. Black. 530.

CHAP. III.

Degrees of certainty.

§ 53. The first degree of certainty, in Lord Coke's enumeration, and which he denotes 'certainty to a *common* intent,' is the lowest which the rules of pleading in any instance allow. This degree is sufficient only in pleas in *bar*, *rejoinders*, and such other pleadings, on the part of the *defendant*, as go to *the action* (*s*); but not in *dilatory* pleas. The second degree, or 'certainty to a *certain intent in general*,' is higher than the former, and is required in *counts*, *replications*, and other pleadings on the part of the *plaintiff*; as also in *indictments* and *informations* (*t*): It being deemed reasonable, that such pleadings as assert a *charge*, either criminal or civil, against the adverse party, should be construed with greater strictness, than those which state his *defence* or *excuse*.

§ 54. More precise explanations of these two degrees of certainty have, however, been attempted. Thus, Mr Justice *Buller* observes, 'By a *common* intent I understand, that when words are used, which will bear a *natural* sense, and also an *artificial* one, or one to be made out by *argument* or *inference*, the *natural* sense shall prevail. It is simply a rule of *construction*, and not of *addition*: *Common* intent cannot *add* to a sentence words which are omitted' (*u*). But where 'certainty to a *certain* intent in *general*' is required, if words are used which will

(*s*) Cowp. 682. Doug. 159. 2 H. Black. 530.

(*t*) Iid. Co. Litt. 303. a. Com. Dig. *Pleader*, C. 24. 2 Lill. Ab. 377.

(*u*) 2 H. Black. 530.

Degrees of certainty.

bear these two senses, they may be taken, it seems, *either* way against the *party pleading;* though as against the *adverse* party, they can be understood only in their *natural* sense: So that if *either* sense will operate *against* the pleader, his pleading is defective (*v*). The same distinguished judge again observes, that by the second degree of certainty is meant, 'what, upon a fair and reasonable construction, may be called certain, *without recurring to possible facts, which do not appear'* (*w*); i. e. without denying, or avoiding by *anticipation*, possible facts, which may operate against him; and on the other hand, without the aid of any supposable facts or circumstances, not alleged by him.

§ 55. These expositions appear correct, as far as they extend: In other words, they conform to the points adjudged, in the particular cases, to which they relate; but if considered as intended to furnish a comprehensive criterion, applicable to all cases to which they may extend, they will often be found, it is believed, to afford but little assistance to the inquirer. The only practicable method, perhaps, of acquiring a competent knowledge of the distinction in question, is a careful and thorough examination of precedents.

§ 56. It is however material to be observed, that neither of these *two first* degrees of certainty

(*v*) Co. Litt. 303. Lawes' Pl. 54.
(*w*) Doug. 159.

CHAP. III.

Degrees of certainty.

requires the pleader to allege any thing more than is necessary to constitute, *primâ facie*, a right of action, or a legal defence (*x*). He is, therefore, not obliged to deny or avoid, by *anticipation*, any of the possible answers which may be given, on the other side, to the matter alleged in his pleading. And therefore in declaring on a contract, the plaintiff is not bound to aver that the defendant, at the time of contracting, was *not* an infant, or *feme covert*—or that the contract was *not* obtained by fraud, or duress, or has not been released—or any other such special matter as might, if alleged and proved on the other side, defeat his action. For if any such matter exists, it is matter of *defence*, to be shown by the defendant. And the same principle governs, in special pleas in bar, and other pleadings to the *action*, on the part of the defendant.—It is necessary indeed for a plaintiff, declaring on contract, to allege that the debt has *not been paid*, or the agreement not performed—not, however, by way of *anticipating* the defence of payment or performance, but because, without such an allegation, no breach of the contract, and of course no *primâ facie* right of action, will appear in the declaration.

§ 57. Certainty of the third sort, or 'to a certain intent in *every particular*,' requires the utmost fullness and particularity of statement, as well as the highest attainable accuracy and precision—leaving,

(*x*) 2 Wils. 100. 2 Burr. 1037. 1 Ld Ray. 400. 1 Saund. 299.

CHAP. III.

Degrees of certainty.

on the one hand, nothing to be supplied by intendment or construction; and on the other, no supposable special answer unobviated (*y*). The rule, requiring this degree of certainty, is a rule not of '*construction*' only, but also of '*addition*;' i. e. it requires the pleader, not only to answer fully what is necessary to be *answered;* but also to *anticipate* and exclude all such supposable matter, as would, if alleged on the opposite side, *defeat* his plea (*z*). This last requisite affords a clear and marked distinction between this, and the two former kinds of certainty. For in those two, nothing more is necessary, in general, than to answer fully the substance of what is *actually affirmed* by the adverse party— or at most to make out a claim or defence, *primâ facie* sufficient; without anticipating other matters, not already appearing in the pleadings, but which may possibly be alleged in reply.

§ 58. This third and highest degree of certainty is required only in such pleas as are *odious* or *unfavourably* regarded in the law: viz. pleas in *estoppel*, and *dilatory* pleas (*a*). The former are so regarded because their effect is to preclude the adverse party from averring even *the truth*, if inconsistent with the *estoppel* pleaded (*b*); and the latter, because their

(*y*) Co. Litt. 352. b.

(*z*) Willes, 554. Lawes' Pl. 55.

(*a*) Bac. Abr. *Pleas*, &c, I. 11. Cro. Jac. 82. 2 Saund. 209. b. 8 T. R. 167. 3 Ib. 185-6. 5 Ib. 487. Doug. 159. 2 H. Black. 530. Willes, 554. Lawes' Pl. 56. 107. 134. Com. Dig. *Estoppel*, E. 4.

(*b*) Co. Litt. 303. a. 352. b. Lawes' Pl. 55.

CHAP. III.

object is to defeat actions upon grounds unconnected with their *merits*.

Degrees of certainty.

§ 59. It has been said, indeed, that the *highest* degree of certainty is required only in pleas of *estoppel* (*c*). So far as regards pleadings which go, on either side, to the *right of action*, the proposition is undoubtedly correct; and in this limited sense it was, probably, meant to be understood. For it is agreed by all, that no other plea of *that* class, except a plea in *estoppel*, requires the highest degree of certainty. It is clear, however, that *dilatory* pleas in general require at least the same certainty as pleas in *estoppel*. If, for example, the defendant is misnamed in the writ or declaration, (as if A. is sued by the name of B.); it is not sufficient for the defendant to allege in his plea, that his name is *not B.*: He must also show in his plea that his true name is A., and must aver that he was, at the time of the writ purchased (*d*), known and called by the latter name; and must, moreover, subjoin a traverse, that he was known or called by the name of B. (*e*) — thus excluding, by *anticipation*, every supposition which could justify the plaintiff in giving him the name of B. This example will illustrate the position, that the rule requiring the highest degree of certainty, is a rule of *addition* as well as construction. (Vid. ch. 5, § 45).

(*c*) 2 H. Black. 530.

(*d*) 1 Salk. 7. Bac. Abr. *Pleas*, &c, F. 3.

(*e*) Willes, 554. 1 Lill. Ent. 6. 2 Chitt. Pl. 418. 3 T. R. 185–6. 5 Ib. 487. Com. Dig. *Abatement*, I. 11. Lawes' Pl. 107. 2 H. Black. 530.

CHAP. III.

Certainty, in what particulars necessary.

As to the parties.

§ 60. The certainty required in pleading relates chiefly to *parties, time, place, and subject-matter.* For certainty, as regards the *subject-matter*, the reader is referred to the Division, *Declaration*, (ch. 4). — The parties should be described by their *proper names* (*f*): Such a description being necessary for the purpose of identifying them. And no other form of description, it seems, can supply the omission of their proper names. If therefore two or more persons are sued, as copartners in trade; a description of them, by their partnership *firm*, or the name of their house, without their proper names, seems clearly insufficient (*g*). For the style of a partnership, being entirely arbitrary, may not contain the proper name of either of its members.

§ 61. But when a *corporation* is a party, the only proper mode of describing it, is by its corporate name (*h*): This being the only name or description, by which a body politic is known in law (*i*). For the law takes no notice of the individual members of a corporation, *as such*, except when the *individual* right of a corporator is the subject in question.

§ 62. When the name of either party, having been once introduced in the pleadings, is afterwards repeated, the repetition of it must be accompanied

(*f*) Com. Dig. *Pleader*, C. 17.
(*g*) 8 T. R. 508.
(*h*) 2 Stra. 787. 2 Ld Ray. 1515. Com. Dig. *Pleader*, C. 18.
(*i*) 1 Black. Com. 474–5.

CHAP. III.

Certainty as to parties.

with some such term of reference, as may *identify* the person named in the latter instance, as the one before named — as by the word 'said,' 'aforesaid,' or some other term of similar import: Otherwise the latter description will be ill for want of certainty (*k*). But when there are *two* or more antecedent persons to whom, or subjects to which it may be referred, the word 'said,' 'aforesaid,' &c, does not alone import sufficient certainty (*l*). In such cases, it is necessary to use the words 'first aforesaid,' 'last aforesaid,' or other terms of equivalent import (*m*).

Certainty as to time.

§ 63. It is a general rule of pleading in personal actions, that the *time* of every traversable fact must be stated (*n*); i. e. that every such fact must be alleged to have taken place on some particular day. This rule seems to be designed merely to promote *certainty* in the pleadings; but in a great proportion of the instances which fall within the rule, very little, if any, practical certainty can result from the observance of it. For where the time is *immaterial*, the pleader is of course not confined in his allegations to the *true time*, nor in his proof to the time alleged (*o*). He is not confined to the true time in *pleading*, where the time is immaterial, because he is not, in such a case, obliged to show in *evidence*

(*k*) 2 Lev. 207. Com. Dig. *Pleader*, C. 18.

(*l*) 8 T. R. 178. 2 East, 66. Cro. Eliz. 267. 2 Ld Ray. 888. 1 B. & A. 327. Com. Dig. *Pleader*, C. 18.

(*m*) 8 T. R. 178.

(*n*) Com. Dig. *Pleader*, C. 19. Yelv. 94.

(*o*) Co. Litt. 283. a. 1 Saund. 24. (n. 1).

CHAP. III.

Certainty as to time.

the precise day, on which the fact alleged took place—which would often, indeed, be impossible. And where the day is not material in *evidence*, it cannot be so in *pleading* (*p*). In such cases, therefore, the adverse party and the court are but little better informed, by the laying of a particular day, of the *actual* time when the fact alleged took place, or to what day the pleader's proof will apply, than if no particular time had been stated in the pleading. Still however it is in general necessary, in point of form at least, to lay a day for every traversable fact, whether the day is material or not; and in the declaration especially, this is necessary for the additional reason, that the cause of action must always appear, by the plaintiff's own showing, to have accrued before the commencement of the suit (*q*).

Time, when immaterial.

§ 64. The precise day on which a material fact alleged in the pleadings took place, is in most cases immaterial, except when the date of a *record*, or other *writing*, or some other fact, the time of which must be *proved* by a written document, is alleged (*r*). For as the day is not an independent *fact*, or substantive matter, but a mere circumstance or accompaniment of such matter; it obviously cannot be in its own nature material, and must therefore be made

(*p*) 2 Stra. 806. 2 Saund. 5. a. (n. 3).

(*q*) Bac. Abr. *Pleas*, &c, B. 5. 1. 1 Saund. 24. a. (n. 1.) 291. c. (n. 1.) 2 Ib. 171. n. 1 Stra. 21.

(*r*) 10 Mod. 313. 1 Saund. 24. (n. 1.) 4 T. R. 590.

CHAP. III.

so, if at all, only by the nature of the fact or matter, in connexion with which it is pleaded.

Time.

§ 65. If then a tort is stated to have been committed, or a parol contract to have been made, on a particular day; the plaintiff is, in neither case, confined in his proof to the day laid; but may support the allegation, by proving that the wrong was done (*s*), or the contract made (*t*), on another day — except that, in each case, the day laid in the declaration, and that proved in evidence, must both be prior to the commencement of the suit. And as the plaintiff is not generally confined, in evidence, to the time stated in the *declaration;* so neither is the defendant, when the time on his part is immaterial, confined to that which is laid in his *plea* (*u*). And the same rule obtains throughout the subsequent pleadings.

§ 66. But though a parol contract has, in strictness, no date, and consequently the time of making it is not, *as such*, material; yet if time enters into the *terms* of such a contract, or is involved in any of its essential parts; the true time must be stated, to avoid a *variance.* Hence, in an action on the statute of usury, in which the plaintiff stated a corrupt agreement, made on the 21*st* of December, 1774, for forbearance from that time to the 23*rd* of

(*s*) Co. Litt. 283. a. Cro. Eliz. 32. 1 Chit. Pl. 383. 1 Saund. 24. (n. 1.) 2 Ib. 5. (n. 3). 295. (n. 2).

(*t*) Stra. 21. 806. 10 Mod. 313. 348. 1 Chitt. Pl. 258. 1 Lev. 110. 111.

(*u*) 1 Saund. 24. (n. 1). 2 Ib. 5. a. b. (n. 3).

Time.

December, 1776, it was resolved, that proof of an agreement made on the 23*rd* of December, 1774, for forbearance for two years, did not support the declaration (*v*). It is to be observed, however, that this declaration was founded, not upon any supposition that, in proving a parol contract, the plaintiff is limited to the day on which it is alleged in the declaration to have been *made;* but upon the ground that the agreement proved, *varied in its terms*, from that stated in the declaration: Since the time of forbearance, counted upon, was an *essential part of the agreement* itself, and entered necessarily into the *description* of it.

§ 67. But in pleading any *written document*—such as a record, specialty, promissory note, bill of exchange, &c, the day, on which it is alleged to bear date, is material, and must therefore be truly stated (*w*): As there will otherwise be a *variance* between the writing itself, and the description of it in the pleading. Thus in debt on bond, if the plaintiff counts upon a writing obligatory, as bearing date on a certain day, and the instrument is actually dated on a different day; the variance will be fatal to the action. For though the date is strictly no part of the *contract*, it nevertheless enters into the description of the *instrument;* and therefore a misstatement of the date describes a *different deed* from that exhibited in evidence. And the same rule obtains,

(*v*) Cowp. 671. et vid. 4 Esp. Rep. 152.

(*w*) 1 Stra. 21. 2 Ib. 806. 10 Mod. 313. 1 T. R 656. 3 Ib. 531. 1 Lev. 110. 111.

CHAP. III.

Time.

whenever the time stated in the pleading, on either side, is to be proved by a *record*, *or written instrument*, referred to in the pleading.

§ 68. Where the date of an instrument is alleged, it is not indispensable to the sufficiency of the pleading, that the time of its *delivery* be stated at all (*x*). For the date being stated, and the time of delivery omitted; the instrument will be *intended* to have been delivered on the day of the date.

§ 69. But if the plaintiff, in an action on a specialty, describes it in the *declaration*, as bearing date on a certain day, without averring the time of its *delivery*; he cannot, in his *replication* allege that it was delivered on a day *different* from that of its date, as stated in the declaration (*y*). For the time of delivery being omitted in the declaration, must be *intended* (as has been suggested already), to have been the *same* as that of the date (*z*): And as the day of the date is material; an averment, in the replication, that the delivery was on a *different* day, would be a *departure*.

§ 70. But where time is not, *primâ facie*, material, it may sometimes be *made* so by the subsequent pleading of the adverse party. Thus, though upon the *face of the declaration*, the day, on which the cause of action is laid, be immaterial; it may

(*x*) Iid. 1 Saund. 291. (n. 1.) Cro. Jac. 420. 2 Ld Ray. 1538.
(*y*) 3 Lev. 348. Cro. Eliz. 773.
(*z*) Cro, Eliz. 773. 890.

nevertheless in many cases, be rendered material in the *subsequent* pleadings, by the matter alleged in them (*a*). Yet whenever the day laid is not, originally, or *primâ facie*, material, but is afterwards made so by the pleading of the adverse party, a deviation from it, (*if necessary*), in any of the subsequent pleadings, is no *departure* (*b*) (18).

§ 71. If therefore the plaintiff in assumpsit lays the promise on a day, which is more than six years before the commencement of the suit, and the defendant pleads the statute of limitations; the plaintiff may reply a promise made *within* six years before the suit was brought (*c*). In this case, though the day, as it appears upon the face of the *declaration*, is not material; the plea nevertheless makes it so, as regards the *subsequent* pleadings, by obliging the plaintiff to allege, in his replication, a promise within six years before the commencement of the suit, for the purpose of taking the case out of the statute. But still as the day is not, upon the *face of the declaration*, material; the deviation from it, in the replication, is no *departure*.

§ 72. Upon the same principles, if the defendant, in an action of trespass, justifies the alleged wrong,

(*a*) 2 Saund. 5. a. b. (n. 3).
(*b*) 1 Lev. 110. 1 Salk. 222–3. Stra. 21. 806.
(*c*) Iid. 16 East, 423.

(18) A departure is a deviation from what is *material*, in the prior pleadings, on the same side. (*Vide* Ch. 8, part 3.)

CHAP. III.

Time.

under the authority of law, (as in the character of sheriff, acting under legal process,) and lays his justification, either on the same day as that mentioned in the declaration, or on another day; the plaintiff also, on *his* part, may in his replication new-assign the trespass, on a day *different* from that stated in the plea or the declaration (*d*). For the justification may be true (since an act *similar* to that stated in the declaration, may have been done, and lawfully done, on the day mentioned in the *plea*); and yet the particular wrong, for which the plaintiff actually seeks redress, may have been committed on a day *different* from that mentioned in the declaration, or the plea; and at a time when the defendant had no legal authority to do the act in question. And thus the time of the alleged trespass, though not *primâ facie* material, is made so by the *plea*. For if the plea be true, it is necessary for the plaintiff—in order to avoid the effect of it, and entitle himself to a recovery—to show, upon the record, a trespass committed at a time different from that covered by the plea. If therefore he were not allowed to vary, in his replication, from the day mentioned in the declaration, he might, (as in the case last before stated,) be ousted, by an evasive plea, of the right which the law allows him of laying the trespass, in his declaration, on whatever day he pleases.

§ 73. It has long been an established general

(*d*) 1 Salk. 222. 1 Freem. 246. 2 Saund. 5. a. b. (n. 3.)

CHAP. III.

Time. When immaterial, must be followed, in the subsequent pleadings.

rule, however, that where the time is *not material* to the defence, the defendant must, in his plea, *follow* the day laid in the declaration: In other words, that the plea must state the matter of the defence, as having accrued on the day mentioned in *the declaration* — (even though that be not the true day) — unless the nature or circumstances of the defence render it *necessary* for the defendant to vary from the day laid in the declaration (*e*). The object of this rule appears to be, to prevent an apparent *discrepancy*, in respect to time, upon the face of the record, where the alleged cause of action, and the defence pleaded, actually occurred at one and the same time, and where the defendant is under no *necessity* of laying his defence on a different day from that mentioned in the declaration.

§ 74. In trespass, therefore, if the defendant pleads a *justification*, he must regularly lay it on the *same* day, on which the trespass is *alleged* to have been done. Nor is he allowed to vary from that day in his plea, unless the defence shows, upon the face of it, that it was *necessary* thus to vary (*f*). Thus, in trespass for an assault and battery, laid on the first of *January*, but actually committed on a different day — as the first of *February* — if the defendant pleads *son assault demesne*, (i. e. necessary self-defence, against an assault by the *plaintiff*) both the first assault and the self-defence must be laid in

(*e*) 1 Salk. 222. 1 Saund. 14. 82. (n. 3.) 2 Ib. 5. a. (n. 3.) 1 Chitt. Pl. 509. 517. Com. Dig. *Pleader*, E. 4.

(*f*) Iid.

CHAP. III.

Time.

the plea, on the first of *January*—or as the usual form is, 'on the day and year in the *declaration mentioned*' (*g*). For if the justification (which *confesses* the alleged battery,) were laid on the first of *February;* the record would exhibit the apparent incongruity of an act done at one time, and justified at another; or, (which is the same thing), of one *identical* act done at *two* different times.

§ 75. But as the general rule, requiring a plea of justification to follow the day mentioned in the declaration, extends only to cases in which the time is *immaterial;* it follows that a justification, unnecessarily varying from the day laid in the declaration, varies only in an *immaterial* point, and is therefore faulty only in *form:* and is consequently good, except on *special* demurrer (*h*).—(Vide *Demurrer*, ch. 9.)

Need not be followed, when a deviation from it is necessary.

§ 76. When, on the other hand, the justification is such as to render it *necessary* to the defence, that the true time be stated in the plea, the law allows the defendant to vary from the time mentioned in the declaration (*i*). And this is always the case, when it is necessary to state the true time, in order to adapt the plea to what is *material* in the defendant's *proof.* In all such cases, the formal objection, arising out of the apparent discrepancy as to time,

(*g*) Iid. 2 Chitt. Pl. 524—533.

(*h*) Stat. 27 Eliz. c. 5. 1 Saund. 14. (n. 2.) 2 Stra. 694. 2 Salk. 642. 1 Lev. 241.

(*i*) 2 Saund. 5. a. b. (n. 3.) 1 Chitt. Pl. 517.

between the declaration and the plea, must yield to the more important principle, that each party must be permitted to frame his allegations according to the exigency of his case. If the rule were otherwise, the plaintiff, by stating in his declaration any other than the true time, might entirely preclude the defendant from availing himself of a just and legal defence.

§ 77. In trespass, therefore, if the defence is, that the act complained of was done by the defendant, as a sheriff, or other officer, acting under the authority of *legal process*, which bears date *after* the day mentioned in the declaration, the defendant may—and to render his plea available, must—lay his justification on some day after the date of the process (*k*). For if the justification were laid on the day mentioned in the *declaration*, (a day *prior* to that of the date of the process,) the process would not, in evidence, support the plea. And thus the time becomes material in the *plea*, though it was not so in the *declaration*.

§ 78. But in such a case, the defendant must, in some form, *traverse* the day laid in the declaration (*l*), i. e. must deny that he was guilty of the alleged wrong, on *that* day, or on any other day than that mentioned in his *plea* (*m*). This traverse is necessary, to make the defence *complete*, or *co-*

(*k*) 2 Saund. 5. a. b. (n. 3.)

(*l*) 1 Saund. 82. (n. 3.) 297. 1 Chitt. Pl. 509.

(*m*) Hob. 104. 1 Chitt. Pl. 534-5. Com. Dig. *Pleader*, G. 1. 2.

CHAP. III.

Time.

extensive with the complaint. For as the plaintiff has an unquestionable right to prove the alleged trespass to have been committed on *any* day, prior to the date of his writ, and of course, on a day different from that mentioned in the plea; it is manifest that, without such a traverse, the plea, which applies the justification to a *single* day only, must leave *unanswered* any trespass, which may have been committed on any such *different* day, and which *may* be the very wrong for which the action is brought: Upon which supposition, the justification, without the traverse, would furnish no defence as to the particular wrong for which the plaintiff claims a recovery.

§ 79. It seems to be settled, however, (though upon this point there is some confusion in the books,) that in the cases contemplated by the last preceding rule, a *direct and formal traverse* of the day laid in the declaration is not necessary, if the plea contains the allegation, *quæ est eadem transgressio;* i. e. that the trespass, justified in the plea, is the *same* as that complained of in the declaration (*n*): That allegation itself being tantamount to a *traverse* or *denial*, that the trespass was committed on any other day, than that stated in the *plea*. And therefore a formal traverse, superadded to that allegation, is held to be not only unnecessary but *improper*, and of course ill, on special demurrer (*o*).

(*n*) 1 Saund. 14. 298. (n. 2.) 2 Ib. 5. a. (n. 3.) Cro. Car. 228. 2 Stra. 694. 1 Lev. 241. 2 Salk. 642. Cro. Eliz. 705. 1 Bulstr. 138. Yelv. 122–3.

(*o*) Iid.

CHAP. III.

Time.

§ 80. If, however, the day stated in the justification is the *same* as that in the declaration, the allegation, *quæ est eadem*, &c, is unnecessary (*p*): The trespass complained of, and that justified, being in such a case *primâ facie identified*, by being laid on the same day; and therefore a traverse, in the plea, of the day laid in the declaration, is improper and ill, in point of form (*q*). And if the plaintiff, in this case, relies on proving a trespass done on a *different* day he must make a *new assignment* of it in his replication (*qq*).

§ 81. But though, where the time in the declaration is *immaterial*, and the justification is, from necessity, laid at a different time, the plaintiff is at liberty to vary, in his replication, as well from the time laid in his *declaration*, as from that stated in the plea: Yet where the day mentioned in the declaration is itself *material*, the plaintiff cannot deviate from it in his replication, without making a *departure*, which would be fatal to his action (*r*). Thus, if the plaintiff declares upon a record, bond, covenant, bill of exchange, promissory note, or other written instrument, described in the declaration as bearing date on a given day, he is not allowed to assign to the document, in his replication, a *different*

Ante, § 70. 71.

(*p*) 2 Saund. 5. a. b. (n. 3.)

(*q*) Id. 8 Mod. 30. Fort. 379.

(*qq*) Bull. N. P. 17. Bac. Abr. *Pleas*, &c, L.

(*r*) 2 Saund. 5. b. (n. 3.) 1 Salk. 222-3. 1 Ld Ray. 121. 1 Stra. 21. 2 Ib. 806. I Lev. 110. 111.

CHAP. III.

Time.

date (*s*). For as the date, mentioned in the declaration, is part of the *description* of the instrument declared upon, the assignment of a different date to the same instrument, in the replication. would be, in effect, the pleading of a *different instrument*, and of course, the substitution of a different *cause of action*, from that stated in the declaration.

§ 82. But in pleading any matter of *discharge*, as a release—accord and satisfaction—a prior judgment or award, deciding the matter in controversy—payment, or tender of a pre-existing debt, or any other defence, operating as a discharge or extinguishment of any *prior* liability—the defendant is never required to follow the day mentioned in the declaration (*t*). And the rule is the same, whether the day in the *declaration* is material or immaterial, and whether it is the true day, or not. For in pleading a defence of this kind, a deviation from the day mentioned in the declaration, introduces upon the face of the record no such apparent *discrepancy*, in regard to time, as in certain cases before stated, a similar deviation would occasion: Since all matter of *discharge* must, from its nature, have accrued *subsequently* to the creation of the duty or liability upon which the action is founded. It is therefore manifest, that in pleading any matter of *discharge*, the defendant not only *may*, but (to make his plea

(*s*) 1 Salk. 222–3. 2 Stra. 806. 2 Saund. 5. b. (n. 3.)

(*t*) 1 Chitt. Pl. 517. 2 Burr. 944. 2 Wils. 150. 173. Plowd. 46. 2 Stra. 994. Com. Dig. *Pleader*, E. 6.

sufficient,) *must*, state the defence as having accrued after the cause of action arose; or, at least, after the wrong complained of was done, or the contract declared upon, was made.

§ 83. It may be proper to add, in this connexion, that when the defendant has been discharged by matter of *record*—as a prior judgment—or by a *written instrument*—as a deed of release; he cannot be confined, in his plea, to the time mentioned in the declaration, for an additional reason, viz. the necessity of stating the time of the discharge, so as to conform to the *date* of the record, or instrument (*u*). For in these, and similar cases, the date is material, on a principle heretofore stated, viz. that a deviation from it would make a *variance*. Ante, § 67.

§ 84. In most cases, and especially when the declaration contains but *one* count, the cause of action is laid on a *single* day only: In which case, the plaintiff can recover only for the wrongs or acts of some *one* day (*v*). For the declaration, in the case supposed, claims no recovery, except for what has taken place on *one* day. And if there is in fact but *one* cause of action, though differently stated in *different* counts, the same day is usually stated in all the counts. And when there is only *one* count in the declaration, the plaintiff cannot recover for acts

(*u*) Vid. reference (*w*), ante § 67, and the authorities there cited.

(*v*) 2 Salk. 639. 1 Ld Ray. 240. 2 Ib. 976-7. 2 Chitt. Pl. 367. (n. s.)

CHAP. III.

or injuries done on *several* days, except in the following cases, and those similar to them (*w*):—

Time.

§ 85. 1. In an action on the case for a *nuisance* or *disturbance* — in which the damage complained of is augmented by the *continuance* of the wrong, the plaintiff is, from the nature of the case, allowed to state the *period* of its continuance, from one given day to another; or, as is the more usual mode, from a certain day named, to the commencement of the suit (*x*): Since the declaration could not otherwise show, nor the plaintiff be permitted to *prove*, the whole *extent* of the injury.

Continuando.

§ 86. 2. In trespass also, when the plaintiff sues for different wrongs of the same nature, committed by *continuation or repetition*, on several different days, he may recover for all of them, on one count, by including in it as many days, or as long a period of time, as his case may require (*y*). But in the application of this rule, there is a difference to be observed in the mode of declaring, between the case of a trespass *continued or renewed* on several different days, and that of *distinct* trespasses *repeated* on different days; or in other words, between *continued* trespasses of a *permanent* nature, and *repeated* trespasses which are *not* permanent.

(*w*) Iid.

(*x*) Vide *precedents* (3 Ld Ray. 260. 292. 324. Plead. Assist. 424. 2 Chitt. Pl. 331—342. 354. 429—437.

(*y*) 2 Salk. 638. 3 Black. Com. 212. Bac. Abr. *Tresp.* I. 2.

Time.

§ 87. When trespasses of one and the same kind, committed on several days, are in their nature capable of *renewal* or *continuation*, and are renewed or continued from day to day — so that the particular injury, done on each particular day, cannot be *distinguished* from what was done on another day — the trespasses are denominated *permanent*. Of this description are trespasses committed by cattle, by trampling down, consuming or destroying, from day to day, the grass, crops or herbage, of any kind, growing upon land (*z*).

§ 88. But when each of several trespasses, committed on different days, is *distinct* from the others, and, terminating in itself, is *incapable* of continuation or renewal, (in which case the injury, committed on any one day, is supposed to be *distinguishable* from the rest), the trespasses, though all of the same nature, are deemed *not permanent*. Thus, if the defendant, has, on each of several different days, felled one or more of the plaintiff's *trees*, or killed several of his *beasts*, or taken and carried away different articles of his personal chattels; the trespasses, in either case, are *not* of a permanent nature (*a*). And from this distinction between trespasses which are permanent, and those which are not so, there results a difference in the mode of *declaring*, when the action is brought for more than *one* day's trespass.

(*z*) 3 Black. Com. 212. Bac. Abr. *Tresp.* I. 2. Ld Ray. 240. 976. 2 Salk. 638. 2 Roll. Ab. 545. 1 Saund. 24. (n. 1).

(*a*) 1 Ld Ray. 239. 2 Id. 975. 2 Salk. 638—9. Bac. Abr. *Tresp.* I. 2. 1 Saund. 24. (n. 1). 3 Black. Com. 212.

CHAP. III.

Time.

§ 89. When the trespasses complained of are all of a *permanent* nature, and are continued on several days, in immediate succession, they may all be laid in one count, with a *continuando* for the whole time—i. e. as having been committed by *continuation*, from one particular day specifically named, to another so named. And if the trespasses, though of a *permanent* nature, were committed on different days, *not* in immediate succession, but with *intervals* of one or more days; they may still be laid with a *continuando*, though not for the *whole* time; but by *continuation*, 'on divers days and times, between' one given day and another (*b*).

§ 90. But if the trespasses alleged are *not* of a permanent nature; they cannot be laid with a *continuando* from one certain day to another; but may be alleged to have been committed, *diversis diebus et vicibus*, ('on divers days and times'), *between* one particular day and another, or between one certain day and the commencement of the suit (*c*). These modes of declaring in trespass for several days, in one count, whether with or without a *continuando*, are allowed, to avoid the necessity of bringing a separate action, or inserting a separate count, for each day's trespass (*d*).

(*b*) Bac. Abr. *Tresp.* B. 2. I. 2. T. Ray. 396. 1 Ld Ray. 239—240. 2 Chitt. Pl. 367. n. s. 2 Salk. 638—9. 1 Saund. 23—4. (n. 1). 3 Black. Com. 212. 1 Sid. 319. Com. Dig. *Tresp.* B. 2. and *vid. precedents* 2 Lill. Ent. 444. 2 Chitt. Pl. 367.

(*c*) Iid.

(*d*) 1 Saund. 24. (n. 1). 1 Roll. Ab. 545.

§ 91. But if trespasses, which, according to the preceding distinctions, do not admit of continuation, are alleged with a *continuando;* the declaration is ill, at least in *form* (*e*): Because it must necessarily appear, from the nature of the wrongs alleged, that they *could not*, in legal contemplation, have been committed by continuation, and consequently, that they could not have been done in the *manner* alleged. But the fault is aided by *verdict* (*f*). For the *continuando* being void, only *one* day's trespass was *legally proveable* under the declaration; and it must therefore be *intended*, that the damages were assessed for no more than *one* day's trespass (*g*).

§ 92. So also, where the plaintiff declared that the defendants, on a certain day named, 'and on divers other days and times, between' that day and the commencement of the suit, committed *an assault* upon him, the declaration — being specially demurred to, — was adjudged ill (*h*): *An assault* being one entire, indivisible act, which cannot be continued, or committed at *different* times. But as it is now held, an allegation that the defendant on a certain day, 'and on divers other days and times, between that day and the day of suing forth the writ, *assaulted* the plaintiff,' &c, is good: Since one may *assault* another at different times, though *an* assault

(*e*) 1 Saund. 24. a. (n. 1). 1 Ld Ray. 240. Bac. Abr. *Tresp.* I. 2. 1 Lev. 210. 2 Salk. 638—9. Esp. Dig. 408.

(*f*) Iid. *Vid.* 2 Mass. R. 50.

(*g*) 2 Ld Ray. 823. 7 Mod. 152. Comb. 427. 1 Freem. 82.

(*h*) Cowp. 828. & Vide 6 East, 391. 395. 1 Saund. 24. a. (n. 1.) 2 Chitt. Pl. 367. (n. s.)

CHAP. III. Time.

cannot be committed at different times *(i)*; A distinction, which must be acknowledged to savour, in some degree, of verbal subtlety.

Ante, §§ 64. 83.

§ 93. It has been stated already, that when a trespass is laid on a certain *single* day, the plaintiff is at liberty to prove that it was committed on *any one* day, before the commencement of the suit. But when trespasses are laid with a *continuando*, he must — if he attempts to prove trespassing acts on more than *one* day — confine his evidence to the *period*, or *some part* of the period, included in the *continuando (k)*; and is not permitted to prove trespasses on *two or more* days, which are *not* comprehended in that period. The reason of this rule appears to be, that although the time, *as such*, is not material; yet the *continuando* is considered as *descriptive* of the alleged trespasses, or at least of the *manner* in which they were committed. And upon this supposition, a deviation, in evidence, from the time stated under the *continuando*, is a deviation from the plaintiff's *description* of the trespasses complained of: Whereas, when only a *single* day is stated in the declaration, it is not regarded as in any sense *descriptive* of the trespasses alleged; but simply as a formal compliance with the general rule of *certainty*, requiring *some* particular day to be alleged. The same rule, which limits the plaintiff's proof, under a *continuando*, to

(i) 2 Bos. & P. 425-7. 6 East, 395. 1 Phil. Ev. (2d ed.) 134. Bull. N. P. 86.

(k) 2 Salk. 639. Bull. N. P. 86. 1 Saund. 24. a. (n. 1.) Esp. Dig. 417-8. Co. Litt. 283. a. 2 Chitt. Pl. 367-8. (n. s.) 1 Ib. 258-9. 16 Mass. R. 470. 2 Stark. Ev. 356. 3 Ib. 1441, note (1).

the time comprehended within it, extends to cases in which several trespasses are laid 'on different days and times' between two different days. The principle of the rule, however, as applied to this latter case, is not altogether so obvious as in the former.

§ 94. But although the cause of action be laid, and properly laid, either with a *continuando*, or 'on divers days and times,' between two certain days; yet if the plaintiff at the trial will, as he may, *wave* the *continuando*, in the former case, or in the latter, his right of recovery, except for a trespass committed on a *single* day; he is at liberty to prove a trespass done on *any one* day before the commencement of the suit. For after such a *waiver*, the declaration will stand as if it had originally alleged but a *single* day.

§ 95. And where several trespasses are *improperly* laid by *continuation*, or 'on divers days,' &c, and the defendant, instead of demurring specially for that cause, pleads to the action; the plaintiff may, at the trial, without any *waiver* on his part, be limited, on the defendant's objection, to the proof of a trespass committed on a *single* day. In such a case, no *waiver* by the plaintiff is necessary: For as he had, by the rules of pleading, *no right*, in the case supposed, to state more than one day in one count; he has of course no right, on the trial, to *prove* more than one day's trespass, except by the defendant's consent or acquiescence.

CHAP. III.

Time. Continuando disused of late.

§ 96. It seems, however, that declaring with a *continuando* is not, at this day, usual in England, even when that form of declaring is admissible. The more customary mode of declaring, it is said, is to lay the trespasses on a given day, 'and on divers other days and times,' between that and another particular day (*l*).

§ 97. When several facts are stated, either in several clauses of an entire sentence, or in several sentences connected by the conjunction 'and', if the time be stated in only *one* of the different clauses or sentences, it will be applied to each of the facts alleged in the succeeding clauses or sentences thus connected (*m*). Thus if the plaintiff, in trespass, declares that the defendant, on such a day, made an assault upon him, *and* took and carried away such a sum of money ; the day stated will be referred, as well to the taking, &c, as to the assault : Such being the fair grammatical construction of the language used.

§ 98. In pleading any *negative* matter, no time need be alleged (*n*): As where the plaintiff avers that the defendant has *not* paid the debt, or performed the duty in question ; or the defendant, that he has *not* done what he covenanted not to do. For no particular day is predicable of that, which has *never* existed. And it may be added, that a negative

(*l*) 1 Saund. 24. (n. 1.).

(*m*) Cro. Jac. 443. Com. Dig. *Pleader*, C. 19. 1 Ld Ray. 576.

(*n*) Com. Dig. *Pleader*, C. 19. Plowd. 24. a. Lawes' Pl. 58.

allegation requires, in general, *no proof:* The burden of proof lying, regularly, on that party, who takes the *affirmative* of the issue (*o*). To this last remark there is indeed an exception, in one or two particular instances, not material to the present subject (*p*).

§ 99. In *real* actions also, there is no necessity of alleging any particular day, in the declaration (*q*). There would indeed be no propriety or congruity, in doing so. For in actions of this class, the declaration does not, as in personal actions, aver any specific *act or fact*, (occurring at a particular time), as the cause of action; but asserts, in substance, only a subsisting *right* or *title* in the plaintiff or defendant, and an adverse holding or denial of his right by the defendant or tenant (*r*).

§ 100. In *ejectment* also, it is held unnecessary to lay the *ouster* on any particular day (*s*): Because —to adopt the reason usually assigned—'so are the precedents.' It is therefore held sufficient, as regards the time of the *ouster*, that it be stated in general terms, as having been committed, *after* the making of the supposed demise, and the plaintiff's entry under it. Perhaps, however, the reason of the rule

(*o*) 1 T. R. 144. 649. 4 Ib. 33. 381. 5 Ib. 616. Bull. N. P. 297-8.

(*p*) Vid. 2 Bl. Rep. 851. Gilb. Ev. 148. Comb. 57. 3 East, 192. 10 Ib. 216. 2 Russ. on Crimes, (2d ed.) 673. 692, note (*f*).

(*q*) 2 Salk. 561. Com. Dig. *Pleader*, C. 19. 1 Saund. 286-7.

(*r*) Vid. *Precedents*, 3 Black. Com. App. No. 1. § 6. Lawes' Pl. App. 212. 3 Chitt. Pl. 620—635.

(*s*) Cro. Jac. 311. 312. Yelv. 182. a. *note*. 2 Chitt. Pl. 396. (n. r.) Esp. Dig. 445-6.

CHAP. III.

Time.

may be, that in the English ejectment, the supposed *ouster* is not *traversable*, and cannot in any way be put in *issue*: The real defendant being obliged, under the 'common rule,' to *confess* the *ouster*, as one of the conditions of his being permitted to appear and defend (*t*). And the general rule, requiring a particular day to be stated in pleading, extends only to *traversable* facts. It is usual, however, in the present forms of declaring in this action, to lay the *ouster* on a particular day (*u*).

Ante, § 62.

§ 101. If, where time is not material, the pleader states an *impossible* day—as the 30th of February; or a day *future* to that of pleading; or a day *inconsistent* with what he has before stated—(as when in trover, the declaration lays the loss of the goods on the *second* day of a certain month, and avers that the defendant 'afterwards,' viz. on the *first* day of the same month, converted them); the effect of the mistake is, in either case, the same as if *no* time whatever had been stated (*v*): For repugnancy or absurdity, in a point *not material*, being but matter of *form*, will consequently, except on special demurrer, be *rejected as surplusage*—according to the maxim, *utile per inutile non vitiatur* (*w*). And the

Post, § 172.

(*t*) 3 Black. Com. App. No. 2. s. 3.

(*u*) 3 Black. Com. App. No. 2. s. 2. 2 Chitt. Pl. 396—400.

(*v*) Carth. 389. Com. R. 12. 5 Mod. 286. Com. Dig. *Pleader*, C. 19. 3 M. 5. Stra. 232. 1095. Cro. Jac. 662. 1 Saund. 116. 286. 1 Lev. 195. *Vide* Yelv. 71. *note* (2). Clayt. 102.

(*w*) Co. Litt. 303. a. Com. Dig. *Pleader*, Q. 9. Vid. Stat. 27 Eliz. c. 5.

time, in the cases now supposed, being *immaterial*, the mistake is aided, except on special demurrer. **CHAP. III.**

§ 102. The third particular, in which certainty, in pleading, is required, is that of *place;* the discussion of which involves the law of *venue.* Under this head, it is a general rule, that the *place* of every *traversable* fact, stated in the pleadings, must be distinctly alleged (*x*): Or, at least, (as the rule is now understood and applied,) that *some* certain place must be alleged for every such fact. This is done by designating the *city*, *town*, *village*, *parish*, or *hamlet*, together with the *county*, in which the fact is alleged to have occurred; and the place, thus designated, is called the *venue* (*y*): The term, '*venue*,' (*vicinage*,) signifying, in strictness, not the *county* in which the action is brought; but the particular *city*, *town*, *parish*, *hamlet*, &c, in which the fact alleged occurred, or is supposed to have occurred, and which is stated as situate in the county named in connexion with it (*z*). In its present acceptation, however, the word *venue* is most frequently used to comprehend, as well the *county*, as the town, parish or other *vicinage*, in which the fact alleged arose, or is stated to have arisen. **Place. (Venue.)**

(*x*) Com. Dig. *Pleader*, C. 20. Cro Eliz. 78. 98. 5 T. R. 620. 1 Stra. 595. Lawes' Pl. 57-8. Bac. Abr. *Venue*, B. Co. Litt. 303. a.

(*y*) 3 Black. Com. 294. 384. Com. Dig. *Pleader*, C. 20. Bac. Abr. *Venue*, A.

(*z*) Iid.

CHAP. III.

Place. (Venue.)

§ 103. But the rule, requiring the laying of a *venue* for traversable facts, though doubtless necessary for the sake of *certainty* in pleading, was, by an ancient principle of the common law, more especially so, for an entirely different reason. For by a general rule of the common law, strictly observed in the ancient practice, and still recognised in *theory*, by legal fiction, every issue in fact, triable by jury, was required to be tried by jurors, not only of the same *county*, but also of the same *venue*, *vicinage*, or *immediate neighborhood*, in which the fact to be tried actually took place (*a*): A rule, founded on the maxim of the common law, *Maximè Vicini Vicinorum facta presumuntur scire*, (the transactions of men are presumed to be best known to those of their *immediate neighborhood*). And this regulation made it necessary, that the *true* place or venue should be alleged; because it could not otherwise appear from the pleading, to what particular vicinage the jury-process should go—or in other words—from what vicinage the jury should come. And upon the establishment of nisi prius trials, (which were held in each county of the kingdom,) it was also required that every matter of fact, put in issue and triable by *jury*, should be *tried*, as well *in* the county (19), as

(*a*) Co. Litt. 125. a. b. *in notis.* Yelv. 12. *n.* 2. Gilb. H. C. P. 70, 83–4. 5 T. R. 620. 3 Black. Com. 359. 384–5. Com. Dig. *Amendment*, H. 1. Lawes' Pl. 27-8. 2 H. Black. 161. Bac. Abr. *Venue*, E. 5 Mass. R. 96.

---

(19) To the ancient common law rule, that every action must be laid in the county, in which the cause of action arose, there

CHAP. III.

Place. (Venue.)

by a jury *of* the county and *vicinage*, in which the fact actually arose (*b*). Hence it became necessary, for the purpose of *trial*, that the *true* place of every traversable fact should be stated in the pleadings: Since it could not otherwise be known from the

(*b*) 2 H. Black. 161. Co. Litt. 125. a. b. Bac. Abr. *Venue*, E. Gilb. H. C. P. 70. 83-4. 3 Black. Com. 359. 384-5. Bac. Abr. *Actions Local*, &c.

---

appears to have been originally, or at a very early period, an exception in the case of actions founded on *personal contracts;* as in account, debt, and covenant broken. Actions of this kind were allowed to be brought in *any* county, in accordance with the maxim, *debitum et contractus sunt nullius loci:* He who is indebted, being a debtor in all places, or wherever he is. (7 Co. 3. a. Com. Dig. *Action*, N. 12. 6. 1 Stra. 612. Cowp. 180. 3 Black. Com. 384. 1 Saund. 74. (n. 2.) But by the stat. 6 *Rich.* 2. c. 2. it is enacted, that in 'writs of debt and account, and all other *such* actions,—if in pleas upon the same writ, it shall be *declared* that the contract thereof was made in *another* county' than that in which the writ is brought; the writ shall *abate*. Under this statute, if it appeared *from the record*, that the contract was made in a county, *other* than that in which the action was laid; the judgment was erroneous. (1 Saund. 74. (n. 2.) But to prevent error, and to avoid the inconvenience of rigidly *abating* the writ, the judges, at a subsequent period, construed the statute as authorizing them, in their discretion, to *change the venue*, under a rule of practice, by ordering the declaration to be altered, and the action laid, and trial had, in the county in which the cause of action arose. (Bac. Abr. *Actions Local*, &c. 2 Salk. 670. 3 Black. Com. 294.) This statute, and that of 4 Hen. 4. c. 18, requiring that attornies 'make no suit in a *foreign* county,' are considered as the source of the authority, which judges now exercise, of *changing venues* in transitory actions.

CHAP. III. record, in what county the issue ought to be *tried* (*c*).

Venue.

§ 104. In the application of this ancient rule, however, a distinction, suggested by general convenience, was soon established between *things local* and *transitory;* and consequently between *local and transitory actions*. In *local* actions, the preceding rules regarding locality of trial were still adhered to; while those of a *transitory* nature became, by an arbitrary laying of the venue, triable in any county, in which the venue was laid in *the pleadings* (*d*). Hence in local actions, the place has ever been, and still is, material; and must therefore be laid according to the truth (*e*). But in actions *transitory*, the ancient rule as to the locality of actions and trials, is now, and has long been, entirely disregarded, or rather *evaded*, to every purpose except the mere *form of laying some venue*, and the power of the court, under special circumstances, to *change* it, i. e. to change the county, on motion. In *transitory* actions, therefore, the plaintiff is at liberty to lay the venue in what county he pleases (*f*).

Vide note 19. ante.

Local and transitory actions.

§ 105. It becomes necessary, therefore, to a correct understanding of the modern law of *venues*, to

(*c*) Iid. Cowp. 176. 2 H. Black. 160–1.

(*d*) 7 Co. 3. Gilb. H. C. P. 84—5. Cowp. 176—7. 3 Black. Com. 294.

(*e*) Com. Dig. *Action*, N. 1. 2. 3. Id. *Pleader*, S. 15. 3 Black. Com. 294.

(*f*) 3 Black. Com. 294. Bac. Abr. *Actions Local*, &c, B. Com. Dig. *Pleader*, S. 9. Cowp. 177. 1 Saund. 74. (n. 2). Gilb. H. C. P. 89—90.

CHAP. III. — Venue.

ascertain in the first place what actions are *local*, and what *transitory*. A *local* action is one, which must still be laid in the county, in which the cause of action actually arose. A *transitory* action may be laid in any county, which the plaintiff may prefer (*g*). The present locality of actions is founded, in some cases, on common-law principles, and in others, on positive enactments of statute-law.

§ 106. Of those which continue local, by the *common* law, are

Local actions.

1. All actions in which the *subject or thing to be recovered*, is in its nature local. Of this class are all *real* actions — actions of *waste*, when brought on the statute of *Glocester*, (6 Edw. 1.), to recover, together with damages, the *locus in quo*, or place wasted — and actions of *ejectment* (*h*). All these are local, because they are brought to recover the seisin or possession of lands or tenements, which are local subjects. And if the place — as the parish, &c, where the land, or subject in demand, is situated — be misstated, the plaintiff will be liable to a nonsuit (*i*), by reason of the mis-description of the *subject-matter* of the suit; because the place enters into the description of it.

§ 107. 2. Various actions, which do not seek the direct *recovery* of lands or tenements, are also local,

(*g*) Bac. Abr. *Actions Local*, &c, A. (a).
(*h*) Iid. Com. Dig. *Action*, N. 1. 7 Co. 2. b. 2 Black. Rep. 1070. Cowp. 176. 7 T. R. 588. 4 Ib. 504.
(*i*) 1 Stra. 595. 3 Lev. 334.

CHAP. III.

Venue. Local actions.

by the common law; because they *arise out* of some local subject, or the violation of some local right or interest. Thus the action of *quare impedit* is local (*k*); inasmuch as the *benefice*, in the right of presentation to which the plaintiff complains of being obstructed, is so. Within this class of cases are also many actions, in which only *pecuniary* damages are recoverable. Such are the *common-law* action of *waste*, and trespass *quare clausum fregit* (*l*); as likewise trespass on the case for injuries affecting things *real*—as for *nuisances* to houses or lands—*disturbance* of rights of way, or of common—*obstruction* or *diversion* of ancient water-courses, &c. (*m*).

§ 108. If however a tortious act, committed in *one* county, occasions damage to land or any other local subject, situate in *another*; an action for the injury thus occasioned, may be laid in either of the two counties, at the choice of the party injured (*n*). Thus, if by the diversion or obstruction of a water-course, in the county of A., damage is done to lands, mills or other real property in the county of B., the party injured may lay his action in either of those two counties.

For local subjects, lying in a foreign country.

§ 109. No action will lie, in any one *sovereign state*, for the recovery of lands or tenements lying

(*k*) 7 Co. 3. a. Com. Dig. *Action*, N. 4. 1 Chitt. Pl. 271.

(*l*) Bac. Abr. *Actions Local*, &c, A. (a). Cowp. 180. 4 T. R 503. 6 East, 598—9.

(*m*) Com. Dig. *Action*, N. 4. 7 Co. 2. b. 2 East, 498—9. 1 Chitt. Pl. 271.

(*n*) 7 Co. 2. b. Co. Litt. 54. a. Com. Dig. *Action*, N. 3. 11. 2 T. R. 241. 7 Ib. 583. 3 Stark. Ev. 1650.

Venue. Local actions.

in another (*o*): Since no common-law court has *jurisdiction* of local causes, arising within a foreign sovereignty. Indeed a judgment, if given in such a case, would be utterly nugatory. For as legal process, issuing from a court of even the highest jurisdiction, is of no authority in any other country or state, than that in which it was issued; a judgment, in the case supposed, could by no possibility be enforced (20). Nor in general can any *personal* action be maintained, in one sovereign state, for a trespass, nuisance, or other injury to *real* property, lying in another (*p*): Such actions being local, (as already stated), because they arise out of *local subjects.*

§ 110. But it has been held that this last rule admits of an exception, where a *local* cause of action, requiring a reparation in *damages* only, arises in a foreign country, in which there are *no regular courts of judicature,* and in which, of course, no legal remedy can be obtained (*q*). In such cases, this

(*o*) Bac. Abr. *Actions Local,* &c, A. (a). Cowp. 176. 1 Chitt. Pl. 269.

(*p*) 1 Stra. 646. 2 Black. Rep. 1070. Cowp. 176. 4 T. R. 503. 7 Ib. 587. 6 East, 598—9.

(*q*) Cowp. 180—1.

---

(20) These remarks, however, are not practically applicable, in their full extent, to the jurisdiction and decrees of courts of *equity.* For these courts, by their power of acting *in personam,* when the parties are within the reach of their process, can in many cases indirectly enforce rights to *real* property, situated in foreign countries. 1 Atk. 19. 2 Ves. 204. 447. 454. Mitf. Pl. 184. 1 Fonbl. Eq. 31. 6 Cranch, 157.

CHAP. III.

Venue.

Local actions.

exception has been allowed in some instances, from *necessity*, to prevent a failure of justice. And as the judgment, in this class of cases, is for *damages* only; there is indeed no practical difficulty in enforcing it—as there would be, if the action were brought for the recovery of a specific *local subject*, situated in a foreign county. Thus where certain houses, erected by the plaintiff on the coast of *Nova Scotia*, had been illegally demolished by the defendant, at a time when no regular administration of justice had been established in that province, and an action of trespass for that injury was brought in the English court of B. R., Lord Mansfield held the action to be maintainable (*r*). But this distinction appears to be now overruled (*s*).

§ 111. The action of *replevin* also, though it lies for damages only, and does not arise directly out of the violation of any local right, is nevertheless *local* (*t*). The reason of its locality—(a reason which applies to no other action for injuries to *personal* chattels)—appears to be the necessity of giving a *local description* of the taking complained of. For, in declaring in replevin, it is necessary to describe, and to describe truly, the *locus in quo*—i. e. the close, house, or common, in which the cattle or goods in question were taken by the defendant (*u*): And as

(*r*) Cowp. 180—1. 4 T. R. 503—4.

(*s*) 4 T. R. 503—4.

(*t*) 1 Saund. 347. (n. 1.) Hob. 16. Willes, 478. 1 Stra. 507-8. 2 Wils. 354. 1 Chitt. Pl. 161. 2 Ib. 364. (n. c. & e.)

(*u*) Iid. Yelv. 185. n. (1). 10 Johns. R. 53.

the necessity of alleging the true *place* of caption involves the necessity of laying the true *town, parish* or *vill*, and of course the true county; the venue and county as well as the close, &c, are consequently *material* (*v*), and the action, of necessity, local. If however replevin lies, by the common law, only for goods *distrained;* there would seem to be another and more fundamental reason for its locality, viz. that the *right of distress*, which the action is intended to contest, is at common law always local.

Venue. Local actions.

§ 112. But *personal* actions, that is to say, actions which seek nothing more than the recovery of *money*, or *personal* chattels of any kind, are in most cases *transitory*, whether they sound in tort or in contract (*w*): Because actions of this class are, in most instances, founded on the violation of rights which, in contemplation of law, have no *locality*. And it will be found true, as a general position, that actions *ex delicto*, in which *mere personalty* is alone recoverable, are, by the common law, *transitory*—except when they are founded upon, or arise out of, some *local* subject (*x*). Thus actions for injuries to the *person*, or to *personal* chattels—as for *assault* and *battery, false imprisonment, slanderous words, libel*, and

Transitory actions.

(*v*) 1 Saund. 347. (n. 1.) Cro. Eliz. 896. Carth. 186. Willes, 478. 1 Stra. 507–8. 2 Mod. 199.

(*w*) Com. Dig. *Action*, N. 12. 1 Chitt. Pl. 273.

(*x*) Com. Dig. *Action*, N. 12. Co. Litt. 282. Cowp. 161. 1 T. R. 571. 2 Black. Rep. 1058. 2 Chitt. Pl. 242. (n. p.)

CHAP. III.

Venue.

Transitory actions.

malicious prosecution (y)—*trespass* for taking away or injuring *personal chattels*, *trover*, *trespass on the case* for *escapes*, *false returns*, *deceit* in the sale of goods, &c, are in general *transitory* (z); and may consequently be laid in any county, even though the cause of action arose within a *foreign* jurisdiction (a).

§ 113. In the case of *Mostyn* v. *Fabrigas* (b), Lord *Mansfield* indeed suggested a doubt, whether trespass for an *assault and battery*, committed out of the realm of England, would lie in the courts of Westminster; because as every such injury involves a *breach of the peace*, it must be alleged to have been committed against the peace *of the king*; and a breach of the peace, considered as a *public wrong*, is confessedly *local*. There appears however no sufficient reason for the doubt here suggested. For the wrong, considered as a *civil* injury, is clearly transitory; and in the subsequent case of *Rafael* v. *Verelst* (c), in which the point in question directly arose, it was held by the court of Common Pleas, that the allegation, '*contra pacem Domini Regis*,' was not traversable in such an action; and that the action, then before the court, which was brought for

(y) Iid.

(z) 2 Salk. 670. 12 Mod. 408. Com. Dig. *Action*, N. 12. Sayer, 54. 1 Wils. 336. 1 East, 114. Cro. Car. 444. 9 Johns. R. 67.

(a) Com. Dig. *Action*, N. 12. Cowp. 161. 2 Black. Rep. 1058. 4 East, 162–3.

(b) Cowp. 176.

(c) 2 Black. Rep. 1058.

an assault, battery and false imprisonment, committed in the dominions of a foreign sovereign prince, was well laid in an English county.

Venue.

Vide note to § 104.

§ 114. Actions *ex contractu* also, as has been suggested already, are in general transitory, by the common law: For '*debitum et contractus sunt nullius loci*' (*d*)—the foundation of which maxim doubtless is, that the *causes* of this class of actions have, in most cases, no natural locality, and therefore follow the person of the defendant. Hence the actions of *debt*, *covenant broken*, *account*, and *assumpsit*, may in general be laid in *any* county (*e*). And the rule is the same, even though the contract were made, and by its terms to be performed, in a *foreign* country (*f*).

On judgment.

§ 115. But debt on *judgment* is local, by the common law, and must be laid in the county in which the record of the judgment remains (*g*). This rule however is founded, not upon the nature of the thing *in demand*, which is money; but apparently upon the locality of the *record*, upon which the action is founded: Records being required to

(*d*) 7 Co. 3. a. Com. Dig. *Action*, N. 12. Tidd, 543–6. 3 Black. Com. 384. 1 Stra. 612. Cowp. 180. 1 Saund. 74. (n. 2.) *vide ante*, Note 19.

(*e*) Iid.

(*f*) Com. Dig. *Action*, N. 12. 2 Salk. 660. Latch, 4. 1 Saund. 74. 241. b. Cowp. 180. 1 Stra. 612. 2 Ld Ray. 1532. 1 Chitt. Pl. 273.

(*g*) Com. Dig. *Action*, N. 6. Hob. 196. 2 Tidd, 1035. 2 Johns. Cas. 381.

CHAP. III.

Venue.

Local and transitory actions.

remain at a fixed place, appointed by law. And hence an action, founded on a judgment, may be considered as arising out of a *local* subject—the record being made local by the law.

On Leases.

§ 116. As to actions arising upon *leases*, and which appear to require a distinct consideration, the common law has established the following general distinction: If the action is founded directly on *privity* of *contract* between the parties; it is *transitory*, and may be laid in any county; even though the land, or subject demised, be situated in a foreign county (*h*): But if the action is founded on *privity of estate*, it is *local*, and must consequently be laid in the county in which the estate lies (*i*). For though money only is recoverable, in either case, yet in the former, the right of action arises exclusively out of the personal *contract*, which is in its nature *transitory*: Whereas in the latter, the action is founded on the *interest* of the parties in the *land* or *property demised*, which is a *local* subject; and for this reason the *action* is local. This general distinction may be illustrated, by the seven following particulars:—

§ 117. 1. The action of debt, or covenant broken, brought by the *lessor* against the *lessee*, or *vice*

(*h*) 7 Co. 2. a. 2 Salk. 651. 1 Saund. 241. b. (n. 6.) 6 Mod. 194. 2 East, 579.

(*i*) 7 Co. 2. a. 3. a. 6 Mass. R. 331. 1 Saund. 241. b. (n. 6.) Carth. 182-3. 6 Mod. 194.

CHAP. III.

Venue. Local and transitory actions.

versâ, is *transitory* (*k*). For these being immediate parties to the *lease;* there exists between them a privity of *contract*, which is the foundation of the action.

§ 118. 2. But debt, or covenant broken, when brought by the lessor against the *assignee* of the lessee, or *vice versâ*, is by the common law *local* (*l*). For the assignee of the lease, though privy in *interest* or estate to the lessor, is a stranger to the *personal contract*, between lessor and lessee; and cannot therefore be charged in favour of the lessor, on privity of *contract;* but is liable, (when liable at all), on privity of *estate*, which is in its nature local. In these latter cases, the *assignee* of the lease, when liable to the *lessor*, on any of the lessee's covenants, is so liable, *because* he holds the *interest* or *estate*, which the lessee had before the assignment; and is consequently liable only on those covenants of the lessee, which '*run with the land*'—or in other words, those which *follow the interest demised* (21). And hence the action is said to be founded on privity of *estate*.

(*k*) 7 Co. a. 2. Bac. Abr. *Actions Local*, &c. A. (a.) 6 Mod. 194. 2 Stra. 776. 2 East, 579. 1 Saund. 241. b. (n. 6.) 2 Salk. 651.

(*l*) Bac. Abr. *Actions Local*, &c, A. (a). 5 Co. 17. 1 Saund. 241. b. (n. 6.) Carth. 183. 2 East, 580.

---

(21) A covenant 'runs with the land', only when the right or obligation, created by it, is attached to the *interest* demised, or to the *estate, out of which* that interest was created; so that the right or obligation devolves, (on an *assignment* of the estate or interest), upon the assignee of the party assigning.

CHAP. III.

Venue.

Local and transitory actions.

§ 119. 3. Upon the same principles, the action of covenant broken, brought by the *assignee* of the lessee, against the *assignee* of the lessor, is by the common law, *local* (*m*): For the action, which is given by the *common* law, between these parties, is founded on privity of *estate*. So also on the other hand, debt or covenant broken, brought *by* the assignee of the lessor, *against* the assignee of the lessee, is local (*n*): For the statute 32 Hen. 8, c. 34, which in this latter instance gives the action, makes it local, by giving to the *assignee* of the lessor, 'the *same* remedy, by action,' as the *lessor himself* has, by the *common* law. And the *lessor's* remedy, by the common law, against the assignee of the lease, being local, (as stated in the last section); that of the lessor's *assignee* is, in the construction of this act, held to be of course local.

§ 120. 4. The action of *debt*, (as for rent arrear), by the *assignee* of the lessor, against the *lessee*, is also local by the common law (*o*). For rent being incident to the *reversion*, and the lessee being in the receipt of the issues and profits of the land, out of which it arises; there consequently exists, between these parties, a privity of *estate*: And the action being founded upon *that* privity — (for the privity of *contract*, between the original parties to the

(*m*) 5 Co. 17, a. 1 Saund. 241. c. (n. 6.) 1 Chitt. Pl. 276.

(*n*) 1 Saund. 241. c. (n. 6.) 1 Salk. 80. 7 T. R. 583. Carth. 182. 2 East, 580. 1 Wils. 165. 3 Mod. 338. 4 Ib. 81. Bac. Abr. *Covenant*, E. 6. Ib. *Actions Local*, &c. A. (a.)

(*o*) 3 Co. 22. b. 1 Saund. 241. c. (n. 6.) 1 Wils. 165. 3 Mod. 338. 4 Ib. 81.

Venue. Local and transitory actions.

lease, is destroyed by the *assignment* of the reversion) — is consequently *local*. And it is here observable, that the *devisee* of the reversion is considered and treated as the *assignee* of the lessor, within the three last rules: The devise being, in legal effect, a *testamentary assignment* of the reversion. And by parity of reason, the devisee of the term is in law the *assignee* of the *lessee*.

§ 121. 5. But the action of *covenant broken*, brought by the *assignee* of the lessor, against the *lessee*, or *vice versâ*, upon an *express* covenant contained in the lease, and running with the land, is made transitory, by the operation of the statute 32 Hen. 8, c. 34 (*p*). For the purpose of explaining this proposition, it may be observed that the action of covenant broken, upon *express* covenants, being founded only on privity of *contract*, will not lie, at *common law*, between the *assignees* of the lessor and those of the lessee; because *that* privity does not exist between them. But the statute above mentioned expressly extends 'the *same remedy*' upon such covenants, to and against the *assignees* of lessors and lessees, as lessors and lessees themselves had by the *common* law (*q*); and according to the construction given to the statute, the remedy afforded by it, to and against assignees, is to be pursued in

(*p*) Bac. Abr. *Actions Local*, &c, A. (a.) *Covenant*, E. 6. 1 Saund. 241, b. (n. 6.) Cro. Car. 183. 1 Lev. 259. 3 T. R. 401-2. 1 Wils. 165. 1 Vent. 10. 2 Keb. 439. 448. 468. 492. — *Cont.* 2 Show. 200. Com. Dig. *Actions*, N. 4.

(*q*) Bac. Abr. *Covenant*, E. 6.

CHAP. III.

Venue. Local and transitory actions.

'the *same manner*', in which the common law gave it to and against their respective *assignors*, (the original *lessors* and *lessees*): And therefore, as actions of covenant broken, between *lessors* and *lessees*, are by the common law *transitory*; it follows that actions, on express covenants between their respective *assignees*, are transitory by virtue of the above statute. And yet, as has been before shown, *debt* by the assignee of the lessor, against the lessee, is local: The action being given by the *common* law, and founded on privity of *estate*.

Ante, § 118.

§ 122. 6. So also, debt or covenant broken, for rent, brought by the lessor, his personal representative or assignee, against the *executor* or *administrator* of the lessee, charging him for rent accruing, *after the lessee's death*, is *local* (*r*). For as the personal representative of the lessee of a term for years is chargeable, during his own possession, as *assignee* of the lease; he is, in this latter capacity, *privy in estate* to the lessor: And therefore, if the action is brought by the *lessor* or his representatives, (in which case the remedy is given by the *common* law); it is local, as being founded on privity of *estate*. And if the action is brought by the lessor's *assignee*; the statute 32 Hen. 8, which gives him the remedy, (for the *common* law gives him none, against the *assignee* of the lease), makes it local, by its own provisions, as before stated, § 119.

(*r*) Bac. Abr. *Actions Local*, &c, A. (a.) 3 Co. 24. Com. Dig. *Actions*, N. 4. 2 Lev. 80. Gilb. H. C. P. 91.

Venue. Local and transitory actions.

§ 123. 7. On the other hand, if the executors or administrators of the lessee, in either of the above cases, are charged *as the representatives* of the lessee, and not *as assignees* of the term, (as where they are sued for rent accruing during the *lessee's life*) ; the action is transitory (*s*). For in such a case they are liable, not by reason of any *interest* of their own in the term, and therefore not upon privity of *estate ;* but upon privity of *contract*, devolving upon them from the lessee whom they represent.

§ 124. It appears, from the preceding distinctions, that where an action, founded on a lease, is given by the *common* law, if an *assignee* of the reversion, or of the term, is party to the suit, it is *local :* Since in all such cases, the action is founded on privity of *estate :* But that where the action is given by *statute*, it may be either local or transitory, as the fair construction of the statute may appear to require.

For use and occupation.

§ 125. Assumpsit for *use and occupation*, though substantially an action for rent, issuing out of a *real* subject, is not, by the law, considered as such, and is therefore *transitory* (*t*) *:* For the plaintiff's *title* being immaterial (*u*), the legal liability of the defendant is considered as a merely *personal* duty, par-

(*s*) 3 Co. 24. Bac. Abr. *Actions Local*, &c, A. (a.) Latch, 262, 271.

(*t*) 6 T. R. 62. 6 East, 348. 2 Chitt. Pl. 8, (n. c.) 174, (n. c.)

(*u*) Sayer, 13. 1 Wils. 314. 2 Ib. 208. 2 Chitt. Pl. 9, (n. c.)

CHAP. III.

taking no more of a *local* quality, than a liability arising from goods sold, labour done, or money lent.

Venue. Local and transitory actions.

§ 126. But though this action is in its nature transitory, and though it is therefore *unnecessary*, in declaring, to state the *place* where the land occupied is situated (*v*) ; yet if the declaration *does*, though unnecessarily, describe the land as lying in a particular place — not by way of *venue* for the promise, but of *local description* ; — the place, thus stated, must be the *true* one, or the plaintiff will be liable to a nonsuit (*w*). For though the *venue*, properly so called — i. e. the place where the contract is alleged to have been made — is immaterial, (the action being transitory) ; yet the place, named for the purpose of describing *the land*, is *material*, as entering into *the description of the cause of action*. And hence, a misdescription of the place where the land lies is in nature of a *variance*, in stating the consideration of the promise. If therefore the declaration describes the land, as lying in the parish of *A.*, when it is actually situate in the parish of *B.*, the plaintiff cannot recover; because the proof will not support the declaration.

§ 127. All *criminal* prosecutions remain local, under the ancient rule of the common law, that

(*v*) 6 T. R. 62. 6 East, 348. 2 Chitt. Pl. 9, (n. d.) 174, (n. e.) 3 M. & S. 380.

(*w*) 6 East, 348. 352. 6 T. R. 62. 1 Taunt. 570. 1 Esp. Rep. 273. 3 Campb. 235. *Vid.* 13 East, 9. 4 B. & A. 619. 3 Stark. Ev. 1571, et seq.

CHAP. III.

Venue. Local and transitory actions.

every issue in fact, triable by jury, must be tried in the county in which the fact to be tried occurred (*x*). For the distinction, since introduced, between local and transitory remedies, was expressly limited to *civil* suits.

§ 128. Hence no *crime*, committed within the territorial limits of one sovereign state, can be tried in any other (*y*). For the *penal* laws of every sovereign state are, in the strictest sense, *local*, and cannot therefore be enforced by the tribunals of any other state (*z*): It being an elementary principle of *public* and municipal *law*, that all offences, considered as *public wrongs*, offend that state only within whose limits they are committed; and no state has a right to punish, for any other offences, than those committed against *itself*.

§ 129. The local actions, thus far enumerated, are all, (except so far as the statute 32 Hen. 8 has prescribed the rule, in certain actions, on *leases*), made local by the principles of the *common* law. But certain other actions, which upon common-law principles are transitory, are, by the English statute-law, required to be brought in the county, in which the cause of action in truth arose; and are thus made local by positive enactments.

(*x*) 7 Co. 2. b. Com. Dig. *Action*, N. 5. 9. 1 Saund. 308. (n. 1.) 2 Black. Rep. 1058.

(*y*) 2 Black. Rep. 1058. Kel. 80. 2 Johns. R. 477. 479.

(*z*) 3 T. R. 733. 1 H. Black. 123.

CHAP. III.

Venue. Local and transitory actions. On penal statutes.

§ 130. Thus, by the statute 21 Jac. 1, c. 4, § 2, all actions and informations, &c, 'for any offence against any *penal statute*,' whether on 'behalf of the king, or any other person,' are required to be 'laid, and alleged to have been committed, in the county where such offence was, in truth, committed, and not elsewhere; or the defendant, upon the general issue, shall be found not guilty' (*a*). When, however, *two* material facts are necessary to constitute an offence against a penal statute, if one of those facts occurred in one county, and the other in another; the action may be laid in either of the two counties, according to the analogy of the *common* law rule in similar cases (*b*). Thus in an action on the statute of *usury*, if the contract was made in the county of *A.*, and the illegal interest received in the county of *B.*; the venue may be laid in either of those counties. It appears to be settled, in the construction of this statute, that it does not extend to any action given, by a penal statute, to the *party aggrieved* by the offence prohibited: So that the action, when brought by such a party, is still *transitory*, as at common law (*c*).

§ 131. By the *common* law then, (as the last observation implies), actions for the recovery of statute-penalties, are transitory (*d*). For though

(*a*) Com. Dig. *Action*, 10. Bac. Abr. *Action*, q. t. C. 1 Chitt. Pl. 276-7. 1 Salk. 373. 5 Mod. 425. 4 Ib. 158.

(*b*) 7 Co. 1. 2 T. R. 238. 7 Ib. 583. 2 Bos. & P. 381.

(*c*) Bac. Abr. *Action*, q. t. C. 1 Show. 354.

(*d*) Iid.

the *object* of every prosecution for such a penalty, is the punishment of the defendant for an *offence;* yet an *action* brought for this purpose, is in form a civil suit (*e*); and as regards the *venue*, as well as in most other respects, the nature or character of every suit, or prosecution, is decided by its *form*. Indeed, a pecuniary penalty is in law considered as a *debt*, due from the offender to the prosecutor, or plaintiff in the action (*f*); and hence the action brought for the recovery of it, and which is usually an action of *debt*, is, by the common law, transitory; on the same principles on which other actions of *debt* are generally so.

Venue.

Venue how laid in the pleadings which follow the declaration.

§ 132. From what has been already stated, of the law of *venues*, (*ante*, s. 104), it results that no suit can be *abated*, nor in any manner defeated, on the ground that the venue is laid in the wrong county, unless the action is in its nature *local*, or is made so by statute (*g*). For in consequence of the distinction between local and transitory actions, it has become an established rule, that in *transitory* actions, the *place* laid in the declaration draws to itself the trial of all *transitory* matters alleged in the subsequent pleadings. And the defendant cannot therefore state, in his plea, any *other* venue for the

(*e*) Cowp. 382. 391. Willes, 597. 1 Wils. 125. 4 T. R. 753. 7 Ib. 257. 3 Ib. 448.

(*f*) Bac. Abr. *Statute*, K. Poph. 175. Palm. 400. Latch, 19. 3 Black. Com. 160–161.

(*g*) 3 Black. Com. 294. Bac. Abr. *Actions Local*, &c. B. Com. Dig. *Pleader*, S. 9. Cowp. 177. 1 Saund. 74. (n. 2). Gilb. H. C. P. 89—90.

CHAP. III.

Venue.

How laid in the plea, &c.

facts which he pleads, than that laid in the declaration; unless the nature of the defence renders another venue *necessary* (*h*); i. e. unless his defence is founded upon something *local*, arising in a different place from that which is laid in the declaration.

§ 133. If therefore, in a *transitory* action, the cause of which is laid in the county of *A.*, (in which county the suit is brought), the defendant pleads any *transitory* matter of defence, as having arisen in the county of *B.;* the plea is ill in form (*i*). For if the defendant might, *without necessity*, thus deviate from the venue laid in the declaration, he would, upon original *common-law* principles, be able to *change* or *oust* the venue in transitory actions; and thus to subvert the rule, which allows the plaintiff, in such actions, to bring his suit in what *county*, and lay his *venue* in what *part* of it, he may choose: Since, if issue was taken upon the plea, in the case supposed, the original rule of the common law would require the *trial* to be had in the county of *B.*

§ 134. If then, in an action of assault and battery, trover, trespass for taking goods, slander, assumpsit, &c, (in all which the place in the declaration is *immaterial*, and the action *transitory*), the defendant pleads any matter of defence, which is *not local*—and lays it at a place not mentioned in the

(*h*) Com. Dig. *Pleader*, E. 4. 3 Lev. 113. 1 Saund. 8. a. (n. 2). 85. (n. 4). 247. (n. 1). 2 Ib. 5. d. e. (n. 3). 2 H. Black. 161. Com. Dig. *Action*, N. 12. *Pleader*, C. 20. 1 Chitt. Pl. 509. Co. Litt. 282. b.

(*i*) Iid.

Venue. How laid in the plea, &c.

declaration; the plea is ill, on special demurrer (*k*). If, for example, in an action of assault and battery laid in the county of *A.*, the defendant pleads *son assault demesne*, in the county of *B.;* or if in trespass for taking goods in the county of *A.*, the plea is a license, in the county of *B.;* or, if in assumpsit on a promise laid in one county, the defendant pleads fraud, duress, accord and satisfaction, usury, &c, in *another;* the plaintiff may with safety demur specially to the plea (*l*). For these several defences, in *whatever place* they may have arisen, are respectively as available, as if they had occurred *elsewhere;* and there can, therefore, be no *necessity* of laying them at any other place, than that stated in the declaration.

§ 135. But although the cause of action be *transitory* — as in the several examples, last stated; yet, if the *nature of the defence is local* — so that the fact, that it arose in a particular county or place, *different* from that stated in the declaration, is *necessary* to be alleged, in order to adapt the plea to the matter of the defence; the defendant is at liberty to *deviate*, in his plea, from the county or place alleged in the declaration (*m*). For if, in such a case, he was confined to the county or venue laid by the plaintiff, he might, by the *false venue* in the declaration, be

(*k*) Iid.

(*l*) Iid. Co. Litt. 282. b. Cro. Eliz. 667. 842. 860. 1 Ld Ray. 120. 3 Lev. 113. 2 Mod. 271.

(*m*) Cro. Eliz. 184. Co. Litt. 282. b. 3 Lev. 113. 227. 1 Ld Ray. 120. 1 Saund. 85. (n. 4). 247. 2 Ib. 5. b. (n. 3). Carth. 326. Hob. 5.

CHAP. III.

Venue. How laid in the plea, &c.

utterly deprived of his defence. For when issue is joined upon a *local* fact, the *place* is of the substance of the issue, and must be proved as laid.

§ 136. Thus, if a sheriff of the county of *A.*, having made an arrest, by authority of law, in that county, is sued for it, in an action of assault and battery and false imprisonment, alleged to have been committed in the county of *B.;* he may, in his plea, justify the arrest, as having been made in the former county (*n*). For as his official authority, existing only in the county of *A.*, was *local;* his defence, which is founded upon that authority, is necessarily so. If then, he were obliged to justify the arrest, as made in the county of *B.;* he would, of course, be reduced to the necessity of proving his authority to arrest in *that* county, (which according to the facts supposed, he could *not* do), or of losing the benefit of a justification, which is in law complete?

§ 137. Upon the same principle, if a constable of the town of *A.*, makes arrest in that town, in virtue of his office, and is sued for it in an action, in which the trespass is laid in the town of *B.*, in the same or a different county; he is allowed to justify the arrest in the town of *A.* (*o*). For the town, which limits his authority, is material to his justification, as is the *county* to that of the sheriff, in the

(*n*) 1 Saund. 85. (n. 4). 247. 2 Ib. 5. b. c. (n. 3). 1 Ld Ray. 120. Cro. Eliz. 174. 184.

(*o*) Iid.

CHAP. III.

Venue.

How laid in the plea, &c.

case last before supposed. The same principle applies to all cases, in which the defence is *local*, and in which the place laid in the declaration is not the *true* one; because in every such case, if issue is taken on the plea, the *place* must be proved as laid.

§ 138. But in all such cases, it is necessary for the defendant to *traverse* the place laid in the declaration: i. e. to deny that he is guilty of the alleged wrong in that place, or in any other than the one stated in his plea (*p*). For the place of the alleged wrong is, by the defendant's plea, made *material* and *traversable*: And it is a general principle, that a party who does not traverse what is material and *traversable*, in his adversary's pleading, tacitly admits it to be true (*q*).

§ 139. By the establishment of the rule, that the *venue* laid in the *declaration* draws to itself the trial of all *transitory* matters, the doctrine of *venues* underwent an essential change. For as, under this rule, no *other venue for transitory* matters can be laid in the subsequent pleadings; there seems now to remain no very substantial reasons for requiring, for the statement of such matters in these latter pleadings, any *venue* at all.

§ 141. In accordance with the principles, which have now been stated, Lord Ch. J. *Eyre*, in deliver-

(*p*) 2 Saund. 5. c d. e. (n. 3). 1 Ib. 85. (n. 4). Ib. 8. a. (n. 2). 1 Sid. 294. Cro. Eliz. 167. 705. 842. Cro. Jac. 45. 372. 3 Lev. 227. Carth. 326.

(*q*) 1 Salk. 91. 1 Wils. 338. Bac. Abr. *Pleas*, &c, *Introd.* Ib. *Pleas*, &c. H. 4. *Vide post*, ch. 7.

CHAP. III.

Venue.

ing the opinion of the court of C. B., in the case of *Ilderton* v. *Ilderton*, (after having recognized the rule, that the *venue* laid in the declaration draws to itself the trial of all *transitory* matters, alleged in the subsequent pleadings), observes that 'the distinction between laying no venue at all, in a *plea*, and being obliged to lay the *same* venue, as is to be found in the *declaration*, will not be a very substantial one'— and that it appears to be 'a *distinction without a difference*' (*r*).

§ 142. It would seem therefore, on principle, that in the pleadings which *follow* the declaration, the laying of a venue for *transitory* matters, is not now necessary, even in point of *form*; and therefore, that the omission of it will not injure those pleadings, even on special demurrer (*s*). Indeed this precise point was adjudged in the case, just referred to, of *Ilderton* v. *Ilderton*; and in the subsequent case of *Neale* v. *De Garay*, the doctrine was approved of, by the Court of King's Bench (*t*).

For local defences.

§143. And since the statutes 16 & 17 *Car.* 2. c. 8.; and 4 & 5 *Ann.* c. 16, § 6. (by which the ancient law regarding *locality of trials* has been still further altered), the laying of a venue, for even *local* matters, in the pleadings *subsequent* to the declaration, appears now to be, in the English law, but

(*r*) 2 H. Black. 145. 161—2. & vid. 7 T. R. 243. 247. 1 Saund. 8. a. Yelv. 12. a. 2 Caines' R. 372. 6 Johns. R. 33.

(*s*) Iid.

(*t*) 7 T. R. 243. 247.

Venue.

For local defences.

mere *form* (22). For by the former of these statutes, it is enacted that 'after a *verdict*, judgment shall not be stayed or reversed, for that there is no right venue; so as the cause were tried by a jury of the proper county or place, where the *action is laid*' (*u*). And this enactment not only cures a wrong *venue*, laid in the *true* county; but also aids, *after* verdict (23), a judgment rendered in a *wrong county;* even though it appear *upon the record*, that the issue was tried in a county, *other* than that in which the matter in issue arose (*v*); whereas, by the ancient law, if it appeared upon *the record*, that the cause of action arose in a county different from that, in which the action was laid; the mistake was incurable, and the judgment erroneous (*w*) (23 *a*), unless the error was waved by both parties, in the manner hereafter mentioned.

Post § 162.

§ 144. The latter of the two statutes above mentioned (4 & 5 *Ann.* c. 16. § 6.) enacts, 'that every *venire facias*, for the trial of any issue, in any action

(*u*) Bac. Abr. *Amendment*, &c, B. 2 Saund. 5. e. (n. 3).

(*v*) 1 Saund. 247. (n. 3). Willes, 431. 7 T. R. 583. 2 Saund. 5. g. (*in notis*). 2 East, 580. 1 Chitt. Pl. 283. 1 Saund. 74. (n. 2).

(*w*) Com. Dig. *Action*, N. 4. 6. 1 Saund. 74. (n. 2). 1 Chitt. Pl. 283.

---

(22) That is, as regards the place of *trial*.

(23) This provision, which applies only to judgments *after verdict*, is by the statute 4 *Ann.* c. 16. § 2. extended to judgments by *confession*, *nil dicit*, or *non sum informatus*. Bac. Abr. *Amendment*, &c. B. 2 Saund. 5. e. (n. 3.)

(23 *a*) And the same rule seems still to be applied to actions, transitory at common law, but made local by *statute*. *Vide* 5 M. & S. 427. 3 ib. 430; and cases there cited.

CHAP. III.

Venue.

For local defences.

or suit, shall be awarded *of the body* of the proper county, where such issue is *triable*' (*x*): The import of which enactment, expressed in more familiar language, is, that the jury, by whom any issue is to be tried, in any particular county, are to be summoned from the county *at large*, without reference to the common-law rule, requiring them to come from the immediate *vicinage*, in which the matter in issue arose: which rule had, indeed, by various evasions and alterations, been greatly relaxed in practice, before the statute of *Anne* was passed (*y*).

§ 145. This latter enactment, by removing the necessity of drawing the jury from the immediate *vicinity*, in which the matter in issue arose, or is alleged to have arisen, has virtually abrogated the ancient law of *venues*, *properly so called* — inasmuch as it has destroyed all distinction between true and false venues, in one and the same *county;* as the statute of *Charles* 2. (*extended* by the *second* section of the 16th chapter of the statute of *Anne*), has rendered all distinction between different *counties*, immaterial after *verdict*, *confession*, *nil dicit*, or *non sum informatus* (24) — provided the trial (in the case of

(*x*) Bac. Abr. *Venue*, D. 3 Black. Com. 360.
(*y*) Co. Litt. 157. 3 Black. Com. 360.

---

(24) A *confession*, (*or cognovit actionem*) is an express acknowledgment, by the defendant, upon the record, of the plaintiff's right of action. (3 Black. Com. 397. 3 Chitt. Pl. 520. 671.) By a *nil dicit* or *default*, is meant, that the defendant offers *no plea* whatever to the declaration, and thus tacitly admits it to be true. (3 Black. Com. 397.) A *non sum informatus* is a suggestion or admission, by the defendant's attorney, that he has

a verdict found), was by a jury of the same county, in which the 'action was *laid*' (25). CHAP. III.

Venue.

For local defences.

§ 146. From the combined operation of these statutes, it has resulted, as has been already suggested, that the laying of a venue for even *local* matters, in the pleadings *subsequent* to the declaration, has become, in effect, matter of form. For the new venue laid for any local matter, in the *plea*, does not now (as formerly) draw to itself the *trial* of such matter; and the consequence of the distinction between things local and transitory has finally been, that in *transitory* actions, the defendant can, by *no plea*, *abate* or *defeat* the suit, on the ground that the venue or county, in the *declaration*, is not the true one (*z*). And since the statute 16 and 17 Car. 2, ch. 8, if the defendant pleads even a *local* defence to a *transitory* action; he can have no opportunity to object to the *county*, in which the action is brought, or to the *venue* laid in the declara- Ante, § 132.

(*z*) 3 Black. Com. 294. Bac. Abr. *Actions Local*, &c. B. Com. Dig. *Pleader*, S 9. Cowp. 177. 1 Saund. 74, (n. 2.) Gilb. H. C. P. 89-90.

---

no instructions to make any answer to the plaintiff, or any defence for his client; and is, therefore, virtually a species of *default*.—(*Id.*)

(25) The statute of *Anne*, having been construed not to embrace actions on *penal statutes*, was by the subsequent act, 24 Geo. 2. c. 18, extended to this latter class of actions (3 Black. Com. 360). Now, therefore, the jury is, by the English law, to be summoned from *the body* of the county, in *all* civil actions. (Lawes' Pl. 28. 29.)

CHAP. III.

tion, till *after verdict;* and then, by the express provisions of that act, the objection is *too late:* The mistake being cured by the verdict.

Venue. For local defences.

§ 147. And in regard to the *venue* laid in the declaration, as distinguished from the *county* (26), in a transitory action, all exception, in any and every stage of the suit, is precluded by the sixth section of the statute of Anne, before recited. There now remains, therefore, no way in which the defendant, in a transitory action, can oblige the plaintiff to change the *county* laid in the declaration, except by *motion*, addressed to the discretion of the court, and which, under circumstances to be hereafter stated, the court has power to grant. Nor is there any mode whatever, in which the defendant, in such an action, can take advantage of a false *venue* laid in the true county.

Post, §§ 151. 152.

§ 148. Since the enactment of these statutes, therefore, it has become the constant practice in England, when issue is taken, even upon a *local* defence laid in a foreign county (a county *other* than that mentioned in the declaration), to try the issue in the county, in which the action is *brought* (*a*) —

(*a*) 1 Saund. 74, (n. 2.) 2 Ib. 5. d. e. (n. 3.) Ld Ray. 330. 1212. 3 Black. Com. 294.

(26) The word *venue*, in its present acceptation, usually includes as well the *county* named, as the *place* or *vicinage* laid within it; though, in strictness, the term signifies the *vicinage* only; in which latter sense, it is, in the present instance, used in the text.

Venue. For local defences.

which practice is subject only to the power of the court, on *motion*, to remove the cause for trial, into the county in which the cause of action arose. It appears then, that according to the English law, as it now stands, and subject to the single qualification just mentioned, the venue, (or rather, the *county*), laid in the declaration, in *transitory* actions, regularly draws to itself the trial, as well of all *local*, as of all *transitory* matters alleged in the *subsequent* pleadings. Hence, if in a *transitory* action, brought in the county of *A.*, issue is joined on any *local* matter of defence, laid in the county of *B.;* the trial is regularly had in the county of *A.* (*b*): The defendant having, in general, no power to change the place of trial, before verdict; and the trial in the county of *A.* being, *after verdict*, aided by the statute of Charles 2, before mentioned.

§ 149. But before that statute was made a trial in the county of *A.*, in the case last supposed, would have been a *mistrial*, and as such, a sufficient ground for arresting the judgment (*c*). So strict, indeed, was the original rule of the common law, in regard to the locality of trials, that if, in a transitory action, the defendant pleaded the general issue to a *part* of the alleged cause of action, and a *local* justification to the *residue;* the general issue must have been Ante, § 133.

(*b*) 1 Saund. 247. (n. 2.) 1 Vent. 22. 263. T. Ray. 181. 2 Saund. 5. e. (n. 3.) 2 Lev. 164. 3 Ib. 394. 7 T. R. 583. Carth. 448. 12 Mod. 8.

(*c*) Gouldsb. 38. 88. Cro. Eliz. 261. (468.) 870. Com. Dig. *Action*, N. 6. 1 Saund. 247. Mo. 257. Hob. 5. 2 Saund. 5. d. (n. 3.)

CHAP. III. tried in the county, in which the action was *laid*, and the justification, in the county laid in the *plea* (*d*).

Venue.

For local defences. § 150. It is however still necessary, notwithstanding the foregoing alterations in the law of venues, that in alleging *local matter*, even in the pleadings which *follow* the declaration, the place in which it arose should be truly stated. Thus, (as in Ante, § 136. a case before supposed), if the sheriff of the county of *A.* makes a lawful arrest, under legal process, or *virtute officii*, in that county, and is sued for it, in trespass for assault, battery, &c, alleged to have been committed in the county of *B.*; it is necessary that he should justify the arrest, as having been made in the county of *A.* (*e*). This is necessary, however, not for the purpose of substituting the true *venue*, for that laid in the declaration, or in other words, not for the purpose of altering the *place of trial*; but for the purpose of rendering the matter of his plea *available*: It being indispensable to the sufficiency of his defence, that the arrest should be shown, in the plea, to have been made within the *local limits of his authority* as sheriff.

Change of the venue. § 151. The power of the court to *change*, on the defendant's motion, the venue laid in the declaration, in transitory actions, has already been incidentally mentioned — a power, supposed to be de-

(*d*) 1 Saund. 247. (n. 1.) Cro. Jac. 87. 127. 3 Lev. 394. Co. Litt. 125. *n*.

(*e*) Cro. Eliz. 174. 184. 1 Saund. 85. (n. 4.) 2 Ib. 5. c. (n. 3.) 1 Ld Ray. 120.

CHAP. III.

Venue. Change of. Ante, note 19.

rived from the statute 6 Rich. 2, c. 2. (*f*). This power, which is discretionary, has been exercised under a rule of practice, by the superior courts of Westminster, from the reign of *James the First*; in whose reign its exercise appears to have commenced (*g*).

§ 152. Under this rule of practice, if the defendant, in a transitory action, will make affidavit that the alleged cause of action arose exclusively in a *foreign* county, the court may, in its discretion, order a change of the venue, and award a trial in the *latter* county—unless the plaintiff will, on his part, undertake to give evidence of some matter, material to the issue. arising in the county in which the action is *brought* (*h*). And if the plaintiff, after having entered into such an engagement, fails on the trial to comply with it, by giving evidence of some matter involved in the issue, and arising in the county in which the action is laid; he will be *nonsuited* (*i*): His failure, in this particular, being a violation of the *condition*, on which the venue in the declaration was allowed to remain unchanged.

§ 153. It is still indispensably necessary, even in transitory actions, that some particular *county* be

(*f*) Vid. Ante, Note 19. 1 Saund. 74. (n. 2.)

(*g*) 3 Black. Com. 294. 2 Salk. 670.

(*h*) 2 Black. Rep. 1032-3. 1 Saund. 74. (n. 2.) Cowp. 410. 2 T. R. 275. 6 East, 433-4. Com. Dig. *Action*, N. 13.

(*i*) Iid.

CHAP. III.

Venue.

laid in the declaration, for the sake of *trial* (*k*). For in every action, in which there is an issue joined, triable by jury, the jury-process must go to *some* particular county. But if *no* county is laid in the declaration, it cannot be known from what county the jury shall be summoned, nor, consequently, in what county or place the trial shall be had.

§ 154. But as the jury now come from *the body* of the county, in which the action is laid; a *venue*, strictly so called, (i. e. a particular *vicinage*,) though universally inserted in the precedents, would seem, in transitory actions, in general, to be not indispensable, on common-law principles, even in the *declaration* (*l*); and so it has been adjudged (*ll*).

Omission of, how aided.

§ 155. By the ancient rule of the common law, the omission of a venue or county, when necessary, appears to have been an incurable defect (*m*), by reason of the strict locality of *trial*, which that rule required. But since the distinction between things local and transitory was fully established, it has long been settled, on *common-law* principles, that if the declaration, in a *transitory* action, mentions *no* venue or county; it is aided by the defendant's pleading to the action, any plea, that *admits* the fact, for

(*k*) Com. Dig. *Pleader*, C. 20. Cowp. 176–7. 5 T. R. 620. 2 Lev. 227. Bac. Abr. *Venue*, C. 3 T. R. 387.

(*l*) 2 H. Black. 161. 2 East, 501. *arg*. 1 Chitt. Pl. 280.

(*ll*) 3 M. & S. 148.

(*m*) Bac. Abr. *Venue*, C. 2 Leon. 22. 1 Chitt. Pl. 283.

CHAP. III.

Venue. Omission of, how aided.

the *trial of which* some particular county ought to have been laid (*n*): Because the fact, when *admitted* by such a plea, requires *no trial*. And therefore, if in debt on bond, the declaration omits to state the *county* in which the instrument was made, and the defendant pleads in bar a release, payment, accord and satisfaction, or any other defence, which *admits* the execution of the bond; the defect is cured by the *plea* (*o*), on the principles last stated. And the same principles apply to all transitory actions, in general, whether sounding in contract or tort.

§ 156. And the omission of a venue or county, in the declaration, in transitory actions, is on *common-law* principles aided on a judgment by *default* (*p*). For all the issuable facts stated in the declaration, being, by the default, *confessed*; no *trial* of them is necessary. And now, by the express provisions of the statute 16 and 17 *Car.* 2. c. 8, the omission of a venue *or county*, in the declaration, is aided by *verdict* (*q*). And the same rule is extended, by the *second* section of the statute 4 and 5 *Ann.* c. 16, to judgments by *confession*, or *non sum informatus* (*r*). It results, therefore, that by these two enactments, the want of a venue or *county*, in the declaration,

(*n*) Bac. Abr. *Venue*, C. Com. Dig. *Pleader*, C. 20. 85. 6 Mod. 222. 2 Ld Ray. 1040. Cro. Jac. 125. 683. Hob. 82. Hardr. 187.

(*o*) Iid.

(*p*) Com. Dig. *Pleader*, C. 20. 1 Lutw. 239. 1 Chitt. Pl. 285.

(*q*) Bac. Abr. *Amendment*, &c, B. 2 Saund. 5. e. (n. 3.) 7 T. R. 587.

(*r*) Bac. Abr. *Amendment*, B.

CHAP. III.

Venue.

in transitory, as also in personal *local* actions, is aided after *verdict*, or on *judgment by confession*, or on *non sum informatus;* as the *common* law had before cured the same omission, on judgment by *nil dicit*, (or default,) or on the defendant's pleading to the action any defence, which *admitted* the truth of the declaration.

Omission of, fatal on demurrer.

§ 157. But, as it is still necessary, in point of form, even in transitory actions, that some county be laid in the *declaration;* the omission of it remains fatal, on *demurrer* (*s*). For as the statutes before mentioned, which cure the defect after *verdict*, *confession*, &c, do not aid it, under a *demurrer ;* the omission, when the declaration is *demurred* to, is left to operate as at common law.

§ 158. But such an omission in the declaration, in transitory actions, is not a ground of *nonsuit*, nor of any objection on the *trial* (*t*). Since no advantage can be taken of defects *apparent* upon the face of the pleadings, but by an issue *in law*. It results then from the preceding rules, that in a transitory action, a demurrer is the *only* mode, in which advantage can now be taken of the omission of a county, in the declaration: All exceptions, in any other form, for such a defect, being, as we have seen,

(*s*) Bac. Abr. *Venue*, C. T. Ray. 181. 2 Wils. 355. 3 T. R. 387. 1 Chitt. Pl. 285. 14 East, 291. *Vide* 5 Mass. R. 94. 98.

(*t*) 2 Wils. 354. 1 Chitt. Pl. 285. 2 East, 499. 3 T. R. 387. 1 Saund. 74. (n. 2.)

excluded by gradual relaxations of the strictness of the ancient rule, and by legislative enactments.

Venue.

Where the cause of action arises abroad.

§ 159. According to the principles of the common law, as already stated, (*ante*, § 112,) a transitory action, the cause of which has arisen in any one country or sovereign state, may in general be brought in any other, in which the defendant may be found (*u*): For duties and liabilities, of a transitory nature, attend the *person* of the party chargeable, wherever he may be. Hence, if a personal contract is made, or a personal tort committed, in the kingdom of *France;* an action will lie against the debtor, or wrongdoer, (if found in *England*,) in an *English* court of general jurisdiction, and may, in general, be laid in *any* English county, without making mention of the place where the cause of action actually arose (*v*). In such a case, it is necessary that *some* English county be laid in the declaration, for a reason heretofore explained; viz. that every action must be laid in *some* particular county in the kingdom for the sake of *trial*. And this legal fiction, like all others devised for the furtherance of justice, cannot be traversed (*w*). Thus, if A. becomes indebted to B., or commits a tort upon his person, or personal property, in the

(*u*) Com. Dig. *Action*, N. 7. Cowp. 161. 177-8. 181. 344. 2 H. Black. 145—161. Co. Litt. 125. a. (n. 1.) 5 T. R. 616. 7 Ib. 243. 1 Saund. 74. (n. 2.)

(*v*) Iid.

(*w*) Cowp. 177-8. 179. 3 Black. Com. 43. 107.

CHAP. III.

Venue.

city of *Paris*, or of *Canton;* an action, in either case, may regularly be maintained against A. in *England*, (if he is there found,) upon a declaration, alleging the cause of action to have arisen in that *English* county, in which the action is laid, without taking notice of the foreign place.

Mode of laying a foreign venue.

§ 160. But to this rule there is one exception, in respect to the *mode* of laying the county: If an action is brought, in an *English* court, on a *specialty*, dated at a place in a foreign country—as at *Amsterdam;* the declaration must describe the bond, as made at *Amsterdam*, for the purpose of avoiding a variance. For if the instrument were described, as having been made in any *English* county; it would not, when produced, correspond to the *description* given of it in the declaration. In this case, however, the name of the foreign place, at which the bond is dated, must be followed, (under a *videlicit*), by that of the county in which the action is laid—as in the manner following:—'At the city of *Amsterdam*, to wit, at *Islington*, in the county of Middlesex' (*x*): The foreign place being named, for the purpose of correctly *describing* the instrument; and the English county, for the sake not only of *trial*, but of *jurisdiction*. For by the theory of the common law, an English court has jurisdiction of such matters only as arise *within the realm*, or in the body of an *English* county—to conform to which *theory*,

(*x*) 2 Salk. 660. Cowp. 161. 177. 178. 2 Ld Ray. 1043. Bac. Abr. *Actions Local*, &c. A. 2 H. Black. 161—2. Com. Dig. *Action*, N. 7. 12. 1 Stra. 612.

the fiction, just mentioned, was invented. And as has been stated already, the fiction employed for this purpose cannot be traversed. For if it were traversable, the jurisdiction might be ousted, at the pleasure of the defendant, and the administration of justice obstructed. CHAP. III. Venue.

§ 161. But the necessity of laying the true place of the execution of written instruments is now, in general, superseded in England, by the practice of dating them, *at large;* i. e. without naming the *place* of execution (*y*). — Actions, the causes of which arise upon the *high seas*, and which are cognizable by the common-law courts, may be laid in any county (*z*). Causes of action arising on the high seas.

§ 162. In most cases, local actions in courts of general jurisdiction, might be tried (even by the common law, and without reference to the statute of 16 & 17 Car. ii. c. 8) in any county, by *consent* of both parties entered upon the record — though the county should appear, from the record itself, to be a wrong one (*a*). For the consent, thus entered, was a waiver on the record, of the error which would otherwise have been fatal to the trial. But unless such consent appeared *upon the record*, it would not, (where the county appeared, from the body of the record, to be a wrong one), prevent error (*b*). Be- Local actions triable by consent in any county.

(*y*) Com. Dig. *Action*, N. 7. 12. 1 Saund. 74. (n. 2).
(*z*) Cowp. 179.
(*a*) Com. Dig. *Action*, N. 11. 1 Chitt. Pl. 271. Cro. Eliz. 664.
(*b*) Iid. Hob. 5. c. n. 2. (*Williams'* ed.) Bac. Abr. *Error*, K. 6.

CHAP. III.

Venue.

cause an error, apparent in the body of the record, cannot be waved, except by what appears on the record itself.—But by the statute above mentioned, (according to the construction given to it by the courts), as has been before shown, such consent on the record is no longer necessary to prevent error.

§ 163. But in actions, brought for the recovery of *lands* or *tenements*—as in *ejectment*—no consent of parties, it seems, can render a trial, in a wrong county, *effectual*, on the principles of the *English* law; though such consent, (while it was necessary), would have prevented error (*c*). For the sheriff of the county, in which the action is tried, to whom only, as it seems, the execution can, in such case, be directed, cannot deliver possession of land lying in another county (*d*). So that there would be, eventually, no means of enforcing the judgment.—In the New-England states, however, this difficulty does not exist; if it does in any of the United States.

Post. c. 5. § 22.

When no venue is necessary.

§ 164. The general rule, (*ante*, § 102), that a venue must be laid for all *traversable* facts, is not universal. *Negative* allegations regularly require no venue (*e*). For place can, with no propriety, be predicated of that, which has no existence. So also, matters which concern the *person* of a party, or of any individual—as his *name*, *title*, &c,—need

(*c*) Palm. 100. 2 Roll. Rep. 166. T. Jon. 199. T. Ray. 372.
(*d*) 1 Chitt. Pl. 284. Cowp. 176. 7 T. R. 588.
(*e*) Plowd. 24. a. 2 East, 503. Lawes' Pl. 58.

not be laid at any particular place (*f*): These also being facts, of which locality is not predicable.

Venue.

§ 165. In alleging wrongs affecting a *local* subject — as the breaking and entering the plaintiff's clóse, in an action of trespass, or the *ouster* in ejectment — a formal *venue* need not be laid for the wrongful act complained of; although it constitutes the *gist* of the action (*g*). For as the description, which is required to be given of the *land*, must state as well the parish, &c, as the county, in which it lies; the place where the act was done will necessarily appear, from that description — which thus, in effect, supplies the venue, without formally laying one. And as upon original principles of the common law, already stated, those facts only, which may be *traversed*, require a venue; it follows that matters of mere *inducement*, or *aggravation*, require none (*h*): Because such matter is not traversable. — The mode of laying the venue, in the *English* precedents, is by placing the name of the county in the *margin*, at the commencement of the declaration, in the following manner: — 'Middlesex, to wit' (*i*).

The requisites of TIME, and PLACE, in pleading, having been thus discussed; it is necessary to proceed to others, of a more miscellaneous character: —

(*f*) 1 Salk. 6. Lawes' Pl. 58.

(*g*) Com. Dig. *Pleader*, C. 20. 2 Black. R. 706. Cro. Jac. 555. 557. 2 Mod. 304. Lawes' Pl. 58.

(*h*) 1 Saund. 74. (n. 1). Com. Dig. *Pleader*, C. 20. Co. Litt. 303. a. Salk. 404.

(*i*) Lill. Ent. *passim*. 2 Chitt. Pl. 1. 2. 3. 4. 141.

CHAP. III.

Miscellaneous rules.

Alleging the evidence of facts, not sufficient.

§ 166. It has already appeared (ante, § 2,) that all facts, *essential* to the right of action or the defence, must, in general, be expressly and substantively alleged. Hence, stating the mere *evidence* of a material fact is not sufficient (*k*). The *fact itself* must be stated; otherwise the allegation will present no subject to which the law can be applied. Besides, such a mode of pleading would, if admissible, refer the matter of *fact* in question to the court, instead of the jury. Thus, if in trover, the plaintiff alleges a property in the goods — the loss — the finding — and a *demand and refusal* — but omits to aver a *conversion;* the declaration is ill: The demand and refusal being only *evidence* of a conversion, which is the *gist* of the action (*l*).

Tacit admissions.

§ 167. Each party tacitly admits all such traversable allegations on the opposite side, as he does not traverse (*m*). For as each party is allowed to deny in some form — (either by a general, or precise traverse) — all material facts alleged against him; the omission, by either party, to traverse any such fact, alleged by his adversary, is justly considered as an *admission* of it.

(*k*) 9 Co. 9. b. Willes, 131. Cro. Eliz. 913. 2 Root, 74. 2 Stra. 793. Cro. Jac. 383. Chitt. on Bills, 186-7.

(*l*) 1 Roll. Ab. 131. Hob. 187. 2 Show. 179. 10 Co. 56. b. 57. a. 3 Burr. 1243. 2 H. Black. 135-6. Cowp. 529. *Contra,* 6 Mod. 212.

(*m*) Bac. Abr. *Pleas,* &c, H. 4. Ib. *Introd.* 2. 1 Salk. 91. 1 Wils. 338.

§ 168. Whatever has been *admitted*, on both sides, in the pleadings, cannot be contradicted, either in the subsequent pleadings, or even by the verdict. For neither party can retract what he has before conceded on the record; and the jury have no authority to find any other facts than such as are put in *issue* (*n*).

Construction of any pleading, most strong against the pleader.

§ 169. Each party's pleading is to be taken most strongly against *himself*, and most favourably to his adversary (*o*). This rule is founded, not only upon the presumption that each party's statement is the most favourable to himself, of which his case will admit; but also upon the obviously reasonable principle, that it is incumbent on each pleader, in stating the ground of his action or defence, to *explain himself fully* and *clearly*. Any ambiguity, uncertainty, or omission in the pleadings, must therefore be at the peril of that party, *in whose* allegations it occurs. If, therefore, the defendant in trespass pleads a general release, without stating the *time* of its execution; it shall be intended to have been made *before* the trespass was committed (*p*). Thus also, if to debt on bond, payable on a given day, the defendant pleads payment or tender, without alleging the *time*; the legal intendment must be, that it was made *after* the day appointed for payment (*q*).

(*n*) Bac. Abr. *Pleas*, &c, *Introd.* Ib. *Verdict*, W. 2 Mod. 6. Willes, 366. Lawes' Pl. 48.

(*o*) Co. Litt. 303. b. Dy. 120. a. Plowd. 29. 202. Com. Dig. *Pleader*, E. 6.

(*p*) Plowd. 46. a. Com. Dig. *Pleader*, E. 6.

(*q*) Plowd. 104. Com. Dig. *Pleader*, E. 6.

CHAP. III.

Surplusage of no effect.

§ 170. *Surplusage* — by which is meant matter, that is altogether superfluous and useless, does not, in general, vitiate the pleadings, even in point of form: The maxim being, *utile per inutile non vitiatur* (*r*). In such cases, the unnecessary matter will be *rejected* by the court, and the pleadings will stand as if it were *struck* out, or had never been inserted.

Effect of unnecessary matter, when repugnant.

§ 171. But where a party pleads *unnecessary* matter, which shows that he has no cause of action, or no legal defence, the matter thus pleaded will be fatal to that which would, otherwise, have been good (*s*). For in this case, the superfluous matter cannot be *rejected, as immaterial;* since it shows that the pleader has, according to his own statement, no cause of action, or no defence. Thus, if in declaring upon a public statute, the plaintiff *so* counts upon it, as to confine himself to its terms as recited, but *misrecites* it, in a material part; the declaration is ill, in substance (*t*), For though the recital of a public statute is *unnecessary;* yet, it being thus recited, and counted upon, the plaintiff must recover upon it, if at all, *as* recited. But, as it must, of necessity, appear judicially to the court, that no such statute, as that recited, exists; it must consequently appear, in the same manner, that the declaration discloses no right of action.

(*r*) Bac. Abr. *Pleas*, &c, I. 4. Co. Litt. 303, b. 2 East, 333. 4 Co. 42. Com. Dig. *Pleader*, C. 28. 29. E. 12. Hob. 208.

(*s*) Iid.

(*t*) Com. Dig. *Pleader*, C. 29. Ib. *Action upon stat.* I. 1 Ld Ray. 382. Plowd. 84. b. Cro. Eliz. 245. Yelv. 127. a. note (1).

Repugnancy, effect of.

§ 172. So also, superfluous matter, when it *contradicts*, or is *inconsistent with facts* before alleged on the same side, vitiates the pleading (*u*). This fault falls properly under the denomination of *repugnancy;* which, as the term imports, is some *contrariety* or *inconsistency* between different allegations of the same party (27).

§ 173. Repugnancy is a fault in all pleading (*v*); and this, upon the obvious principle, that *inconsistent* allegations, in the pleading of either party, destroy or neutralize each other. The rule, however, is to be understood with this difference: If the pleading is repugnant, in a *material* point; it is ill in *substance*, or on *general* demurrer: But repugnancy, in an *immaterial* point, is a fault in *form* only (*w*); and therefore no advantage can be taken of it, except by *special* demurrer. Thus, if in trover, the declaration by mistake alleges the conversion to have taken place on a day *prior* to that, on which the loss of the goods is laid; or if in ejectment, the ouster is laid on a day *prior* to the alleged date of the lease; the repugnancy, in either case, would, at *common* law, (before the statute of *jeofails*), have been fatal,

(*u*) Co. Litt. 303. b. Com. Dig. *Pleader*, E. 12. Lawes' Pl. 63-4. 170. Gilb. H. C. P. 132.

(*v*) 1 Saund. 169. 2 Ib. 291. 1 Stra. 232. 1 T. R. 70. 71. 657.

(*w*) Iid.

(27) Such superfluous matter cannot be considered as mere *surplusage;* for, by *surplusage*, properly so called, is generally meant *such* superfluous matter, as may be *rejected*, or entirely *disregarded*.

CHAP. III.

on general demurrer: But the day being now considered but matter of *form;* the repugnancy is in both cases aided, except on *special* demurrer (*x*).

Ante, § 64.

All things are to be pleaded according to their legal effect.

§ 174. It is laid down as an established rule, that all things must be pleaded according to their *legal effect* (*y*); i. e. must be stated or described, as they operate or take effect, *in law;* although such statement or description should *vary, literally* or in *form,* from the matter of fact to be shown in evidence. This rule relates chiefly to cases, in which a written instrument, drawn in a *form* in which it cannot, by the rules of law, take effect, may nevertheless operate as an instrument of a *different kind:* In which case *ut res magis valeat quam pereat,* the law will so construe it, if possible, as to give it effect, as an instrument of a *different kind* from that, which in its language it purports to be (*z*). For it is an established rule, that a deed shall never fail of effect, if by construction it can be made effectual (*a*).

§ 175. If then a deed, in the form of a contract or conveyance, of one particular species, cannot,

(*x*) Com. Dig. *Pleader,* C. 19. 3 M. 5. Yelv. 94. 3 Black. Com. 394. Carth. 389. Com. R. 12. 1 Saund. 116. 1 Lev. 194. Andr. 250. Stra. 232. 1095.

(*y*) Bac. Abr. *Pleas,* &c, I. 7. Co. Litt. 193. b. Com. Dig. *Pleader,* C. 37. 2 Saund. 96–7. Cowp. 600. Cro. Eliz. 352. Doug. 667. 2 Salk. 574. 1 Ld Ray. 400. Lawes' Pl. 62. 1 T. R. 446.

(*z*) Shep. Touch. 82-3. Cro. Eliz. 352. 2 Salk. 574. 2 Saund. 96. T. Ray. 187. 1 T. R. 446. 4 Mod. 150.

(*a*) Shep. Touch. 82-3. Hob. 277. 2 Saund. 96. n. 1.

CHAP. III.

Pleading according to the legal effect.

from the nature of the thing, operate except *as* a contract, or conveyance, of a *different* kind; it must, according to the above rule, be pleaded, as a deed of the *latter* kind. Thus, if a deed purporting to *give, grant, bargain, sell, and release*, cannot, in the nature of the case, take effect in law, except as a *release;* it must, according to the above rule, be *pleaded* as a *release:* Or if it cannot operate, except as a deed of *bargain and sale;* it must be *pleaded as such* (*b*).

§ 176. And in all such cases, a mistake in stating the legal effect, if it appears upon the face of the pleadings, is fatal on demurrer (*c*); and if it does not thus appear, it is fatal in evidence (*d*). For the court cannot, in either case, give judgment for the pleader, in opposition to his own averments. If, therefore, a deed of feoffment, with livery of seisin, is made by a *joint-tenant* to his co-tenant; it must, according to this rule, be pleaded not as a *feoffment*, but as a *release* (*e*). For a feoffment cannot take effect, as between joint-tenants; since each of them is already seised as well *per tout*, as *per mie*—as well of the *whole*, as of the *half.* So also, if a tenant for life makes a conveyance, in form of *a grant*, to the reversioner; it is, by the same rule, to be plead-

(*b*) Cro. Eliz. 166. 1 Vent. 109. 2 Saund. 97. b. (n. 2.) Co. Litt. 301. b. Carth. 308.

(*c*) 2 Vent. 151. 3 Lev. 291. 2 Saund. 97. c. (n. 2.) 4 Mod. 149. Carth. 253.

(*d*) 1 H. Black. 313. 569. 3 T. R. 182. 481. 2 Stra. 934-5.

(*e*) Com. Dig. *Pleader*, C. 37. 4 Mod. 150. Bac. Abr. *Pleas*, &c, I. 7. Co. Litt. 193. b. 200. b. 2 Saund. 96.

CHAP. III.

Pleading according to the legal effect.

ed as a *surrender* (*f*): The latter being the only form of conveyance, by which the interest of the particular tenant can, by the common law, pass to the reversioner.

§ 177. Under the same rule, if one *covenants to stand seised* to the use of his child, or near relative, for a *pecuniary* or *valuable* consideration; the conveyance must be pleaded, as a deed of *bargain and sale* (*g*). For a covenant to stand seised is not supported by a valuable consideration; but by that only of *natural affection between kindred*, or that of *marriage:* Whereas a conveyance by *bargain and sale* can be supported, by no other than a *valuable* consideration (*h*). Hence, on the other hand, a deed in the form of a *grant*, or of a *bargain and sale*, made to a near relative, and expressed to be in consideration of *natural affection*, must, on the same principle, be pleaded as a covenant to *stand seised* (*i*): Because such a consideration will support *no other* conveyance, than a covenant to stand seised.

§ 178. And a single deed, made by two persons, having distinct interests in the subject of it, may enure to *two different intents or effects*. Thus if a tenant for life or years, and the reversioner, join in a deed of conveyance, in the form of a deed of *bargain and sale*; it will, as against the reversioner,

(*f*) Bac. Abr. *Pleas*, &c, I. 7. 4 Mod. 151. Comb. 190.

(*g*) Carth. 308. 3 Lev. 291. 4 Mod. 149. 2 Vent. 149.

(*h*) 2 Black. Com. 342.

(*i*) 2 Wils. 22. 75. Willes, 673. 682. 4 Mass. R. 135. 2 Saund. 97. a. (n. 1.) Bac. Abr. *Pleas*, &c, I. 7. 2 Vent. 149. 260. 266.

Pleading according to the legal effect.

take effect as a *bargain and sale*, and *quoad* the tenant, as a *surrender*. In such a case therefore, the conveyance should, by the above rule, be *pleaded* according to its twofold legal effect — viz. as a *bargain and sale*, on the part of the reversioner; and as a *surrender*, on that of the tenant (*k*).

§ 179. Within the same general rule, a *covenant* by a creditor, with his debtor, never to sue for the debt, should be pleaded, not *as* a covenant, but as an *acquittance* (*l*). For, *as a covenant*, it cannot *bar* an action for the recovery of the debt; although it would entitle the debtor to *damages*, in a cross action of covenant broken: Since a covenant is no bar to an action brought upon a different contract, unless the former contains words of *defeasance* (*m*).

§ 180. So also, when a bill of exchange is payable, in its terms, to the *order of a fictitious* payee, the holder, in declaring upon it, must, by the same rule, describe it as a bill payable to *bearer* (*n*): This being the only form in which it can take effect.

§ 181. But the rule itself, (*ante*, § 174), of which the preceding examples are given, as illustrations — though generally laid down as being *imperative* — ought rather to be expressed, as *permis-*

(*k*) 1 Ld Ray. 400. Lutw. 569.

(*l*) Cro. Eliz. 352. 1 Show. 46. 1 Roll. Ab. 939. 1 T. R. 446. 8 Ib. 170-1. Willes, 109, *note*. 17 Mass. R. 581.

(*m*) 1 Lev. 152. 6 T. R. 737. 8 Ib. 483. Esp. Dig. 306.

(*n*) 1 H. Black. 313. 569. 2 Ib. 194. 288. 3 T. R. 178. 282. 335. 481.

CHAP. III.

Pleading according to the legal effect.

sive. And the more proper form of stating the rule, would be, that where the form and legal effect of an instrument differ, it *may be* pleaded, according to its legal effect. For, though this latter is confessedly the more scientific and approved mode of pleading, in all such cases; yet the pleader *may*, at his option — instead of stating the legal effect — *recite* the instrument, *in hæc verba*, and refer its legal operation to the court (*o*). For if, when the form of the deed differs from its legal effect, and it is stated according to that effect, the court can perceive from the instrument, that it supports the statement, *in evidence;* there appears to be no sufficient reason, why — when the deed is recited, *in hæc verba* — its legal effect may not be recognized by the court, upon the face of *the pleadings*.

Ante, s. 176.

§ 182. If however the pleader undertakes to state the legal effect, and *misstates* it; the mistake will be fatal (*p*): As if a deed, which can operate in law only as a *release*, or *surrender*, is pleaded as a *grant*, or *bargain and sale*, or *vice versâ*. For in such a case, the allegation, professing to state the legal effect, is essentially *untrue*.

Immaterial and impertinent averments.

§ 183. There is an important distinction to be observed, between *immaterial* and *impertinent* averments: viz. that the former must, in many cases, be

(*o*) 1 Ld Ray. 400. 403. 404. Lutw. 569. 2 H. Black. 11. 3 Lev. 292. 8 Johns. R. 374.

(*p*) 3 Lev. 291. 2 Saund. 97. c. (n. 2). 4 Mod. 149. Carth. 253. 1 H. Black. 313. 516. 3 T. R. 182. 474. 481. 2 Stra. 934—5. 3 B. & A. 66.

precisely proved; whereas the latter require no proof in any case (*q*).

Impertinent averments.

§ 184. For the purpose of explaining this distinction, it must be premised, that an *impertinent* averment is a statement of matter altogether *foreign* to the merits of the cause, and which might, therefore, be *entirely struck out*, without injury to the pleading (*r*). Of such matter, no proof can ever be required. An *immaterial* averment, (as contradistinguished from an *impertinent* one), has been variously described; but not always with sufficient precision. In the case of *Bristow* v. *Wright*, (Doug. 665), Lord *Mansfield*, in commenting upon the distinction between these two species of averments, observes, 'The distinction is between that, which may be rejected as *surplusage*, and which might have been *struck out* on motion, and what cannot. Where the declaration contains *impertinent matter*, *foreign* to the cause, and which the master, on a reference to him, would strike out, that will be rejected by the court, and need not be proved. But if the *very ground* of the action is misstated; as where you undertake to recite that part of a deed on which the action is founded, and it is misrecited; that will be fatal.'

§ 185. This language, though sufficiently descriptive of an *impertinent* averment, affords rather a

(*q*) Doug. 667. 2 Black. Rep. 1104. 3 T. R. 643. 5 Ib. 496. 2 East, 446. 451. 497. 3 Bos. & P. 456. 461. 2 McNall. Ev. 501. 513.

(*r*) Doug. 667. 2 Black. Rep. 1104. 3 T. R. 644—5.

CHAP. III.

particular *example*, than a general definition or description of an *immaterial* one. The following is therefore submitted, as a substantially correct description of the latter: —

Immaterial averments.

An *immaterial* averment is one, alleging, with *needless particularity* or *unnecessary circumstances*, what is material and necessary, and which might properly have been stated *more generally*, and without such circumstances or particulars: Or in other words, it is a statement of *unnecessary particulars*, in *connexion with, and as descriptive of, what is material.*

When necessary to be proved.

§ 186. Immaterial averments, and the necessity of strictly proving them, may be illustrated by the case before mentioned, of *Bristow* v. *Wright* (Doug. 665). This was an action, brought on the statute 8 *Ann.* c. 14. § 1. by a landlord against a sheriff, for taking in execution, and removing from the demised premises, the goods of the tenant, without leaving effects sufficient to satisfy a year's rent. The declaration stated the demise, which it described as reserving a certain annual rent, payable '*by four even and equal quarterly payments*,' &c. On the trial, a parol demise was proved; but it appeared that there was no stipulation with regard to the *time or times* of paying the rent; and for this cause, it was resolved by the court of King's Bench, that the plaintiff could not recover. For though it was confessedly unnecessary to state the time or times of payment, in the declaration — in other words, though this part of the statement was *immaterial;*

yet, as it was indispensably necessary to allege a *contract*, reserving the rent: (so that the *entire* statement of the reservation could not be struck out, without destroying the declaration); and as the appointment of certain particular times of payment was stated as a *constituent part* of the contract, which was in its nature entire; a failure to prove such an appointment, was a failure to prove the contract as stated, and consequently a *variance*. The contract proved was not the contract alleged in the declaration.

§ 187. The same rule, in regard to immaterial averments, was recognized in the case of *Savage, q. t.* v. *Smith* (2 Black. Rep. 1101. 1104). That was an action of debt against a bailiff, for extorting illegal fees, on a writ of *fieri facias*. The declaration described the *fi. fa.*, as having been issued, on a judgment recovered in B. R. at a specified term, for £51, 12, 0, debt, and £6, 10, 0, costs. But the plaintiff having failed, on the trial, to prove such a *judgment*, the court held, that admitting it to have been *unnecessary* for the plaintiff to state any judgment, (*Ib.* 1104. and *vid.* 5 T. R. 498), that is to say, admitting the statement, in that particular, to have been *immaterial;* yet being made, as *descriptive of the foundation* of the *fi. fa.;* it was necessary to be proved as made (*s*). The omission of such proof was indeed of the nature of a *variance*.

(*s*) *Acc.* 12 Mod. 127. 3 T. R. 646. 5 Ib. 497. 3 Bos. & P. 456. 461. 5 Price, 540. 2 B. & A. 767. 1 M. & S. 204.

CHAP. III.

When not necessary to be proved.

§ 188. The rule that immaterial averments must be strictly proved, is however by no means universal, though it appears to have been formerly so understood: The *principle* of the rule manifestly embraces, (it is conceived), no other averments of that class, than those of which a *variance* may be predicated. And the rule itself, it seems, is now to be understood as limited by that principle.

§ 189. The rule, then, as limited by the more modern authorities, appears to be, that no *immaterial* averment requires precise proof, unless the failure of such proof would occasion a *variance* between the pleading and the proof: Or (in different language), strict proof of such an averment is not, at this day, necessary, unless the subject of the averment is a *record* — a *written instrument* — or, (as I conceive) an *express contract* (*t*): Inasmuch as these are in strictness the only subjects of variance, (properly so called), when the mistake in the pleading is in a point *not in itself material* (28). It is here observa-

(*t*) 3 T. R. 645. 5 Ib. 496. 2 East, 452. 502. 4 Ib. 400. 5 Esp. Rep. 8.

(28) The editor of the second English edition of Douglas's Reports observes, in a note annexed to the case of *Bristow* v. *Wright*, that the rule requiring *immaterial* averments to be strictly proved, is now confined to the cases of 'records and *written* contracts.' This assertion appears to have been founded upon a casual remark of Mr J. *Buller*, (3 T. R. 646,) that 'perhaps the rule will be found to extend to all cases of *records and written* contracts.' (*Vid.* also 3 Cranch, 209). But that learned judge did not profess, in this occasional remark, formally to define the

ble, that the decisions in the two cases before stated, of *Bristow* v. *Wright* and *Savage* v. *Smith*, both come within the range of the rule, as thus restricted. For the immaterial averment in question, in the former case, was descriptive of an *express contract*, as that in the latter was of a *record*.

§ 190. But where, in an action on a policy of insurance on a ship, the declaration contained an averment, that she sailed upon her voyage, *after* the making of the policy; whereas she actually sailed *before* it was made — it was held by the court of B. R. unnecessary for the plaintiff to prove the averment, as made (*u*): Because it was not a statement of any part of the *contract*, but of a *collateral* fact, which (as there was no warranty, or representation, in regard to the time of sailing), could not affect the right of action.

(*u*) 5 T. R. 496.

---

precise extent of the rule. Indeed, he had before, and in immediate connexion with the observation just cited, extended it to 'contracts', generally; as Lord *Kenyon* had done, in the same case. Nor, on principle, does there appear any reason for confining the rule to the limit expressed in the note to *Bristow* v. *Wright:* Since a *variance* may occur, as well in the statement of a *parol* contract, as in that of a *written instrument or record.* But what appears decisive against such a restriction of the rule is, that the averment, which was held fatal to the action, in *Bristow* v. *Wright*, (the leading authority in support of the Editor's rule), was an averment, made in stating a *parol* lease. *Vid.* Yelv. 195. b. (n. 1.)

CHAP. III.

§ 191. Thus also, where in an action of debt, brought on the statute 11 Geo. 2, c. 19, § 3, to recover double the value of goods, which were removed by the defendants, to prevent a distress for rent, the declaration averred that *such a certain sum* (£57), was due, as rent in arrear — the court of B. R. resolved, that the plaintiff was not bound to prove that particular sum as the amount due (*v*). For the averment of a *particular sum*, as the amount in arrear, being immaterial, and not descriptive of the terms of the *contract*, (as a statement of the rent *reserved* would have been), was not within the rule requiring precise proof of immaterial averments (*w*).

Defects, on one side, aided by the adverse pleading.

§ 192. If one of the parties expressly *avers*, or *confesses*, a material fact, before omitted on the other side; the omission is cured. For the defect, in the pleading of the one party, is thus supplied by the other; and it may thus be made to appear, from the pleadings on *both* sides, taken together, that he, on whose part the omission occurs, is entitled to judgment; although his own pleading, taken *by itself*, be insufficient (*x*). Thus where in trespass, the plaintiff complained of the defendant for taking a certain iron hook, without alleging *possession* in himself (which in that action is material), the de-

(*v*) 3 T. R. 643.

(*w*) Vid. 3 Cranch, 193. 208-9.

(*x*) Esp. Dig. 588. Com. Dig. *Pleader*, C. 85. 1 Sid. 184. Cro. Car. 288. Aleyn, 7. 6 Binn. 24. 9 Pick. 62. *Cont.* Gouldsb. 187. 3 Caines' R. 73.

CHAP. III.

fendant's plea, in which he confessed and justified the taking of the hook from the *plaintiff's hand*, was held to aid the declaration; inasmuch as it expressly *acknowledged* the plaintiff's possession (*y*).

Showing a primâ facie cause of action, &c, is sufficient.

§ 193. In general, it is not necessary for either party to allege more than will constitute, *primâ facie*, a sufficient cause of action or defence (*z*) (29). It is therefore in general unnecessary for a party to deny or avoid, by *anticipation*, all or any of the possible facts, which might furnish sufficient answers in law to his own allegations. For this would not only lead to extravagant prolixity, but would be found *impracticable*.

§ 194. Thus also, in declaring on a contract, it is unnecessary to aver that the defendant, at the time of making it, was of *full age* — or was not a *feme covert* — or, that the contract was not obtained by *fraud*, or *duress* — or, that it was not founded upon an *usurious*, or other *illegal* consideration — or to anticipate any other *special* matter of defence (*a*). For if any such matter of defence exists, it is for the *defendant* to show it.

(*y*) 1 Sid. 184.
(*z*) 2 Wils. 100. 1 Saund. 299. 1 Ld Ray. 400. Doug. 159. 1 Vent. 217.
(*a*) Plowd. 376. 564. 1 Vent. 217. 1 Saund. 298-9.

(29) An exception to this rule has been already mentioned, as obtaining in two particular instances: viz. in pleading *estoppels*, and generally, in *dilatory* pleas, (*Vid. Dilatory Pleas, post.* ch. V.) Co. Litt. 352. b. 303. a. 2 H. Black. 530

Ante, ch. 3, § 57.

CHAP. III.

Yet, in declaring on a contract, the plaintiff must aver that it has not been *performed;* though performance is special matter of *defence*, on the defendant's part. But this allegation, in the declaration, is necessary, not for the purpose of *excluding, by anticipation*, the defence of performance ; but for that of showing a *primâ facie right of action.* For without an allegation of non-performance, no complete right of action can, in such a case, appear upon the face of the declaration.

New matter, what.

§ 195. All facts alleged in pleading, which go in *avoidance* of what is before pleaded, on the opposite side, are called *new matter.* In other words, every allegation made in the pleadings, subsequent to the declaration, and which does not go in *denial* of what is before alleged on the other side, is an allegation of *new matter.*

Must conclude with a verification.

§ 196. And it is a general rule of the common law, that all new matter must be followed by a *verification*, or, as it is frequently termed, an *averment* (*b*) : A verification being an *averment*, or affirmation, that the pleader is prepared to *verify*, or *prove*, the matter alleged by him ; and is expressed in the following form: 'And this he is ready to verify' (*c*).

§ 197. The necessity of concluding new matter with a verification, arises from the right, which each

(*b*) 3 Black. Com. 309. Lawes' Pl. 114. 145. 223. Cowp. 575. 1 Saund. 102. 103. Doug. 58.

(*c*) 3 Black. Com. 309.

party has, (until a proper issue, closing the pleadings, is tendered), to *answer* the allegations on the other side, by new matter of his own, or otherwise, as the exigency of his case may require. And to secure this right to each party, the pleadings, on both sides, must be *kept open* to such answer, until they are closed by an issue, in the manner above-mentioned. And a *verification* is, in general, the conventional and only mode known to the law, of keeping them thus open.

§ 198. There is one instance, however, in which new matter need not conclude with a verification, and in which the pleader may pray judgment, without it: viz. Where the matter pleaded is merely *negative* (*d*). For a negative in general requires no *proof;* and it would therefore be impertinent or nugatory for him, who pleads negative matter, to declare his readiness to *prove* it. To an action on a *negative* covenant, therefore, the defendant may plead merely that he has not done what he covenanted against, and pray judgment, without a verification.

And by a positive, and anomalous, provision, in the English statute 5 Geo. 2, a *bankrupt* may plead his bankruptcy in bar, and conclude, (though the matter pleaded is *new*, and merely *affirmative*), to the *country* (*e*).

(*d*) Willes, 5. Lawes' Pl. 145.
(*e*) Lawes' Pl. 145. 227.

CHAPTER IV.

OF THE DECLARATION OR COUNT.

CHAP. IV.

Declaration, requisites of.

SECTION 1. THE declaration, or count, as has been before stated, (Chap. II.), is an *amplification or exposition of the original writ*, with the addition of all necessary circumstances, not expressed in the writ (*f*): In other words, it is a detailed statement of the complaint, or cause of action, which, in the writ, is presented in a more general form.

Difference between declaration and count.

§ 2. The terms 'declaration' and 'count' are frequently used, especially in the older books, as convertible terms; but practice has introduced the following distinction: Where the plaintiff's complaint embraces only a *single* cause of action, and he makes only *one* statement of it, that statement is called, indifferently, a 'declaration', or a 'count'; though the former term is the more usual, at the present day. But where the suit embraces two or more causes of action, (each of which requires, of course, a distinct statement); or when the plaintiff makes two or more different *statements* of one and

(*f*) Co. Litt. 17. a. 303. b. 3 Black. Com. 293. Com. Dig. *Pleader*, C. 7. Bac. Abr. *Pleas*, &c. B. 1.

the same cause of action ; each several statement is called a *count*, and all of them, collectively taken, constitute the *declaration*.

§ 3. In all cases, however, in which there are two or more counts — whether there is actually but *one* cause of action, or *several* — each count purports, *upon the face of it*, to disclose a distinct right of action, unconnected with that stated in any of the other counts: So that, upon the face of the declaration, there appear to be as many different *causes of action*, as there are counts inserted. And therefore, whether a plaintiff, whose declaration contains more than one count, claims a recovery upon *one* right of action only, or upon several, cannot appear, except in evidence. *Practically*, however, the defendant can seldom be left in doubt on this point.

§ 4. One object proposed, in inserting two or more counts in one declaration, when there is in fact but *one cause* of action, is, in some cases, to guard against the danger of an *insufficient statement* of the cause, where a doubt exists as to the *legal sufficiency* of one or another of two or more different modes of declaring. But the more usual end proposed, in inserting more than one count, in such a case, is to accommodate the *statement* of the cause, as far as may be, to the possible state of the *proof* to be exhibited on the trial: Or to guard, if possible, against the hazard of the *proof's varying* materially from the statement of the cause of action: So that if one or more of the several counts should

Several counts, use of.

CHAP. IV.

not be adapted to the evidence, some other of them may be so (*g*).

§ 5. The plaintiff has, in every case, a *right* to insert, in his declaration, as many counts, (each one being in itself single), as he pleases (*h*); and in actions *on the case* (especially in *assumpsit*), it is the usual practice to insert, though often unnecessarily, two or more (*i*). But where counts, clearly superfluous, are inserted, they may, in the *English* practice, be struck out by order of the court, and the plaintiff be compelled to pay the costs (*k*).

§ 6. And if any one of several counts in a declaration be proved, (although the proof of all the others should fail); the plaintiff must recover upon it, unless it be radically insufficient in law (*l*). For by maintaining *one* good count, he establishes a complete right of recovery. And for the same reason, if on demurrer to the *whole* declaration, any one of the counts is adjudged sufficient in law; the plaintiff will be entitled to judgment on that count — though all the others be defective.

What the declaration must allege.

§ 7. The declaration, being the statement of those facts on which the plaintiff founds his right of recovery, must of course allege *all that is essential*

(*g*) 3 Black. Com. 295.
(*h*) Lawes' Pl. 73.
(*i*) 3 Black. Com. 295. Lawes' Pl. 73.
(*k*) Cas. Temp. Hardw. 129. Lawes' Pl. 61. 73.
(*l*) Com. Dig. *Pleader*, Q. 3. 3 Black. Com. 295. 1 Saund. 286. (n. 9.) 2 Ib. 171. d. (n. 1.) 380. (n. 14.) 1 Mod. 271.

to his right of action (*m*). For he can recover only *secundum allegata et probata;* and can legally *prove* no material fact, which the declaration does not allege.

§ 8. The first and most comprehensive rule, in respect to the requisites of a declaration, is that it must show a *title*, (i. e. *a right of action*), in the plaintiff (*n*). If then the declaration, which is the *foundation* of the suit, is insufficient in law to warrant a judgment in the plaintiff's favour; no *subsequent* allegation on his part can entitle him to a recovery (*o*). He must recover upon the grounds, on which he *first* places his claim, or not at all.

§ 9. If, therefore the declaration, though otherwise sufficient, discloses any fact, which shows that at the *commencement* of the suit (1) the plaintiff had

(*m*) Bac. Abr. *Pleas*, &c. A. B. 1. Doct. Pl. 85.
(*n*) Com. Dig. *Pleader*, C. 34. Bac. Abr. *Pleas*, &c, B. 1.
(*o*) Bac. Abr. *Pleas*, &c, B. 1.

(1) The suit is considered as *commenced*, from the issuing of the writ (3 Black. Com. 273. 285. 7 T. R. 4. 1 Wils. 147): but where the *teste*, or date of the writ is *fictitious*, the true time of its issuing may be averred and proved, whenever the purposes of justice require it: As, to let in a plea of *tender*, or of the statute of *limitations*. (Bac. Abr. *Tender*, D. 1 Stra. 638. 1 Wils. 147. Peake Ev. 259.) In the usual practice of the Court of King's Bench, however, the suit is not deemed to be commenced till the filing of the *bill*, (or declaration) which is considered in that court as the *original*. (Cowp. 454. 456. 1 Wils. 147. 2 Burr. 960. 8 Mod. 343. 1 Vent. 28.)

CHAP. IV.

no right of action; he cannot have judgment (*p*).: As where in debt on an obligation, it appeared from the declaration, that the writ bore date *before* the time of payment appointed in the deed. For the cause of action, which entitles a party to recover by suit, must be *complete* at the time when the suit is *commenced*, (*vide ante, note* 1). If it is not *then* complete, the complaint of the plaintiff must of necessity be either *untrue*, or *insufficient in law*.

§ 10. For any matter, accruing *after* the commencement of the suit, the plaintiff therefore cannot recover (*q*) — except that *interest*, on demands carrying interest, is recoverable up to the time of the *judgment*, under the name of *damages* (*r*). For the interest is regarded as only incident to, or part of, *the debt;* and that interest, which accrues after the commencement of the suit, being inseparable from the rest, is consequently recoverable in no other way (*s*).

§ 11. So also, if the declaration *omits* the averment of any fact, which is of *gist* of the action —(as, if no *consideration* be alleged, in assump-

(*p*) Cowp. 454. Bac. Abr. *Pleas*, &c, B. 5. 7 Co. 24-5. Cro. Eliz. 325.

(*q*) 2 Saund. 171. c. (n. 1.) Cowp. 454.

(*r*) 2 Burr. 1085. 1087. 2 T. R. 58. Doug. 376. Chitt. on Bills, 214. Toller on Ex. 286-7. 2 Saund. 171. c. (n. 1.) 8 Johns. R. 446.

(*s*) 1 Esp. Rep. 110. 2 New Rep. 206. n. 3 Johns. R. 229. 5 Ib. 271.

sit (2) — no conversion in trover, &c); the omission is fatal (*t*). CHAP. IV.

§ 12. The *gist* of the action is that, without which there is *no cause* of action. It comprehends, therefore, whatever is *indispensable in law* to a right of recovery (*u*). Hence, if any thing of this kind be omitted, no title can appear from the declaration; and the defect is of course incurable (*v*). Gist of the action.

§ 13. Whenever therefore the right of recovery depends upon a *condition precedent*, the declaration must aver performance of it, (or what is equivalent to performance), to entitle the plaintiff to recover (*w*). For in every such case, performance of the Condition precedent.

(*t*) Bac. Abr. *Pleas*, &c, B. 1. Doct. Pl. 85. 1 Sid. 184. Bull. N. P. 33. 2 Salk. 519. 640. 7 T. R. 348. 351. n. 5 Ib. 143. Com. Dig. *Assumpsit*, H. 3. 6 East, 568. 8 Ib. 9. 2 Bos. & P. 79.

(*u*) Bac. Abr. *Pleas*, &c, B. 1. Doct. Pl. 85.

(*v*) Bac. Abr. *Pleas*, &c, B. 1. 3 Black. Com. 395. 4 T. R. 472. 2 H. Black. 201. Doug. 683.

(*w*) 7 Co. 10. a. Bac. Abr. *Pleas*, &c, B. 5. (2.) Com. Dig. *Pleader*, C. 51. 70–75. Plowd. 25. b. Yelv. 134. n. 1 T. R. 645. 7 Ib. 125. 1 Saund. 320. 2 H. Black. 574.

---

(2) In assumpsit on bills of exchange and promissory notes, however, the mere statement of the facts, which create the defendant's *liability*, dispenses with the necessity of stating the consideration. (2 Bos. & P. 79. 1 Chitt. Pl. 295.) For these instruments, like specialties, afford *primâ facie internal evidence* of a consideration, and consequently dispense in general, with the proof of it. And what need not be *proved*, need not be alleged. (2 Ld Ray. 758. 3 Salk. 70. 1 Black. Rep. 487. 2 Black. Com. 445. Kyd on Bills, 48. 3 Burr. 1516. 1523. Chitt. on Bills, 9. 51. 201. 209.

CHAP. IV.

condition, or what the law holds equivalent to it, is a constituent and indispensable part of *the* right of action — or that, without which there can be no cause of action.

§ 14. Thus, in an action against the indorser or drawer of a bill of exchange, if the declaration does not allege a *demand* of payment, at the proper time, on the drawee, or acceptor — or omits an allegation of due *notice* to the defendant, of the refusal of payment by the former; the omission is fatal (*x*). For such demand and notice are implied *conditions*, the performance of which, by the holder, is essential to the liability of the indorser or drawer.

Notice and request, when to be alleged.

§ 15. And in all cases, in which actual notice of any fact to the defendant, or a special request, is, either by the terms or the nature of the contract, the *condition* of his liability; such notice, in the one case, and such request, in the other, is of the *gist* of the action, and must therefore be specially averred in the declaration (*y*). For without such averment, no complete right of action can appear from the declaration.

§ 16. And whenever an *actual* request is necessary to be stated, the general averment, 'although

(*x*) Doug. 683. Chitt. on Bills, 132-3. 188-9. 202-3. 5 Burr. 2670. 1 T. R. 712.

(*y*) Com. Dig. *Pleader*, C. 69. 73. Sav. 72. 1 Saund. 33. (n. 2). 2 Keb. 126. 1 Stra. 88. Hob. 68. Com. Dig. *Condition*, 10. 11. 14 East, 500. 16 Ib. 110. 1 Campb. 425. 5 T. R. 409.

often thereunto requested,' is not sufficient (*z*): That averment being but matter of form, and not traversable.

Conditions subsequent.

§ 17. It is never necessary, by the common law, for the plaintiff, in his declaration, to state, or in any manner to take notice of any condition *subsequent*, annexed to the right which he asserts (*a*). For the office of such a condition is, not to *create* the right on which the plaintiff founds his demand; but to *qualify* or *defeat* it. The condition, therefore, if performed or complied with, furnishes matter of *defence*, which it is for the *defendant* to plead. Thus in debt on bond, it is not necessary for the plaintiff, in his declaration, to state or count upon any other than the *penal* part of the instrument; leaving the condition to be pleaded by the *defendant*, if it affords him any defence; as it does, if performed (*b*). For the penal part of the bond, alone, constitutes *primâ facie*, a right of action.

§ 18. The plaintiff *may*, however, in an action on bond, count as well upon the condition, as upon the penal part; but if he declares in this manner, he must allege the breach of the condition in his *declaration*, instead of *replying* it, (as he must, when he counts only on the penal part), in answer to the

(*z*) 1 Saund. 33. (n. 2). 1 Stra. 88.

(*a*) Com. Dig. *Pleader*, C. 57. 7 Co. 10. a. b. 11. a. Bac. Abr. *Pleas*, &c, B. 5. (2). 1 T. R. 638. 1 H. Black. 254. 2 Ib. 574.

(*b*) Iid. 2 Chitt. Pl. 151—3.

CHAP. IV.

defendant's plea (*c*). The declaration, when framed in the former manner, is called a *special* one.

How much of a deed must be set out.

§ 19. It is a general rule, that in declaring upon a deed or other instrument, consisting of several distinct parts, the plaintiff is required to state only so much of the instrument, as constitutes, *primâ facie*, a complete right of action (*d*). And if any other part of the instrument furnishes the means of defeating the action; it is matter of *defence*, of which the defendant may, on his part, avail himself for that purpose.

Exceptions in covenants, &c.

§ 20. But in declaring upon a covenant, or upon articles of agreement, an *exception*, (if there be any), in the *body* of the covenant, &c, must be set out, and the subject-matter of the exception must be excluded from the breach assigned (*e*).

If then A. covenants to convey to B. a certain farm, *except* one particular close; B., in an action on the covenant, must state the *exception*, as well as the rest of the covenanting clause; and, in assigning the breach, must aver that A. has not conveyed the farm, *except* the one specified close. For the exception enters into the *description of the covenant;* and the corresponding exception, in the assignment of the breach, is necessary to show that the breach

(*c*) Bac. Abr. *Pleas*, &c, B. 1. Doct. Pl. 84. 2 Chitt. Pl. 152—7.

(*d*) 8 East, 7. 6 Ib. 567. 1 Chitt. Pl. 300—1. 352. Doug. 667. 1 Saund. 233. (n. 2).

(*e*) T. Jon. 125. Esp. Dig. 300.

is within the covenant. If the declaration should set out the covenant to convey the farm, without stating the exception; there would be a *variance:* And if the exception, though stated in the description of the covenant, were omitted in the assignment of the *breach;* no breach, within the covenant, would appear in the declaration: Since all the land, *not* embraced in the exception, might have been conveyed, consistently with the truth of such an assignment.

Proviso in covenants.

§ 21. But if A. covenants to convey to B. a certain farm, with a *separate proviso*, that on A.'s performing a certain act, he shall not be bound to convey one particular close, parcel of the farm; B. in declaring on the covenant need not take notice of the *proviso* (*f*). For it does *not* enter into the description of the covenanting clause, on which the action is founded; but is in nature of a condition *subsequent*, of which A. may avail himself in his defence, if he has performed the act mentioned in the proviso.

In statutes.

§ 22. A distinction, analogous to that above stated, prevails in declaring on *statutes.* In an action founded on a penal statute, the subject of any exception, in the *enacting* or *prohibitory* clause of the act, must in the declaration be excluded by averment: But of any *proviso* or qualification, in a *separate substantive* clause, the declaration need not take

(*f*) T. Ray. 65. 1 Lev. 88. Esp. Dig. 300.

CHAP. IV.

notice (*g*). In the first case, the exception is an essential part of the *description of the offence* or thing prohibited; in the latter, the proviso, &c, is only distinct matter of *defence*. Thus, if a statute enacts that if any person, *not having a certain qualification*, (as a freehold estate), shall kill certain game, he shall incur a certain penalty; the declaration, in an action on the statute, must aver that the defendant had *not* such a freehold. But if the act contains a separate *proviso*, that if he shall have obtained a *license* for the killing from a magistrate, he shall not be liable to a conviction; it need not be stated that he had no such *license*.

Certainty as to subject-matter.

§ 23. The declaration, like all other pleadings, must contain certainty (*h*). This requisite, so far as regard *parties*, *time* and *place*, has already been considered. But the certainty required in stating the *subject-matter*, or *matter* in *demand*, remains to be explained.

§ 24. The subject-matter of a suit embraces all the *material facts*, which constitute the cause of action; and consequently comprehends, (according to the nature of the case), the *contract* declared upon, and the breach of it — or the *wrong* complained of, and its injurious consequences — or the *property*, of which a recovery is sought, or in respect to which

(*g*) 1 Burr. 153. 1 T. R. 141. 6 Ib. 559. 7 Ib. 27. 8 Ib. 542. 1 East, 646. 2 McNall. Ev. 544.

(*h*) Bac. Abr. *Pleas*, &c. B. 1. Hob. 295. Co. Litt. 303. a. Com. Dig. *Pleader*, C. 21. 5 Co. 35.

the alleged injury and damage have been done. But the requisite of certainty respects only the *manner* in which these particulars are to be stated. And in most cases, when the pleader understands what *facts* are necessary to be stated, there is very little difficulty in alleging them with the requisite *certainty;* which, in general, consists merely in alleging them so *distinctly* and *explicitly*, as to exclude ambiguity, and make the meaning of the averments clearly intelligible.

§ 25. From the nature of this subject, it is impossible to point out, by any definite general rule or rules, the *precise* degree of certainty, which may be necessary, in all cases, in setting out the subject-matter; and hence very little on this point is found in the law, except what may be collected from particular examples.

§ 26. The only general rule of extensive application, in respect to this kind of certainty is, that the subject-matter of the action must be described in the declaration, with *convenient* certainty; and that no greater certainty is required, than the subject will *conveniently* admit of (*i*): Or in other words, that if the averments are so made, that the adverse party, the counsel, the jury, and the judges, can fully *understand* the subject-matter; the declaration is

(*i*) Bac. Abr. *Pleas*, &c, B. 5. (5). 1 Stra. 637. Ld Ray. 588. 1410.

CHAP. IV.

sufficiently certain (*k*). In the application of this rule to individual cases, the court is necessarily left, in some degree, to the exercise of its *discretion;* but a more definite general rule could not perhaps be framed.

§ 27. In actions *ex contractu*, the declaration must distinctly state the nature and essential parts of the contract, either in the terms of it — or in substance, and according to *its legal effect* — together with the breach (*l*). And except in the case of contracts *under seal*, and negotiable instruments, the *consideration* must also be stated; as the contract will otherwise appear from the declaration to be *nudum pactum* (*m*). — Hence in an action on a deed, a description of it, as 'a *certain* bond', without further particulars, is not sufficient (*n*); since such a description would not *identify* the bond sued upon.

§ 28. So in assumpsit for wages, alleged to be due in consideration of the plaintiff's performing 'a *certain* voyage', without describing it, the statement of the consideration is too uncertain (*o*). — And a justification, alleged to be 'by virtue of a *certain*

(*k*) Lawes' Pl. 53. 2 Bos. & P. 267. Co. Litt. 303. a. Com. Dig. *Pleader*, C. 17.

(*l*) 1 Saund. 233. (n. 2.) 2 Ib. 305. (n. 13.) 366. Doug. 669. 1 T. R. 240. 4 Ib. 560. 5 Ib. 498. 1 Chitt. Pl. 299. 351.

(*m*) 6 East, 567. 8 Ib. 7.

(*n*) 1 Bos. & P. 100. 102. 1 Chitt. Pl. 240.

(*o*) 2 Bos. & P. 116, & *Vid.* Ib. 265. 13 East, 102.

writ,' without setting it out, would be ill for want of certainty (*p*). CHAP. IV.

§ 29. And the words 'duly', 'lawfully', &c, without a statement of the *special facts* of which they are predicated, have, in general, no effect (*q*). For such terms are not only indefinite; but affirm matter of *law*, instead of *fact*, and consequently are not *traversable*.

§ 30. In ejectment, the town, city, parish, &c, and the county in which the land lies, must be stated in the description of the land (*r*). In some of the United States, the boundaries or abuttals are also a usual part of the description. Great precision was indeed formerly required, in describing the land, in ejectment; but the rule is much relaxed in the modern practice. Such precision is now held unnecessary — especially, as according to the present doctrine, the lessor of the plaintiff must, at his peril, *show* the land to the sheriff, on the execution (*s*).

§ 31. In trespass *quare clausum fregit* also, the close must be described, as lying in a certain parish and county named; and it is held advisable to set out also the abuttals, or *name* of the close (*t*) — In the United States, in which closes, or parcels of

(*p*) 1 Saund. 298. n. 1. 1 Chitt. Pl. 227. 240.
(*q*) 9 Co. 25. a.
(*r*) Cro. Eliz. 465. 3 Lev. 334. 5 Burr. 2673. 2 Chitt. Pl. 394-400.
(*s*) Stra. 71. 1063. 1 Burr. 629. Cowp. 350.
(*t*) 2 Black. R. 1089. 2 Chitt. Pl. 382-8. Bull. N. P. 89.

CHAP. IV.

land, are not in general known by particular ancient *names*, a description by *abuttals*, or by lines and distances, would seem generally indispensable. And any mistake, in a description by *abuttals*, is fatal; although the parish and county be truly laid (*u*). For the abuttals, when given, are a *local description of the injury* complained of.

§ 32. In some cases, where the facts, which constitute the alleged cause of action, are supposed to lie in the knowledge of *the defendant*, but not of the plaintiff, less particularity of statement is required in the declaration, than would otherwise be necessary (*v*). Thus, in an action by a lessor against an *assignee* of the term, it is sufficient, as regards the defendant's interest; to aver in general terms that the estate of the lessee came to him 'by assignment': For the plaintiff is not supposed *to know all* the particulars of the defendant's derivative title: Whereas, in an action *by* the assignee against the lessor, the declaration must state specially *all* the mesne assignments, down to himself: For the assignee, being privy to them, is presumed to be *able* to state them specifically; and therefore is not allowed to allege his title *generally* (*w*).

§ 33. Most of the questions, which have arisen in regard to certainty in stating the subject-matter,

(*u*) 1 T. R. 479. 2 Chitt. Pl. 387. *note* (n).

(*v*) 3 T. R. 767. 8 East, 85. Com. Dig. *Pleader*, C. 26. 42.

(*w*) 1 Saund. 112. n. 1 Chit. Pl. 353. 2 Ib. 196-7. 6 Mod. 72. *Vid.* Bac Abr. *Pleas*, &c, I. 3.

have related to the description of *personal chattels*, in actions for injuries to that species of property. CHAP. IV.

In these, however, as in other cases, the rule before stated now generally prevails: viz. that the property must be described with as much certainty, as it will *conveniently* admit of; and that no greater certainty than this is necessary (*z*). Ante, § 26.

§ 34. In the action of *detinue*, indeed, *great minuteness* of description has been considered necessary; because the goods are to be specifically restored to the plaintiff, on the execution (*a*). It appears, indeed, to have been deemed necessary to describe the goods so minutely, that the sheriff might be able to identify them, by the *mere description* given of them in the writ of execution. And when the action of detinue was first superseded by that of *trover*, as great precision and minuteness of description were deemed necessary in the latter, as in the former action (*b*).

§ 35. But it is now established, that in trover, trespass, and other actions in general, for injuries to personal chattels, nothing more than *convenient* certainty is necessary in the description of them (*c*).

(*z*) *Vid. ante*, § 26, references (i. k.) 1 Vent. 114. 317. 1 Ld Ray. 588. 2 Stra. 809. 1 Lev. 301. 2 Ib. 176. Bac. Abr. *Pleas*, &c, B. 5. (5).

(*a*) 10 Co. 57. 2 Saund. 74. b. (n. 1). Willes, 120. 3 Black. Com. 152. 2 Salk. 654.

(*b*) 2 Saund. 74. a. (n. 1). Cro. Eliz. 865. 5 Co. 34. b.

(*c*) 2 Saund. 74. a. (n. 1). 2 Stra. 809. Bull. N. P. 37. Esp. Dig. 588. Ld Ray. 588. 1219. 12 Mass. R. 505.

CHAP. IV.

In these actions then, it is necessary to describe the goods, by specifying distinctly their *kind* or *kinds*, together with their *number*, *weight* or *measure* (*d*); and this is regularly all that is required for the purpose of certainty, in describing them. But number, quantity, &c, alleged in the declaration, does not regularly require strict proof, and need not therefore be *truly* stated, except when alleged in the recital or statement of a *record*, *written instrument*, or *express contract* (*e*). For except in these cases, the statement of a wrong number, &c, does not occasion a *variance*. And in the cases now under consideration, (trover, trespass, &c.), if the plaintiff proves the wrongful taking away, or conversion, of *any part* of the goods duly described in the declaration, he is entitled to recover *pro tanto*.

§ 36. And when the subject to be described is supposed to comprehend a *multiplicity* of particulars, a *general* description is sufficient; not only because the plaintiff may probably be *incapable* of describing them specifically; but also because a detailed description of them, if practicable, would produce great and inconvenient *prolixity* in the pleadings. Post. ch. 6. s. 112. Hence where a declaration in trover alleged the conversion of 'a library of books,' without naming their number, titles or quality, the description was held sufficiently certain (*f*). And in an action for

(*d*) 5 Co. 34. b. Bac. Abr. *Trespass*, I. 2. (1).

(*e*) Lawes' Pl. 48—9. 4 T. R. 314. Cro. Car. 262. 2 Black. Rep. 1104. Doug. 669.

(*f*) 3 Bulstr. 31. Carth. 110. 2 Burr. 772. 8 T. R. 459. 1 Bos. & P. 640. Bac. Abr. *Trover*, F. 1. Sty. 25. Gilb. H. C. P. 122.

the loss of goods, by the burning of the plaintiff's house, the goods may be described by the simple denomination of 'goods,' without any designation of their quantity, or kind (*g*); and it seems that in such a case, the words 'divers goods' would be sufficient.

Ante, § 32.

Value when necessary to be stated.

§ 37. In actions for injuries to property, whether consisting of personal chattels, or chattels annexed to the realty, (as growing crops, &c), the *value* of the property, or at least *some* value, must be alleged (*h*). This is required, not strictly as matter of *description*, to identify the property; but because it is incumbent on a plaintiff claiming damages, to show in his declaration the *amount* of the damage which, according to his own statement of the case, he has sustained; and to this end, he is required to allege the *value*, or what he claims to be the value, of the property converted, destroyed or otherwise injured; and thus to furnish (according to his own showing), a *primâ facie rule* of damages. But as he is not obliged to state the *true* value; the rule requiring it to be stated would seem to be of no great practical use.

'Vi et armis,' when necessary to be alleged.

§ 38. In actions for *forcible* injuries—as assault and battery, false imprisonment, and other trespasses—the declaration must allege the wrongful

(*g*) 1 Keb. 825. Plowd. 85. 118. 123. Cro. Eliz. 837. 1 H. Black. 284. 3 Bulstr. 31. Finch's Law, 48.

(*h*) Bac. Abr. *Trespass*, I. 2. (1). *Trover*, F. 1. 2 Lev. 230. Cro. Jac. 147—8. 1 Sid. 39.—*Cont.* Esp. Dig. 588. *Dub.* Cro. Jac. 130.

CHAP. IV.

act to have been committed 'with force and arms,' and 'against the peace' (*i*).

And by the common law, the omission of these words was an incurable defect (*k*). For every defendant, on conviction, in a civil action, of a *forcible* wrong alleged to have been committed *vi et armis*, &c, was obliged to pay a *fine* to the king, for the *breach of peace* implied in the act; and was subjected to the judgment of *capiatur pro fine*, under which he was liable to be arrested and imprisoned, until the fine was paid. But if the words expressive of the force were omitted in the declaration, the judgment of *capiatur* could not be rendered; and consequently, payment of the fine could not be enforced: So that if the omission of the words in question had not been held incurable, even by verdict, the crown would, by such omission, have been defrauded of the fine; and the *judgment*, which the wrong required, would have been changed into another species of judgment, (a *miserecordia*), not adapted to the action (*l*).

§ 39. And though now, by the statute 5 W. & M. c. 12, the judgment of *capiatur pro fine*, in civil actions, is abolished; yet as that statute prescribes a *substitute* for the fine, in all actions for forcible injuries (viz. the payment of a fixed sum by the

(*i*) Bac. Abr. *Tresp.* I. 1. 2 Salk. 636. 640. 1 Saund. 81. 82. (n. 1.) 140. (n. 4). F. N. B. 196. Com. Dig. *Pleader*, 3 M. 7.

(*k*) Iid.

(*l*) 3 Black. Com. 398. App. 12. Hob. 180. *Vide post.* §§ 81. 82.

plaintiff, on signing judgment — which sum he recovers back by the judgment); and as it seems that this substitute cannot be exacted, unless the wrong is laid '*vi et armis*', &c; the better authority appears to be, that these words are now as necessary to give effect to the provisions of the statute, as they were, for a different reason, (i. e. to warrant a judgment of *capiatur*), by the common law (*m*).

§ 40. According to some opinions, however, the words '*vi et armis*', though confessedly necessary in all cases of trespass, were even by the *common* law, (before the statute 4 Ann. c. 16), only matter of *form* (*n*). But the better opinion appears to be, that they were necessary in *substance* (*o*). Now however the omission of those words, and also of the words '*contra pacem*', may, after *verdict*, be supplied by amendment, under the statute 16 & 17 Car. 2, c. 8, § 1. And by statute 4 & 5 Ann. c. 16, the omission of the words *vi et armis* and *contra pacem*, is expressly aided, except on *special demurrer* (*p*).

§ 41. In declaring upon a contract or conveyance of any kind, to the validity of which a *deed* is, by common law, necessary, (as a grant, covenant, &c), the plaintiff must *count upon* the deed; i. e. he must allege the contract, &c, to be by *deed*, or

Deeds, when to be counted on.

(*m*) Bac. Abr. *Tresp.* I. 1. 1 Saund. 82. (n. 1). Com. Dig. *Pleader*, 3 M. 7. — *Cont.* 2 Ld Ray. 985.

(*n*) Cro. Jac. 130. 2 Salk. 636. 640. Carth. 66.

(*o*) Bac. Abr. *Tresp.* I. 1. 1 Saund. 82. (n. 1.)

(*p*) Bac. Abr. *Amendment*, &c. B. Ib. *Tresp.* I. 1.

CHAP. IV.

under *seal*: otherwise the declaration will be insufficient (*q*). This is necessary, on the general principle, heretofore stated, that the declaration must allege *all* that is essential to a right of action. For, as the contract, &c, in the case now supposed, cannot exist in law, except by deed; a declaration, not alleging it to be by deed, will show no right of action.

§ 42. In all cases falling within this last rule, it must appear in the declaration, in some form, that the contract, &c, is under *seal* (*r*). But certain terms of technical import — such as 'indenture', 'deed', or 'writing obligatory' — supersede the necessity of an express averment that the contract, &c, is under *seal* (*s*): Because each of these words, *ex vi termini*, imports a sealed instrument. It is therefore a sufficient compliance with the rule, to aver that the defendant, by his 'certain deed', or 'certain writing obligatory', covenanted, granted, &c. But describing the instrument merely as a 'certain writing' is not sufficient; as such a description does not legally designate a deed (*t*): No other than a *sealed* instrument being a deed.

(*q*) 2 Wils. 376. 6 Co. 38. 43. b. 2 Salk. 519. Cro. Eliz. 571. 2 Stra. 814. Esp. Dig. 298. 1 Saund. 276. (n. 1.) 1 N. Rep. 104. 1 M. & S. 573.

(*r*) Iid.

(*s*) 1 Saund. 291. (n. 1.) 320. (n. 3.) 4 Leon. 175. Cro. Eliz. 737. Cro. Jac. 420. 1 Stra. 512. 6 Mod. 306. 1 Vent. 70.

(*t*) Cro. Eliz. 571. 1 Saund. 291. (n. 1.) 3 Lev. 234. 2 Ld Ray. 1537-8. Com. Dig. *Pleader*, 2 W. 9. 14.

§ 43. But where an action is founded upon a contract or conveyance, which at common law is valid, *without* deed or writing, but which the statute-law requires to be *written*, (as on any of the contracts embraced by the statute of *frauds and perjuries*), the declaration need not *count upon*, or take notice of the writing (*u*). — Thus if an action is brought on a promise by one person to pay the debt of another — or upon a promise by an executor or administrator, to pay a debt due from his testator or intestate ; the declaration need not aver that the promise, or any note or memorandum of it, is *in writing*, even if such be the fact (*v*). For the statute of *frauds*, (which in each of these cases requires the promise to be written), though it introduces a new rule of *evidence*, does not alter or affect the manner of *pleading* (*w*): And as the promises were, before the statute, valid without writing, and might therefore have been well declared upon at common law, without counting upon any writing ; the same mode of declaring upon them is still good. It is sufficient in these cases, therefore, to show the writing in *evidence*. It may be added, that in this class of cases, the writing required by the statute is not regarded as an *instrument creating* the right asserted in the declaration; but as mere *evidence* of

CHAP. IV.

Contracts, required, by statute, to be written, how to be declared upon.

(*u*) Bull. N. P. 279. 2 Salk. 519. 1 Saund. 9. a. (n. 1.) 276. (n. 1.) 11 Price, 504. 3 Burr. 1890. 2 Show. 88. 12 Mod. 540. Bac. Abr. *Statute*, L. 3. *Agreement*, C. 1 Caines' R. 45. 4 Johns. R. 237. 4 Greenleaf, 1.

(*v*) Iid.

(*w*) 1 Saund. 9. a. (n. 1.) 211. (n. 2.) 276. (n. 1.) 3 T. R. 156. 2 Salk. 519.

CHAP. IV.

a *parol* contract (*x*). This rule extends to declarations upon *all* the several kinds of promises and agreements contemplated by the above statute (*y*).

§ 44. On the same principle, a *lease*, or an *assignment* of a lease, or a conveyance with *livery* of *seisin*, in fee, in tail, or for life, may be pleaded without the allegation of any *deed* or writing, even if the conveyance, &c, were actually made by deed, &c (*z*): Because, by the *common* law, no writing of any kind is necessary to such conveyance, &c (3); and consequently no writing need be alleged, in *pleading* it.

Confessed, by demurrer, to be in writing.

§ 45. And if, to a declaration upon any promise or agreement within the statute of *frauds*, the defendant *demurs;* he by demurring confesses the promise, as being *in writing*, — however the fact may be (*a*). For as the demurrer, by confessing the promise, precludes *all proof* of it — so that the plaintiff cannot exhibit a written agreement in evidence, if he has one; the law must intend that the

(*x*) 7 T. R. 350-1. n. Cowp. 289.
(*y*) Iid.
(*z*) Co. Litt. 121. b. 9. a. (n. 1). 1 Saund. 276. (n. 1.)
(*a*) Cowp. 289. 7 T. R. 350-1. n.

(3) If, however, the action is *founded immediately upon any stipulation* in the deed, (as upon a covenant in it), the deed must be pleaded, by the rule of the common law. For the deed itself necessarily enters into *the description* of any *covenant*, &c, contained in it. (1 Saund. 276. n. 1. Cro. Eliz. 571. 1 Lev. 88.) Besides, a covenant cannot exist, except by deed.

promise, thus confessed, is one which the plaintiff has the means of proving by *legal evidence* — i. e. that it is in writing. If it were otherwise, the plaintiff, though possessed of written evidence of the promise, would lose the whole benefit of it by the defendant's demurring.

§ 46. But if any agreement within the statute of *frauds* is pleaded *in bar* of an action; the plea, it is held, must show that the agreement, or some note or memorandum of it, is in writing *(b)*. — Thus if in assumpsit, by A. against B., the defendant pleads that the plaintiff has accepted, in satisfaction of his demand, an agreement by C. to pay the debt; the plea must show that C.'s agreement is in writing. For the plea *confesses* a cause of action, or legal claim, once existing in favour of the plaintiff; and this cannot be barred or destroyed, it is said, by any substituted claim, which is not itself shown to be such as will *support an action*.

How to be pleaded in bar.

§ 47. When a contract or conveyance, unknown to the common law, but authorized by statute, and by the statute required to be in writing, is to be stated in any stage of the pleadings, it must be alleged to be *in writing* *(c)*.

Devises, how to be pleaded.

(b) T. Ray. 450. T. Jon. 158. Bull. N. P. 279. 1 Saund. 276. a. (n. 2). 2 Wils. 49. Roberts on St. of Frauds, 203. *note*. *Vid.* 2 Salk. 519, Evans' *note*. Lawes' Pl. in Assump. 90.

(c) Plowd. 376. 12 Mod. 540. 2 Salk. 519. Bac. Abr. *Statute*, L. 3. 1 Saund. 276. a. (n. 2).

CHAP. IV.

Thus where a party declares upon, or otherwise pleads, a *devise* of real property, he must aver that the devise was made *in writing*. This is necessary, upon the same general principle before mentioned, Ante, § 41. that the pleader must allege *all* that is essential in law, to the right which he asserts in pleading. For a devise of realty, being unknown to the *common law;* no form of pleading it could, by the ancient common law, be prescribed. And as the statute of *Wills*, (32 Hen. 8. c. 1), which first authorized such devises, required them to be *in writing;* no right, under a devise not in writing, could ever have existed in the law: And therefore no devise could ever have been well pleaded, without an averment that it was *in writing:* Since all that is necessary to its validity, or legal existence, could not otherwise have appeared from the pleading.

§ 48. And the same reasons, which require a devise to be pleaded as being in writing, render it equally necessary to allege an observance of *all the other requisites*, prescribed by statute as essential to its validity: These requisites being expressly made as indispensable to the validity of such instruments, as writing itself. And hence, he who now pleads a devise, must aver not only that it is *in writing*, as provided by the statute of *Wills* (32 Hen. 8); but also that it is *signed and attested*, according to the provisions of the statute of *frauds* (29 Car. 2, c. 3, § 5). For this latter enactment, relating to the same subject-matter as that of the statute of Wills, and being in effect only *supplementary* to it, is to be taken notice of in pleading, as if it formed *a part* of the elder statute (*cc*).

CHAP. IV.

Declaration good in part, and in part ill.

§ 49. A declaration, though consisting of a single count, may be good as to *part* of what the plaintiff demands, and ill for the residue: In which case, if the whole be demurred to, the plaintiff may have judgment for the part which is good (*d*) (4). Thus, if in covenant broken, the declaration assigns two breaches, one of which is well assigned, and the other ill — or if in trover for two chattels, one of them is sufficiently described, and the other not so; the plaintiff may, in either case, have judgment for that which is well pleaded (*e*). For in these, and all similar cases, that part of the declaration, which is sufficient, shows of itself a complete right of action, which cannot be destroyed by the part which is worthless.

§ 50. A declaration may be *general*, or *special* (*f*). Thus in debt on bond, a declaration,

(*cc*) Bac. Ab. *Statute*, L. 3. Syst. Pl. 439. 2 Chitt. Pl. 231. *Vid.* 6 Taunt. 628.

(*d*) Bac. Abr. *Pleas*, &c, B. 6. 1 Saund. 286. (n. 9). 2 Ib. 380. (n. 14). Cro. Jac. 557. Com. Dig. *Pleader*, C. 32. Lawes' Pl. 59. 60. 1 Salk. 218. 11 East, 565. 3 Caines' R. 89.

(*e*) Iid. 6 Johns. R. 65.

(*f*) Bac. Abr. *Pleas*, &c, B. 1. Doct. Pl. 84.

(4) It is assumed in this rule, that the demand in the declaration is *divisible* into two or more distinct claims, of which one alone constitutes a right of action — as in the examples which follow in the text. For if a declaration founded on one *indivisible* demand, (as on a *single* promise, or a *single* breach of covenant, or the conversion of a *single* chattel), is ill in part, it is necessarily so *in toto*.

CHAP. IV.

counting on the penal part only, is *general:* But if it sets out both the penalty and the condition, and assigns the breach; it is *special.* In assumpsit also, if the declaration states only a *general* legal liability and a general promise to pay, in the form of a common count; it is *general:* If it alleges a *special* express agreement, and a *specific* consideration, according to the usual forms of declaring upon express promises; it is *special.*—And a declaration may contain both special and general counts.

Declaration must pursue the writ.

§ 51. The declaration must *agree with,* or *pursue,* the complaint made in the writ (*g*). For the writ is the foundation of all the subsequent proceedings, and indeed confers upon the court all its *authority* to proceed, in each particular action. Besides, the declaration is, or ought to be, merely an enlarged *exposition* of the writ; and must of course follow up the same complaint, as is contained in the writ. If, therefore, the declaration varies from the writ—as if the writ sounds in *tort,* and the declaration in *contract,* or *è converso*—the latter is an abandonment of the complaint in the writ; and the court has, strictly, no authority to proceed in the suit. In such a case, the declaration itself is said to 'abate the writ' (*h*).

Ante, ch. 2, § 4.

Of the Joinder of Parties in one Declaration.

I. Joinder of plaintiffs.

§ 52. Under this head, it may be premised, that the *remedy* or redress, which the law affords in any

(*g*) Bac. Abr. *Pleas,* &c, B. 4. Doct. Pl. 84. Hob. 180.
(*h*) Bac. Abr. *Pleas,* &c, B. 4. *Abatement,* I.

given case, for the violation or deprivation of a legal right, belongs exclusively to him or them, *whose* right has been violated, or is withheld.

Joinder of plaintiffs.

If then, the right of action is in *one* person only, another may not be joined with him, as plaintiff in the action (*i*). For he whose sole right is violated, cannot, by joining another person in his complaint, make the defendant liable to a *stranger*. This rule extends both to actions *ex contractu*, and *ex delicto*. (Vid. note (5). *post*. § 56).

§ 53. When the *several* rights of two or more persons are violated, even by one and the same act or wrong, — (as if the same slanderous words are spoken, by one and the same person, at the same time and place, and in the same sentence, of A. and B.; or if the persons of A. and B. are both injured, or their *several* interests violated, by one and the same tortious act) — they cannot regularly, in either case, *join* in an action for the injuries thus occasioned (*k*). For there is no *joint* right violated.

On this principle, tenants *in common* cannot join, in a *real* action, or in *ejectment*, to recover the lands which they hold in common (*l*): Their interests

(*i*) Com. Dig. *Abatement*, E. 15. Godb. 440. Hob. 72. Cro. Car. 300. 408. 575.

(*k*) Bac. Abr. *Pleas*, &c, B. 2. Gouldsb. 76. Keilw. 55. a. Ow. 106. Cro. Car. 512. Bac. Abr. *Slander*, S. 1. Yelv. 129. Co. Litt. 145. b. 2 Saund. 117. (n. 2.)

(*l*) 2 Black. Com. 194. Co. Litt. 197. 2 Wils. 232. 2 H. Black. 387. 2 Black. Rep. 1077. Bac. Abr. *Joint Tenants*, &c. K.

CHAP. IV.

being not *joint*, but *several.* (*Vide note* (5), *post.* § 56.)

Joinder of plaintiffs.

§ 54. If however slanderous words are spoken or written of *two partners* in trade, as such—i. e. if the slander or libel affect their *joint* interest as *traders*, and occasion *special damage ;* they may join in an action for the injury. For the interest, and the injury sustained, are joint. And there appears to be no reason why the same rule should not hold, if the words were in themselves actionable, and *no special* damage alleged. For the damage, *implied* or *presumed* in the latter case, would be joint, in every sense in which *special* damage can be so (*m*).

§ 55. Where a cause of action accrues in right of a *feme covert*, if the right is such as would, on the husband's death, (he dying first), survive to her; they must both, regularly, join as co-plaintiffs in the action (*n*). For she cannot sue alone, by reason of the legal disability of *femes covert* thus to sue; and if the husband alone could maintain the action, he might, in certain events, deprive her of her sole right of recovery after his own death.

(*m*) 3 Bos. & P. 150. 3 Bing. 452. 2 East, 426. 2 Saund. 117. a. (n. 2.) 2 Selw. N. P. 1162. Yelv. 129, *notis* Metcalf. *Vid. etiam* 17 Mass. R. 182; and *Collins* v. *Barrett*, mentioned by Best, C. J. in 3 Bing. 456.

(*n*) 1 Roll. Ab. 347. 2 Wils. 424. 3 T. R. 631. 1 Bulstr. 21. Lane, 53-4. 1 Fonbl. Eq. 309. Bac. Abr. *Baron & Feme*, K.

CHAP. IV.

Joinder of plaintiffs.

§ 56. If the right of action is in *two* or more persons *jointly*, they all may and ought to join, as plaintiffs in the action, whether it be *ex contractu* or *ex delicto* (*o*). For on the general principle, first premised (*Ante*, § 52), one person ought not to be allowed to sue alone, for the *whole* of that, of which he is entitled to only a part; and on the other hand, the defendant ought not to be subjected more than once, for one and the same cause or thing. On this principle, *joint creditors*, whether by record, specialty, or simple contract, must all join in an action to recover the debt (*p*). So also, in general, *joint tenants* and *coparceners* must, respectively, join in actions to recover the estate, which they respectively hold together (5); and in all actions for injuries to their joint property (*q*).

(*o*) Com. Dig. *Abatement*, E. 8. *Pleader*, 2 V. 2. 1 Saund. 153. 291. f. (n. 4.) Bac. Abr. *Pleas*, &c. B. 2. Co. Litt. 164. a. 5 Co. 18. b. 2 Stra. 820. 1146.

(*p*) 5 Co. 18. b. Yelv. 177. 1 Saund. 155. 291. f. (n. 4.) 1 Sid. 238. 1 Vent. 34. 3 T. R. 782.

(*q*) Bac. Abr. *Joint Tenants*, &c, K. Co. Litt. 180. b.

---

(5) It appears to have been long considered as an established rule of the common law, that joint-tenants and coparceners must, respectively, all join in actions relating to their respective estates. But in some recent cases, it has been held, that in *ejectment* they may either join or sue *severally*, at their election. (12 East, 39. 57. 6 Ib. 173. 11 Ib. 288. 2 Caines' R. 169): Inasmuch as a *several* demise, by one of the tenants, to the plaintiff in the action, is a *severance* of the joint-tenancy or coparcenary. In the state of Connecticut, joint-tenants, coparceners, and tenants in common, have immemorially joined, or severed, at their election, both in ejectment, and disseisin. (1 Root, 246. 4 Day, 298. 303.)

CHAP. IV.

Joinder of plaintiffs.

§ 57. And although tenants *in common* cannot join, in real actions, or in ejectment — because their *interest* is several; yet in personal actions, in which *damages* only are recoverable — as in trespass *quare clausum fregit*, in case for a *nuisance* to their land, and in all actions for injuries to *personal chattels* — they must all join (*r*). For in such cases, as the damages are *entire*, and will *survive* entire, to the surviving tenant; they are in effect *joint*, and so, consequently, is the right of action,

§ 58. It has already been stated, that where the right of action is in two or more, jointly — as joint obligees, covenantees, &c, the action must be brought by all of them. So also, where one covenants with, or otherwise binds himself to, two or more persons, *jointly and severally*, if it appear from the contract, that their *interest* is joint; they must all, if living, join in the action (*s*). Thus if A. conveys land to B. and C. *jointly*, and covenants with *both, and each* of them, (thus making the covenant joint and several), that he is well seised, &c; B. and C. must join, in an action on the covenant (*t*). For when the *interest* of the covenantees is joint, the right of recovery is so: And the defendant ought not to be subjected to *two* suits, for one and the same *entire* cause or thing.

(*r*) Litt. § 315. Cro. Jac. 231. Co. Litt. 198. a. Yelv. 162. Com. Dig. *Abatement*, E. 10. Bac. Abr. *Joint-Tenants*, &c. K.

(*s*) 5 Co. 18. b. 19. a. 1 East, 497. 1 Saund. 153. & n. 1. Bac. Abr. *Obligation*, D. 3.

(*t*) Iid.

§ 59. But upon such a covenant, (or, as it seems, even on one that is *joint only*), if it appears from the deed, that the *interest* of the covenantees is *several*; they may sue in separate actions (*u*). For the interest of the covenantees being several; the *right* to be asserted by action, is consequently several.

CHAP. IV.

Joinder of plaintiffs.

If then A., by one and the same deed, leases *Black-acre* to B. and *White-acre* to C., and covenants as to the *whole*, with both and each of them; B. and C. may each maintain a several action on the covenant. And the rule, it seems, would be the same, if the covenant had been with *both* the convenantees only, and not with *each* of them (*v*).

§ 60. Where one is bound by contract, to two persons, (as B. &. C.), *severally, and only* severally, (their interest being also several), they not only may, but it seems must, sue upon it separately (*w*). For the case is, in effect, that of two *distinct contracts*, though contained in one instrument. And in such a case, B. and C. might, each in his own sole action, declare upon the obligation as one made to himself *alone*, without naming the other: This form of declaring being according to the *legal effect* of the contract (*x*).

Ante, ch. 3. § 174. 180.

(*u*) 5 Co. 18. 19. Bull. N. P. 157-8. 2 Mod. 82. 1 Saund. 154. (n. 1.) 2 Ib. 116. a. b. (n. 2.) 1 East, 497. Yelv. 177.

(*v*) 5 Co. 18. 1 Saund. 154. (n. 1.) Yelv. 177. *Metcalf's* ed. n. 1.

(*w*) Cro. Eliz. 729. Mo. 667. Yelv. 25.

(*x*) Iid.

CHAP. IV.

Joinder of plaintiffs.

§ 61. On the *death* of one of two or more *joint* obligees, promisees, &c, the action must be brought by the survivor, or, (if there be more than one), by *all* the survivors (*y*). For by the common law, rights of action, vested *jointly* in several persons, survive entire, on the death of any of them, to the survivors, and ultimately to the last survivor (*z*): But while there are several survivors, the right of action, as between themselves, continues *joint*.

If therefore, one of two *joint* obligees in a bond dies; his executoror administrator can neither join, in an action upon it, with the survivor, nor sue alone, at law, for the part which belonged to his testator or intestate (*a*). For the *remedy*, at law, survives *entire* to the surviving obligee; who however receives the share of the deceased obligee in the avails of the suit, as *trustee* to the personal representatives of the latter, and must therefore account for it with them (*b*).

§ 62. But when the contract is with two or more *severally*, and their interest is several, no right of survivorship accrues between them. In this case therefore, each, on his own death, transmits his several interest, and right of action, to his own re-

(*y*) 1 Saund. 291. f. (n. 4). 2 Salk. 444. Carth. 170. Comb. 474. 1 Bos. & P. 445. 1 East, 497.

(*z*) Iid.

(*a*) 1 East, 497. 1 Bos. & P. 445.

(*b*) 1 Ves. 242. 252. 1 Ld Ray. 340. Toller on Ex'rs. 155. 163. 444—5.

Joinder of plaintiffs.

presentatives (*c*): The case being, in effect, the same as if a separate contract had been made with *each* of the original parties, for his part of the debt or demand.

Executors, &c.

§ 63. Where there are two or more *executors*, named in a will, they must all, if living, join as plaintiffs, or at least be named as such, in actions brought in right of the testator (*d*). For their rights and interests, as executors, are in so strict a sense *joint*, that they are all considered in law as constituting but *one* officer or representative (*e*). And where one of several co-executors, when named as co-plaintiff, refuses to join in pursuing the action, he may be summoned and *severed*, i. e. *separated* from the suit — after which, the others may proceed in the action without him (*f*): Since the judgment of severance makes him a *stranger* to the right of action.

§ 64. On the death of one of several co-executors, the executor of the deceased executor can not join in actions, with the surviving original executors, nor sue *at law*, at all, in right of the first testator (*g*). For rights of action survive entire,

(*c*) Cro. Eliz. 729. 2 Burr. 1197. 1 Saund. 154. (n. 1).

(*d*) Off. Ex. 42. 9 Co. 37. Toller on Ex. 41. 45. 446. 1 Saund. 291. g. Com. Dig. *Abatement*, E. 13.

(*e*) Off. Ex. 259. Godolph. 134. Toller on Ex. 243. 359. 3 T. R. 558. Com. Dig. *Administration*, G.

(*f*) Cro. Car. 420. Toller on Ex. 446. Carth. 61. Dyer, 319. b.

(*g*) Bac. Abr. *Executors*, &c, G. 1 Ves. 10. 3 Atk. 509. Toller on Ex's. 363.

CHAP. IV.

between co-executors, as between *original* parties having joint rights of action.

Joinder of plaintiffs.

§ 65. *Co-administrators* also must all, if living, join in actions, like co-executors (*h*); and for the same reason, viz. that their right to sue is *joint.* And on the death of one of them, the right survives to the others, as in the case of executors (*i*).

II. Joinder of defendants.

§ 66. In regard to the joinder of *defendants*, it is a general principle, that where a legal right has been violated, or is withheld, by the *joint* act or *joint* default of two or more persons, they *may* all be joined as defendants in one action, whether it be *ex contractu* or *ex delicto.* And if the action be *ex contractu*, they *must* all, if living, be thus joined; although in actions *ex delicto*, they may generally be joined or not, at the option of the party injured. The reason of the distinction is, that in *contracts*, if the obligation or duty be *joint* only; the non-performance or default, and consequently the *liability*, must be so: whereas if a *tort* is committed by several; the wrong, and the liability, may be treated as joint *or* several, at the election of the aggrieved party. For the act of *each* of the wrong doers is deemed the act of all; and on the other hand, the acts of *all* are, in law, the acts of *each.*

(*h*) Com. Dig. *Abatement*, E. 14. Ib. *Pleader*, 2 D. 10. Toller on Ex's. 448.

(*i*) Bac. Abr. *Executors*, &c, G. 2 Vern. 514. Lovelass, 21.

CHAP. IV.

Joinder of defendants.

On contracts.

§ 67. If therefore two or more persons bind themselves, by a joint contract of any kind; they must all, if living, be joined as defendants, in an action for the breach of it (*k*). And the rule was formerly held to be the same, in actions *ex quasi contractu*—as in actions against carriers, or other bailees, for *negligence or breach of trust* (*l*). But it is now held to be unnecessary, in this class of actions, to join, as defendants, all the parties who are liable, *unless* the action is founded on contract, so that to support it a contract between the parties to the suit must be proved. If the action is so founded, all must be joined as defendants, though the action is in form *ex delicto*. This principle reconciles all the recent cases (*m*). Thus, if in an action against carriers, the plaintiff declares against them on the *custom of the realm*, and alleges a breach of duty imposed by that custom; he alleges a *breach of law*, which needs not the aid of a *contract* to enforce it, and of course he need not sue all the persons who are liable: Otherwise, if he declares on *contract*.

§ 68. And if one of several persons, bound by a *joint* contract, dies; the action must be brought against the survivor; or if there be more than one

(*k*) Bac. Abr. *Obligation*, D. 4. 5 Co. 19. 1 Saund. 154. (n. 1). 291. (n. 2). 5 Burr. 2611. 2 Black. Rep. 947.

(*l*) Carth. 162—3. 1 Freem. 499. 1 Saund. 291. d. n. 6 T. R. 369.

(*m*) 5 T. R. 649. 2 N. Rep. 365. 454. 3 East, 62. 12 East, 89. 452. 6 M. & S. 385. 6 Moore, 141. 3 Brod. & Bing. 54. *Vid.* 5 B. & A. 653.

CHAP. IV.

Joinder of defendants.

survivor, against all of them (*n*). For joint liabilities survive entire, *against* survivors, as do joint rights, in their *favour*. And therefore, the personal representative of the deceased party is not liable, at law, either as a co-defendant with the survivor, or in a separate action (*o*).

§ 69. But if two bind themselves by contract, *jointly and severally;* they may both be joined as defendants in one action; or either, or each of them, may be sued in a separate action (*p*). For when the contract is in this form, the obligation, created by it, may be treated as either joint or several, at the election of the party, who is entitled to recover for the breach of it. For the liability, considered as *several*, is virtually the same as if it had been created by two several and *distinct contracts*, for the performance of one and the same duty. The plaintiff is ultimately entitled, however, to only one satisfaction in the whole.

§ 70. If *three* persons bind themselves by a *joint and several* contract; they may be sued jointly or severally, as in the last case (*q*): But *two* of them cannot be sued together, in one action, while they

(*n*) 1 Saund. 291. (n. 2). 2 T. R. 477—8. 6 Ib. 365. 5 Esp. Rep. 32. 1 Salk. 393. *Vid.* 4 B. & A. 374.

(*o*) Carth. 105. 1 East, 400. 2 Burr. 1196. 2 Vern. 99.

(*p*) Bac. Abr. *Obligation*, D. 4. 1 Saund. 153. (n. 1). 291. e. (n. 4). 2 Vern. 99. 8 Mod. 166. 1 Stra. 76. 553. Yelv. 27. 1 Sid. 238.

(*q*) Iid.

Joinder of defendants

are all living, without the other (*r*). For the plaintiff must treat the contract as *altogether* joint, or *altogether* several. An action, *partly* joint, and *partly* several, *quoad* the parties liable, being unknown in the law. But in the case, now supposed, if the plaintiff sues two, and only two of the three, in one action; he, by joining the two, treats the contract so far as *joint;* while by not joining the third, he treats it as *several.*

§ 71. When two or more bind themselves *jointly and severally*, if either of them dies, his personal representative is liable to an action at law upon the contract (*s*). For if the plaintiff elects to sue upon the contract as *several;* its legal operation, (as has been before stated), is the same as if the parties, originally bound, had made, each a several contract for the performance of the same duty. — When two or more bind themselves *severally*, and not otherwise, the rule is of course the same. (*Post.* ch. 5, § 114.)

§ 72. But in neither of these last cases, can the executor of the deceased party be joined in an action with the survivor (*t*). For as the former can be subjected at law, only when a *several* liability devolves upon him; it is manifest that he cannot be liable *jointly* with any of the original parties. Be-

(*r*) Hardr. 198. Bac. Abr. *Obligation*, D. 4. 1 Sid. 238. 2 Ib. 12. Cro. Eliz. 494. 3 T. R. 782. 1 Saund. 291. e. (n. 4.)

(*s*) Carth. 171. 2 Lev. 228. 2 Burr. 1196.

(*t*) Carth. 171. 2 Lev. 228. 1 Chitt. Pl. 37.

CHAP. IV.

Joinder of defendants.

sides, a judgment against the executor must be *de bonis testatoris;* whereas against the survivor, it would be *de bonis propriis:* So that no one final judgment, (and the law allows but one, in one action), would be adapted to such a joinder of defendants.

§ 73. Where a right of action exists against *co-executors*, as such, all those of them, who have *acted* in the execution of the trust, must be joined in the action; but those, who have not administered, may be omitted (*u*). For though the liability of co-executors is *joint;* yet a stranger or creditor is presumed not to know who, or how many they are, except from their *acts;* and is therefore not bound to take notice of any others, than those who administer.

In tort.

§ 74. If several persons join in committing a *trespass*, or *tort* of any kind; the party injured may generally, at his election, sue them all *jointly*—or each, or either of them, in a several action—or any number of them, less than the whole, together (*v*). For *torts*, in which several join, may be considered, Ante, § 66. in regard to the wrong-doers, either as *wholly* joint, or *wholly* several—or as joint in respect to part of them, and several, as to the others: Since the act of any one of the wrong-doers may be regarded in

(*u*) Off. Ex. 95. 1 Lev. 161. 3 T. R. 557. 1 Sid. 242. Toller on Ex. 471.

(*v*) Bac. Abr. *Pleas*, &c. B. 2. Ib. *Actions in Gen.* B. Carth. 171. 294. 361. 5 T. R. 649. Com. Dig. *Abatement*, F. 8. 6 Taunt. 29.

law, either as his own sole act, or as the act of either, or of all, or of any number of them.

CHAP. IV.

Joinder of defendants.

§ 75. In general also, if several are sued, as for a *joint* tort; one or more of them may be convicted, and subjected in damages, although others of them be acquitted (*w*).

§ 76. To the general rule, that joint wrong-doers are suable severally, as well as jointly, there is an exception, where a personal action *ex delicto* concerns, or arises out of, *real property* held by two or more persons together. Hence, if one of two joint tenants, parceners, or tenants in common, is sued alone, for not setting out *tithes* accruing from the land held by both; or for the neglect of any other duty, arising from their holding in common; the non-joinder of the other tenant is pleadable in *abatement* (*x*). The reason of the rule probably is, that in every such suit, the rights and interest of *both* tenants are necessarily in question: A reason not applicable to cases, in which a tort, committed by several, does *not* arise out of, or concern any joint or common estate of their own.

§ 77. Two persons are not suable in one action, for distinct torts committed by them *severally*, against one and the same person: There being,

(*w*) 1 Saund. 291. d. (n. 4.) 1 Salk. 32. 6 T. R. 766.

(*x*) 5 T. R. 651. 2 Black. Com. 182. 1 Saund. 291. e. (n. 4.) Com. Dig. *Abatement*, F. 6. *Vid.* 14 Johns. R. 426. 4 Pick. 308. 10 Mass. R. 377–9.

CHAP. IV.

Joinder of defendants.

in such a case, no *joint* wrong (*y*). Thus, if A. and B. at the same time and place, utter the same slanderous words concerning C.; the latter cannot, for this cause, join them as defendants in one action (*z*): For the act of *speaking* cannot be a *joint* act.

§ 78. But two or more may be joined as defendants, in an action for publishing a *libel* (*a*): This being an act, which any number of persons may commit *jointly*.

The same rule applies, and for the same reason, to actions for *malicious prosecution* (*b*). And in this, as also in the last case, any one of the wrong-doers may be sued alone; or the whole, or any number of them, may be joined in one action, as in other cases of joint wrongs.

Joinder of causes of action.

§ 79. It is laid down as a general rule of the common law, that where several causes of action, of the *same nature*, exist between the same parties, all accruing to the plaintiff in the *same right*, and against the defendant in the *same character* or capacity, they may all be joined, by several counts, in

(*y*) Bull. N. P. 5. 2 Saund. 117. a. (n. 2.) 1 Bulstr. 5. Esp. Dig. 504. Bac. Abr. *Pleas*, &c. B. 2. Cro. Jac. 647. Palm. 313.

(*z*) Iid.

(*a*) 2 T. R. 199. 2 Burr. 985. 2 East, 426.

(*b*) 2 Saund. 117. a. (n. 2.) Bac. Abr. *Pleas*, &c. B. 2. Ib. *Actions in Gen.* B. Latch, 262. Bull. N. P. 5. *Vid.* 17 Mass. R. 182. Hammond on Parties, 85. 86.

CHAP. IV.

one declaration (*c*). For there is no principle of law, limiting a suit to a single cause of action; and where several rights of recovery can be enforced, as well by one action as by several, a joinder of them is advantageous to both parties, and favoured by the policy of the law. By causes of action 'of the same nature', are here meant such as require, at common law, *the same judgment;* viz. a *capiatur*, or a *misericordia*.

Joinder of causes of action.

Ante, § 38.

§ 80. The meaning of the above general rule then is, that where several distinct causes of action, existing between the same parties, and accruing in the manner mentioned in the rule, *all* require, at common law, either the judgment of *capiatur*, or that of *misericordia*, they may all be joined in one declaration (*d*).

§ 81. If therefore A. has several causes of action against B., arising upon several *bonds* — or upon several *covenants*, though contained in several different deeds — or upon several different *promises*, even though some of them be in writing, and others not; all the demands, in each of these cases respectively, (if they accrue in the manner before mentioned), may be joined by as many different counts, in one declaration (*e*). For they all require,

(*c*) Com. Dig. *Action*, G. 8 Co. 87. b. 1 Wils. 248. 2 Ib. 319. Bac. Abr. *Pleas*, &c, B. 3. Comb. 244.

(*d*) Iid.

(*e*) Com. Dig. *Action*, G. Bac. Abr. *Pleas*, &c, B. 3. *Actions in Gen.* C. 1 T. R. 276. 2 Wils. 319. 1 Ib. 252. 2 Saund. 117. c. 1 Vent. 366.

CHAP. IV.

Joinder of causes of action.

at common law, the same judgment: viz. a *miseri cordia*. It may be added, that the several rights of action, in each of the cases, now supposed, all require the same *general issue*.

§ 82. In the same manner, several *trespasses* — as assault and battery, false imprisonment, and trespasses upon property, either real or personal — may all be joined (*f*). For all the several causes of action require, at common law, the same *judgment*, (viz. a *capiatur*); and the same general issue, (*not guilty*), is adapted to all of them.

Ante, § 38.

§ 83. Upon the same principle, several trespasses *on the case ex delicto* — as slander, trover, malicious prosecution, fraud, breach of trust by bailees or agents, nuisance, disturbance, &c, — may all be joined (*g*). For all these require the judgment of *misericordia*, at common law; and *not guilty* is the proper general issue to all of them.

§ 84. It is not indispensable, however, in order to justify the joinder of different causes of action, that they should all require the same *general* issue: In other words, the fact that they require *different* general issues is, *per se*, no objection to their joinder; although, (as will presently appear), the fact

(*f*) 8 Co. 87. b. 2 Saund. 117. b. (n. 2.) 6 Cranch, 226. Bac. Abr. *Pleas*, &c, B. 3. Com. Dig. *Action*, G. 4. Bac. Abr. *Actions in Gen.* C.

(*g*) Com. Dig. *Action*, G. 1 Wils. 252. 2 Ib. 319. 3 Ib. 349. 456. Hob. 6. Cowp. 230. Doug. 678. 3 East, 70. 1 T. R. 274. 277.

of their requiring different *species* or *forms of action*, is so.

Joinder of causes of action.

Hence, debt on *judgment* — debt on *specialty* — and debt on *simple* contract — may all be joined in one action (*h*); although the general issue, in the first case, is *nul tiel record* — in the second, *non est factum* — and in the third, *nil debet*. For the same judgment, (a *misericordia*) being adapted to all the three rights of action; their joinder is warranted by the express terms of the first general rule, (*Ante*, § 79) — to which the difference in the *pleas* is not considered as affording sufficient ground for an exception.

§ 85. Upon the same principle, *debt* and *detinue* may be joined in one action (*i*); although they require different general issues. For not only is the judgment, at common law, the same in both; but the actions of debt and detinue are essentially the same in character: The only material difference being, that one is brought for a sum of *money*, and the other for the recovery of specific chattels (6).

(*h*) 1 Vent. 366. Cro. Car. 316. 2 Saund. 117. b. (n. 2.) Bac. Abr. *Pleas*, &c. B. 3. 1 Wils. 252. 1 T. R. 276. 13 Johns. R. 462.

(*i*) Bac. Abr. *Pleas*, &c, B. 3. 5 Mod. 92. 2 Saund. 117. b. (n. 2.) 1 Wils. 252.

---

(6) Some doubt has been expressed, of the original correctness of the rule allowing debt and detinue to be joined in one action. (2 Saund. 117. b. n. 2.) But the rule itself is well established by

CHAP. IV.

Joinder of causes of action.

§ 86. On the other hand, where several causes of action require *different judgments*, at common law — as where the judgment of *capiatur* is adapted to one of them, and a *misericordia* to the other — the rule is universal, that they cannot be joined in one action (*k*). For there can be but *one* judgment *quod recuperet*, in one action; and if such causes of action were joined, no one judgment, known to the law, would be adapted to *all* of them.

§ 87. For this reason, a count in *trespass* for an injury either to person or to property, can never be joined with trespass *on the case*, even when the latter arises *ex delicto* (*l*). Thus assault and battery, false imprisonment, or trespass upon property of any kind, cannot be joined with trover, slander, fraud, malicious prosecution, or any other wrong unaccompanied with *force* (*m*). For though all these causes of action require the same *general issue*; yet trespass and case require, at common law, different *judgments* — the former a *capiatur*; the latter a *misericordia*.

§ 88. *Trespass* can, in no instance, be joined in one action with any kind of *contract* (*n*). For such

(*k*) Gilb. H. C. P. 7. Com. Dig. *Action*, G. 2 Saund. 117. b. (n. 2.) 1 Salk. 10.

(*l*) Bac. Abr. *Actions in Gen.* C. 1 Ld Ray. 273-4. 2 Saund. 117. e. (n. 2.)

(*m*) Iid. (*n*) Iid.

authority; and from the reasons suggested in the text, it would seem that no general *principle* is violated by it.

a joinder would require, not only different *judgments*, at common law, but also different *general issues*.

Joinder of causes of action.

§ 89. And the general rule (*Ante*, § 79) that where several causes of action, all require the *same judgment*, at common law, they may all be joined in one declaration, is not *universally* true. For a joinder of different demands is never allowed, where it would occasion the blending of different *forms* or *species* of action, even though the *same judgment* would be adapted to all of them.

§ 90. And therefore, *debt*, *covenant broken*, *account*, and *assumpsit*, cannot be joined in one action, nor can either of them, it seems, be joined with any of the others — although they are all founded on contract, and all require the same judgment, at common law: viz. a *misericordia* (*o*). For as, (with the exception of the two first), they require different *general issues*; and more especially, as the *forms* of action adapted to them are essentially different; the joinder of them, or of any of them, would tend to confusion and perplexity in the administration of justice.

§ 91. *A fortiori*, *tort* of any kind, though unaccompanied with force, (as trespass on the case, *ex delicto*), can never be joined with any separate de-

(*o*) Bac. Abr. *Actions in Gen.* C. 1 Chitt. Pl. 199.

CHAP. IV.

Joinder of causes of action.

mand founded on *contract* (*p*). Thus *trover*, *slander*, &c, can never be joined with *debt*, *covenant broken*, *account*, or *assumpsit*—although the judgment of *misericordia* is, at common law, adapted to all of them (*q*). For these two classes of actions are different from each other, not only in form and species, like those last mentioned; but *generically* different.

§ 92. It has been said, however, to be a *universal* rule, that when several causes of action, accruing between the same parties, and in the same capacities, all require, not only the *same judgment*, at common law, but *also the same general issue*, they may be joined in one action (*r*). That this position is *generally* true, there can be no doubt—as is manifest from various examples already given: But its *universality* appears at least questionable. For it seems agreed that *debt* on bond, and *covenant broken*, cannot be joined (*ante*, § 90); though the same judgment, at common law, and the same general issue, are common to both of them. And in tort, *quære*, whether an English *ejectment* can be joined with *any* count in simple trespass? (*s*).

§ 93. But distinct causes of action, though of the same nature, and between the same parties, cannot be joined, unless they all accrue to the plain-

(*p*) 1 Vent. 366. Bac. Abr. *Actions in Gen.* C. Willes, 118. 1 T. R. 276—7. Carth. 189. 3 Wils. 354. 6 East, 335.

(*q*) Iid.

(*r*) 1 T. R. 276. & *vid.* 2 Saund. 117. c. (n. 2).

(*s*) Bac. Abr. *Actions in Gen.* C. Thel. Dig. 191. Hob. 249. 1 Brownl. 235.

Joinder of causes of action.

tiff in one and the *same right*, and against the defendant in one and the same capacity. And therefore an *executor* cannot join a promise, made to his *testator*, with one made to *himself*, in his own individual capacity (*t*): The principal reason of which is, that on the finding of entire damages, it would not appear from the record, how much of the amount found was assessed *as assets*, in right of the *testator*, and how much, in the plaintiff's *individual* right. Indeed the two claims, accruing in these two different rights, belong in effect to *different persons*. Another objection, indeed, to such a joinder is, that the rule in regard to *costs*, on the two counts, would be different in the event of the suit's failing: An executor, when suing *as such*, and solely in right of his testator, not being liable to *costs*. But this last consideration seems not now to be regarded as decisive (*u*).

§ 94. The joinder supposed, in the example last given, is not termed a misjoinder of *causes of action*, (for these are of precisely the same nature in both counts); but a misjoinder of *counts*. In strictness, however, it seems most to resemble a misjoinder of *plaintiffs*: The two different *capacities*, in which the plaintiff sues, being analogous to the joinder, as plaintiffs, of two different *persons*, having several distinct rights.—In the application of the above

(*t*) 2 Saund. 117. d. 1 Salk. 10. 1 T. R. 489. 3 Ib. 659. 4 Ib. 277. 1 Wils. 171. 3 Bos. & P. 7. 2 Stra. 1271.

(*u*) 6 East, 411. 412.

CHAP. IV.

rule, there has been some diversity of opinion, and consequent confusion in the adjudged cases (*v*).

Joinder of causes of action.

§ 95. It appears at length, however, to be established, notwithstanding some opinions to the contrary (*w*), that where a declaration *by* an executor or administrator, consists of several counts, which in their own nature admit of a joinder — if the whole avails of a recovery upon all of them would be *assets* in his hands; the counts, (so far as depends upon the *capacity* in which the plaintiff sues), are well joined (*x*): Because, in every such case, the causes of action, laid in the several counts, all accrue to the plaintiff in one and the same *right* — that of his *testator*, or *intestate*.

§ 96. On the other hand, different counts, charging the defendant in two different capacities, cannot be joined in one action. And therefore, a demand *against* an executor or administrator, *as such*, (i. e. charging him for any duty of his *testator*, or *intestate*), cannot be joined with another, accruing against him in his own *personal* capacity (*y*). Thus, in an action against an executor or administrator, a count on a bond or promise made by his

(*v*) 6 East, 409. 410. 411. 2 Saund. 117. c. d. (n. 2). 1 Wils. 172.

(*w*) 2 Saund. 117. d. (n. 2). & *vid.* 7 T. R. 358—9.

(*x*) 6 East, 405. 3 Ib. 104. 5 Ib. 150. 2 Lev. 165. 3 Ib. 60. 1 T. R. 487. 3 Ib. 659. 660. 4 Ib. 281. 2 Saund. 117. d. (n. 2). 208. 6 Taunt. 453. 5 Price, 412. 7 Ib. 591.

(*y*) 2 Saund. 117. d. (n. 2). Hob. 88. & *notis* Williams. 2 Lev. 228. 4 T. R. 347. 2 Bos. & P. 424. 1 Chitt. Pl. 205. Archb. Civ. Pl. (Amer. ed.) 175.

testator, or *intestate*, cannot be joined with a count on a bond or promise made by *himself* in his own *personal* capacity. For the judgment, required on the first count, would be *de bonis testatoris*, &c, and that on the second, *de bonis propriis*. Such a joinder, however, would not be a misjoinder of *causes of action*, (these being both of the same nature); but a misjoinder of *counts*.

Joinder of causes of action.

§ 97. The joinder of causes of action, or of counts, which the law does not allow to be joined, is fatal to the declaration, not only on demurrer, but on motion in arrest of judgment after verdict, or on writ of error (*z*). For the joinder would, if sanctioned, require, in the one case, *two* final judgments of different kinds, and in the other, two of the same kind, in one action: Whereas the law allows but *one* such judgment, in any civil action. But if, where counts are misjoined, a verdict is found for the plaintiff on one count, or on two or more counts that are well joined, and for the defendant on the other, or others; the misjoinder is cured (*zz*).

Post. c. 8, § 31.

§ 98. In connexion with the last rule, it is proper to remark, that *misjoinder* of causes of action, or

Misjoinder of causes of action.

(*z*) Bac. Abr. *Pleas*, &c, B. 3. Mo. 419. 1 T. R. 274. 1 H. Black. 108. 2 Bos. & P. 424. 1 Salk. 10. Carth. 436. 7 Taunt. 581.

(*zz*) 2 M. & S. 533—overruling 3 Lev. 99. 2 Ib. 101. T. Ray. 233. *Vid.* 11 Mod. 196. 256. 1 Brownl. 235. Hardr. 166. 3 T. R. 433.

CHAP. IV.

counts, which is a radical fault, is essentially different from *duplicity*, which is but matter of *form*:

Misjoinder of causes of action, or counts, consists in joining, in different counts in one declaration, several different demands — which the law does not permit to be joined — to enforce several *distinct*, *substantive* rights of recovery: As, where a declaration joins a count in *trespass* with another in *case*, for distinct wrongs — or one count in *tort*, with another in *contract*.

Duplicity in the declaration.

§ 99. *Duplicity* in a declaration consists in joining, in one and the *same count*, different grounds of action, of different natures, or of the same nature, to enforce only a *single* right of recovery. This is a fault in pleading, only because it tends to useless prolixity and confusion, and is therefore only a fault in *form*.

Thus where the plaintiff declared, in *one count*, that whereas he had bailed to the defendant a horse, to be ridden from L. to E., and there to be safely redelivered to the plaintiff; the defendant, *intending to deceive* the plaintiff, rode the horse from L. to E., and *from E. to L.* again; and by riding so far, *abused* the horse, &c; and also, that the defendant had *refused to redeliver* the horse on demand, and *converted him* to his own use — it was held that the declaration was demurrable, for *duplicity* (a). For the declaration, in one count, stated two or three

(a) Cro. Car. 20. Bac. Abr. *Actions in Gen.* C.

distinct grounds of action, sounding in both *contract* and *tort ;* though the plaintiff's loss, or damage sustained, entitled him to only a *single, entire* right of recovery — which he might have enforced, by declaring in only one form of action.

§ 100. So also, if the obligee in a penal bond declares upon it *specially*, by setting out the condition, and assigns more than one breach; the declaration is, by the common law, *double* (*b*). For by the common law, *one* breach works a forfeiture of the whole penalty; which is all that could be forfeited by any number of breaches.

How amenable.

§ 101. When a declaration is ill, for *misjoinder* of causes of action, the plaintiff may, with leave of the court, *amend* it on payment of costs, by *striking out* one or more of the counts, and thus leaving upon the record but one count, or such only as are rightly joined (*c*). And if the declaration has not been *demurred* to, he may also cure the mistake, by entering a *nolle prosequi* upon one or more of the counts (*d*).

§ 102. But it has been several times held, that *after* demurrer to a declaration, for such a misjoinder, the plaintiff cannot cure the mistake by enter-

(*b*) Com. Dig. *Pleader*, C. 33. 2 Co. 4. a. 1 Saund. 58. (n. 1.) 2 Vent. 198.

(*c*) 4 T. R. 347-8. 360.

(*d*) Iid. 1 Saund. 207. c. (n. 2.) 285. (n. 5.) 1 Chitt. Pl. 206.

CHAP. IV.

ing a *nolle prosequi* upon any of the counts (*e*): Since to permit this, would enable him, by his own act, and without paying costs, to defeat a demurrer well taken, and for a sufficient and *substantial* cause.

Consolidation of actions.

§ 103. Where one brings several suits, upon several distinct demands, which *might* all have been joined in one action, the court may, upon the defendant's motion, compel a *consolidation* of them — that is to say, may order all the declarations in the several actions, to be inserted, as so many *counts*, in one declaration (*g*): It being unreasonable that the defendant should be harassed with several suits, where one would answer all the purposes of justice.

The interposition of the court, for this purpose, is however discretionary (*h*): An order for consolidating actions being only a matter of *practice.* But when a consolidation is ordered, the costs of the application are, regularly, to be paid by the *plaintiff* (*i*). For the institution of several suits, where all the ends of justice might have been attained by one, is considered as vexatious and oppressive.

(*e*) 4 T. R. 347. 360. 1 H. Black. 108. 1 Saund. 207. c. (n. 2.) *Cont.* 1 Bos. & P. 157. 2 Ib. 77.

(*g*) Bac. Abr. *Pleas*, &c, B. 3. Comb. 244. 2 T. R. 639. Com. Dig. *Action*, I.

(*h*) 2 Stra. 1149. 1178. Com. Dig. *Action*, I.

(*i*) 2 T. R. 639. Tidd, 556.

Of Avowries and Cognizances.

§ 104. In connexion with the *declaration*, it is proper to present a brief outline of *avowries and cognizances*, which are pleadings on the part of the defendant in *replevin*, and are peculiar to that action (*k*). These pleas are introduced in this connexion, because they both partake of the nature, as well of *declarations*, as of special pleas *in bar* (*l*). For they not only justify, by way of *defence*, the taking of the goods or cattle, the taking and holding of which, by the defendant, is complained of by the plaintiff in replevin; but also demand a judgment *quod recuperet*, viz. for the *return* of the goods, &c, to the defendant — or as the case may be, for *damages* — for the security or satisfaction of some claim, asserted by the defendant against the plaintiff; as *rent* due to the former, or damage done to him, by the cattle distrained and replevied (*m*). Avowries and cognizances.

§ 105. *Avowries and cognizances* are substantially the same, and differ from each other only in name, and form. When the defendant in replevin justifies, and claims a return of the goods, &c, or damages, in *his own* right, or in that of his *wife*, he begins his pleading, by averring that he 'well *avows*

(*k*) 3 Black. Com. 150. Lawes' Pl. 78.

(*l*) Iid. 2 Saund. 195. Esp. Dig. 360. Bac. Abr. *Replevin*, A. K.

(*m*) Bac. Abr. *Replevin*, A. K. 3 Black. Com. 150. Lawes' Pl. 78.

CHAP. IV.

Avowries, &c.

the taking' of the goods, &c, and then proceeds to state his claim — as *rent* due, *damage* done by the plaintiff's cattle, &c (*n*): But when he justifies, as bailiff or servant to *another*, and in the latter's right, he begins by saying, that he 'well *acknowledges* the taking', &c; and then proceeds, as in the former case (*o*). In the case first stated, the plea is called an *avowry;* in the latter, a *cognizance:* These two denominations being derived, it seems, from the *terms*, in which the pleas respectively commence.

§ 106. When the defence in replevin consists of matter of *justification only*, without claiming a judgment *quod recuperet*, an avowry, or cognizance, is not only unnecessary, but improper; since a *simple* justification (as in trespass, &c) is, in such a case, all that the nature of the defence can require (*p*).

But when the defendant makes an *avowry*, or *cognizance*, it partakes of the nature of a *declaration*, and both parties are virtually *actors*, or plaintiffs. An avowry, &c, is of the nature of a declaration, not only in the *recovery* which it demands; but also in this — that it may be the subject of a plea in *abatement*, and is not required to conclude with a *verification* (*q*).

(*n*) 2 Chitt. Pl. 508. 513. 3 Black. Com. 150.

(*o*) 2 Chitt. Pl. 509. 513. 3 Black. Com. 150.

(*p*) Com. Dig. *Pleader*, 3 K. 12. Lawes' Pl. 86.

(*q*) Bac. Abr. *Replevin*, A. 1 Salk. 94. 2 Wils. 117. Lawes' Pl. 82. Cro. Eliz. 530. 798. Carth. 122. 6 Mod. 103. Yelv. 148–9.

§ 107. Under the statute 4 Ann. c. 16, § 4, allowing a defendant to plead several different pleas to one declaration, the defendant in replevin may plead several *avowries*, &c ; and on the other hand, the plaintiff in replevin may plead several pleas *in bar* of the avowry, &c (r).

CHAP. IV.

Avowries, &c.

Post. c. 8, § 18.

It is unnecessary, however, to treat of avowries, in the present connexion, in *detail:* Since, *as declarations*, they are governed by the same general rules as other declarations, in personal actions; and *as special pleas in bar*, must have the same properties or requisites, as other pleas of that class.

(r) Lawes' Pl. 82.

CHAPTER V.

OF DILATORY PLEAS.

CHAP. V.

Vid. ch. 2. § 34.

SECTION 1. DILATORY pleas, as usually distinguished, for the purpose of settling the *order* of pleading, are,

I. To the *jurisdiction* of the court:

II. To the *disability of the person*,

1. Of the plaintiff, and
2. Of the defendant:

III. To the *count*, or *declaration*:

IV. To the writ — viz.

1. To the *form* of it, and
2. To the *action* of it (*s*). — But this division of pleas to the *writ* is seldom if at all regarded, it seems, in modern practice. — (*Vide post. note to* § 138.)

Defendant may plead two or more of them.

§ 2. Any or *all* of these pleas may be used, *successively*, in one and the same case, if pleaded within the time allowed for dilatory pleas by the rules

(*s*) Co. Litt. 303. Reg. Pl. 54. 1 Tidd, 572. Bac. Abr. *Pleas*, &c, A. 3 Inst. Cler. 5. Lawes' Pl. 37.

of practice (*t*). This rule, however, means only, that when a dilatory plea has been overruled, the defendant is still at liberty to plead, (within the proper time), any *other* plea, which, in the above enumeration, is *subsequent* to that which has been overruled. The rule is, therefore, to be understood with the two following restrictions; 1. That the latter plea be not *repugnant* to the former; and 2. That the defendant do not *invert* the established *order* of pleading — or in other words, that the latter plea be not such as is *waved* by the former (*u*).

§ 3. But after any dilatory plea has been overruled, no second plea of the *same kind, or class*, can be admitted (*v*). If it were otherwise, dilatory pleas might, except for the restrictions imposed by positive rules of *practice*, succeed each other beyond all definite limits.

But not at the same time, to the same point.

§ 4. Nor is the defendant allowed to plead simultaneously, to the same thing or point, *two* dilatory pleas of the same kind, (as two *outlawries* of the plaintiff), or two of the same *class*, (as *outlawry* and *alienage*). For this would amount to *duplicity*, which the rules of pleading forbid (*w*).

(*t*) Co. Lit. 304. a. Carth. 8. 9. Bac. Abr. *Pleas*, &c. K. 1. 1 Tidd, 572. Lawes' Pl. 107. Com. Dig. *Abatement*, I. 3. 4.

(*u*) Com. Dig. *Abatement*, I. 4.

(*v*) Bac. Abr. *Abatement*, M. Ib. *Pleas*, &c. K. 1. Hetl. 126. 12 Mod. 230. Doct. Pl. Introd. V.

(*w*) Lawes' Pl. 108. Com. Dig. *Abatement*, C. I. 3. 4. Tidd, 589. 3 Ld Ray. 183. Bac. Abr. *Abatement*, O.

CHAP. V.

§ 5. Neither can he plead, at one time, two dilatory pleas of *different* classes or degrees, either to the *whole*, or to the *same* part, of the writ, or matter in demand (*x*). For such pleading would be not only double, but incongruous: Since the plea, which is *subsequent* to the other in the order of pleading, would be, as will presently appear, a *waiver* of the other.

Defendant may plead two, or more, to different points.

§ 6. But the defendant may plead, at the same time, two different dilatory pleas, either of the same class, or of different classes, to *different* points — as different parts of the matter in demand (*y*). For as the pleas go to *different points*, they do not constitute *duplicity;* and for the same reason, they are not *incongruous*, even if they are of different classes, unless one of them has before been waved. The defendant, therefore, may plead simultaneously the nonjoinder or misjoinder of a party, as *plaintiff*, to one count; and the nonjoinder of another person, as *defendant*, or other matter of abatement, to the other.

§ 7. He may also, at the same time, plead a *dilatory* plea, as to part of the matter in demand, and in *bar*, as to the residue: As nonjoinder of a party, to one of two counts in assumpsit, and *non assumpsit*, or a special plea in bar, to the other (*z*):

(*x*) Com. Dig. *Abatement*, C. I. 3. Lawes' Pl. 108. Co. Litt. 303. a.

(*y*) Com. Dig. *Abatement*, I. 5. Lawes' Pl. 107.

(*z*) Lawes' Pl. 107—8. 2 Bos. & P. 420. *Vid.* 10 Mod. 285.

Different pleas to different counts being virtually, as they appear upon the record, pleas to different *demands*, or causes of action (1).

Order of dilatory pleas.

§ 8. The *order* to be observed, in pleading the several dilatory pleas before enumerated, is the same as that in which they are named in the enumeration; and this order is dictated by the principle, that the pleading of any one of the pleas, in that enumeration, is a tacit *waiver* of those of the preceding class or classes. Thus, a plea of the second class waves those of the first; one of the third class waves those of the first and second; and the same principle prevails through the whole series.

§ 9. But as the only object of the foregoing minute division, and subdivision of dilatory pleas, is to show their *priorities in the order of pleading;* and as these priorities, and the several offices of dilatory pleas, may be sufficiently explained, under the *threefold* division, heretofore mentioned (ch. 2, § 34); the latter, as being the more simple, will be still pursued.

Kinds of dilatory pleas.

§ 10. *Dilatory* pleas then, according to the division under which they are now to be considered, and have already been classed, in a former part of this Treatise, are—I. Pleas to the *jurisdiction of*

(1) In the States of Connecticut and Massachusetts, it has heretofore been customary to assign any number of causes of abatement, in one and the same plea. (Story's Pl. 59—60).

CHAP. V.

the court: II. Pleas to the *disability of the plaintiff:* III. Pleas *in abatement* (*a*).

§ 11. It is here to be observed, that what are termed pleas *in abatement*, in this threefold division of dilatory pleas, comprehend all those which, in the more minute division (*ante*, § 1), follow pleas *to the person of the plaintiff*. All dilatory pleas, therefore, which go to the disability of the person of the *defendant*, and all those which follow that class of pleas, in the latter division, are here to be considered as pleas *in abatement*, properly so called. But pleas founded upon a defendant's *privilege*, exempting him from suits, except in a *particular* court, are here considered as pleas to the *jurisdiction of the court*. (See *post*. § 16).

Restriction of dilatory pleas.

§ 12. Dilatory pleas having been formerly used for the mere purpose of *delay*, and without any foundation in fact; it is enacted, by the statute 4 *Ann*. c. 16, § 11, that no plea of this class shall be received without *affidavit* made of its *truth*, or of some matter, which shall induce the court to *believe* it true (*b*). But this enactment, though universal in its terms, is applicable only to pleas alleging *extrinsic* matters: As those, appearing upon the face of the record, can require no proof (*c*).

(*a*) 3 Black. Com. 301.

(*b*) Bac. Abr. *Pleas*, &c, E. 2. Ib. *Abatement*, O. 2 Saund. 210. e. Sayer, 293. 3 Wils. 51.

(*c*) 3 Bos. & P. 397. 2 Ld Ray. 1409. 1 Chitt. Pl. 452.

I. *Of Pleas to the Jurisdiction.*

§ 13. A plea to the *jurisdiction* is one which denies that the court has jurisdiction of the cause (*d*).

This is the *first* plea, in the regular order of pleading, on the part of the defendant (*e*). The defendant therefore, if he would except to the jurisdiction of the court, in any case in which the exception must be taken, if taken at all, *by plea*, must do it before he offers any other plea: For in such a case, a plea of any kind, which refers to the court any *other* question than that of its own jurisdiction, (which last every court must, from the necessity of the case, decide for itself, in the first instance), is a tacit admission that the court has a right to judge in the cause; or in other words, that it *has jurisdiction:* And thus all exception to the jurisdiction is waved (*f*).

Pleas to the jurisdiction, the first in the order of pleas.

In every such case also, a plea to the jurisdiction must, for a similar reason, be pleaded, if at all, before a *general* or even a *special imparlance* (*g*). But for the distinctions on this head, see ch. 2, §§ 17. 18. 19.

§ 14. Want of jurisdiction may arise, at common law, from either of several causes — as 1. from

Causes of exception to the jurisdiction.

(*d*) Bac. Abr. *Pleas*, &c, E. 1. 2.
(*e*) Bac. Abr. *Pleas*, &c, A. E. 1. 2. Co. Litt. 303.
(*f*) Iid. Co. Litt. 127. b. Hob. 164.
(*g*) 2 Saund. 2. (n. 2). Tidd, 418.

CHAP. V. what may properly be termed *privilege of tenure;* under which head falls the plea of *ancient demesne:* 2. from some *privilege of the defendant,* by which he is exempted from liability to suits, in the court in which the action is brought: 3. from the cause of action's having arisen *out of the limits* of the court's jurisdiction: 4. from a want of power in the court to take cognizance of the *subject-matter* of the suit.

Ancient demesne.

§ 15. I. When land, sued for in any of the superior courts, (as the King's Bench, Common Pleas, &c), is held in *ancient demesne,* the defendant may plead that fact, to the jurisdiction of the court (*h*): *Ancient demesne* being a peculiar and privileged species of tenure, cognizable only in the court *of the manor,* of which the land so held is parcel (*i*).

This plea, I trust, is unknown to the laws of any of the United States: Since no such tenure or court, it is presumed, exists in any of them.

Privilege of attorney, &c.

§ 16. II. If an *attorney,* or other *officer* of one of the superior courts of Westminster, is sued *alone,* and in his own individual capacity, in another court, in any action that the court, of which he is an officer, is *competent to try;* he may defeat the suit, by pleading his privilege, as an officer of the court to which he belongs (*k*). This privilege is allowed, on the

(*h*) Com. Dig. *Abatement,* D. 1. 2 Leon. 190. Sty. 273. 3 Lev. 182.

(*i*) 2 Black. Com. 93. 3 Woodes. 12.

(*k*) Com. Dig. *Abatement,* E. 4. 2 Bulstr. 207. 2 Salk. 544. Andr. 44. Bac. Abr. *Abatement,* C.

presumption that the constant attendance of these officers, in *their own* courts, is necessary to the due administration of justice.—But as this privilege, also, is presumed not to exist in any of the United States; the more particular rules relating to it are here omitted.

§ 17. III. It is, in some cases, a good plea to the jurisdiction, that the cause of action *arose out of the local limits* of the court's jurisdiction; in others, it is not so. And on this head the following distinctions are to be observed:

Cause of action arising out of the court's jurisdiction.

§ 18. 1. In courts of *limited* jurisdiction,—i. e. courts whose jurisdiction extends only to causes of action actually arising within certain local limits—it is a good plea to the jurisdiction, as well in *transitory* as in *local* actions, that the cause of action did not accrue within those limits (*l*). Most of the *city courts*, in the United States, are believed to be thus limited in their jurisdiction.

In such cases, however, it is not necessary for the defendant to *plead* to the jurisdiction: Since the exception may be taken under the *general issue* (*m*). For the legal presumption being *against* the jurisdiction of such inferior courts; it is necessary for him, who sues in one of them, to *allege* that

(*l*) Bac. Abr. *Pleas*, &c, E. 1. Gilb. H. C. P. 188-9. 1 Roll. Ab. 545-6. Bac. Abr. *Courts*, D. 4.

(*m*) Bac. Abr. *Pleas*, &c, E. 1. 1 Lill. Ab. 366. 1 Saund. 98. (n. 1.) Gilb. H. C. P. 188-9. 2 Ves. 357. 6 East, 601.

the cause of action arose within its jurisdiction. If this allegation is omitted, his declaration is ill; and if the allegation, being made, is not *proved*, he is liable to a nonsuit (*n*).

§ 19. 2. Courts of *general* jurisdiction, (as the Superior Courts of Westminster, in England), have cognizance of all *transitory* actions, wherever the cause of action may have accrued: Since all such actions, in general, follow the *person* of the defendant (*o*). The same extent of jurisdiction appertains not only to the several Superior Courts, (or highest courts of ordinary jurisdiction), of the several states, which compose the United States; but to various other courts, of subordinate authority, in many of the states, and probably in all of them.

§ 20. 3. But it is a good exception to the jurisdiction of courts, even of the superior class, that the cause of action, when *local*, accrued in a *foreign* state, or in any place where the process of the court cannot run (*p*).

§ 21. Thus, to an action of trespass *quare clausum fregit* — or an action for rent arrear, against the *assignee* of a lease — or any other action, in

(*n*) 2 Inst. 231. 1 Roll. Ab. 545-6. Bac. Abr. *Pleas*, &c, E. 1. Gilb. H. C. P. 188-9.

(*o*) Com. Dig. *Action*, N. 7. Cowp. 161. 177-8. 344. 2 H. Black. 145-161. 5 T. R. 616. 7 Ib. 243. Ante, ch. 3, § 159.

(*p*) Bac. Abr. *Pleas*, &c, E. 1. Ib. *Actions Local*, &c, A. 1. 2 Bl. Rep. 1070. 4 T. R. 503. 7 Ib. 587. 1 Stra. 646. Ante, ch. 3, § 108.

general, arising out of the *realty*, it is a good plea to the jurisdiction of a court, even of general jurisdiction, that the land, on which the wrong was committed, or out of which the action arose, lies in a *foreign* country or state (*q*). And the same rule extends to *all local* actions, in general, the causes of which arose in a foreign state (2). — In the application of this rule, in the United States, the several states are, in relation to each other, *foreign*.

§ 22. In an action, brought for the recovery of a *local subject*, (as land), situated in a foreign country, or beyond the reach of the process of the court, *a plea* to the jurisdiction cannot, however, on principle, be *necessary* for the purpose of ousting the jurisdiction. For, as the judgment, demanded in such an action, being *in rem*, would, if rendered, be utterly nugatory (since the subject could not be reached by any process of the court); the exception may be taken in any stage of the proceedings (*r*).

§ 23. But in *local* actions which are *personal*, and in which, of course, the judgment demanded may be enforced against the *person*, *or goods* of the defendant (as in trespass *quare clausum fregit*, debt for rent against the *assignee* of a term, &c), — if the

(*q*) Com. Dig. *Abatement*, D. 3. 1 Salk. 80. 1 Show. 191. Carth. 182.

(*r*) Cowp. 176. 7 T. R. 587-8. 1 Chitt. Pl. 284.

---

(2) For the enumeration and description of *local actions*, in general, see *ante*. ch. 3, § 105 to § 131.

cause of action accrued in a foreign state, or where the process of the court cannot run, it appears to have been formerly deemed necessary, even in a Superior Court, to *plead* to the jurisdiction (*s*). And such is now the rule, in relation to *this* class of local actions, in the courts of Westminster, when the cause of action accrued in *Wales*, or in a *County Palatine*, where, though within the kingdom of England, the ordinary process of the court does not run (*t*).

§ 24. It seems now, however, that where a local action, not requiring a judgment *in rem*, (as trespass *quare clausum fregit*, for an injury to land lying in a foreign country), is brought, even in a Superior Court, exception may be taken to the jurisdiction, under the *general issue* (*u*).

§ 25. 4. It is a fatal objection to the jurisdiction of any court, that it has not cognizance of the *subject-matter* of the suit — i. e. that the *nature* of the action is such as the court is, under no circumstances, competent to try (*v*): As if a *real* action were brought in B. R.: or a cause, exclusively of *admiralty* jurisdiction, in any court of common law. In any such case, neither a plea to the jurisdiction,

(*s*) 1 Salk. 80. 1 Show. 191. Carth. 182. Com. Dig. *Abatement*, D. 3.

(*t*) Bac. Abr. *Pleas*, &c, E. 1. 1 Chitt. Pl. 427. Cowp. 172. Andr. 198.

(*u*) 4 T. R. 503. & vid. 6 East, 583. 598–9. 7 T. R. 587.

(*v*) 10 Co. 68. 76. b. 1 Vent. 133–4. Hardr. 478. 481. 8 Mass. R. 87. 12 Ib. 367.

nor any other *plea* would be *necessary*, to oust the jurisdiction of the court. The cause might be dismissed on motion; and even without motion, it would be the duty of the court to dismiss it *ex officio*. For the whole proceeding would be *coram non judice*, and utterly *void*.

Mode of pleading to the jurisdiction.

§ 26. As to the *mode of pleading* to the jurisdiction, there is an essential difference to be observed, between a plea to the jurisdiction, in a court of *limited*, and one of *general* jurisdiction: In a court of the former class, it is sufficient to plead *negatively*—i. e. to show, by proper allegations, that the court has *not* jurisdiction: Whereas in a *superior* court, it is necessary, both at law, and in equity, and as well in criminal as in civil cases, not only to show that the court has *not* jurisdiction; but also to point out, specially, some *other court* which has it (*w*). For if it does not appear that a remedy can be had in some other tribunal; that very fact will, in general, confer jurisdiction upon a superior court; as there would otherwise be, for aught that would appear, a failure of justice. But it seems manifest, for reasons which have already been stated, that neither in this, nor in any other way, can jurisdiction be ultimately given to any court, which has not cognizance of the *subject-matter*, or where the action is brought for the recovery of *real* property, lying in a *foreign* country, or where the process of the court cannot run.

(*w*) Yelv. 13. 1 Ves. 202. 2 Ib. 357. 2 Burr. 1047. Cowp. 172. Doct. Pl. 234. 6 East, 583. 598. 601. 3 Mass. R. 26.

CHAP. V.

§ 27. A plea to the jurisdiction must be signed by the defendant *in person.* For if signed by an attorney, who is an officer of the court, he is supposed to have signed it by *leave* of the court; and the asking of leave is considered as a tacit *admission* of the jurisdiction (*x*). But such an implied admission obviously cannot aid the jurisdiction, except in cases, in which the objection to the jurisdiction must be taken, if at all, by *plea* to the jurisdiction, and can be taken in *no other* way.

§ 28. In *ejectment,* according to the English practice, a plea to the jurisdiction cannot be pleaded, except by *leave of court* (*y*): Because without such leave, the real defendant is, by the 'common rule', obliged to plead the *general issue.* — Under the more simple forms of this action, which prevail in some of the United States, no such leave is necessary.

§ 29. A plea to the jurisdiction concludes to the *cognizance* of the court, by praying judgment, if the court will take 'cognizance, (or have further cognizance)', of the suit — or, in more technical language, 'of the plea aforesaid' (*z*).

(*x*) Bac. Abr. *Abatement,* A. Ib. *Pleas,* &c, E. 2. 6 Mod. 146. Lawes' Pl. 91. 6 Pick. 371.

(*y*) 1 Black. Rep. 197. 2 Burr. 1046. 3 Wils. 51. 8 T. R. 474.

(*z*) Bac. Abr. *Pleas,* &c, E. 1. 3 Black. Com. 303. 1 Wentw. Pl. 19. 2 Chitt. Pl. 412. 3 T. R. 186. 5 Mod. 146. Lawes' Pl. 109.

§ 30. Whenever jurisdiction cannot be *given* to the court, by the defendant's omitting to plead to the jurisdiction, or by consent of parties, the *plaintiff* in the suit may assign for error the want of jurisdiction; although he, himself, chose to resort to the court for redress (*a*). For in such a case, nothing can give validity to the judgment.

When the plaintiff may assign the want of jurisdiction, for error.

II. *Of Pleas to the disability of the Plaintiff.*

§ 31. There are certain *legal disabilities*, which disqualify the subjects of them to prosecute suits; and which are therefore pleadable 'to their disability' as plaintiffs. Some of these entirely defeat the suit; while others only *suspend* it, *quousque* — until the disability be removed.

These disabilities, as they exist in the law of England, are the following:

§ 32. I. *Outlawry* (3). — That the plaintiff is an *outlaw*, is pleadable to his disability: One of the effects of a judgment of outlawry being, to disable the outlaw to assert any civil right in a court of justice, while that judgment remains in force (*b*).

Outlawry.

(*a*) 2 Cranch, 126.

(*b*) Bac. Abr. *Abatement*, B. Litt. § 197. Co. Litt. 128. a.

(3) As this disability, and those which follow it, to that of *excommunication*, inclusive, can be of little practical importance in the United States; little more concerning these, than a mere enumeration of them, will be presented in this Treatise.

CHAP. V.

§ 33. If the disability existed, when the *cause of action accrued;* it has the effect of *totally defeating* the suit (*c*); which, in such a case, was improper in its commencement. But the disability, when it commences *after* the accruing of the cause of action, is only a *temporary* impediment, which does not absolutely *destroy* the suit. For as the action in this case is *rightly commenced;* the supervening disability has no other effect, than that of *suspending* the proceedings in it, until the impediment is removed; and this can be done, only by a *reversal* of the judgment of outlawry, or a *pardon* (*d*).

§ 34. If *two* sue as co-plaintiffs, in a personal action, a plea that *one* of them is an outlaw, will, if established, defeat or suspend the suit, as to *both* (*e*). For as they sue *jointly*, and of course assert a *joint* right; they must recover *jointly*, or not at all, in that suit.

How pleadable.

§ 35. That the plaintiff is an outlaw, is *always* pleadable to his *disability*, and in some cases it can be pleaded in no other way; in others, it may be pleaded either to his disability, or in *bar* (*f*). And the distinction between these different cases, is the following: —

(*c*) Lawes' Pl. 102-3.

(*d*) Bac. Abr. *Abatement*, B. 1. Lawes' Pl. 103. 12 Mod. 400.

(*e*) Com. Dig. *Abatement*, E. 2.

(*f*) Bac. Abr. *Abatement*, L. Co. Litt. 128. b.

§ 36. If the *right of action* is not *forfeited* by the outlawry — (as where the action is for an injury to the person; such as *battery*, *slander*, &c; and in general, where the damages demanded are altogether presumptive) — this defence goes only to the *disability* of the plaintiff, and is not pleadable in *bar* (*g*): Because rights of action, of this kind, are not in their nature forfeitable by crimes.

§ 37. But a judgment of outlawry, which works a *total forfeiture* of the outlaw's property, (as where he is outlawed on a charge of *felony*), may, in general, be pleaded either to his disability, or in bar, in all suits in which he asserts *a right of property* (*h*). For by such a judgment, the right of action is itself, by the common law, forfeited to the crown or state.

Attainder.

§ 38. II. *Attainder* of treason or felony, by the common law, disables the party attainted, to prosecute any civil action, and may therefore, (like a judgment of *outlawry* for such an offence), be pleaded to his disability, when plaintiff in a suit (*i*). For by the attainder, the traitor or felon is *civilly* dead (*k*).

(*g*) Bac. Abr. *Outlawry*, D. 4. (3.) Ib. *Abatement*, L. Co. Litt. 128. b. 1 Chitt. Pl. 473. 5 Co. 109. 2 Lill. Ab. 333. Ow. 22. 3 Lev. 29.

(*h*) Bac. Abr. *Outlawry*, D. 4. (3). *Abatement*, L. Com. Dig. *Pleader*, 2. G. 4. 1 Chitt. Pl. 473. Lawes' Pl. 38. 104.

(*i*) 3 Black. Com. 301. 4 Ib. 112. 380—2. Com. Dig. *Abatement*, E. 3.

(*k*) 4 Black. Com. 380. 3 Inst. 213

CHAP. V.

Præmunire, &c.

§ 39. III. IV. V. *Præmunire*, (or the offence of maintaining the *Papal* power in the realm of England)—*Popish recusancy*—and *Monachism*, i. e. being a *Monk professed*, are, by the common and statute law of England, respectively pleadable to the plaintiff's disability (*l*). But neither of these disabilities, I trust, is recognized by the laws of any of the United States.

§ 40. VI. *Excommunication* is also, by the law of England, a civil disability, and as such pleadable to the person of an excommunicated plaintiff, suing either in his own right, or in the character of executor or administrator (*m*). The excommunication of the plaintiff does not however *destroy* the suit, but merely *suspends* it until the plaintiff has obtained *absolution* (*n*). This disability also is unknown to the laws of this country.

Alienage.

§ 41. VII. *Alienage* is, in some actions, pleadable to the disability of the plaintiff; but not in all. In regard to the extent of this disability, there exists a distinction, first, between alien *enemies* and aliens in *amity;* and secondly, between the *species of actions*, which the latter can, and cannot, maintain.

(*l*) 3 Black. Com. 301—2. 4 Ib. 112. Com. Dig. *Abatement*, E. 5.

(*m*) Godolph. 85. 3 Black. Com. 301. Bac. Abr. *Abatement*, B. 2.

(*n*) Bac. Abr. *Abatement*, B. 2. *Vid.* St. 51 Geo. III, c. 127.

§ 42. An alien *enemy* can in general maintain, in his own right, *no* action; real, personal or mixed. This rule extends, as well to *prisoners of war* detained here, as to all other subjects of a hostile power (*o*). For, as a general rule, such an alien, being out of the protection of the laws of the state, with which his own is at war, can have no civil remedies under them.

§ 43. This rule, however, does not extend to an alien enemy residing here, under a *license, protection, or safe conduct*, from the executive government (*p*). For such license, &c, places him under the protection of the law, and substantially upon the same footing as that of an alien *friend*.

§ 44. The question whether an alien enemy, not thus protected by the government, can maintain suits in the character of *executor* or *administrator*, has been a subject of considerable debate, and diversity of opinion (*q*). The better opinion appears to be, that he cannot (*r*). For, without adverting to the several reasons, urged in the books, on either side of the question, it may be sufficient to observe, that his right to sue here, in any capacity, would

(*o*) Bac. Abr. *Abatement*, B. 3. *Aliens*, D. 2 Stra. 1082. 6 T. R. 23. 49. 8 Ib. 166. 4 East, 502.

(*p*) Bac. Abr. *Abatement*, B. 3. *Aliens*, D. 1 Salk. 46. 4 Mod. 405. 1 Ld Ray. 282. 2 Stra. 1082. 8 T. R. 166. 10 Johns. R. 69.

(*q*) Cro. Eliz. 142. 684. Skin. 370. Carter, 193. Bac. Abr. *Aliens*, D. *Executors*, &c, A. 4.

(*r*) Co. Litt. 129. b. 1 Salk. 46. 1 Ld Ray. 282. Toll. on Ex'rs. 32.

CHAP. V.

seem of course to give him the additional right, not only of holding such *personal intercourse and communication* with his counsel and others here, as the policy of the laws of war forbids, between the subjects of belligerent states; but also of *appearing personally* in the court, in which his action is brought, and of remaining, during its pendency, within the territories of the state at war with his own: A right, which no alien enemy, not protected by the government of the state with which his own is at war, can possess.

'*Alien enemy*' may be pleaded, as well in *bar*, as to the plaintiff's disability (*s*). For the law recognizes, in such alien, no *right of action* during the war.

§ 45. Under the plea, that the plaintiff is an alien enemy, the burden of proof is on the *defendant* (*t*). For every suitor is presumed to be under the protection of the law, and of ability to maintain his suit, until the contrary is shown. Hence the plea must allege, not only that the plaintiff is an alien enemy; but also, that he has no *license, safe-conduct*, or *protection*, from the government of the kingdom or state, in which the suit is brought (*u*): An example of the highest degree of certainty

(*s*) Bac. Abr. *Abatement*, B. 3. *Aliens*, E. Co. Litt. 129. 6 T. R. 24. 4 East, 407. 410. Com. Dig. *Abatement*, K. 1 Bos. & P. 222. (n. a.) 2 Ib. 72. 2 Chitt. Pl. 425—6. 1 Ib. 470. 473. 3 Inst. Cler. 16. *Vid.* 10 Johns. R. 183. 11 Mass. R. 26. 119.

(*t*) 2 Stra. 1082. *Vid.* also 8 T. R. 166. 4 Mod. 405.

(*u*) 8 T. R. 166. 4 Mod. 405. 3 Inst. Cler. 16. 2 Chitt. Pl. 425—6. *Vid.* 2 Gallison, 127—129; *semb. cont.*

required in pleading. (*Vid. post.* §§ 66. 67. and *ante*, ch. 3, §§ 57. 58).

§ 46. An alien-*friend*, being under the protection of the law, may in general maintain actions of any kind, either in his individual or representative character; except in so far as his legal incapacity to hold certain species of property disables him to sue for the recovery of it, or for damage done to it.

He may, therefore, maintain actions for the recovery of *debts*—for injuries to his *person*—and in general, actions of any kind relating to personal chattels (*v*). In these several cases, therefore, alienage is no disability.

§ 47. In *real* and *mixed* actions, however, alienage is held a good plea to the disability of the plaintiff, even though he be an alien-*friend* (*w*). For in both these actions, *real* property is recovered; and as no alien can, it is said, *hold* such property, it follows that he cannot *recover* it by suit (4).

(*v*) Cowp. 171. 3 Black. Com. 384. 2 H. Black. 162. Yelv. 198. Bac. Abr. *Aliens*, D. Co. Litt. 129. b. 2 Kent's Com. 54.

(*w*) Bac. Abr. *Abatement*, B. 3. *Aliens*, D. Co. Litt. 129. b.

(4) The common law rule, disabling aliens to hold real property against the *sovereign* or *state*, has been adopted to its full extent, in most of the United States. In some of them, however—as in Pennsylvania, Kentucky, and probably in some of the new states—the rule has been somewhat relaxed; (Vid. New Edinb. Encyclop. *Am. ed.* Art. *Alien*, by *Duponceau*). And *private statutes*, enabling foreigners to hold lands, like na-

CHAP. V.

§ 48. But this rule seems to require some qualification. For though no alien can *inherit* real estate; an alien friend can, nevertheless, take it by *purchase*, and, as a purchaser, hold it against all others than the *king* or *state*—and even against these, until *office-found* (*x*) (5). It would seem, therefore, that *until* office-found, he may sue for and recover it; and so it has been held, in this country (*y*) (6).

§ 49. In ejectment also, brought by an alien-*friend* in *his own* right, his alienage is regularly pleadable to his disability, as in real and mixed actions; because he cannot, in general, hold even a term for years, in his own right (*z*).

(*x*) Co. Litt. 2. b. 5 Co. 52. 9 Ib. 141. Pow. Dev. 316. 4 T. R. 300. 4 Cruise's Dig. 22. Esp. Dig. 439. 3 Dallas, 305—6. n. 1 Mass. R. 256. 12 Ib. 143. 7 Cranch, 603. 2 Kent's Com. 53.

(*y*) 1 Mass. R. 256. 7 Cranch, 603.

(*z*) Poph. 36. Co. Litt. 2. b. Bac. Abr. *Aliens*, C. 2 Black. Com. 297. 1 Roll. Ab. 194.

---

tive citizens, are sometimes passed by our state-legislatures. This is usually done, indeed, as a matter of course, in favour of *femes covert*, who are foreigners, on a prayer that they may be enabled to hold *dower* in the inheritable estates of their American husbands.

(5) By 'office-found,' is here meant, a certain species of *inquisition* or *verdict*, finding a person to be an alien; upon which finding, the estate purchased by him vests in the crown or state.

(6) According to the terms of the statute of Connecticut, on this subject, no alien is capable of '*purchasing* or holding' land in the state. Probably, however, nothing more than an affirmance of the common law rule was intended by this enactment.

But to this rule there is one exception: An alien-friend, being a *merchant*, may hold, in his own right, a term for years, in a house or building, for the convenience of merchandizing (*a*). This exception is allowed, for the encouragement of trade and commerce. And as an alien-friend may, in the capacity of *executor* or *administrator*, hold a term for years, in the right of others, who are not aliens; he is of course capable, in either of those capacities, of suing for the recovery of it (*b*).

Coverture.

§ 50. VIII. *Coverture.* When a *feme covert* sues, otherwise than as co-plaintiff with her husband, her coverture is generally pleadable to her disability (*c*). The principal reason of her inability to sue alone, appears to be, that if she were permitted thus to sue, the result of the suit might impair both the property of the *husband*, and his marital rights: Since both might be put in hazard, by a judgment against her.

§ 51. But if the husband has *abjured the realm*, or is *banished*, or is, from any cause, *civilly dead;* this disability of the wife ceases, and she may consequently sue alone (*d*). For in such cases, the husband, though actually living, is regarded as hav-

(*a*) Iid.

(*b*) Cro. Car. 8. Bac. Abr. *Aliens*, D.

(*c*) Com. Dig. *Abatement*, E. 6. Bac. Abr. *Abatement*, G. Co. Litt. 132. 3 T. R. 631.

(*d*) Bac. Abr. *Abatement*, G. Com. Dig. *Abatement*, E. 6. Co. Litt. 132. 1 Black. Com. 469.

CHAP. V. ing *no civil rights;* and the wife is, therefore, in contemplation of law, a *feme sole.*

§ 52. And if a *feme sole,* being plaintiff in a suit, marries while it is *pending*; this supervenient coverture may, by the common law, be pleaded to her disability (*e*). For by this act, she is disabled to proceed *further* in the suit, on the same principles, on which a prior marriage would have disabled her to sue at all.—But by a statute provision, in the States of Connecticut and Massachusetts, if a *feme sole* plaintiff marries, *pendente lite,* her husband may appear, suggest the marriage upon the record, and then proceed in the suit, jointly with her.

§ 53. The plaintiff's coverture is pleadable, only as a *dilatory* plea. It is no defence in *bar* (*f*): Because the fact of her coverture goes neither in denial nor avoidance of the *cause of action;* but simply in denial of her legal ability to commence or prosecute the suit, alone.

Infancy. § 54. IX. *Infancy.* That the plaintiff is an infant, is pleadable to his disability, unless he appears by *guardian,* or his *prochein amie,* (next friend) (*g*). For he cannot declare or appear *in person,* by rea-

(*e*) 3 Black. Com. 316. Bac. Abr. *Abatement,* G. 4 Serg. & R. 238. 17 Mass. R. 342.

(*f*) 3 T. R. 631. Carth. 124.

(*g*) Co. Litt. 135. b. 2 Saund. 117. f. (n. 1). 3 Black. Com. 301—2. Bac. Abr. *Infancy,* &c, K. 2. 7 Johns. R. 373. 2 Connect. R. 357.

son of his supposed want of judgment to conduct a suit; nor by *attorney*, on account of his legal inability to make a power of attorney.

CHAP. V.

Infancy.

§ 55. By the common law, if an infant plaintiff appears by attorney, and, (no plea to his disability being interposed), judgment is given, either *against* or *for* him; it is error, and the judgment may be reversed by writ of error (*h*).

But by the English statutes 21 Jac. 1, c. 13, § 2, and 4 Ann. c. 16, § 2, if judgment, in such a case, is *for* the infant, upon verdict, or by confession, *nil dicit*, or *non sum informatus*; it is valid (*i*).

§ 56. And by the common law, where an infant sues as *co-executor* with an adult, both may appear by attorney (*k*). For the suit being *en auter droit*, the personal rights of the infant are not affected by it; and therefore the adult is permitted to appoint an attorney for both.

§ 57. Any person, in general, being of full age and *sui juris*, may name himself next friend to an infant plaintiff (*l*); and in that character, may institute a suit in the name of the latter. But to

(*h*) Cro. Jac. 4. Cro. Eliz. 424. 1 Roll. Ab. 287. Carth. 123. 2 Saund. 212. (n. 4). Bac. Abr. *Infancy*, &c, K. 1. 2.—*vid. cont.* Cro. Jac. 441.

(*i*) 2 Saund. 212. (n. 5).

(*k*) 2 Saund. 212. 213. Bac. Abr. *Infancy*, &c, K. 2. Carth. 123. 1 Roll. Ab. 288. Cro. Eliz. 542. 2 Stra. 784.

(*l*) 1 Eq. Ca. Ab. 72. Bac. Abr. *Infancy*, &c, K. 2.

CHAP. V.

guard the infant against injury from mismanagement, the court exercises the power of admitting, or dismissing, the next friend (*m*).

Plaintiff not in esse.

§ 58. X. That the person, named as plaintiff, is not (or rather that he *never was*) *in rerum naturâ*, is a good plea of this class (*n*); as where he is a *fictitious*, or *imaginary* person. For in such a case, there is, in fact, *no* plaintiff.

And if one of several co-plaintiffs is an imaginary person; that fact, pleaded as to *him*, will defeat the *whole* suit (*o*). For where several persons sue, as *joint* plaintiffs, they must, regularly, recover, if at all, *jointly*. (*Vid. post.* Pleas in *abatement*, § 107.) (6).

§ 59. But where a suit is brought in the name of a person *once existing*, but who is dead, at the commencement of the suit, a plea that he was not *in esse when the writ was purchased*, is said to be ill (*p*): The proper plea, in such a case, being, that

(*m*) Stra. 304. 709. Bac. Abr. *Infancy*, &c, K. 2. 1 Ld Ray. 232. Comb. 331.

(*n*) Com. Dig. *Abatement*, E. 16. 17. Lawes' Pl. 104. 1 Wils. 302. 1 Chitt. Pl. 435–6. 6 Pick. 370. 19 Johns. R. 308.

(*o*) Com. Dig. *Abatement*, E. 16.

(*p*) Ib.

---

(6) There is an exception to this general position, when there is a *summons and severance*, in personal actions, and also, in many cases, where one of several co-plaintiffs *dies after* the commencement of the suit. (*Vid. post. Pleas in Abatement*, §§ 91. 92.)

he was *dead* at the time. — This diversity, in the form of pleading, seems intended merely to mark the difference between the case of a person, named as plaintiff after his *death*, and that of a plaintiff altogether *imaginary*.

§ 60. That the plaintiff was never *in esse*, seems also to be a good plea in *bar* (*q*). For that a *right of action* should exist, in favour of an *imaginary* person, is plainly impossible (7).

§ 61. Pleas to the disability of the plaintiff *conclude*, by praying judgment; 'if the said A. B. the plaintiff, ought to be answered' — or, (when the disability operates only as a *temporary suspension* of the suit), 'that the plaint may remain without day, &c', i. e. until the disability be removed (*r*).

(*q*) Vid. 1 Bos. & P. 44. Bro. Ab. *Misnomer*, 93.
(*r*) 3 Black. Com. 303. Tidd, 585. Lawes' Pl. 109.

---

(7) That the nominal plaintiff, in the English *ejectment*, is fictitious, is however not pleadable, in any form. His fictitious character is an essential part of the machinery of that action; and the fiction, being devised for the advancement of *justice*, cannot be contradicted. Indeed, the real defendant has generally no opportunity to plead the fact: Since he is obliged, under the consent-rule, to plead the *general issue*. Vid. 4 M. & S. 301. 19 Johns. R. 169.

III. *Of Pleas in Abatement.*

Pleas in abatement, nature of.

§ 62. The term 'abatement', in the language of pleading, signifies *prostration*, or *demolition;* and hence, to 'abate' a writ, is to *prostrate* or *destroy* it (*s*).

§ 63. Pleas in abatement, in most instances, extend only to the *writ*, when the suit is commenced by original writ (*t*). In some cases, however, pleas of this class may be pleaded to the *count*, even when the suit is thus commenced (*u*).

§ 64. But defects or mistakes, *apparent* upon the face of the declaration, *independently of any reference to the writ*, are not pleadable in abatement (*v*): The proper mode of taking advantage of such faults being by *demurrer.* On the contrary however, certain mistakes in the *declaration*, when *not* apparent upon *the face of it*, (such, for example, as *misnomer*, *variance* from the writ, &c), are proper subjects of a plea in abatement. (Ante, ch. 2, § 34.) (8).

(*s*) Co. Litt. 134. b.
(*t*) 3 Black. Com. 301–3.
(*u*) 3 Black. Com. 301–3. Com. Dig. *Abatement*, G. 1. Doct. Pl. 1. Lawes' Pl. 102. 105.
(*v*) 1 Salk. 212. Willes, 478.

(8) In respect to the precise office and extent of pleas in abatement, there is some confusion, or apparent inconsistency, in the

§ 65. When the suit is commenced by *bill*, the defendant may plead in abatement of the 'bill', as

books. Pleas of this class are sometimes mentioned in a manner implying that they extend only to the *writ*, and that *no* defects in the *count* can be reached by them. But this limitation of their effect is clearly too unqualified. It is indeed universally true, that a plea *to the writ*, if properly framed for its purpose, is a plea *in abatement:* But it is not always true, *è converso*, that a plea in abatement can extend to the *writ only;* for by the common law, various matters of abatement are pleadable to the *declaration* — though in consequence of certain modern rules of practice, in the English C. B. and B. R. pleas in abatement, *to the declaration*, are, to a great extent, virtually abolished in those courts. And the change, thus introduced, between the ancient and modern practice, appears to be the chief cause of the apparent inconsistency above alluded to. — To explain, somewhat more particularly, what is here suggested, it may be observed, that pleas in abatement, *to the count*, which were frequent in the ancient practice, were founded chiefly upon some defect, mistake, or informality, appearing either in the *recital of the writ*, in the declaration, (which *recital* was then deemed necessary, in all cases) — or upon some *variance* between the count and the writ. (Lawes' Pl. 105. 1 Saund. 318. n. 3. Cro. Eliz. 829. 185. 330. 198.) But in the year 1654, a rule of court was established by the English C. B. ordering that thenceforth 'declarations in actions upon the *case*, and general statutes, other than debt, should not repeat the original writ, but only *the nature of the action*' (1 Saund. 318. a. (n. 3.) Lawes' Pl. 105–6.) And it seems that the more recent practice has somewhat extended the operation of the rule (Carth. 108. 1 Saund. *ub. sup.*) The consequence has been, that in cases affected by this rule, all pleas in abatement, founded upon the *recital* of the writ in the count, have been abolished. And no advantage can be taken of any *variance* between the writ and the count, but by obtaining *oyer of the original writ*, (Com. Dig. *Abatement*, H. 1.) But by a more recent rule of C. B. and B. R. established in the 12 Geo. 2, and 19 Geo. 3, (*Vid. post.* § 101,) it was ordered, *that oyer of the original should not thence-*

CHAP. V.

he may of the 'writ', when it is commenced by writ. In the former case, the plea prays judgment of the *bill*, as in the latter it does of the writ (*w*).

Requisites of.

§ 66. It has been stated in a former chapter (vid. ch. 3, §§ 57. 58), that in pleas of this class — as in all other dilatory pleas, the greatest *precision* and *certainty* are required, because dilatory pleas are odious, or at least not favoured. Hence, the least inaccuracy or defect, in pleas of this kind, is fatal (*x*).

§ 67. It is a *general* rule, founded upon the same principle, that a plea in abatement must 'give the plaintiff a better writ' (*y*); i. e. it must be so pleaded as to *enable* the plaintiff, (in a subsequent suit for the same cause), to supply the defect, or avoid the mistake, upon which the plea is founded. Thus,

(*w*) 3 Black. Com. 303.

(*x*) Cro. Jac. 82. 3 T. R. 185-6. 5 Ib. 487. 8 Ib. 167. 2 Saund. 209. b. Com. Dig. *Abatement*, I. 11. Willes, 554. 1 Lill. Ent. 1. 6. 2 H. Black. 530.

(*y*) Com. Dig. *Abatement*, I. 1. 2. Lawes' Pl. 39. 103-4. 8 T. R. 515. 1 Lill. Ent. 6. Willes, 554. 2 Chitt. Pl. 418. *Vid.* Yelv. 112. (n. 1.) 6 Pick. 369. Archb. Civ. Pl. (Amer. ed.) 334.

---

forth be granted. And the effect of this rule has been, to abolish all pleas in abatement, founded upon any *variance* between the declaration and the writ. Thus, pleas in abatement *to the count*, are, in the modern practice of those two courts, almost unknown. — When, indeed, as is most usual in B. R., the suit is commenced *by bill*, no distinction can exist, between pleas to the *writ* and to the count. For in these cases, the *bill itself* is the only original; and all pleas in abatement are *to the bill.* Vid. *post.* §§ 82–84.

if the defendant pleads that he is misnamed, or that a wrong addition is given him, in the writ; he must show, in his plea, what his true name or addition is; and thus enable the plaintiff to avoid a similar mistake in a subsequent suit (*z*). And this rule is applied to indictments, as well as to civil actions (*zz*).

§ 68. The causes or grounds for pleading in abatement, may be either *intrinsic*, or *extrinsic* — either *apparent* upon the face of the writ, &c; or *not* thus apparent (*a*). **Causes of.**

These causes, in the order here proposed, are

§ 69. I. *Misnomer*, and want or mistake of *addition.* — If the defendant is sued, or declared against, by a wrong name; he may plead the mistake in abatement (*b*). The object of this rule is, to prevent mistakes and confusion as to the *identity* of the person sued. A party may however sue, or be sued, by *any* name by which he is *known and called*, at the commencement of the suit (*c*); though it be not his baptismal, or original name. For he **Misnomer, &c, of defendant.**

(*z*) Bac. Abr. *Misnomer*, &c, F. 1 Salk. 6. 7. Willes, 554. 1 Lill. Ent. 6.

(*zz*) 6 M. & S. 88.

(*a*) Lawes' Pl. 102. 106.

(*b*) 3 Black. Com. 302. 1 Salk. 7. 3 East, 167. Bac. Abr. *Abatement*, D.

(*c*) Willes, 554. 2 Wils. 367. 1 Bos. & P. 60. 1 East, 542. 2 Chitt. Pl. 590.

CHAP. V.

may be as fully identified by the former, as by the latter.

Misnomer, &c, of defendant.

§ 70. Where there are several co-defendants, the true proper name of *each* of them must be given. Describing them, even when sued as partners, by the style or name of the *co-partnership*, (as 'A. B. & Co.') seems clearly not sufficient. For the name of a co-partnership is altogether *arbitrary*, and may not express the proper name of any one of the individual partners (*cc*).

§ 71. By the common law, no other personal description of a party, sued or suing, was required, than his proper name, (including both his name of baptism, and surname), unless his dignity, or degree, were as high as that of *knight* — in which case, his degree was a necessary *addition* to his proper name: The title of *knight*, and all those above it, being deemed *parcel* of the proper name (*d*). And this rule extends to both the plaintiff and defendant. But the statute of *additions* (1 Hen. 5, c. 5), requires, that in all personal actions, appeals and indictments, there shall be added to the name of the *defendant*, his title, mystery, estate or degree, (as, 'knight' — 'gentleman' — 'esquire' — 'yeoman' — 'spinster', &c), and his place of abode (the town, hamlet, &c) and the county in which he resides, or

(*cc*) 8 T. R. 508. 1 Leach's Cr. Cases, 240. 1 Chitt. Pl. 256.

(*d*) Bac. Abr. *Misnomer*, &c, B. 2. 2 Roll. Ab. 469. Comb. 189.

Misnomer, &c, of defendant.

has resided (*e*). The title, &c, thus added to the defendant's name, is called his 'addition'; and the absence of this addition, or the giving of a wrong one, in the writ, is pleadable in abatement (*f*). But the addition of the defendant's degree, *or* mystery, with his present *or* late place of abode is held sufficient (*g*). Where there are several co-defendants, the proper addition must be given to *each*, except where husband and wife are co-defendants—in which case the latter requires no addition (*h*).

§ 72. But this statute extends only to *personal* actions, appeals, and indictments. *Real* actions are not within its purview; probably because the defendant is supposed to be sufficiently identified, by his proper name and the *possession* of the land in question (*i*).—By the 'appeals', mentioned in the statute, are meant those *criminal* prosecutions, which are so called.

§ 73. At common law, neither want of addition, nor misnomer, was pleadable to an indictment for *felony*: The prisoner being identified by his personal presence (*k*). But the rule, as now altered by the above statute 1 Hen. 5, is the same in indictments for felony, as in personal actions. The plea to such

(*e*) Bac. Abr. *Misnomer*, &c, B. 2. 3 Black. Com. 302. Lawes' Pl. 106.

(*f*) Iid.

(*g*) 2 Ld Ray. 1541. Stra. 556. 816. 924.

(*h*) Bac. Abr. *Misnomer*, &c, B. 1 Chitt. Pl. 247.

(*i*) Bac. Abr. *Misnomer*, &c, B. 2. 6 Mod. 85.

(*k*) Bac. Abr. *Abatement*, D. *Indictment*, G. 2.

CHAP. V.

Misnomer, &c, of defendant.

an indictment however, can in general be of little avail, eventually, to the prisoner; since the court will, as a matter of course, detain him in custody, till another indictment can be framed and found against him (*l*).

§ 74. Misnomer, or want of addition, in describing *one* of *two* defendants, is not pleadable by the other (*m*). For the former may, if he pleases, admit himself to be rightly named and described; (as he does of course, by not pleading the mistake himself in abatement); and his co-defendant cannot object to such admission.—The same rule holds in indictments against several (*n*).

§ 75. If a defendant, in pleading misnomer, gives himself, in the commencement of his plea, the same name by which he is sued; (as if A. B., when sued by the name of C. D., begins his plea, by saying, 'And the said C. D. comes and defends,' &c); his plea is ill (*o*). For, by calling himself 'C. D.', in the first instance, he is *estopped* to aver that that is not his true name. He should begin, by saying, 'And A. B., against whom the plaintiff has sued out his writ, by the name of C. D., comes,' &c (*p*).

(*l*) 2 Hale, P. C. 176. 238. 1 Chitt. Crim. Law, 203.

(*m*) Bac. Abr. *Misnomer*, &c, G. *Abatement*, D.

(*n*) 2 Hale, P. C. 177. Bac. Abr. *Misnomer*, &c, G.

(*o*) 2 Saund. 209. b. 5 T. R. 487. Comb. 188. Lawes' Pl. 92. Carth. 207. 1 Show. 394.

(*p*) Iid. 2 Chitt. Pl. 416. 417. 1 Lill. Ent. 1.

Misnomer, &c, of defendant.

§ 76. And if the recognizance of bail gives the defendant the *same* name by which he is sued, (though a wrong one); he is estopped to aver that it is a misnomer (*q*). For by the entry of the recognizance in this manner, he places upon the record the name, given him in the writ, *as his true name.* And the rule is the same, even though the defendant himself does *not join* in the recognizance (*r*). For although the recognizance, in such a case, is not in strictness the defendant's *act;* yet being by his *procurement*, he is concluded by it.

§ 77. If one executes a specialty, by a wrong name; it is held that he must be sued upon it, by the same name by which the instrument is executed; and that his true name should be added, under an *alias* (*s*). For he is estopped by the deed to deny the name, by which he executed it; and if sued by his true name, there would be a *variance* between the deed and the writ.

Misnomer of plaintiffs.

§ 78. Misnomer of the *plaintiff* is also pleadable in abatement (*t*): And the plea may be answered, by the same replication, as when the misnomer is of the defendant (*u*). But the want of *addition*, or a wrong one, in the description of the plaintiff, is no cause of abatement, except as at *common* law (*vid.* § 71). For the statute of *additions* does not

(*q*) Willes, 461. 1 Salk. 8. 2 Chitt. Pl. 590. 2 New Rep. 453.
(*r*) 2 New Rep. 453.
(*s*) 2 Stra. 1218. 1 Bulstr. 216. Bac. Abr. *Misnomer*, B. 1.
(*t*) Com. Dig. *Abatement*, E. 18. 1 East, 542.
(*u*) 1 East, 542.

CHAP. V. extend to *plaintiffs* (v) — because there was supposed to be no danger of mistakes in regard to their identity.

§ 79. Misnomer, &c, as such, is pleadable only in *abatement* (w). It is no plea in *bar;* because it does not deny the *cause of action;* nor can it be assigned for error, unless it has been pleaded in abatement, and overruled. For if not thus pleaded, the exception is waved, as all matters of mere abatement are, if not pleaded in abatement (x).

Post. § 100.

§ 80. To a plea of misnomer, (whether of the plaintiff, or defendant), it is a good replication, that at the commencement of the suit, he was *known and called*, as well by the name, by which he sues or is sued, as by that set forth as his true name, in the plea (y).

§ 81. In the State of Connecticut, and probably in many of the United States, no other *addition*, than his place of abode, need be given to either of the parties; but this must be given to both; and of course to all the co-parties, plaintiffs or defendants.

§ 82. In concluding this head of abatement, it is proper to remark, that in the English Court of

(v) Bac. Abr. *Misnomer*, &c, B. 2.

(w) Bac. Abr. *Misnomer*, &c, E. Carth. 124. Comb. 188. 1 Bos. & P. 40. 6 M. & S. 46.

(x) 6 T. R. 766. 2 H. Black. 267. 299. 1 Salk. 2.

(y) 2 Wils. 367. 1 East, 542. 1 Bos. & P. 60. 2 Chitt. Pl. 590. Willes, 554.

Common Pleas, and (when the suit is by *original*), in that of the King's Bench also, pleas in abatement, founded upon the want, or the falsity, of the defendant's *addition*, are now virtually abolished, by the operation of a *rule of practice*, (established in the former of those courts, in the 11 & 12 Geo. 2. and in the latter, in the 19 Geo. 3), ordering that *oyer* shall not thenceforth be granted *of the original* writ (*z*). For no addition is given, or required to be given, to either party, in the *declaration;* and its omission or falsity, in the writ, cannot be shown, without an inspection of the *writ itself*. And as *oyer* of the writ (*a*), is now unattainable, in the two courts above mentioned, under the above rule of court; a plea, in either of those courts, founded upon the want of addition, &c, must of necessity fail (*b*). — The effect of this rule, indeed, has been the abolition, in those courts, of all pleas, which cannot be verified without *oyer of the writ*. (*Vid. post.* § 101.)

§ 83. Yet if any thing, which, in the writ, would be matter of abatement, appears in the *declaration;* it may be pleaded to the *writ* — the above rule of court notwithstanding. If, for example, there is a misnomer, or a nonjoinder or misjoinder of parties, in the *declaration;* the mistake may be safely pleaded, as a fault in *the writ*. For the declaration is conclusive against the plaintiff,

(*z*) Doug. 227. 1 Saund. 318. a. (n. 3).
(*a*) 2 Salk. 701. Lawes' Pl. 105—6. 1 Saund. 318. a. (n. 3).
(*b*) 1 Saund. 318. a. (n. 3). Lawes' Pl. 105—6. 1 Chitt. Pl. 440.

CHAP. V. that the parties, and the names given them, are the same in the *writ*, as in *itself:* Because the plaintiff, by averring the contrary, would himself necessarily disclose a *variance* between the declaration and the writ, which would be fatal to the suit. And thus, without any examination of the writ, the defendant may, in cases like these, abate it *through the medium of the declaration.*

§ 84. When the suit is commenced by *bill*—which is itself considered as the *original*, and of which there is no occasion for *oyer*—the above rule of court has no effect.

And where—as in the practice of the courts of some of the United States—the writ and declaration are *embodied*, as parts of one and the same instrument, no such rule can exist (*c*).

Coverture. § 85. II. *Coverture* of the defendant.—If a *feme covert* is sued without her husband, she may plead her coverture in abatement (*cc*). This defence is allowed, for the protection of her *privilege*, and of the husband's *rights*; both of which might be violated by a recovery against her.

§ 86. But this plea is no defence, where the husband, though actually living, is *civilly dead*—as, where he is *banished*, or has *abjured* the realm, or is an *alien enemy*, and out of the realm, &c. For

(*c*) *Vid.* 5 Mass. R. 285.
(*cc*) Com. Dig. *Abatement*, F. 2. Co. Litt. 132. b. 1 Salk. 7.

Coverture of defendant.

in either of these cases, the wife is in law considered as a *feme sole* (*d*). And whenever she is, from any cause, regarded in law *as sole*, this plea cannot avail her (*dd*).

§ 87. If a woman, being sued while sole, marries pending the suit; she cannot plead this supervenient coverture, in abatement, or at all (*e*). For it would be manifestly unreasonable, to allow her to defeat, by her own act, a suit *rightly commenced* against her.

§ 88. When a *feme covert* is sued alone, she can plead her coverture only *in abatement* (*f*). For the defence does not deny the *right of action;* and therefore, if she omits to plead it as a *dilatory* plea, she *waves* it, so far as regards her own privilege, and tacitly admits that she is liable to be sued alone.

She must also plead her coverture *in person* (*g*): Because she is legally incapable of appointing an *attorney*.

(*d*) Com. Dig. *Abatement*, F. 2. Co. Litt. 132. b. 133. a. 1 Salk. 116. *Vid. ante*, ch. 5, § 51.

(*dd*) *Vid.* 3 Campb. 124. 15 Mass. R. 31. 6 Pick. 89. 5 Ib. 461. 11 East, 304, *notis* Day. 2 Kent's Com. 132. 214. *n.* 3 Barn. & Cress. 291.

(*e*) Bac. Abr. *Abatement*, G. 1 Lill. Ab. 526. 2 Stra. 811. 2 Ld Ray. 1525. Cro. Jac. 323. 1 Ves. 182. 2 Rol. Rep. 53.

(*f*) Com. Dig. *Abatement*, F. 2. 3 T. R. 631. Carth. 12.

(*g*) 2 Saund. 209. c. (n. 1). 1 Lill. Ent. 1. 2 Chitt. Pl. 415. 425.

CHAP. V.

§ 89. But she can, by no admission or omission, wave any right of her *husband:* And therefore, if she omits to plead her coverture, *he* may, at any time, come in and plead it in *bar* (*h*).

And if both of them omit to plead it, and judgment is given against her; the judgment may be reversed, by writ of error, in which they must both join, as plaintiffs in error (*i*). If the writ of error is in the name of either of them *alone*, it may be *quashed* (*k*). For the wife cannot prosecute it alone, by reason of her legal disability; nor can the husband alone, because *her* rights, as well as his own, are involved in it.

Death of parties.

§ 90. III. *Death of Parties.*—By the common law, the death of a sole plaintiff or sole defendant, *pendente lite*, abates the suit (*l*): There being, after such an event, but *one* party to the action. And if, after the death of either party, final judgment should be given, for or against him; it would be *erroneous* (*m*) — as being for or against a party not *in esse*. But by the statute 17 Car. 2, c. 28, it is enacted, that the death of either party, '*between verdict and judgment*, shall not be alleged for error, so as judg-

(*h*) Bac. Abr. *Abatement*, G. Sty. 280. 1 Salk. 400. 3 T. R. 631. 5 Ib. 681.

(*i*) Iid. 3 Esp. Rep. 19. 4 Mass. R. 661.

(*k*) 3 Esp. Rep. 19. Bac. Abr. *Error*, B.

(*l*) Bac. Abr. *Abatement*, F. Com. Dig. *Abatement*, H. 32.

(*m*) Carth. 338—9. T. Ray. 59. 463. Bac. Abr. *Pleas*, &c, Q.

ment be entered within two terms, after such verdict' (*n*). CHAP. V.

Death of parties.

§ 91. By the common law also, if one of several *plaintiffs* dies, pending the suit; it will, in most cases, abate (*o*). For by joining in the suit, they assert a *joint* right of recovery, which, as such, is destroyed by the death of either of them.

§ 92. But this last rule does not apply, in its full extent, to such personal actions as admit of *summons and severance*, and in which an entire, indivisible thing is to be recovered (9). For in such actions, after one of two co-plaintiffs has been summoned and severed, he ceases to be *a party;* and the other becomes a sole plaintiff, prosecuting for the whole amount, or matter in demand, and therefore if the severed plaintiff afterwards *dies*, pending the action, his death has no effect upon the suit (*p*).

(*n*) Bac. Abr. *Abatement*, F.

(*o*) Bac. Abr. *Abatement*, F. *Joint-Tenants*, &c, K. 10 Co. 134. 6 Ib. 26. Com. Dig. *Abatement*, H. 33.

(*p*) Bac. Abr. *Abatement*, F. Cro. Eliz. 652.

(9) *Summons and severance* is a proceeding, by which one of several persons named as co-plaintiffs, in a writ, is, on his neglecting to appear and prosecute, summoned to appear, &c, and if he refuses to join in prosecuting the suit, is *separated* from it, by a judgment of *severance.* As to what cases admit of summons and severance, see Off. Ex'r. 96. 104. 6 Co. 25. Bac. Abr. *Summons* & *Severance*, F. Co. Litt. 139.

CHAP. V.

Death of parties.

If one of several, named as co-plaintiffs, was dead at the *issuing* of the writ; the fact may be pleaded in abatement (*q*). For it *falsifies* the writ.

§ 93. If one of several *co-defendants* dies, pending the suit; his death is, *in general*, no cause of abatement, even by the common law (*r*). For by being sued together — (a proceeding in which they are passive) — co-defendants do not, like co-plaintiffs, either assert or admit any thing, which requires them all to act or proceed jointly: And hence, on the death of one of them, if the *cause of action* is such, as would *survive* against the survivors, (as is almost universally the case); the plaintiff may, by suggesting the death upon the roll, proceed in the same suit, against the latter.

§ 94. The inconvenience of abatement, by the death of parties, is now, in a great measure, remedied, by the statute 17 Car. 2, c. 8, and by the 8 & 9 W. 3, c. 2, §§ 6 & 7; by which last it is enacted, 'that if there be *two or more* plaintiffs or defendants, and one or more of them should die, if the cause of such action should survive *to* the surviving plaintiff or plaintiffs, or *against* the surviving defendant or defendants; the writ, or action, shall not be thereby abated. But such death being suggested upon the record, the action shall proceed at the suit of the surviving plaintiff or plaintiffs, against the surviving defendant or defendants': And that

(*q*) Bac. Abr. *Abatement*, F.
(*r*) Hardr. 113. 151. Cro. Car. 426. Bac. Abr. *Abatement*, F.

Death of parties.

'if any *plaintiff* happen to die, after an interlocutory judgment, and before a final judgment obtained therein; the said action shall not abate by reason thereof; if such action might, originally, be prosecuted or maintained *by* the executors or administrators of such plaintiff; and if the *defendant* die, after such interlocutory judgment, and before final judgment therein obtained, the said action shall not abate, if such action might originally be prosecuted or maintained *against* the executors or administrators of such defendant; and the plaintiff, (or if he be dead after such interlocutory judgment), his executors or administrators shall and may have a *scire facias* against the defendant, if living after such interlocutory judgment, (or if he died after,) then against his executors or administrators, to show cause why damages, in such action, should not be assessed and recovered by him or them.'

§ 95. Under the former of these statutes, (that of 17 Car. 2), the death of a party, *after verdict*, does not abate the suit; but judgment in pursuance of the verdict, may be entered, (within the time prescribed, by the act), as if the death had not intervened (*s*). And under the latter statute (8 & 9 W. 3), if a *sole* plaintiff dies, after an interlocutory judgment (10), and before final judgment in an ac-

(*s*) 1 Salk. 42. 1 Sid. 385. Toll. on Ex'rs. 442-3.

(10) The interlocutory judgment, contemplated in the above enactment, is such an one, as leaves nothing more, to be ascertained, than the *amount to be recovered*, in damages, or otherwise

CHAP. V.

Death of parties.

tion, the cause of which would have *survived to* his personal representatives — or if a *sole* defendant dies, after such a judgment in an action, the cause of which would have survived *against* his personal representatives (11) — the suit shall not abate; but on a *sci. fa.* prayed out, as prescribed in the act, the suit may proceed to final judgment: And if one or more of several co-plaintiffs die, pending an action, the cause of which would have survived *to* the surviving plaintiffs — or if one or more of several co-defendants die, pending an action, the cause of which would have survived *against* the surviving defendants; the suit shall not, in either case, abate; but — such death being suggested upon the

— as, where a demurrer to the declaration, or to the plaintiff's evidence, has been *overruled* — or, where the defendant has submitted to a judgment by *default, non sum informatus, nil dicit,* &c; in each of which cases, nothing more is necessary to be done, as preparatory to final judgment, than to ascertain *how much* the plaintiff is entitled to recover. (Vid. 1 Lill. Ent. 647. 6 Mod. 144. 4 T. R. 431. Toll. on Ex'rs. 443.) The statute of Connecticut prevents the suit from abating, when the death happens in any stage of the suit — whether *after* or *before* an interlocutory judgment.

(11) When a cause of action is such as, on the death of either of the sole parties to it, might have been *originally prosecuted* by or against his personal representatives, it is one, which *would survive* to or against such representatives, within the meaning of the above distinctions: But when it could *not* have been thus originally prosecuted, it is one which *would not* thus survive. But *what* particular causes of action do, or do not, thus survive, is an inquiry, which falls appropriately under a different title — that of *Executors* and *Administrators.*

record — the action shall proceed between the surviving parties.

Death of parties.

§ 96. It will be perceived, that the second clause in the above statute, (viz. that which provides against abatement, by the death of a *sole* party), extends only to *personal* actions — i. e. such as survive to or against *personal* representatives. *Real* actions therefore still abate, as at common law, on the death of a *sole* plaintiff or defendant (ante, § 90). But real actions, in which there are *several* co-plaintiffs or co-defendants, and of which the causes are such, as *survive* to or against the surviving parties, are within the purview of the first clause of the act.

Variance.

§ 97. IV. *Variance.* — There are divers instances, or particulars, in which variance is pleadable in abatement — as where the *count* varies from the *writ* — or, where the writ varies from the *record*, *specialty*, or *instrument*, on which the action is brought (*t*). For in the one case, the count does not maintain or pursue the writ; and in the other, the writ is not adapted to the cause of action.

§ 98. As to variance between the writ and the count, this diversity is to be observed: If the variance is in matter of mere *form*, (as in time, or place, when that circumstance is *immaterial*, or in

(*t*) Com. Dig. *Abatement*, G. 1. H. 7. 9. 6 Co. 14. 2 Wils. 85. 395. Cro. Eliz. 722. 1 H. Black. 249.

CHAP. V.

Variance. any other particular which is so); advantage can be taken of it, only by plea *in abatement* (u): But if the variance is in matter of *substance* — (as if the writ sounds in *contract*, and the declaration in *tort*, or *è converso* — or if the writ demands one *thing*, or subject, and the declaration another); advantage may be taken of it, even by motion in arrest of judgment (v). For as it is *the writ*, which gives authority to the court to proceed in any given suit; it is obvious, that the court can have *no authority* to hear and determine a cause, *substantially* different from that mentioned in the writ.

§ 99. In the states of Connecticut and Massachusetts (w), it has heretofore been customary to plead in abatement any variance between the record or instrument declared upon, and the description of it in the *declaration*. But the more proper mode of taking exception for such a variance, is either by objecting to the record, &c, as *evidence*, under the general issue — and in that way, compelling a nonsuit (x) (because the record or writing, offered in evidence, will appear to be a *different* one from that declared upon); or by reciting it upon the record, on oyer, and then *demurring* to the declaration (y): This latter course being justified, on the ground that

(u) Yelv. 120. Latch, 173. Bac. Abr. *Abatement*, I.

(v) Hob. 279. Cro. Eliz. 722.

(w) Story's Pl. 59. 60.

(x) 4 T. R. 612. 687–8. 1 ib. 656. 1 Bos. & P. 7. 1 Saund. 154. n. Doug. 665. Cowp. 766–7.

(y) 1 Saund. 317. Com. Dig. *Pleader*, 2. 3. Hob. 18. Lawes' Pl. 98–9.

the instrument, &c, thus recited, on *oyer*, becomes in effect, part of the *declaration* (*z*). CHAP. V.

§ 100. Though, as heretofore stated, no advantage can be taken of *misnomer, as such*, except by plea in abatement; yet when misnomer occasions a *variance* (as, if A. B., having executed a bond by his true name, is sued upon it, and declared against by the name of C. D.); advantage may be taken of the mistake, *as a variance*, in either of the two modes last before mentioned: i. e. under the *general issue*, or by *demurrer, on oyer* (*a*): Though if the mistake is treated, by the defendant, as a *misnomer*, (in which case, no use is made of the *instrument*, in evidence or otherwise); he must plead it in *abatement*.

§ 101. Pleas in abatement, for any variance between the writ and the count, are now, however, practically abolished in England, in C. B. and (where the suit is by original) in B. R. also, by a rule of practice heretofore mentioned (*b*), refusing *oyer* of the original writ. And the operation of this rule extends to all pleas in abatement which cannot be proved without an *examination* of the original writ (*c*).

(z) 1 Vent. 43. 1 Saund. 316. Carth. 513. 6 Mod. 28. 237.
(*a*) 4 T. R. 611. 612. 3 Bos. & P. 559. 1 Campb. 195.
(*b*) Ante Note 8 to § 64, and § 82.
(*c*) Lawes' Pl. 97..105. 1 Saund. 318. (n. 3.) 3 Bos. & P. 395. 7 East, 383, 6 T. R. 363. 1 Chitt. Pl. 440.

CHAP. V.

V. *Nonjoinder and Misjoinder of Parties.*

§ 102. In what cases, two or more persons ought or ought not to be joined as co-parties, (either as plaintiffs or defendants), in one suit, has been already explained (*ante*, ch. 4, § 52 to 78). The present inquiry is, in what manner *advantage is to be taken* of a mistake, in respect to the proper parties.

Nonjoinder and misjoinder of parties.

§ 103. Under this head, it may be laid down as a universal rule, applicable both to actions *ex contractu* and *ex delicto*, that if one person sues alone, when the right of action is in *two or more*, jointly (*d*) — or if two or more sue as co-plaintiffs, when the right of action is in *one* of them only (*e*); the mistake is pleadable *in abatement:* Because, without reference to the merits, the suit is, in both cases, brought in an *improper manner*, in regard to the parties.

§ 104. On the other hand, if one is sued alone, when by law another should have been joined with him, as co-defendant — or if two or more are sued together, when by law the action should have been brought against *one* of them only; the nonjoinder

(*d*) Com. Dig. *Abatement*, E. 8–14. 1 Salk. 4. 7 T. R. 243. 1 Saund. 291. (n. 4.) Co. Litt. 164. a. 189. a. 195. b. 198. a.

(*e*) Com. Dig. *Abatement*, E. 15. Cro. Eliz. 143. 1 Leon. 315.

in the one case, and the misjoinder in the other, is, in all cases, pleadable in the same manner (*f*)

CHAP. V.

Nonjoinder, &c, of parties.

§ 105. In some cases, falling under the two last rules, the exception can be taken *only* by plea in abatement: In others, it may be taken, at the election of the defendant, either by pleading in abatement, or under the *general issue*; or, as the case *may* be, by *demurrer* on oyer — by motion in *arrest of judgment* — or by writ of *error*.

§ 106. And for the purpose of determining, in any given case, whether a mistake in the joinder or nonjoinder of a party, is pleadable *only* in abatement — or whether advantage may be taken of it, under *the general issue* — the following distinction, it is believed, will be found to furnish the true criterion: —

If the proof, which supports the objection arising from the nonjoinder or misjoinder of a party, goes *in denial* or *disproof of the declaration*, or of any material allegation in it; advantage may be taken of the mistake, as well under the *general issue*, as by plea in abatement (for whatever denies the declaration, goes to support the general issue): But if the proof, which shows the mistake, is *not inconsistent* with any material part of the declaration; the exception can be taken, only by a *plea in abatement*: Because whatever does *not* contradict the declara-

(*f*) 5 Burr. 2611. 1 Saund. 153. (n. 1.) 291. b. (n. 4.) 5 T. R. 651. Com. Dig. *Abatement*, F. 6. 2 East, 574. 1 Chitt. Pl. 75-6.

CHAP. V.

tion, does not conduce to support the general issue (12).

Nonjoinder &c. of plaintiffs:

To apply this distinction; first, to the nonjoinder or misjoinder of parties, as plaintiffs —

In contract.

107. In an action on CONTRACT, if one of the co-parties to it sues alone, when the right of action is in himself *and another* — or if two or more sue together, when the right of action is in *one* of them only; advantage may be taken of the mistake, as well under the *general issue*, as by plea *in abatement* (*g*). If therefore, upon an obligation or promise, made to A. and B. jointly, A. sues alone, as on a contract made with himself only — or if on a contract made with A. *only*, he and B. sue, as on a contract made with both of them; the suit may be defeated, in either of the above modes. For in each of these cases, there is a *variance:* The contract, offered in evidence, being *not the same* as that declared upon. In other words, the fact, (or proof), that the right of action is *joint*, in the former case, or that it is *not* so, in the latter, goes in *disproof* of the declaration.

(*g*) 1 Saund. 291. f. (n. 4.) 1 Chitt. Pl. 209, & *seq.* 1 Taunt. 7. 1 Bos. & P. 75. 2 Stra. 820. 1146. 2 T. R. 282. 5 ib. 709. 1 Esp. Rep. 183. Bull. N.P. 152. Peake Ev. (2d. ed.) 205. 2 Mass. R. 510. 6 Pick. 360.

---

(12) It is not pretended that all the cases conform to this distinction; but on principle, it appears to be the only correct one.

CHAP. IV.

Nonjoinder, &c, of plaintiffs: In contract:

§ 108. And if in either of the two last cases, the action is founded upon a *written instrument* ; advantage may be taken of the mistake, not only in either of the two modes just mentioned, but in another also: viz. by praying *oyer* of the instrument, reciting it, *verbatim*, upon the record, and *demurring* to the declaration (*h*). For it is a general principle, that a written instrument, pleaded by one party, when thus recited on the record by the other, becomes *parcel* of the former party's *pleading*.

§ 109. And if in an action, on *contract*, brought by a sole plaintiff, it appears, upon the face of the *declaration*, or of any other pleading on the plaintiff's part, that another ought to have been joined as co-plaintiff; the mistake is incurable, even by verdict (*i*) If therefore, in an action of debt, covenant broken, or assumpsit, brought by A. alone, it appears from *his own* pleading, that the contract was made with himself and B. *jointly*, and that B. is *still living*, (as he is presumed to be, unless the contrary appears, in the declaration) ; the defendant may demur, *without* reciting the contract ; or may, after verdict, move in arrest of judgment, or reverse a judgment against him, on writ of error (*k*). For in this case, as it appears from the plaintiff's *own showing*, that he alone has no right of action ; the defendant is not

(*h*) 1 Saund. 153. (n. 1.) 291. f. (n. 4.) 1 Bos. & P. 67. 1 Chitt. Pl. 209.

(*i*) 1 Saund. 153. (n. 1.) 291. b. (n. 4.) Esp. Dig. 304. 2 Stra. 1146. 1 Bos. & P. 67. 74. 1 East, 497.

(*k*) Iid.

CHAP. V.

under the necessity of showing the mistake, by *pleading* the fact which has occasioned it.

Nonjoinder &c. of plaintiffs: In contract:

And undoubtedly the same rule must apply to an action, brought by *two* plaintiffs, on a contract which appears, from their own pleading, to have been made with *one* of them only.

§ 110. But the general rule, that if one of two persons, having a joint right of action *ex contractu*, sues alone, advantage may be taken of the mistake, under the *general issue*, does not extend to actions brought by one, suing in a *representative* capacity. Hence, if one of two *co-executors* sues alone, on a contract made with their testator, advantage can be taken of the nonjoinder of the other only by plea *in abatement* (*l*). For as the executors are not parties to the contract; the nonjoinder of one of them occasions no *variance*, and does not in any respect involve a *contradiction* of the declaration: Inasmuch as the fact that there is another executor, who should have been joined as co-plaintiff, is not inconsistent with the description, in the declaration, of the contract made with the *testator*.

In tort.

§ 111. In an action EX DELICTO, if one sues alone, when another should have been joined — (as where one of two joint-tenants, or of any two persons, whose *joint* right has been violated by a tort, sues for it, without joining the other) — advantage can

(*l*) 1 Saund. 291. g. (n. 4.) 3 T. R. 558. 1 Chitt. Pl. 8, note (*g*) 13.

CHAP. V.

Nonjoinder, &c, of plaintiffs: In tort:

be taken of the nonjoinder of the latter, *only* by plea in abatement (*m*): Because the fact, that another was interested jointly with the plaintiff, does not go in support of the *general issue*. For proof that the right violated was *joint*, is no proof that the defendant has not injured the plaintiff's property: Nay, it *admits* that fact; and shows merely that the injury was not to his *sole* property. But this latter fact does not disprove the *declaration*.

§ 112. In this last case however, the defendant may prove, under *the general issue*, the interest of the other party, who is not made co-plaintiff in the suit — not, indeed, for the purpose of defeating the action; but for that of taking off *a moiety* of the *damages* (*n*). For otherwise, the plaintiff might recover damages to the *whole* amount of the injury; and still leave the defendant liable, for a moiety of them, to the other party in interest (*o*).

§ 113. If *two* sue together, in tort, when the right of action is in *one* of them, only — (as if, for a trespass upon the sole property of *A.*, he and *B.* sue, as co-plaintiffs); advantage of the misjoinder may be taken, either in abatement, or under the

(*m*) 6 T. R. 766. 1 Saund. 291. f. g. h. (n. 4.) Cro. Eliz. 554. Godb. 172. Latch, 152. 5 Co. 18. b. 5 East, 407. 2 Stra. 820. 1 Johns. R. 471. 6 ib. 108. 1 Wend. 380. 6 Mass. R. 462. 2 ib. 511. 11 ib. 419.

(*n*) 5 East, 407. Peake Ev. (2d ed.) 205.

(*o*) 7 T. R. 279.

CHAP. V.

general issue (*p*): Because the fact, that A. is the sole owner of the property, *contradicts* the declaration; since it proves that the trespass committed, was not upon joint property of *A. and B.*, and consequently, is not the trespass complained of.

As to the joinder or nonjoinder of *defendants*—

Nonjoinder, &c, of defendants: In contract:

§ 114. In an action on *contract*, if one is sued alone, where another ought by law to have been made co-defendant with him—(as if A. is sued alone, on a joint obligation or promise, made by himself and B); advantage can be taken of the nonjoinder of B. only *in abatement*; unless the mistake appears, (as hereafter mentioned), from the *plaintiff's own pleading* (*q*). For the obligation is *A's* act, though not his *sole* act; and the promise is his, though not his *sole* promise. The fact then, that B. is a co-obligor, or co-promissor with A., does not prove that the obligation, in the one case, is not *A's act*, nor that *A. did not promise*, in the other (13); and therefore does not *disprove the declaration.*

(*p*) Cro. Eliz. 143. 473. Gouldsb. 77. Clayt. 121. Bac. Abr. *Tresp.* I. 2. (3). *Lacy* v. *Barns & al.* Sup. C. (Connecticut.) 1805. M. S. 6 Pick. 222. Gow. on Partnership, 159.

(*q*) 5 Burr. 2611. 2 Black. Rep. 947. 5 T. R. 651. 7 ib. 313. 1 Saund. 291. b. (n. 4.) 2 N. Rep. 365. Cowp. 832. 5 Co. 119. 1 Bos. & P. 72. 18 Johns. R. 459. *Cont.* 2 Salk. 440.

(13) It is suggested by Mr Serjeant *Williams*, (1 Saund. 291. f. g. (n. 4), that since the nonjoinder of one of two joint *promissors as defendant*, is held to be only matter of *abatement*, the rule ought, for the sake of consistency, to be the same as to joint

CHAP. V.

Nonjoinder, &c, of defendants: In contract:

The rule is the same, and for the same reason, where two only are sued upon a *joint and several* contract, made by *three*, or more (*r*). For the fact, that another or others bound themselves by the same contract, does not prove that the *defendants did not* contract, as stated in the declaration.

§ 115. But in an action on contract, if it appears from the face of the *declaration*, or of any other pleading on the part of the *plaintiff*, that a person, not made defendant in the suit, was a joint contractor with the defendant, and that such person is still living, (as he must be presumed to be, unless the contrary is alleged); the nonjoinder of him as defendant, is a good ground of *demurrer*, or motion

(*r*) 1 Saund. 291. e. (n. 4.) Bro. Ab. *Obligation*, 94. Yelv. 27. a. *note*. 1 Peters, 73.

---

promissees; i. e. that the nonjoinder of one of two joint *promissees as plaintiff*, should be pleadable in *abatement only*. But with submission, are not the two cases essentially different? If A. & B. make a joint promise, it is nevertheless true, that *each* of them promises: And if so, it follows, that a declaration on the promise, against A. alone, alleging that *he* promised, is not disproved by the admission, that B. promised *jointly with him*. But if a promise is made *to* A. & B. jointly, it would seem not correct, to say that there is a promise to *each* of them: And therefore, a declaration by A. alone, alleging the promise to have been made *to* him, without naming B. as a co-promissee, is falsified, by proof that the promise was made to *both of them jointly*. In other words, there is a *variance* between the declaration and the proof. — Such, at any rate, is the principle of the distinction recognized by the authorities — a distinction, which, it is believed, is *not* 'without a difference.'

Nonjoinder, &c, of defendants: In contract:

in *arrest of judgment* — and (if judgment be given for the plaintiff), may be assigned for *error* (*s*). For in this case, the pleading of the plaintiff himself shows, that he has no right to recover in the suit, *as it is brought;* and as the mistake appears upon the record, by his *own showing;* there is no need of the defendant's *pleading* it. (*Vid. ante*, § 109.)

§ 116. If, on a contract made by one person only, he and *another* are sued, as upon a contract made by *both*, the misjoinder is a good ground of defence, under the *general issue* (*t*). For the contract made is *not the same*, as that declared upon. The proof of the former therefore *disproves* the declaration.

And in an action against *two* as joint contractors — as in assumpsit against A. & B. as joint promissors — if the jury find that A. promised, but that B. did *not;* A. may arrest the judgment (*u*). For the contract declared upon, is disproved, by the verdict (*v*). And when the action is thus brought against *two*, upon a contract made by *one* of them only, the plaintiff cannot enter a *noll. pros.* as to the other, and then proceed against the party bound,

(*s*) 5 Burr. 2614. 1 Saund. 153. (n. 1.) 291. b. c. (n. 4.) 6 T. R. 769. 1 Vent. 34.

(*t*) Clayt. 114. 1 East, 48. 2 Day, 272. 2 New Rep. 454. 11 Johns. R. 101. 1 Esp. Rep. 363.

(*u*) 3 East, 62. 1 Keb. 284. Carth. 361. 3 Brod. & Bing. 54.

(*v*) 1 Keb. 284.

alone (*w*). To allow this, would be to enable the plaintiff, by his own act, not only to defeat a good defence upon the merits; but also virtually to *substitute* one action for another — or rather, to transform an action against A. & B., into an action against A. alone.

Nonjoinder, &c, of defendants: In contract:

In tort.

§ 117. If several are sued for a TORT, committed by *one* of them only; the joinder of the others is no ground of *abatement*, nor can advantage be taken of it, as a *misjoinder*, in any way (*x*). For of co-defendants, in actions *ex delicto*, some may be *convicted*, and others *acquitted;* and the proper plea for those not actually guilty, is the *general* issue. But a plea *in abatement*, by one of the defendants, that the wrong in question was committed by the *others*, without his concurrence, is ill; because it is, in effect, the *general issue*, which is pleadable only *to the action*.

§ 118. If, on the other hand, one is sued alone, for a *tort* committed by himself and *others jointly;* the nonjoinder of the others is, in general, no ground of exception, either in abatement or otherwise (*y*). For a tort, committed by several, may regularly be treated as *joint* or *several*, or as *partly* joint, and *partly* several, at the election of the plaintiff. And as he consequently has, by the general rule, the

(*w*) 4 Taunt. 470. 3 Esp. Rep. 76. 5 Ib. 47. *Cont.* 5 Johns. R. 160. 1 Pick. 500.

(*x*) 1 Saund. 291. d. (n. 4.)

(*y*) Bac. Abr. *Tresp.* G. 1. & I. 1. 8 Co. 159. 1 Saund. 291. d. (n. 4.) 3 East, 62.

CHAP. V.

Nonjoinder, &c, of defendants: In tort.

right by law, to sue *any one* of them only — or all — or any number of them together — or *each* of them, in a several action; the nonjoinder of any of the wrong-doers is no defence, in any form.

§ 119. But there is an exception to the last rule, where one is sued alone in tort, upon a cause of action, arising out of, or concerning, *real property* held jointly, or in common, by himself and another. In this case, the nonjoinder of the other tenant is pleadable in abatement, although the action sounds in *tort* (*z*). For the probable ground of this exception to the general rule, see ch. 4, § 76.

§ 120. When a suit is defeated, by a plea in abatement, for the nonjoinder of another person, who should have been made a co-defendant; the latter may, in a subsequent action for the same cause, and in which he is made such, plead in abatement, that still another ought to have been sued (*a*). And in case of several successive suits for the same cause, *each new* defendant, disclosed in the next preceding suit, by a plea in abatement, may plead, in the same manner, that another, still, should have been joined, as defendant (*b*). For the new defendant cannot be deprived of his right thus to plead, by the omission of the defendant, or defendants, in the prior suit, to disclose the names of *all* those,

(*z*) 5 T. R. 651. 1 Saund. 291. e. (n. 4.) 2 Black. Com. 182. Com. Dig. *Abatement*, F. 6.

(*a*) 3 East, 70–1.

(*b*) Ib.

who ought to have joined in it. And the same rule holds, throughout any series of actions in which new joint contractors are successively disclosed.

§ 121. But *the same* defendant, who, in a prior suit, has pleaded the nonjoinder of *one* joint contractor, cannot plead, when afterwards sued on the same contract as co-defendant with the latter, that there is still *another* joint contractor, who should have been made defendant (*c*). This he is *estopped* to do, by his plea, in the preceding suit: For he ought, by his plea in *that* suit, to have 'given the plaintiff *a better writ*,' by naming *all* the joint contractors.

VI. The *Pendency of a prior suit*, for the same cause.

Pendency of a prior suit.

§ 122. It is, in general, a good plea in abatement, that there is a prior action, (similar, or concurrent), pending between the same parties, for the same cause (*d*). For the law, which 'abhors a multiplicity of suits,' will not permit a defendant to be harassed, by two or more actions for the same thing, where a complete remedy might be obtained by one of them. The object of the rule is to prevent *vexation*.

(*c*) Ib.

(*d*) Thel. Dig. 270. Com. Dig. *Abatement*, H. 24. Bac. Abr. *Abatement*, M. 5 Co. 61—2. Doct. Pl. 10. 67.

§ 123. To give effect to this plea, it is not necessary that both suits be of the *same kind:* It is sufficient for this purpose, that they are *concurrent* (*e*). Thus, in replevin, it is a good plea in abatement, that a prior action of *trespass*, for the same taking, is depending. And when trespass and trover are *concurrent*, the pendency of one when the other is brought, is pleadable in abatement of the latter (*f*). For the *vexation* is the same, as if both suits were of the same kind. And the identity of the cause of action, in the two cases, may be shown by *averment.*

§ 124. But where the cause of action is not *the same* in both suits, the pendency of the first will not abate the second (*g*). Such a case is not within the reason, or even the terms, of the above general rule. Hence, in debt on a bond secured by mortgage, the pendency of a prior action of *ejectment*, for the land mortgaged, is no cause of abatement (*h*).

§ 125. It is immaterial whether the first suit is pending, or not, at the time of the defendant's *pleading* in abatement of the second. If the first was pending, when the second was *commenced;* the latter may be abated, as being *vexatious ab initio* (*i*).

(*e*) Iid.

(*f*) Bac. Abr. *Abatement*, M. Hob. 184. Hutt. 3. Doct. Pl. 10. Com. R. 595.

(*g*) 5 Co. 61—2. Hob. 184. Com. Dig. *Abatement*, H. 24.

(*h*) Doug. 417. 2 Atk. 344. Pow. on Mortg. 417.

(*i*) Doct. Pl. 10. Bac. Abr. *Abatement*, M. 3 Inst. Cler. 118. Gilb. H. C. P. 255—6. 5 Mass. R. 177.

And on principle, it seems, that this plea can never prevail, except in cases where the latter suit is *vexatious*. CHAP. V.

§ 126. Hence, where it appears that the first action must have been *ineffectual*, the courts of Connecticut have often determined that its pendency shall not abate the second (*k*): Because in such a case, the latter is not *vexatious*.

§ 127. The plea of a prior suit pending, for the same cause, is good, although there be a *new* defendant added in the second: As where the first action is against *A. only*, and the second against *A.* & *B.* (*l*). And by the opinion of three judges, (*Holt*, Ch. J. doubting), it was held that the second suit must abate, as to *both* defendants (14).

And when, on the other hand, one of two or more defendants in the first action is *omitted* in the second—(as if the first action is against A. & B.

(*k*) 1 Root, 355. 562.

(*l*) Carth. 96—7. Comb. 144. 1 Show. 75. Ham. N. Prius. (Am. ed.) 96. Hob. 137.

(14) Where the liability of the defendants is *several*, as well as joint, (as in an action for a joint *tort*), *qu.* whether the second action ought, on principle, to abate *quoad the new* defendant. For *he* is not, in fact, subjected to vexation by the second suit; and the action is, by the supposition, of such a nature, as might be prosecuted against himself alone. Such, however, was the action, in the case referred to, in the text. Was not Ld *Holt's* doubt, then, well founded?

and the second against A. *only*)—it seems manifest that the second must abate: The case being plainly within the reason of the general rule.

§ 128. On a writ of *partition*, the defendant may, by the common law, plead in abatement the pendency of a prior writ of the same kind, brought by himself against the *plaintiff* in the second, for a partition of the same land (*m*): Because the same end, which the plaintiff in the second suit seeks to attain, may be fully attained in the first.—But since the statute 8 & 9 W. III, c. 39, there can be *no plea in abatement* in any suit for partition of lands (*mm*).

§ 129. By the English law, the pendency of a prior action, in an *inferior* court, is not pleadable in abatement of another, brought in one of the *Superior* Courts of Westminster (*n*). This rule seems to have originated in the general authority of the latter courts to *supersede* the jurisdiction of the former, upon the application of defendants in the inferior courts (14 *a*).

(*m*) Gilb. H. C. P. 260. Bac. Abr. *Abatement*, M. Dy. 92. b. *Cont.* 1 Brownl. 158.

(*mm*) 2 Lill. Ab. 357. 3 Black. Com. 302.

(*n*) 5 Co. 62. Bac. Abr. *Abatement*, M. 2 Wils. 87. Com. Dig. *Abatement*, H. 24.

(14 *a*.) From the language of Ch. J. *Eyre* (Fitzg. 313), it might perhaps be inferred, that the reason of this exception to the general rule is the presumed *want of jurisdiction* in the inferior court. (See also 1 Chitt. Pl. 443. n. r). But upon this suppo-

§ 130. It is no cause for abating an *indictment*, that a prior indictment is pending against the defendant, for the same offence. Because the court, in the exercise of its *discretionary control* over prosecutions by indictment, may *quash the first* (o). The same is true of *informations for crimes* filed *ex officio*, by a prosecuting officer (oo).

§ 131. But this rule does not extend to the case of two informations *qui tam*, &c, for the same offence. For on such an information, the situation and rights of the prosecutor are analogous to those of the plaintiff in a civil suit; and the court has, therefore, no such discretionary power over them, as it exercises over indictments (p).

Defects in the writ.

§ 132. VII. In general, any *irregularity*, *defect* or *informality*, in the terms, form, or structure, of the writ, or in the mode of issuing it, is a ground of abatement (q).

(o) 2 Hawk. P. C. c. 34, § 1. Cro. Car. 147. Fost. 104, & *seq.* 2 East, 226.

(oo) Doug. 240.

(p) 2 Hawk. P. C. c. 26, § 63. Doug. 240, (n. 1.) 2d ed.

(q) Com. Dig. *Abatement*, H. 1-6. Lawes' Pl. 106.

---

sition, there would seem to be no propriety in limiting the exception to prior suits in *inferior* courts; since a prior suit, pending even in a *superior* court, not having *jurisdiction* of it, would, on principle, afford no cause for abating a second suit for the same cause, in any other court. Upon the same supposition, a replication, alleging jurisdiction in the inferior court, would seem to be a good answer to the plea.

CHAP. V.

§ 133. The defects or mistakes, which fall within this general description, are quite multifarious, and hardly admit of an explanation in detail. Among those usually enumerated, are any *uncertainty* or *repugnancy* — want of *date*, or an *impossible* date — want of *venue*, or, in *local* actions, a *wrong* venue — a *defective return*, &c, &c (*r*). The return is 'defective', when the time, between the date of the writ and the return-day, is too short to afford the defendant such *notice*, in regard to time, as the law requires (*s*).

§ 134. If the writ is made returnable to any other than the *first* term of the court, after it issues, when there is sufficient intervening time for its return to that term; it may for this cause be abated; but a plea in abatement, in such a case, is *unnecessary*. For the writ is *void*, and therefore liable to be set aside, *on motion* (*t*) (15).

(*r*) Com. Dig. *Abatement*, H. 1-17. Lawes' Pl. 106.

(*s*) Com. Dig. *Abatement*, H. 15. 2 Keb. 461. 2 Wils. 117. 6 Pick. 370.

(*t*) 3 Wils. 341. 2 Salk. 700. 1 Root, 315. 316. 5 Mass. R. 100.

---

(15) It is necessary to the protection of the defendant, that the writ should be considered as *void*, and not as *merely abateable*. If the rule were otherwise, no advantage could be taken of the irregularity, until the arrival of the term, to which it is made returnable — which might be at any future term, however remote; and the defendant might consequently be held to bail, or imprisoned, during the whole intermediate period. But the writ being *void*, all acts done in obedience to it, are so: And the defendant, if arrested under it, is entitled to an immediate discharge.

§ 135. If the sheriff's *return of service*, as indorsed by him upon the writ, is defective *upon the face of it* — (as if it appears, from his indorsement, that the defendant has not had *sufficient notice* of the suit); this is a ground of abatement, or for setting the writ aside, on *motion* (*u*). But if *sufficient upon the face of it;* the defendant cannot falsify it, on a plea in abatement; and his only remedy is an action against the sheriff, for a *false return* (*v*). For it is a general rule of the common law, that such *official* acts shall not be falsified, except by a proceeding, to which the *officer* is a party, and which is commenced for the *direct* and *express* purpose of falsifying it.

§ 136. In the state of Connecticut, however, if the service is *actually defective*, the defendant has always been allowed to *prove* it so, under a plea in abatement, even in *contradiction* of the officer's indorsement.

§ 137. VIII. That *the action is misconceived*, is pleadable in abatement: As if *assumpsit* is brought, when *account* is the only proper remedy; or *trespass*, when *case* is the proper action (*w*). But a plea in *abatement*, for this cause, is unnecessary and unusual. For if the mistake appears upon the face of the

Action misconceived.

(*u*) Com. Dig. *Abatement*, H. 15. 2 Wils. 117.

(*v*) 2 Stra. 813. T. Jon. 39. 1 Black. R. 393. Com. Dig. *Retorn*, G. 4 Mass. R. 478.

(*w*) Com. Dig. *Abatement* G. 5. 1 Show. 71. Hob. 199. Lawes' Pl. 106. Tidd, 579.

CHAP. V.

declaration, it is fatal on *demurrer;* and if not, advantage may be taken of it under the *general issue.*

Commenced too soon.

§ 138. IX. That *the right of action had not accrued*, at the commencement of the suit, may be pleaded in abatement (*x*): As, when an action on contract is commenced, *before* the time, appointed for performance. This plea also is seldom used, and for the same reason, as is mentioned under the last head.

The foregoing enumeration of pleas in abatement comprehends all the principal causes or grounds of abatement, known to the common law (15 *a*).

(*x*) 2 Lev. 197. Benl. 57. Cro. Eliz. 325. Hob. 199. Com. Dig. *Action*, E. 1.

(15 *a*) What are here called pleas 'in abatement', without further discrimination, comprehend all those pleas, which, under the more minute and complex classification of dilatory pleas, presented in the first section of this chapter, follow pleas to 'the person of the *plaintiff*.' And the nine foregoing kinds, or classes, of pleas in *abatement*, enumerated in the present chapter, (from § 69 to § 138, inclusive), are under that more minute classification, denominated as follows: — 1. The plea of *coverture* of the defendant, and that of the *death* of a party, are pleas 'to the *person*' — i. e. the person of the defendant, in the first case, and of either party, in the second. — 2. The plea of *variance* between the count and the writ, or between the writ and the instrument, &c, declared on, is a plea 'to the count'; (as all writs were formerly recited at full length in the *count*). — 3. The pleas of *misnomer*, want of *addition*, &c — of *nonjoinder*, or *misjoinder* of parties, and pleas founded on any *repugnancy*, *defect* or *informality*, upon the face of the writ, are pleas 'to the *form* of the writ'. — 4. The plea of a *prior*

Ante, § 64, (n. 8.)

§ 139. When a plea in abatement is true, in point of fact, and sufficient in law, (in which case the writ must abate), the *plaintiff* may — in order to prevent unnecessary delay and expense — enter a *cassetur breve*, or *cassetur billa;* i. e. may pray that his writ or bill may be *quashed*, to the intent, that he may sue out a better writ, or exhibit a better bill, for the same cause (*y*). And judgment will, of course, be entered according to his prayer. Whenever the defect is such as cannot be amended, this is the more eligible course for the plaintiff.

Nolle prosequi.

§ 140. There is also another mode, in which the plaintiff may, in general, after a plea in abatement, and in most other stages of the suit, put an end to his own action, in whole, or in part; viz. by entering a *nolle prosequi* (*z*) — which is an entry upon the record, that he will no further prosecute his suit against the defendant, in respect either to the *whole*, or some *part*, of his alleged cause of action.

(*y*) Lawes' Pl. 166. 7 T. R. 698. 3 Anst. 935. Tidd, 633. 1 Chitt. Pl. 454. 2 Ib. 590.

(*z*) Lawes' Pl. 166. Tidd, 617. 620-1. 1 Bos. & P. 157. *Vid.* 1 Peters, 74, *& seq.*

---

suit pending for the same cause — that the action is *misconceived* — or that the suit was commenced before the right of action had accrued, is a plea 'to the *action* of the writ.'

CHAP. V.

Of the mode of pleading in abatement and the effect of the plea (16).

§ 141. If matter of mere abatement is pleaded in *bar;* or if matter, which goes only in bar, is pleaded in *abatement;* the plea, in either case, is ill (*a*). For otherwise, all distinction between these different classes of pleas would be confounded. In the former case too, judgment *in chief* must be given for the plaintiff (*b*); since the plea, which is necessarily ill, is to *the action.* There are, however, as has before been shown, (*ante*, §§ 37. 43), certain defences, which are good, either in abatement *or* in bar; and to these the above rule is, of course, inapplicable.

The plea, how to begin, and conclude.

§ 142. A plea in abatement, for matter *apparent* upon the face of the writ, should, in general, both *begin* and *conclude*, by praying 'judgment of the writ,' (or 'of the writ and declaration'), and that the same may be quashed: But where the cause of abatement is *extrinsic*, the plea, it is said, should not

(*a*) Com. Dig. *Abatement*, I. 12. 14. 4 T. R. 227. 2 Saund. 209. c. d. (n. 1.) 1 Mod. 239.

(*b*) 2 Ld Ray. 1020. 1 East, 634.

(16) The great degree of *certainty and accuracy*, required in dilatory pleas of all kinds, has been before explained, (ante, §§ 66. 67, and ch. 3, §§ 57. 58). The rules on this subject need not, therefore, be here repeated.

begin, but only *conclude*, with this prayer (*c*). The precedents, however, do not all appear to conform to this distinction (*d*). If the action is by *bill*, the plea should, in like manner, pray 'judgment of *the* bill' (*e*).

The plea how to begin, and conclude.

§ 143. When the plea goes to the *person* of the defendant, (as if it be, that she is a *feme covert*), the form of praying judgment is, 'whether the defendant ought to answer'—or 'ought to be compelled to answer' (*f*): It being rather the *personal privilege* of the defendant, than any fault in the writ itself, that constitutes the ground of exception.

§ 144. Any mistake, in the form of *beginning* or *concluding* a plea in abatement, is fatal to the plea (*g*). Great accuracy is therefore required, in these two, as well as in all other particulars. Upon these two, indeed, depends the *character* of the plea, as distinguished from a plea to *the action*.

§ 145. The character of a plea depends, regularly, upon the form of its *commencement and conclusion*: or (which is the same thing), upon the nature of the *judgment* which it prays, in its commence-

(*c*) Lawes' Pl. 108—9. Com. Dig. *Abatement*, I. 12. 2 Saund. 209. a. d. (n). 2 Chitt. Pl. 415. Tidd, 577. 584. 3 Black. Com. 303.

(*d*) 1 Chitt. Pl. 451. 2 Ib. 413—420. Bac. Abr. *Abatement*, P.

(*e*) 2 Saund. 209. d. Holt, 3. 5 Mod. 144. Tidd, 577. Com. Dig. *Abatement*, I. 12.

(*f*) Lawes' Pl. 109. Tidd, 584. 2 Saund. 209. d.

(*g*) 2 Saund. 209. c. d. 1 Chitt. Pl. 445. 3 T. R. 185. 1 B. & A. 173.

CHAP. V.

The plea how to begin, and conclude.

ment and conclusion. So that if these are *alike* (both in abatement, or both in bar); they are decisive of the character of the plea, whatever may be its *matter* (*h*).

§ 146. If therefore, the defendant pleads matter, which goes only *in bar* (as a release), but begins and concludes *in abatement*, (as by praying judgment of the *writ*); the plea is in *abatement* (*i*). And the same commencement and conclusion, which the plea requires, are to be followed in the *replication*, *rejoinder*, &c, until an *issue* is tendered; and those, tendering an issue, require the same *commencement*.

§ 147. And on the other hand, if the matter pleaded goes only *in abatement*, (as *misnomer*, or any informality in the *writ*), but begins and concludes *in bar*; the plea is *in bar* (*j*). (17).

§ 148. But when the beginning and conclusion of the plea *differ*, (the former being *in abatement*, and the latter *in bar*, or *è converso*), there is some confusion in the books — not indeed as to the *legal* sufficiency of the plea, which is ill of course, by

(*h*) Ld Ray. 593. 1019. Bac. Abr. *Abatement*, P. Latch, 178. 2 Saund. 209. c. d. (n. 1). Lawes' Pl. 107. Tidd, 583—4.

(*i*) Iid. 6 Taunt. 587.

(*j*) 1 Sid. 189. 190.

(17) By a plea 'in abatement,' in these distinctions, regarding the different characters of pleas, is meant a *dilatory* plea of any kind.

reason of the discrepancy—but as to the effect of the discrepancy, upon the *character* of the plea, and consequently upon the mode of *answering* it, and the kind of judgment to be rendered upon it.

The plea how to begin, and conclude.

According to the weight of authority, however, the following appear to be the correct distinctions:—

§ 149. When the beginning and conclusion thus differ, the *subject-matter* of the plea would seem to be the most simple and most obvious criterion of its character. And such is the established rule, when the application of this criterion would favour the *plaintiff;* though it is otherwise, when the same criterion would operate in favour of the *defendant:* A distinction, derived from the policy of discouraging *dilatory* pleas.

§ 150. Thus if matter, which goes only *in bar,* begins in abatement and concludes in bar—or *è converso;* it is a plea *in bar* (*k*), by reason of its *subject-matter*—and being ill, by reason of the discrepancy between its commencement and conclusion; the plaintiff, by demurring as *in bar,* (i. e. by concluding his demurrer, with a prayer of his *debt,* or *damages*), is entitled to *final* judgment upon it.

§ 151. So also, if matter, which goes only in *abatement,* begins in bar, and concludes in abate-

(*k*) Ld Ray. 593. 1018. 2 Saund. 209. c. d. (n. 1). 6 Mod. 103.

CHAP. V.

The plea how to begin, and conclude.

ment, or *è converso;* the plaintiff *may* demur, as *in bar* (*l*). And if he thus demurs, he entitles himself to *final* judgment (18). But if issue is joined, on such a plea, and found for the *defendant;* the judgment will be, as on a plea in *abatement*, viz. that the writ be quashed; though if the same issue were found for the *plaintiff*, he would be entitled to judgment *in chief* (*m*).

§ 152. If a plea of matter, which goes indifferently either in bar *or* in abatement, differs in its commencement and conclusion; the plaintiff may, with equal propriety, demur to it, either *as* in bar, or in abatement (*n*). For the beginning and conclusion *neutralize* each other, as regards the character of the plea; and its *subject-matter*, (as it may operate either way), furnishes no criterion. The judgment will therefore follow the nature of the *prayer*, with which the demurrer concludes. It is obvious, then, that the course, most advantageous to the plaintiff, is to demur to the plea, as *in bar;* as by thus demurring, he will entitle himself to judgment *quod recuperet.*

(*l*) 1 Chitt. Pl. 446. 456—7. 2 Saund. 209. d. (n. 1). 1 East, 634. 10 Johns. R. 49.

(*m*) 1 Chitt. Pl. 446. 1 East, 634. 2 Saund. 209. d. (n. 1). 2 Ld Ray. 1018.

(*n*) Bac. Abr. *Abatement*, P. 1 Vent. 136. 3 Mod. 281.

---

(18) The rule, allowing the plaintiff to demur in this manner, originated in the same anxiety of courts of justice to *discourage* dilatory pleas. Were it not for this reason, the *matter* of the plea would determine its character, as under the last preceding rule.

Error assignable on the judgment, given on dilatory pleas.

§ 153. On a judgment, rendered upon any *dilatory* plea, *error* may be assigned, as well as upon a final judgment. But matter of mere abatement, if *not pleaded* in abatement, cannot be assigned for error (*o*). For if not thus pleaded, it is *waved* — as it would be unreasonable that a suit should be defeated, in its latter stages, by an exception, which might have been taken *in limine*.

§ 154. For a similar reason, it is an established rule, that to a *scire facias*, or debt on *judgment*, the defendant is not allowed to plead in abatement, (nor indeed in bar), any thing, which he might have pleaded in the original action (*p*).

Defendant may not demur in abatement.

§ 155. A defendant cannot 'demur in abatement' (*q*). This rule appears, from the application of it in the books, to have two different meanings, or to be applied in two different senses: 1. That the defendant cannot *demur*, for defects or mistakes in the *writ* (*r*) (19): 2. That he cannot plead *in abatement*, for the insufficiency of the *declaration* (*s*).

(*o*) 10 Mod. 166. 6 T. R. 766. Carth. 124. Com. Dig. *Abatement*, I. 36. 2 H. Black. 267. 299. Bac. Abr. *Error*, K. 5.

(*p*) Bac. Abr. *Abatement*, O. 1 Salk. 2. 310. 1 Atk. 292. 2 Stra. 732. 1 Wils. 258. 1 Saund. 219. c. (n. 8.) Co. Litt. 303.

(*q*) Bac. Abr. *Abatement*, P. 1 Salk. 220. Willes, 410. 479. 6 Mod. 195. 198. Andr. 147.

(*r*) Plowd. 73. n. 6 Mod. 198.

(*s*) Plowd. 73. n. Willes, 410. 479. Lawes' Pl. 172. Gilb. H. C. P. 259.

---

(19) It was formerly held otherwise. (Plowd. 73. Dy. 341).

CHAP. V.

The former he cannot do, because a demurrer never reaches the *writ;* nor the latter, because no advantage can be taken of insufficiency in *the pleadings*, by a plea *in abatement* (*ante*, ch. 2, § 34). And on the plaintiff's joining in the demurrer, in the one case, or demurring to the plea, in the other, *final* judgment will be given in his favour (*t*) (20).

General prayer of judgment, sufficient.

§ 156. Although, as we have seen, the prayer of a *wrong* judgment, in the conclusion of a plea, makes the plea faulty; yet a mere prayer of judgment, not specifying any particular *kind* of judgment, is sufficient (*u*). For it is the duty of the court to render such a judgment as the *legal effect* of the pleading requires.

The writ may be abated, in part only.

§ 157. A writ may be abated as to *part* of what the plaintiff demands, and stand good for the residue (*v*). Thus, in debt on two bonds, or assumpsit on two promises, the defendant may plead, as to *one* of them, the nonjoinder of a co-obligor, or co-promissor, and thus abate the writ, *quoad* that one bond or promise *only*. And a judgment, thus abat-

(*t*) Plowd. 73. n. 6 Mod. 198. Willes, 411.
(*u*) 2 Lev. 19. 1 Saund. 97. Willes, 410. 411. 4 East, 502. 509.
(*v*) Lawes' Pl. 106-7. 2 Saund. 210. a. (n. 1.) 2 Bos. & P. 420. Com. Dig. *Abatement*, N. Bac. Abr. *Abatement*, L.

---

(20) But if a prisoner, indicted of a *capital* offence, demurs in abatement; the judgment is only a *respondeat ouster*, (2 Hawk. P. C. c. 31, § 6): A rule founded on the benignity of the law, *in favorem vitæ*.

ing the writ *in part*, may be given on a plea, praying that the *whole* may be abated (*w*): It being the duty of the court to give the plea its proper effect, if the judgment prayed is of the *right kind*.

Judgment on pleas in abatement, not conclusive of the merits.

§ 158. As a plea in abatement does not go to the *merits* of the cause; a judgment upon it does not, in general, conclude either party, *quoad the cause of action*, and is therefore *no bar* to a subsequent action for the same cause (*x*): The general principle, upon which a prior judgment bars a subsequent action, being, that the *merits* of the controversy have been already decided in the former suit.

But the above rule does not hold, when the judgment upon a plea in abatement goes *in chief*—as, in some cases, it does (*y*). For such a judgment is, in its nature, conclusive as to the *right of action*.

What judgment pleas in abatement require.

§ 159. As to the *judgment*, to be rendered on pleas in abatement, the distinctions are the following: —

1. If the plea is determined in favour of the *defendant*, upon an issue either in law or fact; the judgment is, that the writ, (or, as the case may

(*w*) Iid.

(*x*) Com. Dig. *Action*, L. 4. Bac. Abr. *Pleas*, &c, I. 13. 4 Co. 43. a. 6 Ib. 7. 8. 8 Ib. 37. b. 98. 2 Vent. 170.

(*y*) Iid.

CHAP. V.

be, the bill), be *quashed* (z). And this judgment, though it does not decide the *right of action*, puts an end to the suit; unless the mistake, on which the plea is founded, may be, and is, corrected by amendment — in which case, the amended writ, (or bill), becomes a new one, and the suit may then proceed.

2. If the plaintiff prevails, on a *demurrer* to the plea; the judgment is *interlocutory*, viz. a *respondeat ouster* — that the defendant answer over (a); under which judgment, he may plead any plea, *subsequent* (in the order of pleading) to that, which has been overruled. (*Post.* ch. 9, § 41.)

3. If an issue in *fact* is joined on a plea in abatement, and found for the *plaintiff*; *final* judgment is awarded in his favour (b): A rule, which extends to all *dilatory* pleas (21). The object of the rule appears to be, to discourage *false* dilatory pleas.

(z) Bac. Abr. *Abatement*, P. Yelv. 112.

(a) 2 Saund. 211. (n. 3.) Yelv. 112. Bac. Abr. *Abatement*, P. 3 Black. Com. 303. 1 Vent. 22. 137.

(b) Com. Dig. *Abatement*, I. 15. 1 East, 544. 2 Wils. 368. 1 Lev. 163. 1 Vent. 22. Yelv. 112. T. Ray. 119. 1 Ld Ray. 594. 2 Saund. 211. (n. 3.)

---

(21) This rule does not extend to the case of indictments for *capital* offences. In such cases, if an issue in fact, joined on a plea in abatement, is found *against* the prisoner; the judgment, (*in favorem vitæ*), is a *respondeat ouster:* So that he is still permitted to plead to the *merits*, (2 Hawk. P. C. c. 23, § 128. 8 East, 107).

§ 160. In the state of Connecticut, the Supreme Court of Errors, in the year 1818, recognized the following distinction, as established by the ancient usage of the state: viz. If an issue in fact, joined on a plea in abatement, is tried by the *jury*, and found for the plaintiff; *final* judgment shall be given for him: But if the issue is tried by the *court*, (as, by the statute-law of the state, it may be, with the mutual consent of the parties); the judgment shall be a *respondeat ouster*: A distinction, for which it seems difficult to assign any satisfactory reason. CHAP. V.

CHAPTER VI.

OF PLEAS TO THE ACTION.

PART I.—*Of the General Issue, and Special Issues; including also Immaterial and Informal Issues.*

CHAP. VI. PART I.

Of issues in general.

SECTION 1. AN *issue*, in pleading, is defined to be a *single*, *certain*, and *material* point, issuing out of the allegations of the parties, and consisting, regularly, of an *affirmative* and *negative* (*c*) (1). The word 'issue,' (*exitus*), in the sense in which it is applied to pleading, signifies *end*, *termination*, or *conclusion* (*d*); and is thus applied, because an issue brings the pleadings to a *close*.

§ 2. The above definition comprehends, as well issues in *law*, as in fact. As to the former, however,

(*c*) Co. Litt. 126. a. Com. Dig. *Pleader*, R. Bac. Abr. *Pleas*, &c, G. 1. 5 Peters, 149.

(*d*) 3 Black. Com. 314. Finch's Law, 396.

---

(1) This definition describes a *good* issue. But when a direct affirmative and negative are predicated of an *immaterial* fact, they form what is called, in law, *an issue*, though a bad one, as being *immaterial*. An issue *in law*, however, can never be immaterial: Since it reaches back through *all* the pleadings, and puts their sufficiency, (in point of substance, at least), in issue. *Vid. Demurrer*, ch. 9.

Issue.

nothing further need be observed at present, than that when an issue in law is said to consist of a *single* point, the proposition does not mean that such an issue involves, necessarily, only a *single* rule or principle of law — or that it brings into question the legal sufficiency of a *single fact* only: The meaning of it is merely, that an issue in law reduces the whole controversy to the single question, whether the facts, confessed by the issue, are *sufficient in law* to maintain the action, or the defence, of the party who alleged them — instead of leaving the controversy, (as is done in most courts, under any other system of jurisprudence than that of the common law), open to a discussion *at large*, of all the various matters of both fact and law, which may, on each side, be brought to bear upon the cause. The *singleness* of issues in *fact*, (as will appear hereafter), admits of a similar explanation.

Must consist of an affirmative and negative.

§ 3. According to the strict original rule of the common law, every issue in fact, (with the exception of one or two anomalies), must consist of a *direct* affirmative allegation, on one side, and a *direct* negative, on the other (*e*). For of two affirmatives, or two negatives, though *inconsistent* with each other, the latter denies the former only *argumentatively;* and argumentative pleading, (as has been shown before, ch. 3, § 28), is not allowable. Thus, if a defendant pleads that his co-defendant is *dead;* a replication that he is '*alive*,' does not form a pro-

(*e*) Co. Litt. 126. a. 2 Black. Rep. 1312. 8 T. R. 278. Bac. Abr. *Pleas*, &c, G. 1. 5 Peters, 149.

CHAP. VI. PART I.

Issue.

per issue — for the reason just assigned (*f*). The replication should be, that the co-defendant '*is not dead;*' or, 'that he is alive, *without this*, that he is dead'— a form of negation, to be explained hereafter, under the head of *Traverse*.

§ 4. In one or two modern cases, however, the above rule has been somewhat relaxed. Thus, where the defendant pleaded that he was born in *France*, a replication that he was born in *England*, was held to form a good issue (*g*): And it is said, in the report last cited, to be sufficient, 'if the second affirmative is *so* contrary to the first, that the first cannot, *in any degree*, be true:' Any relaxation of the original rule tends, however, in some degree, to looseness and uncertainty in the formation of issues; and breaks in upon that *simplicity* and uniformity in their structure, which it is important to preserve. And it may be added, that no relaxation of the rule appears to be demanded, either by necessity or convenience; since a strict conformity to it is, of all modes of producing a regular and precise issue, the most natural, simple, and easy.

§ 5. One original exception to the above general rule, as to the formation of issues, occurs in the instance of a *writ of right*. The general issue to the count upon that writ, is, and ever has been, formed by *two affirmatives:* The averment on one side being, that the demandant has greater right than the

(*f*) Sav. 86. 1 Vent. 213.
(*g*) 1 Wils. 6. 2 Stra. 1177.

tenant; and on the other, that the tenant has greater right than the demandant — or, (more precisely), the demandant 'demands' the tenements as his right and inheritance; and the tenant, by way of denial, 'prays recognition to be made, *whether* he himself, or the demandant, has greater right,' &c (*h*). But by reason of the irregular and imperfect form of this plea, it is technically called, 'the *mise*,' as distinguished from general 'issues,' strictly so called (*i*).

§ 6. The other anomalous issue, before referred to, occurs in the general plea of denial, to a count in *dower;* which, to the extent of the interest demanded, is strictly analogous to a count upon a *writ of right* (*k*). The count in dower merely 'demands the third part of —— acres of land, &c, *as the dower*' of the demandant, 'of the endowment of J. S., heretofore her husband,' &c; and the general issue is, that J. S. was *not seised* of such estate, &c, that *he could endow* the demandant thereof, &c (*l*): A mode of negation, that is merely *argumentative.*

These two anomalies appear to form the only original exceptions to the general rule, that every issue must consist of a *direct* affirmative, and a *direct* negative. And the only reason for these exceptions

(*h*) Lawes' Pl. *App.* 232—3. 3 Black. Com. 195—6. 305. Ib. *App.* No. I, § 6. 2 Stra. 1177. 3 Chitt. Pl. 652.

(*i*) Iid.

(*k*) 3 Black. Com. 183.

(*l*) 2 Saund. 329. 330. Stearns' Real Actions, 473. 475.

CHAP. VI. PART I.

would seem to be, that they are conformable to the ancient precedents.

Issue.

§ 7. An issue, taken upon the declaration, is either *general* or *special*. The former is called the *general issue;* the latter, a *special* issue (*m*). Some respectable authorities, however, add a *third*, which they denominate a *common issue* (*n*)—a name given to no other than the single plea of *non est factum*, when pleaded to an action of *covenant broken;* for the reason of which, *vid. post.* note 2, page 308.

§ 8. The *general issue* denies all the material allegations in the declaration (*o*); by which are meant all those, which the plaintiff may be required to *prove:* Or, (more precisely), it *enables* the defendant to contest all such allegations, in evidence; and actually puts the plaintiff upon the proof of all, or any of them, which are thus contested. A *special* issue denies only some particular *part* of the declaration, which goes to the *gist* of the action (*p*). This distinction, between *general* and *special* issues, applies only to the *declaration:* An issue, joined upon any of the pleadings which *follow* the declaration, being called simply, 'an issue', without further description.

(*m*) Co. Litt. 126. a. Bac. Abr. *Pleas*, &c, G. 1.

(*n*) Tidd, 598. Lawes' Pl. 110. 113. *vid.* 8 T. R. 282.

(*o*) Bac. Abr. *Pleas*, &c, G. 1. Lawes' Pl. 110. 3 Black. Com. 305.

(*p*) Co. Litt. 126. a. Lawes' Pl. 112. 113. 145.

I. Of the *general issue* —

General issue.

§ 9. Though this plea denies all that is material in the declaration; the denial is not usually expressed in the *precise terms* of the allegations denied; but by a shorter, and more simple *formula*, which is tantamount to a specific and literal negation of all and each of them. Thus in the action of trespass — however numerous the acts complained of may be — the general plea of 'not guilty', (i. e. that the defendant *is not guilty* of the said trespasses, &c, or of any part thereof), is equivalent to an allegation that he *did not*, with force and arms and against the peace, commit the acts complained of, or any of them. And a similar explanation might be given of all other general issues.

§ 10. The general issues, in the principal actions now in use, are the following: —

In personal actions *ex delicto*, in general, whether sounding in trespass or case, and whether founded on misfeasance or nonfeasance, and including *eject-ment*, the general issue is, 'Not guilty' (*q*).

In *replevin*, the general issue is 'Non cepit' (*r*):

In *disseisin*, '*Nul tort, nul disseisin*' (*s*):

In *detinue*, '*Non detinet*' (*t*):

(*q*) Bac. Abr. *Pleas*, &c, G. 1. I. 1. 3 Black. Com. 305. App. No. II. § 4. Gilb. H. C. P. 57.

(*r*) Bac. Abr. *Replevin*, I. 2 Chitt. Pl. 508.

(*s*) 3 Black. Com. 305.

(*t*) 2 Chitt. Pl. 495.

CHAP. VI. PART I.

In *debt* on simple contract, '*Nil debet*' (*u*); or, against an *executor* or *administrator*, '*Non detinet*' (*v*):

In *debt* on *specialty*, '*Non est factum*' (*w*):

In debt on *judgment* or *recognizance*, '*Nul tiel record*' (*x*):

In debt on a *penal statute*, the more appropriate general issue is *nil debet*; because it corresponds to the *form* of the action (*y*). But as the object of the action is to enforce a penalty for an alleged *offence*; it seems that 'Not guilty' may be substituted for '*Nil debet*' (*z*).

In *covenant broken*, the general issue is the same as in *debt* on specialty—'*Non est factum*' (*a*); or at least, this is the only *general* plea, which goes in bar of the action (2).

(*u*) 3 Black. Com. 305. 2 Chitt. Pl. 459.
(*v*) Bac. Abr. *Pleas*, &c, I. 1. 2 Mod. 266. 1 Chitt. Pl. 476.
(*w*) Iid.
(*x*) 3 Black. Com. 330. 331. 2 Chitt. Pl. 488.
(*y*) 1 T. R. 462. 1 Chitt. Pl. 481. 2 Ib. 459. 2 Mass. R. 522.
(*z*) Mo. 302. 914. Cro. Eliz. 257. 621. 766. Noy, 56. Bac. Abr. *Pleas*, &c, I. 1. 1 T. R. 462. 5 Mass. R. 270.
(*a*) 2 Chitt. Pl. 496.

---

(2) According to respectable authorities, (Tidd, 593. Lawes' Pl. 113. 1 Chitt. Pl. 482), there is, to a declaration in *covenant broken, no* general issue: Since the plea of *non est factum*, which denies the *deed* only, and not *the breach*, does not put the *whole* declaration in issue. And therefore, it is said, that this plea, when used in this particular action, is to be called '*the common issue.*' It must indeed be admitted, that there is a difference between the effect of the plea of *non est factum*, in covenant broken, and in *debt* on specialty. A valid bond, or single bill, necessarily creates a

In *assumpsit*, the general issue is 'Non assumpsit' (*b*): Or, when the action is against an *executor* or administrator, 'that the said E. F. deceased' (the testator, or intestate), 'did not undertake, or promise', &c. 'Not guilty' was also formerly held to be a proper general issue in assumpsit (*c*); because the action, being entitled '*trespass* on the case', was deemed to partake of the nature of an action *ex delicto*. But as the action is, in substance, founded exclusively on *contract;* the last mentioned plea is not now considered as a proper answer to it;

(*b*) 3 Black. Com. 305. 2 Chitt. Pl. 423.
(*c*) Bac. Abr. *Pleas*, &c, G. 2. I. 1. 1 Lev. 142. 2 Stra. 1022. Esp. Dig. 167.

---

present debt; and the plea in question, by denying the deed, necessarily and *directly* denies the alleged *debt:* Whereas a *covenant* does not necessarily create, in the covenantee, a right to *damages;* because a breach may never occur. And though, if there be no covenant, there can be no *breach;* yet a denial of the covenant denies the breach, only by *consequence*, and not *directly*. As however *non est factum* is confessedly a *good* plea, in covenant broken, and also the most general form of denial, of which the action admits; there appears to be little use in distinguishing it, by the anomalous appellation of a 'common issue.' Indeed, the only peculiarity which distinguishes it, in this action, from other general issues — viz. that it does not put the *whole* declaration directly in issue — would seem rather to bring it within the description of a *special* issue. At any rate, if it is necessary or proper to give this plea, in the action of *covenant broken*, the peculiar denomination of a *common issue;* it would seem equally so, to distinguish the same plea by the same name, when pleaded to a *special* declaration, in debt *on a penal bond*. For the same reason, which authorizes its peculiar designation in the former action, exists, to the same extent, in the latter.

CHAP. VI. PART I.

but is still held to be aided by *verdict*, as being only an *informal* issue (*d*).

In *debt* for *rent* on a demise, '*rien en arrere*'; (nothing in arrear), as well as *nil debet*, is a good general issue (*e*). For the former plea, as well as the latter, directly denies that any rent is due; and is, therefore, a direct denial of the alleged *debt*.

§ 11. But in *covenant broken* for rent, (in which the covenant itself is set out, and the action founded upon it), '*rien en arrere*', is not a good plea (*f*): Because it impliedly confesses both the *covenant* stated, and the *breach*, and alleges nothing in *avoidance* of either: Whereas, in the preceding case of *debt* for rent, though reserved by *deed*, it is neither necessary nor usual to allege the *deed;* and if alleged, it is but *inducement*, and therefore need not be directly *answered* in pleading. And the *gist* of the action of debt being the mere fact *of rent in arrear;* the plea of *nil debet*, or *rien en arrere*, as it is a direct denial of that part, is a proper general issue (*g*).

On a similar principle, *nil debet* is not a good plea to debt on bond (*h*); and the plea is ill, on *general*

(*d*) Iid.

(*e*) Cowp. 588. 2 Chitt. Pl. 486. z. Bac. Abr. *Pleas*, &c, I. 1. 2 Saund. 297. (n. 1.) 2 Ld Ray. 1503. 2 Chitt. Pl. 486.

(*f*) Cowp. 589. 2 Chitt. Pl. 486. n. c.

(*g*) 2 Saund. 297. (n. 1) Cowp. 589. Bull. N. P. 170. 2 Chitt. Pl. 486. n. e.

(*h*) 2 Johns. R. 183. 8 Ib. 82. 2 Wils. 10. Cun. R. 75.

demurrer: It being *the nature* of the plea, and not the *manner* of pleading it, that is defective (*i*).

'Nil debet' to debet on bond, effect of.

§ 12. But if *nil debet* is pleaded to debt on bond, and the plaintiff, instead of demurring, accepts the plea, and joins in the issue; the defendant is at liberty to prove any and every special matter of defence, which might be proved under the same plea, in debt on *simple* contract (*k*) — such as *want of consideration, payment, release, usury, infancy,* &c. For the plaintiff, by accepting the plea, founds his demand solely upon the *defendant's being indebted;* and thus waves the *estoppel,* or *conclusive* evidence of that fact, which the deed would have furnished against the defendant, under the plea of *non est factum.*

§ 13. Yet when in *debt,* the plaintiff counts upon a deed only as *inducement* to the action, *nil debet* is a good plea — as, in the before mentioned case of *debt for rent,* due on a deed of lease (*l*). For, in this case, *the subsequent occupation* of the defendant, under the demise, is the *gist* of the action; because rent is considered as a *profit, issuing out of land;* and when it is sued for, as a *debt,* the law considers the debt as arising out of the *receipt of the issues and profits* by the tenant, and not from the *deed.*

(*i*) 2 Wils. 10. Esp. Dig. 224.

(*k*) 5 Esp. Rep. 38. 1 Chitt. Pl. 478. *Vid.* 4 McCord, 380.

(*l*) 1 Saund. 276. (n. 1). 2 Ib. 297. (n. 1). 1 New Rep. 109. 2 Chitt. Pl. 174. n. z.

CHAP. VI. PART I.

Goes to to the count only.

§ 14. The general issue, being a plea to *the action*, refers to the *count*, and not to *the writ*. Hence, if in account, the writ charges the defendant as receiver, *generally*, and the count, as receiver *by the hands of A.;* the plea, 'never receiver,' denies only that the defendant was receiver *by the hands of A.;* and the plaintiff is not permitted to give evidence of the defendant's being his receiver in any other way (*m*).

§ 15. The *conclusion* of the general issue, as well as all issues in fact, must conform to the particular *mode of trial*, prescribed by law, for the determination of the matter in issue. And the mode of trial depends, in all cases, upon the *nature of the fact* to be tried; as facts of different kinds require different modes of trial.

Different modes of trying.

§ 16. The different modes or species of trial, established by the common law, in civil cases, are, 1. by *record*; 2. by *inspection*, or *examination;* 3. by *certificate;* 4. by *witnesses*, (without the intervention of a jury); 5. by *wager of battel;* 6. by *wager of law;* 7. by *jury* (*n*). These different methods of trial, except the *first* and the *last*, being now either obsolete, or rarely in use in the United States (3);

(*m*) Co. Litt. 126. a. Bac. Abr. *Pleas*, &c, G. 1.
(*n*) 3 Black. Com. 330—348.

---

(3) Certain facts — as that of *marriage* in particular — are *proveable*, in the courts of our country, generally, by *certificate;*

it seems unnecessary, in this Essay, to treat particularly of any of them, except the two last mentioned. As to the others, it will be sufficient to refer to the explanation given of them, in the commentaries of Sir W. Blackstone, vol. 3, pp. 330—348 (4).

CHAP. VI. PART I.

By record.

§ 17. The trial *by record* takes place, whenever a record is directly put in issue, by the plea of *nul tiel record* (o). This plea, (the only one by which a record can be *directly* put in issue), concludes with a *verification;* and the issue is then, (*regularly* and *usually*) closed by the adverse party's *re-affirming* the existence of the record, and praying that it may be inspected by the court (p). For a record is of too high a nature to be tried by a jury, or in any other way, than by *itself*—i. e. by the court, on personal *inspection* of it.

By jury.

§ 18. But most issues in fact are tried by *jury:* And therefore when any matter, *not* of record, is

(o) 3 Black. Com. 330—1.

(p) Lawes' Pl. 146. 148. 226. 236. 2 Chitt. Pl. 488. 602. Com. R. 533. 2 Wils. 113. 114. 2 T. R. 443. 5 East, 473. *Vid.* 2 Bos. & P. 302. Steph. Pl. 255.

---

but I am not aware that the issue upon such fact ever *concludes* to the certificate.

(4) In the State of Connecticut, any issue in fact, in a *civil* case, may, by the agreement of both parties, be tried by *the court.* But when the issue is to be thus tried, the *agreement* of the parties must be suggested, in the conclusion of the plea tendering the issue; and this is done in the form following: 'Of this the said C. D. *by agreement*, puts himself upon the court'—or, 'This the said A. B. *by agreement*, prays may be inquired of, by the court.'

CHAP. VI. PART I.

denied by the general issue, the plea, in general, (in all cases, indeed, where no one of the other modes of trial, above enumerated, is necessary), concludes to *the country*, i. e. the jury (*q*). And all issues in fact, whether general or special, if triable by *jury*, conclude in the same manner (*r*).

§ 19. The *form* of concluding a plea to the country, when the denial is on the part of the *defendant*, (as is always the case, when the general issue is pleaded), is as follows: 'And of this the said C. D. *puts himself* on the country.' But when the denial is on the part of the *plaintiff*, (i. e. when he puts in issue the defendant's allegations), the established form of the conclusion is in these words: 'And this the said A. B. prays, may be *inquired of* by the country' (*s*).

But where the denial or traverse, though it come on the part of the plaintiff, is in *negative* terms (as when he denies the defendant's affirmative allegations), he may conclude in the *former* of these modes: It being deemed somewhat incongruous, to pray that a *negative* 'may be *inquired* of' (*t*). And as the mere mode of concluding to the country is, essentially, but *matter of form*; either of the above

(*q*) 3 Black. Com. 315. Co. Litt. 126. a. Bac. Abr. *Pleas*, &c, G. 1.

(*r*) Iid.

(*s*) 3 Black. Com. 313. Bac. Abr. *Pleas*, &c, G. 1.

(*t*) 10 Mod. 166. 1 Lev. 281. Rast. Ent. 20. b. 36. 324.

formulæ might now, perhaps, be used without hazard, by either party (*u*).

The similiter.

§ 20. Whenever one of the parties concludes to the country, and thus refers the trial to the jury, the issue is *joined*, and made ready for trial, by the opposite party's adding, 'and the said A. B.' (or 'C. D.') 'does the like' (*v*). This addition, which, from its concluding word, is called the *similiter*, merely expresses the concurrence of the party, to whom the issue is tendered, with his adversary, in referring the trial to the jury. It is however, in strictness, no part of *the pleadings;* since it neither affirms nor denies any *fact*, in maintenance of the action, or the defence.

§ 21. The *similiter* would therefore seem, on principle, to be only matter of *form;* and as such, the omission of it would seem to be aided by verdict. And so it has been determined, in the states of Connecticut and Massachusetts (*w*). Indeed the Connecticut *postea* distinctly states, that the parties *joined* in referring the issue to the jury — the only fact, which the *similiter* is designed to show.

In the English courts, however, judgment has formerly been arrested after verdict, by reason of

(*u*) 10 Mod. 166. Steph. Pl. 248. *Vid.* 7 Pick. 117.
(*v*) 3 Black. Com. 315. Co. Litt. 126. a, Lawes' Pl. 147-8.
(*w*) 2 Day, 392. 9 Mass. R. 533.

CHAP. VI. PART I.

the omission of the *similiter* (*x*). But the setting aside of verdicts, for this cause, has, in later times, been complained of as unreasonable, in the courts of Westminster; and the omission has consequently been allowed, upon the slightest possible grounds, to be *supplied* after verdict, by way of *amendment* (*y*). At this day indeed, the court, it seems, will, after verdict, *as a matter of course*, allow the record to be amended, by the insertion of the *similiter*, when omitted, if the allowance be not inconsistent with *the justice* of the case (*z*).

'Modo et formâ', effect of.

§ 22. The words 'in manner and form', &c, which are regularly used in tendering an issue, either general or special, are sometimes of the *substance* of the issue, and sometimes merely words of *form*. When they are of the *substance* of the issue, they put in issue the *circumstances*, alleged as concomitants of the principal matter denied by the pleader; (such as *time*, *place*, *manner*, &c): When *not* of the substance of the issue, they do *not* put in issue such circumstances (*a*). And to determine when they are of the substance of the issue, and when not so. the established criterion is, that when the circumstances of *manner*, *time*, *place*, &c, alleged in connexion with the principal fact traversed, are *originally* and *in themselves material*, and therefore

(*x*) 2 Saund. 319. a. (n. 6.) Yelv. 65. n. 8 Mod. 376. Stra. 641. 1117. 3 Brod. & Bing. 1. 6 Moore, 51.

(*y*) 3 Burr. 1793. Cowp. 407. 1 New Rep. 28.

(*z*) 2 Bing. 384. & vide 2 Chitt. Rep. 25. 1 Stark. R. 400. (323.) 6 Greenleaf, 327.

(*a*) Bac. Abr. *Pleas*, &c, G. 1. Lawes' Pl. 120. Hardr. 39.

necessary to be *proved* as stated, the words '*modo et formâ*' are of the substance of the issue, and *do* consequently put those concomitants in issue: But, that when such concomitants or circumstances are *not* in themselves material, and therefore not necessary to be *proved* as stated, the words '*modo et formâ*', are *not* of the substance of the issue, and consequently do not put them in issue (*b*). The result then is, that these words may always be safely used, in tendering an issue; because, in their legal effect, they always put in issue all *material* circumstances, and *no other* (*c*).

§ 23. Hence if one party pleads a feoffment *by deed*, and the other traverses the feoffment, *modo et formâ* as alleged; the deed, as well as the enfeoffing act, is put in issue (*d*): And therefore proof of a feoffment *without* deed, is inadmissible, under this issue. For though a feoffment without deed is good, at common law; yet when it is pleaded *as by deed*, the deed becomes material, as an essential part of the conveyance.

§ 24. But in trespass for an assault and battery, alleged to have been committed with *swords, daggers*, &c, if the defendant pleads not guilty 'in manner and form'; the plaintiff is at liberty to prove a battery, committed with *any other* weapon. And

(*b*) Lawes' Pl. 120. Latch, 92–3.
(*c*) 2 Saund. 319. (n. 6.) Lawes' Pl. 49. 120.
(*d*) Litt. § 483. Co. Litt. 281. b.

CHAP. VI. PART I.

the same rule holds, on an indictment for *murder*, alleging a mortal wound to have been inflicted, with any particular weapon: The form or species of the *instrument* of the battery or homicide, being an immaterial circumstance (*e*).

§ 25. So also when *time, place, number, quantity,* &c, alleged in the declaration, are not in themselves *material,* and therefore not necessary to be proved *as alleged,* the general issue, with the words, '*modo et formâ*', does not put them in issue (*f*). And where a misstatement, in any of these particulars, does not occasion a *variance,* they are in general *immaterial.*

§ 26. And it seems, that the words, 'in manner and form', &c, though almost universally used, in tendering an issue in fact, are in no case, indispensable, even in point of *form,* to the legal sufficiency of the issue, or traverse, in which they are employed (*g*).

§ 27. Under the present head, it may be proper to treat of *immaterial* and *informal* issues, whether general or special in their character.

Immaterial issues.

An *immaterial* issue is one, which, *passing by what is material* in the previous pleading, is joined

(*e*) 2 Hale, P. C. 185. 291. 9 Co. 67. 4 Black. Com. 196. 2 M'Nall. Ev. 520. 522. 1 Russ. on Crimes, 467. (2d ed.)

(*f*) Lawes' Pl. 48-9. 120. Cro. Eliz. 12. 13. Cowp. 260. 3 Lev. 334. Com. Dig. *Pleader,* G. 1.

(*g*) Com. Dig. *Pleader,* G. 1. Lawes' Pl. 120.

on an immaterial point; i. e. a point not decisive of the right of the cause (*h*): As where issue is tendered upon matter of mere *form*, or upon matter of *inducement* or *aggravation*, or upon what is *impertinent*, or not alleged in the adverse pleading. Thus, if in assumpsit against an executor, on a promise of his testator, the defendant pleads that *he, himself*, did not promise; or if in *debt* on bond, the defendant pleads *not guilty;* or in *trover*, that he did not *find* the goods in question; the issue tendered is *immaterial*, and of course ill *in substance;* since the finding either way cannot enable the court to discover which party is entitled to judgment (*i*). And such an issue, being radically defective, is not aided by *verdict* (*k*). (*Vid. Arrest of Judgment, post.* ch. 10).

Informal issues.

§ 28. When a *material* allegation is traversed in an *improper or inartificial manner*, the issue, taken upon it, is called an *informal issue* (*l*). This defect is aided, after verdict, by the statute 32 H. 8, ch. 30.

But if the party, to whom such an issue is tendered, *demurs* for the informality, instead of joining in the issue; the demurrer must be *special*, by the sta-

(*h*) Bac. Abr. *Pleas*, &c, G. 2. 3 Black. Com. 395.

(*i*) Iid. 2 Vent. 196. Carth. 371. 2 Mod. 137. 139. 2 Saund. 319. a. (n. 6). Gilb. H. C. P. 147. 1 Wils. 338.

(*k*) Iid. 3 Pick. 124.

(*l*) Bac. Abr. *Pleas*, &c, G. 2. N. 5. 2 Saund. 319. a. (n. 6). Gilb. H. C. P. 147.

CHAP. VI. PART I.

tute 27 Eliz. ch. 5; though the rule was otherwise, at common law.

Negative pregnant.

§ 29. Under the class of informal issues, may be considered such as are joined upon a *negative pregnant*, or an *affirmative pregnant*. The former is a *negative* allegation, involving, or admitting of, an *affirmative implication* (*m*), or at least, an implication of some kind, *favourable* to the adverse party (5). An *affirmative pregnant* is an *affirmative* allegation, implying some *negative*, in favour of the adverse party (*n*).

§ 30. As a general rule therefore, an issue cannot properly be joined upon a *negative pregnant* (*o*): Because the *affirmative* implication, to which it is open, destroys the effect of the denial, or traverse. Thus, if the defendant pleads in bar a release, made *since the date of the writ;* and the plaintiff replies, that the said supposed writing 'is not his act, *since the date* of the writ;' the replication is a *negative pregnant*. For it admits, by implication, a release made *before* the date of the writ, and which would

(*m*) Lit. Rep. 65. Com. Dig. *Pleader*, R. 5. 2 Lill. Ab. 274. Bac. Abr. *Pleas*, &c, N. 6.

(*n*) Iid.

(*o*) Co. Litt. 126. a. 303. a. Cro. Jac. 87. 560. Lawes' Pl. 113. 114.

(5) An issue of this kind is here classed with *informal* issues, because the ground of objection to it is, not that it is *defective in substance*, as not involving what is *material or issuable;* but that it improperly includes, *with* what is material and issuable, what is *unnecessary* and *improper* to be put in issue.

be as effectual a bar to the action, as one made afterwards. (*Vid.* ch. 7, §§ 34. 35).

§ 31. An issue, joined upon a *negative pregnant*, differs from an *immaterial issue*, properly so called, in this:—That the terms of the former include, *regularly*, as well what is *not* material, (as *time*, *place*, *manner*, &c), as what is so; and in all cases, leave it *uncertain*, which of two or more things the pleader intends to *contest*: Whereas a traverse, tendering an issue, *strictly immaterial*, includes *only* what is *immaterial*. Thus, in the example last given, of a plea of release, after the date of the writ, the traverse, in the replication, extends as well to *the time*, alleged in the plea, and which is immaterial, as to *the release itself*: And as it does not appear, from the terms of the traverse, upon which of those points the plaintiff intends to rest his defence; the replication may be considered as ill, for this *uncertainty*. The proper mode of traversing the release would have been, by replying that it was 'not his act, in *manner and form*,' &c; or, that it 'was not his act,' without the subsequent words.

§ 32. The same explanation may be applied to the following case:—In replevin, the defendant avowed the taking of the plaintiff's cattle for rent arrear, reserved on a lease; alleging, that on the *first* day of Nov., in the 18th year of the reign of the king, he demised to the plaintiff, &c: The plaintiff pleaded to the avowry, that the avowant,

CHAP. VI. PART I.

'*on the said first day of Nov.*, in the said 18th year, &c, did not demise,' &c, in manner and form, &c. In this case, the traverse of the plaintiff was a *negative pregnant;* as it included the time of the demise, which was *immaterial.* But the avowry being itself defective; the case was decided on other grounds (*o*). The traverse should have been, that the avowant 'did not demise, in manner and form.'

§ 33. Again: Where in trespass for cutting the plaintiff's trees, the defendant pleaded, that he cut them by command of the plaintiff; a replication, that the defendant 'did not cut them by command of the plaintiff,' was held to be a *negative pregnant*—as the denial extended as well to the act of *cutting the trees*, as to the command (*p*).

The traverse should have been limited to the alleged *command*, in one of the forms last mentioned.

How aided.

§ 34. By the statute 32 H. 8, c. 30, an issue, joined on a *negative pregnant*, is aided by a verdict for either of the parties (*q*).

But by the common law, such an issue is not thus aided, unless the finding shows *for which* party

(*o*) 2 Saund. 317. 2 Lev. 11.

(*p*) Bac. Abr. *Pleas*, &c, I. 6. Doct. Pl. 256. & *vid.* Com. Dig. *Pleader*, R. 5. 2 Leon. 197. Cro. Jac. 87. Steph. Pl. 381—384.

(*q*) Co. Litt. 126. a. 303. a. Cro. Jac. 87. 312. Gilb. H. C. P. 147. 2 Saund. 319. (n. 6).

judgment ought to be given (*r*). But generally, at least, and probably in all cases, a verdict *for* the party, who tenders the issue by a negative pregnant, will *not* show for which party judgment ought to be given: Whereas, a verdict for the party, *to whom* the issue is tendered, will, regularly, show (if there is no substantial defect in the *previous* pleading, on *his own* part), that *he* is entitled to judgment. Thus, in the first example already given, of an issue of this kind, (*ante*, § 30)—where the defendant pleaded a release *since the date of the writ*, and the plaintiff denied, in his replication, that he had released 'since the date of the writ'; a verdict for the *defendant* would have shown that he was entitled to judgment; although a finding the other way would have decided nothing. And in each of the other foregoing examples, (*ante*, § 32. 33), a verdict finding the *affirmative* of the issue, would have shown that he, *to whom* the issue was tendered, was entitled to judgment, unless some substantial fault could be found in his *own previous* pleading.

§ 35. If however the party, to whom issue is tendered on a negative pregnant, *demurs* for that cause, instead of joining in the issue tendered; the demurrer must, under the English statutes of jeofails (27 Eliz. c. 5, & 4 Ann. c. 16), be *special* (*s*). But by the *common* law, which in general treats substan-

Post. ch. 9, § 9.

(*r*) 3 Black. Com. 395. 2 Vent. 196. 2 Stra. 994. Cun. R. 71. 106. 2 Burr. 944. 1 Ib. 302. 7 Mod. 231. 2 Wils. 173.

(*s*) Bac. Abr. *Amendment*, &c, B. *Pleas*, &c, I. 6.

CHAP. VI. PART I.

tial and formal defects with equal rigor, a negative pregnant is ill, on *general* demurrer. Statutes of *jeofails*, substantially like those last mentioned, or at least like the former of them, exist in many, and probably in all, of the United States.

§ 36. But where the affirmative, implied in a negative allegation, is such as *would not maintain the pleading on the other side*, it does no harm, and affords no ground of exception. In such a case, therefore, the negative allegation is not called a *negative pregnant* (*t*). Hence, when in debt for labour done, the plaintiff alleged that the defendant retained him *in husbandry*, and the defendant pleaded that he did not retain the plaintiff *in husbandry;* the plea, though tacitly admitting a retainer of a *different kind*, was held good: Since proof of any other retainer, than *in husbandry*, would not maintain the count; as it would be a variance. So also, if the defendant pleads title to the freehold, under a devise from J. S.; alleging that J. S. died seised in *fee-simple*, and the plaintiff replies that J. S. did not die seised *in fee-simple;* the replication, though open to the implication that he died seised *in tail*, or of the largest estate *less* than a fee-simple, would, doubtless, not be faulty by reason of this implication: Because proof of any other estate in the testator, than a fee-simple, would not support the defendant's plea of title under the devise.

(*t*) Com. Dig. *Pleader*, R. 6. Lawes' Pl. 114.

§ 37. The same principles are applicable to *affirmatives* pregnant. The following may be taken as an example of such an allegation: If to an action of assumpsit, which is barred by the statute of limitations in *six* years, the defendant pleads, that he did not undertake, &c, within *ten* years, a replication that he did undertake, &c, 'within ten years', would be an *affirmative pregnant* (*u*): Since it would impliedly admit that the defendant had *not* promised within six years. And as no proper issue could be tendered upon such a plea, the plaintiff should, for that reason, *demur* to it.

Affirmative pregnant.

§ 38. The *general issue*, as already mentioned, (*ante*, § 8), covers the whole declaration, and thus enables the defendant to contest *all* the plaintiff's material allegations (*v*).

In some cases, however, even according to the ancient and most rigorous principles of pleading, the general issue may properly be pleaded, when none of the *facts* alleged in the declaration are intended to be *actually* denied under it. Such is the case, where the action is founded on a bond, or other specialty, which is void at common law, through an *absolute incapacity* in the obligor. Thus, if an action is brought on a bond, or other deed, executed by a *feme covert;* she may plead *non est factum;* and proof of her coverture will support the

What defences are admissible under the general issue.

(*u*) 2 Ld Ray. 1099. 6 East, 387.
(*v*) Bac. Abr. *Pleas*, &c, G. 1. 3 Black. Com. 305.

General issue, defences under.

plea (*w*). But the defence of coverture, in this case, is considered *in the law*, as going *in denial* of the declaration. For her incapacity to bind herself, by any contract, being *absolute* and *total;* she is regarded, as being *not a moral agent* in executing the instrument; and it is therefore not considered as *her act.* And according to what appear to be the more reasonable opinions, the same rule applies, and for the same reason, to the deed of an *idiot* or a *lunatic;* but on this point, the authorities are not all agreed (*x*).

§ 39. But if the legal incapacity of the party executing the specialty, on which the action is founded, is only *partial* or *qualified*—as if the suit is on the bond of an *infant;* he cannot give his infancy in evidence, under the plea of *non est factum;* but must plead it *specially* (*y*). For the legal incapacity of an infant not being *absolute;* a bond executed by him is considered as *his act*, though avoidable by him; and therefore, proof of his infancy does not support the plea that the instrument is *not his act.* The defence is inconsistent with the plea.

§ 40. The rule is the same, in the case of a bond obtained by *duress.* For it is *the act* of the

(*w*) 5 Co. 119. 2 Wils. 341. 347. 1 Pow. on Cont. 97. Gilb. Ev. 162. Com. Dig. *Pleader*, 2. W. 18.

(*x*) 2 Vent. 198. 2 Stra. 1104. 1 Ld Ray. 315. 2 Salk. 675. 4 Co. 123. Wilmot, 155. Chitt. on Cont. 260. 3 Day, 90. 15 Johns. R. 503. 5 Pick. 431.

(*y*) 3 Burr. 1805. 1 Salk. 279. Gilb. Ev. 162-3. Com. Dig. *Pleader*, 2. W. 22.

General issue, defences under.

party making it, though *avoidable*, as in the preceding case (*z*). The duress must, therefore, be pleaded *specially;* as the defence would *contradict* the general issue. For the latter plea *denies* the execution of the bond; but the defence of duress *admits* it.

§ 41. So also, where a specialty is declared void by *statute*, for any cause — as, for *usury*, *gaming*, or other illegal consideration — the obligor, or maker of the deed, cannot avail himself of the statute, under *the general issue;* but must *plead it specially*, i. e. he must plead specially the facts, which bring the case within the statute (*a*). For the instrument, though it creates no legal obligation, is nevertheless, as in the preceding cases, *his act;* and the special matter of the defence is therefore *inconsistent* with the plea of *non est factum.*

§ 42. But *fraud*, in the execution of a deed, may be proved under the plea of *non est factum:* As, where one is, by a *deception* practised upon him, induced to execute an instrument, materially *different* from what he believed it to be — *ex. gr.* a *bond*, instead of a *release* — or an obligation for £100, instead of one for £10 (*b*). For in such a case, proof

(*z*) 2 Black. Com. 296. 5 Co. 119. a. Com. Dig. *Pleader*, 2. W. 19. 20. Bull. N. P. 172.

(*a*) 5 Co. 119. a. Hob. 72. 1 Stra. 498. 2 Black. Rep. 1108. Com. Dig. *Pleader*, 2. W. 23. Gilb. Ev. 163.

(*b*) 2 Black. Com. 308. 2 Co. 3. 9. b. Shep. Touch. 70–1. 4 Cruise's Dig. 27. 2 T. R. 765. 3 Ib. 438.

CHAP. VI. PART I.

of the fraud goes directly to support the plea: Inasmuch as the instrument, thus obtained, is not in law *the deed* of the party sealing it.

General issue, defences under.

§ 43. Thus also, the *want of complete delivery* — as in the case of an *escrow*, where the condition, on which it was to be delivered over, is not complied with — *loss of the seal* — *erasure* — *interpolation*, or *any alteration*, in general, after the delivery — are, respectively, good evidence under the plea of *non est factum* (c). The two first of these grounds of defence are founded on the principle, that without a complete delivery, or without a seal, no deed can exist in law; and consequently if an instrument, originally sealed, loses its seal, though after delivery, it ceases, *ipso facto*, to be *a deed* (6). As to the other grounds of defence last mentioned, it may be observed, that where a deed, originally valid, is *altered after its delivery*, it is no longer *the same instrument*, which the maker executed.

§ 44. According to the strict, original principles of the common law, no defences would appear to be admissible, in any case, under the general issue, except such as go in denial *of the truth of the declaration:* And therefore all special matters of defence,

(c) 5 Co. 23. a. 11 Ib. 27. a. b. 28. b. Doct. Pl. 259. 262. 2 Show. 28-9. Gilb. Ev. 109.

---

(6) Where the seal is lost or destroyed, otherwise than by the act of the party, claiming under it, he may be relieved against the accident, *in equity*.

which admit, but go in *avoidance* of, the declaration, would seem to require *special* pleas in bar, as being *inconsistent* with the general issue.

General issue, defences under.

In the original common law actions.

§ 45. In the original *common-law* actions of *debt* on specialty — *covenant broken* — *account* — *detinue* — *trespass* — and *replevin*, the above principle has generally been observed; and therefore in these actions, matters of *avoidance* have in general been, as they still are, inadmissible defences, under the general issue, except in so far as the principle, excluding them under that issue, has been relaxed by statute provisions, or rules of court. Hence in these actions, any defence, which does not imply a *denial* of the material facts, or of what are alleged as such, in the declaration, must be *specially pleaded.*

In trespass on the case.

§ 46. But in actions of *trespass on the case*, which, as having originated in the *equity* of the statute of Westm. 2, (13 Edw. 1) are regarded as *equitable* actions, a more liberal, or rather a more lax mode of pleading, has, with some exceptions, been allowed (*d*). Hence, in this comprehensive class of actions, whether arising *ex contractu* or *ex delicto*, many defences, which go merely *in avoidance* of the declaration, have been admitted under the *general issue.*

In assumpsit.

§ 47. In the action of *assumpsit* especially, this is eminently the case. For in this action, not only

(*d*) 3 Burr. 1353. Bac. Abr. *Pleas*, &c, G. 2. Yelv. 174. b. (n. 1.)

CHAP. VI. PART I.

General issue, defences under.

such defences as deny the allegations in the declaration — but almost all matters of avoidance — such as *coverture* — *infancy* — *usury*, or other illegality — *duress* — *payment* — *release* — a *specialty* given for the debt — a *judgment* rendered for either party, in a former action for the same cause — an *award of arbitrators*, deciding the right in question — and *accord and satisfaction* (7), are respectively good defences, under the plea of non assumpsit (*e*).

§ 48. This practice appears to be a very wide departure from the general principle abovementioned, except where the action is founded upon an *implied* promise; in which case, it may, in theory at least, be reconciled with that principle, by adverting to the peculiar nature of the action of *indebitatus assumpsit*. For in that action, as the promise, laid in the declaration, is a mere *inference or conclusion of law*, from the *debt or legal liability*, alleged as its consideration, (which inference the law *continually*

(*e*) Bac. Abr. *Pleas*, &c, G. 2. 2 Burr. 1010. 3 Ib. 1353. 1 Stra. 498. Ld Ray. 566. 787. Doug. 108. 2 H. Black. 143. 5 East, 230. 4 Esp. Rep. 181. Com. Dig. *Accord*. 12 Mod. 377. Chitt. on Bills, 197–8. 1 Chitt. Pl. 472–3.

---

(7) It has been questioned by some, whether *accord* and *satisfaction* can be given in evidence, under *non assumpsit*. But the same *reason*, which justifies the admission of the other enumerated defences, under the same plea, most clearly extends to this: Since it goes in *extinguishment* of the debt. And the weight of authority is on the same side of the question. (12 Mod. 377. 1 Ld Ray. 566. Com. Dig. *Accord*. Bac. Abr. *Accord*. 5 East, 230. 4 Esp. Rep. 181.)

General issue, defences under.

raises, while the legal liability remains, and no longer); it results, that whatever disproves a *subsisting* debt, or legal *liability* at the time of plea pleaded, disproves the alleged *promise*. And the existence of the *debt*, &c, at the time of pleading, may be disproved, by showing, either that it *never existed*, or that it has been, by any means, *extinguished* before that time. As therefore, each of the several defences, enumerated in the last section, goes to the proof of the one or the other of these two points; it follows, that they all, in their legal effect, go in *denial* of the alleged promise, and consequently in support of the plea of *non assumpsit*.

§ 49. From the preceding remarks it will also be apparent, that in the action of *indebitatus assumpsit*, the plea of *non assumpsit*, though expressed in the past tense, does not mean that the defendant did not *actually promise*, as stated in the declaration, (for the action is not founded on a promise *in fact*); but that he is at *the time of pleading*, *not indebted* to the plaintiff, or not in law *liable to the demand*, made in the declaration.

§ 50. It is quite apparent, however, that the reasons, just assigned for allowing such a latitude to the general issue, in *indebitatus assumpsit*, and which are founded on the *peculiarities* of that action, are inapplicable to the action of assumpsit on *express* promises; and consequently, that the special matters of defence, before mentioned, or at least such of them as accrue *subsequently* to the making of the

CHAP. VI. PART I.

General issue, defences under.

promise, are, *on principle*, *inadmissible*, under *non assumpsit*, in the latter action. And so the rule appears to have been, formerly, in practice (*f*). But through inadvertence, in not attending to the distinction between the two forms of assumpsit, or from some other cause, the rule has been now long established, that *all* the defences, which are admissible under the general issue, in the one form of action, are so in the *other*.

§ 51. But even in *assumpsit*, the *statute of limitations* — *tender* — *set-off* — and *bankruptcy*, are, on common-law principles, inadmissible defences, under the general issue, and must therefore be pleaded specially (*g*). For these defences, respectively, admit the *debt*, or *gist* of the action, and go in denial of the *remedy only*.

§ 52. In *indebitatus assumpsit*, (and now in all actions of assumpsit), the plea of *non assumpsit*, as before explained, appears to have the same comprehensive and legal effect, as that of *nil debet* in debt on simple contract; and therefore the same defences appear, on principle, to be admissible, under both these issues; as in most instances they are (*h*).

§ 53. It is held, however, that the *statute of limitations*, though inadmissible under *non assumpsit*,

(*f*) 1 Mod. 210.

(*g*) 1 Ld Ray. 153. Tidd, 375. 1 Saund. 283. (n. 2). Chitt. on Bills, 198.

(*h*) Cro. Eliz. 140. 222. 5 Mod. 18. 1 Salk. 284. 2 Phil. Ev. 94. 1 Saund. 283. (n. 2).

is a good defence, in debt on simple contract, under the plea of *nil debet* (*i*); because the plea is in the *present tense*. But so, *in effect*, is the plea of *non assumpsit*. And if the reason of the rule, which excludes this defence under the latter plea, is a sound one; the same rule, it would seem, ought to be applied to the latter (*k*).

General issue, defences under.

Advantage may also be taken of the statute of *frauds and perjuries*, under the plea of *non assumpsit*, by excepting to all parol evidence offered in support of the declaration (*l*).

In case, ex delicto.

§ 54. In those actions on *the case* also, which arise *ex delicto*, matters of *mere avoidance* have, to a very considerable extent, been admitted in evidence, under the general issue. It would be difficult, however, to discover any precise *principle*, by which this practice may be justified, or any definite general rule, by which to limit its precise extent. Indeed, the practice appears to be, in a great measure, an arbitrary departure from the original principles of the law, and as such, to rest on *authority*, rather than any known legal reason.

§ 55. According to this practice, however, (whatever may have been its origin), the rule has now become general, that in actions *on the case*, *ex*

(*i*) 1 Saund. 283. (n. 2). 1 Ld Ray. 153. 566. 1 Salk. 278. Com. Dig. *Pleader*, 2 W. 16.

(*k*) *Vid.* 1 Chitt. Pl. 476. 1 Saund. 283. (n. 2). 2 Mass. R. 87.

(*l*) 1 Bro. C. C. 93. 1 Chitt. Pl. 470.

CHAP. VI. PART I.

General issue, defences under.

delicto, the defendant may prove, under the plea of *not guilty*, almost every special matter of defence, which conduces to show, that *at the time of pleading, he is not liable* to the plaintiff's demand (*m*). Ex. gr. a *license*, or any other *justification* (*n*)—a *former recovery*—*release*—*accord and satisfaction*, &c (*o*).

§ 56. These special defences, however, and all others which *confess* the truth of the declaration, *may be specially pleaded*, instead of being given in evidence, under the general issue: A rule, which holds in assumpsit also. For regularly, no plea which *admits* the truth of the declaration can be said to amount to *the general issue;* though the matter of it might have been given in evidence, under that issue (*p*).

§ 57. In the single case of *trover*, however, it has been held that there is but *one* good special plea to the action, viz. *release:* All other such pleas amounting, it is said, to the *general issue* (*q*). And if we are here to understand the word 'release,' not as meaning exclusively a *formal, technical* release or acquittance, but as including *whatever extinguishes* or *discharges* a right of action once exist-

(*m*) 3 Burr. 1353. 1 Black. R. 388. 1 Wils. 45. 1 Chitt. Pl. 486—7.

(*n*) 8 East, 308. 2 Mod. 6. 7.

(*o*) 2 Mod. 276. 3 Ib. 166. Com. R. 273. 1 Wils. 44. 175. 2 Phill. Ev. 108. Bac. Abr. *Pleas*, &c, I. 1. 1 Keb. 305.

(*p*) 1 Ld Ray. 88-9. 1 Salk. 394. 5 Mod. 18. Carth. 356. Lawes' Pl. 112. Tidd, 591. 599.

(*q*) Bac. Abr. *Pleas*, &c, I. 1. 1 Keb. 305. Yelv. 174. a. (n. 1). Reg. Pl. 268.

General issue, defences under.

ing — as *accord and satisfaction*, a *former recovery*, or a *former bar*, an award of *arbitrators*, &c, (and in this sense the term appears to have been used); the position will appear to be not destitute of a foundation in principle. For as the *conversion*, which is the gist of the action in trover, is, *ex vi termini*, a *tortious* act, which cannot in law be *justified* or *excused;* it is manifest that any plea alleging matter of *justification* or *excuse*, (as a *license* from the plaintiff — an *authority* derived from the law, &c), is equivalent to the plea of *not guilty;* since it must involve a denial of the conversion.

§ 58. In *slander*, the defendant is allowed to prove, under the general issue, that the words were spoken by him *as counsel* in a cause; or in honest *confidence*, and for a justifiable reason — (as in fairly giving the character of a servant); or to show any other fact, in general, which conduces to prove that the words were not uttered *maliciously* (*r*): *Malice* being, in this action, of the gist of the action (8).

(*r*) 2 Selw. N. P. 929. 1066. 1 Saund. 131. (n. 1). Cro. Jac. 90. 1 B. & A. 232. 1 M. & S. 644. 15 Mass. R. 50. 57. 4 Ib. 1. 2 Pick. 310. Bull. N. P. 8. 1 T. R. 110. 1 Bos. & P. 525. 1 Campb. 267. 3 Johns. R. 180.

---

(8) Yet the defendant, in slander, is not allowed to prove the *truth* of the words, under the general issue, (2 Stra. 1200. Bull. N. P. 9. Willes, 20. 1 Saund. 130. (n. 1). 1 T. R. 748. 1 Bos. & P. 525. 2 Ib. 225. (n. a). Com. Dig. *Pleader*, 2 L. 2): Though the truth of the words plainly conduces to rebut the legal presumption of *malice*.

CHAP. VI. PART I.

All these and similar defences *may* however be pleaded specially (*s*).

General issue, defences under.

But it seems impossible to reconcile all the different rules admitting and excluding special matters of defence, under the general issue, in *actions on the case*, either with the strict principles of the common law, or with each other.

§ 59. The universal principle which, by the common law, renders any given evidence admissible under any given issue, is its relevancy to the issue — i. e. its conduciveness, or tendency, *to prove* the affirmative or negative of the issue. And according to this principle, no evidence is admissible, on the part of the defendant, under the *general issue*, except such as conduces to disprove *the declaration*. But in actions *on the case*, as has been shown, many deviations from this simple principle have been sanctioned by courts of justice; and various similar deviations from the same principles have been introduced, and extended to *other* actions, both in England (*t*) and in the United States, by legislative enactments, and rules of court, for the purpose of enlarging the office of the general issue, and of allowing the defendant to give in evidence, under it, many special matters of defence, which, as being *inconsistent with it*, are by the strict original rules of the common law, required to be pleaded specially.

(*s*) 1 Saund. 130-1. (n. 1).
(*t*) Com. Dig. *Pleader*, E. 13.

§ 60. Instead of pleading the *general issue*, the defendant may, in some cases, effectually answer the declaration by a *special issue* — i. e. by directly denying some one material and traversable allegation in the declaration, and concluding to the country (*u*).

Special issue.

§ 61. A *special issue*, however, is not adapted to all cases. Its proper use is limited to those cases, in which the declaration alleges at least *two* distinct substantive facts, both of which are essential to a right of action. In such a case, a denial of *one* of those facts — though it does not put the whole declaration in issue — is nevertheless as complete an answer in law to the whole right of action, as the general issue itself would be. For where two or more facts are necessary to constitute a right of recovery, it is self-evident, that a denial of any *one* of them is a denial of the entire right of recovery.

§ 62. Thus, in assumpsit on a special agreement, where the right of action depends upon *a condition precedent*, and where the declaration specially alleges, as it must, performance of the condition — the defendant may, instead of pleading the general issue, deny the alleged *performance* of the condition *only*, and put himself upon the country (*v*). If, for example, the plaintiff's right of action depends upon

(*u*) Yelv. 195. Lawes' Pl. 112. 135. Gilb. H. C. P. 61. Com. Dig. *Pleader*, R. 2. Bac. Abr. *Pleas*, &c, G. 3. H. 1.

(*v*) Doct. Pl. 203. Gilb. H. C. P. 60-1. 139. 148. 1 Chitt. Pl. 467.

CHAP. VI. PART I.

Special issue.

previous *notice* of some fact, to the defendant, or upon a special *request;* the defendant may take a special issue upon the allegation of such *notice*, in the one case, or such *request*, in the other. This mode of pleading *in assumpsit* is now, however, in a great measure obsolete: Since every allegation, which might be denied by a special issue, may, in that action, be contested under the *general issue.*

§ 63. But in some cases, special issues are still not only proper, but necessary — as where, in *covenant broken*, or other action on a *specialty*, performance of a *condition precedent* is alleged in the declaration. For in such a case, the defendant cannot contest the alleged performance of the condition, under the plea of *non est factum.* So also, in an action of covenant broken against a lessee, for not repairing a building, and in which the declaration alleges that the building was left *ruinous and out of repair*, the defendant may take issue upon this allegation, by averring that the building was *not* ruinous or out of repair, and conclude to the country (*w*) (9). For this defence would not maintain the plea of *non est factum.*

(*w*) 2 Chitt. Pl. 501.

(9) This last plea supposes *no* repairs to *have been necessary:* For if the defendant has *actually made* the repairs required by his covenant; his answer to the declaration should be a *special* plea, averring that he *did repair*, &c, and concluding with a *verification*, (2 Chitt. Pl. 501. n. y). For in this case, the defence would be *performance*, which is matter of avoidance.

CHAP. VI. PART I.

Special non est factum.

§ 64. In actions founded on deeds, the defendant *may*, instead of pleading *non est factum* in common form, allege any special matter, which *admits the execution* of the writing in question, but which shows, nevertheless, that it is not *in law his deed;* and may conclude with *non est factum:* As that the writing was delivered to J. S. as *an escrow*, to be delivered over, on a certain condition, which has not been complied with, 'and *so* is not his act': Or, that the writing *has been altered* by the plaintiff, since its delivery, 'and *so* is not his act': Or, that the defendant was, at the time of making the writing, a *feme covert;* 'and so it is not her act' (*x*).

This anomalous plea is called, indifferently, 'a *special non est factum*', or 'the general issue, *with an issint*'—the latter denomination being derived from the Norman word, 'issint' (*so*), in the language of the plea (*y*).

§ 65. In a plea of this kind, the latter part, (the *non est factum*), is merely an *inference* from the special matter which precedes it: The word '*so*' being used in an illative sense, and conveying the same meaning as the word, 'therefore'. The special matter then merely shows *how* and *why* the instrument is not the defendant's act; and on the trial of the issue, the evidence on both sides is confined to the *special matter* alleged. For under a

(*x*) Bac. Abr. *Pleas*, &c, H. 3. I. 2. Gilb. Ev. 164-6. Sav. 71. 72. Bridgm. 100. 1 Vent. 9. 210. 1 Salk. 274. 4 B. & A. 441.
(*y*) Iid.

CHAP. VI. PART I.

plea of this kind, the special facts so alleged, and no others, are put in issue.

Special non est factum.

§ 66. It is manifest, therefore, that if the facts, specially stated in this plea, are not such as to show that the instrument is, in law, *not* the defendant's *deed*, or, (which is the same thing), not such as would, in evidence, maintain the general issue, when pleaded in its general and usual form; the plea is ill, and demurrable (*z*). For as the facts, specially alleged, present *all* the grounds of the defence specifically, *upon the record;* the question of their sufficiency in law arises upon the face of the pleadings, as upon a plea merely special. If therefore the defendant pleads, that he was compelled by *duress* to execute the writing — or that, at the time of executing it, he was an *infant* — and concludes with the general issue; the plea is ill, and demurrable. For, as has been seen, (ante, §§ 39. 40), these defences, like all others which render the instrument merely *voidable*, do not maintain that issue (*a*).

§ 67. The effect of a demurrer to a *special non est factum* is strictly analogous to that of a demurrer to *evidence*. The question of law, raised by the latter, is, whether the facts shown *in evidence* are sufficient in law to maintain the issue in fact, in favour of the

(*z*) Gilb. Ev. 164–5. *Vide* 4 Esp. Rep. 255. 6 Mod. 217.

(*a*) 5 Co. 119. Plowd. 66. Gilb. Ev. 162. Com. Dig. *Pleader*, E. 30.

party exhibiting the evidence (*b*). And the question of law, raised by a demurrer to a *special non est factum*, is, whether the facts, specially alleged *in the plea*, are sufficient in law to maintain the general issue, (with which it concludes), in favour of the party pleading them.

Special non est factum.

§ 68. The conclusion of this plea with the general issue, seems plainly to indicate that it ought to be referred to the *jury;* and the better authority appears to be, that it must be closed to the *country* (*c*). But this conclusion, it may be observed, does not prevent the plaintiff from *demurring* for the legal insufficiency of the special matter, which precedes the *non est factum*. For though a conclusion to the country, on either side, puts an end to the *pleadings;* it does not preclude a *demurrer* by the party, to whom the issue is tendered.

§ 69. According to some opinions, however, a special *non est factum* may, and should, conclude with a *verification* (*d*). But such a conclusion would alter the essential character of the plea, and convert it into a mere *special plea amounting to the general issue*, which is, regularly, inadmissible. Besides, it is difficult to discover any use or propriety in leaving the plea open to an answer. It cannot be necessary, to

(*b*) Doug. 218. 225. Bull. N. P. 313. *Vid.* ch. 9, part 2.

(*c*) Plowd. 66. 3 Keb. 26. Bro. Ab. *General Issue*, pl. 26. 1 Vent. 9. 210. Bac. Abr. *Pleas*, &c. I. 2. Com. Dig. *Pleader*, E. 32. 1 Salk. 274.

(*d*) Gilb. Ev. 164-5. Noy, 112.

CHAP. VI. PART I.

the end of giving the plaintiff an opportunity to *take issue* on the special facts stated in the plea (for these are put in issue by the plea itself); nor to enable him to make a special replication; for whatever could be specially replied, may be given in evidence *in disproof* of the plea.

OF PLEAS TO THE ACTION.

Part II. — *Of Special Pleas in Bar.*

Special pleas in bar.

§ 70. A *special* plea in bar, as usually defined, is one which *admits* the truth of the declaration, but alleges special matter in avoidance of it (*e*). Of this class are such pleas, as that of *release*, *accord and satisfaction*, *payment*, *tender*, a *justification* of any kind, the statute of *limitations*, or of *usury*, &c — all which, like many others, confess, but *avoid*, the allegations in the declaration.

§ 71. But it is not universally true, (though generally so), that a special plea in bar goes, merely and exclusively, in confession and avoidance of the plaintiff's allegations. For in some instances, such a plea concludes with a *traverse* of part of the declaration (*f*). It may be added too, that a spe-

(*e*) Bac. Abr. *Pleas*, &c, (Introd. 2.) Lawes' Pl. 37-8. 115. 129.
(*f*) Hob. 104. 2 Chitt. Pl. 510. Bac. Abr. *Pleas*, &c, H. 3.

cial plea in bar, alleging matter of *estoppel*, neither confesses nor denies the truth of the declaration; though, like other pleas in bar, it virtually denies the *right of action* (*g*), by denying the plaintiff's right to *allege* the facts stated in the declaration. (Vid. ch. 2, § 39.)

§ 72. For the purpose then of defining, more precisely, a special plea in bar, it may perhaps be sufficient to say, that it is a plea, which alleges *new or special* matter, in bar of the action, and concludes with an *averment* (10). It admits, on general principles heretofore explained, (ch. 3, § 67), the truth of all the plaintiff's *traversable* allegations, which it does not traverse, and goes in *avoidance* of what it admits (*h*).

§ 73. Special pleas in bar are usually in *affirmative* language; but not universally so. To a *negative* covenant, for example, the plea, by which the defendant shows that he has kept his covenant, is

(*g*) 3 Black. Com. 308. Willes, 13. Lawes' Pl. 38. 130. 140. 161. 170. 3 East, 346.

(*h*) Bac. Abr. *Pleas*, &c, H. 4. 1 Salk. 91. 1 Wils. 338.

---

(10) The term, 'averment', when used as above, to express the *manner of concluding* any pleading, signifies *the* averment, 'this he is ready to verify'; and in this sense is synonymous with the word, 'verification'. But in its more general acceptation, it has the same meaning as the word 'allegation'.

CHAP. VI. PART II.

in the *negative;* as that he has *not* done what he covenanted against (*i*).

Must conclude with a verification.

§ 74. As every special plea alleges *new* matter; it must, regularly, conclude with a *verification* and a prayer of judgment (*k*). For, according to a principle heretofore stated, (ch. 3, §§ 196. 197), all pleading, subsequent to the declaration, and alleging new matter, must be *left open*—in order that the adverse party may have an opportunity to answer it, as he pleases.

§ 75. But there is no necessity of concluding any plea, *merely negative*, with a verification: It may conclude with a prayer of judgment *only* (*l*). For a verification, being an *offer to prove* the allegations to which it refers, cannot, in strictness, be required of him who pleads in the negative; because he, who takes the *negative* in pleading, is, regularly, not bound to *prove* it: The tender of proof, by the general rule, being upon him who takes the *affirmative*.

§ 76. When the defendant alleges *distinct* matters of defence to *different parts* of the declaration, or cause of action (as where in an action to recover

(*i*) 3 Black. Com. 309. Co. Litt. 303. b. Bac. Abr. *Pleas*, &c, I. 3.

(*k*) 3 Black. Com. 309. 310. Lawes' Pl. 145. 159. 1 Saund. 103. (n. 1.) Carth. 337. 2 Wils. 66. 2 T. R. 576. 2 Burr. 772. Cowp. 575.

(*l*) Co. Litt. 303. a. Willes, 6. 7. Lawes' Pl. 145.

a debt, he pleads payment of part, and a tender of the residue), he may either conclude each distinct matter of defence, with a separate verification, or all of them together, with a *single general* one (*m*).

§ 77. It is said to be a universal rule, that every good defence to the action, which cannot be pleaded *specially*, may be given in evidence under the *general issue* (*n*). It must follow, therefore, on the other hand, that every such defence, which *cannot* be given in evidence under the general issue, may be *specially pleaded*. Otherwise the defence, though admitted to be sufficient in law, would necessarily be lost to the defendant.

Amounting to the general issue, not in general allowed.

§ 78. But a special plea, *amounting to the general issue*—i. e. a plea alleging new matter, which is in effect *a denial* of the truth of the declaration—is, in general, improper and inadmissible (*o*). If therefore in trespass, the defendant pleads specially an *alibi*—or *title* in himself or a stranger, to the property in question—or in trover, that he took the goods as a *distress* for rent, &c, the plea is improper: Because in each of these cases, the matter pleaded is virtually a denial of the truth of the declaration. The proper plea, therefore, in each of them, would have been the general issue (*p*). So

(*m*) 1 Saund. 336. b. 339. (n. 8.) 1 Salk. 298. 312. Carth. 43.

(*n*) Lawes' Pl. 111.

(*o*) 10 Co. 95. a. Com. Dig. *Pleader*, E. 14. 3 Black. Com. 309. Bac. Abr. *Pleas*, &c, G. 3. Co. Litt. 303. b. Hob. 127. 1 Salk. 394. Cro. Car. 157.

(*p*) Iid. Yelv. 174. b. (n. 1).

CHAP. VI. PART II. also, where in trover, the defendant pleaded *title* in himself, to the goods, the plea was held ill, as amounting to a denial of the *conversion*, which is the gist of the action, and therefore as tantamount to the *general* issue (*q*).

§ 79. The ground of objection to a plea of this kind is, that it tends to unnecessary *prolixity* in the pleadings, and refers to the *court*, instead of the jury, matter of mere *fact*—matter which goes in *denial* of the declaration, and not in *avoidance* of it (*r*). The fault in the plea, however, is not in its *substance*—(for whatever denies the declaration is *substantially* a sufficient answer to it); but in its *form* only (*s*).

When allowable.

§ 80. But the above general rule is subject to three exceptions, or qualifications:—

1. A special plea, amounting to the general issue, is good, if it contains special matter of *justification* (*t*): In other words, an *entire* special plea, answering the *whole* declaration, and alleging matter of *justification*, is good; although, as to *part* of the declaration, it amounts to the general issue. For

(*q*) Cro. Car. 157.

(*r*) Hob. 127. Bac. Abr. *Pleas*, &c, G. 3.

(*s*) 10 Co. 95. a. Bac. Abr. *Pleas*, &c, G. 3. Com. Dig. *Pleader*, E. 14. Hob. 127. & note (2) by Williams. 1 Freem. 39.

(*t*) 3 Lev. 40. Bac. Abr. *Pleas*, &c. G. 3. *Trespass*, I. 3. (2) Cro. Eliz. 268. Esp. Dig. 318.

matter of *justification* is matter of *law* (11), which ought to be referred, by the plea, to the *court*. And therefore such matter, when it goes in avoidance of a *material part* of the declaration, is allowed to be pleaded specially; though, as to some *other part* of the declaration, it may amount to a mere denial. For, as the matter of *one entire* plea cannot be separated, by a reference of one part of it to the jury, and of the other to the court, and as it would be at least as improper to refer matter of law to the jury, as matter of fact to the court; the defendant is allowed to refer *the whole* to the latter. Thus, in trespass for entering the plaintiff's close, treading down his grass, and driving his beasts to places unknown, so that they could not be replevied, the defendant pleaded that the *locus in quo* was his own waste, (in which, as appeared in another part of the pleading, the plaintiff had a right of common); and that the beasts of the plaintiff were there, intermixed with the beasts of strangers, which had no right there; and that because the latter could not there be separated from the plaintiff's beasts, the defendant drove them all to a pound in the waste, to separate them, and having separated them, left the plaintiff's beasts in the waste: On demurrer to this plea, as amounting to the general issue, the

(11) In this, as in other rules, pointing out what should, and what should not, be pleaded specially, 'matter of *law*' is synonomous with 'matter of *avoidance*,' as distinguished from matter of *denial*. Hence, whatever amounts to a *denial* of the adverse party's allegations, is termed 'matter of *fact*,' whatever *confesses and avoids* them, 'matter of *law*.'

CHAP. VI. PART II.

court held, that though the allegation, that the *place where* was the *defendant's* waste, was a mere *denial* of his alleged entry into *the plaintiff's* close; yet as it was a necessary part of the defendant's *justification, in driving the plaintiff's beasts to the pound,* (which was part of the alleged trespass); the plea, being *entire*, was good (*u*) (12).

§ 81. 2. The general rule under consideration admits of another exception, (or rather an *evasion*), in *trespass qu. cl. fr.* and *assise*—in which, though a simple plea of a possessory *title* in the defendant is ill, as amounting to the general issue; he may, nevertheless, plead that defence, if the plea gives *colour* to the plaintiff (*v*). To give colour to the plaintiff, is to assign to him, in the plea, some *colourable* (i. e. *defective*), but *fictitious* title, of which (it being matter of law), the jury is incompetent to judge—in order to justify, in opposition to it, a special statement of the *defendant's* title; so that the question, which is the *better* title of the two, may appear, upon the face of the plea, as a question of *law* (*w*). And thus, by alleging a *fictitious* and *defective* title in the plaintiff, which

(*u*) 3 Lev. 40.

(*v*) 3 Black. Com. 309. Lawes' Pl. 51. 126—7. 150. 10 Co. 90. 91. 8 T. R. 404. Bac. Abr. *Pleas*, &c, I. 8. *Trespass*, I. 2.

(*w*) Iid. Com. Dig. *Pleader*, 3. M. 40. 41. 2 Chitt. Pl. 555—6.

(12) The more simple and better mode, however, of pleading in such a case, would be to plead, as to that part of the declaration, which the defence *contradicts*, *not guilty;* and to plead the special matter of justification, in avoidance of the *other* part only.

cannot be traversed, the defendant is enabled to plead specially what, *in fact*, is neither more nor less than the general issue. He may, for example, plead a possessory title in himself, under a feoffment with livery, from A. (which plea would, *by itself*, amount to the general issue), provided he adds, that the plaintiff entered, claiming title under *colour* of a certain prior deed of feoffment, *without livery*, by which nothing passed: In which case, the title, alleged in the plaintiff, is clearly defective, at common law (*x*).

§ 82. The colourable title alleged to be in the plaintiff, in a plea of this kind, is not traversable (*y*). Indeed if the title, which the defendant alleges in himself, is in law a sufficient bar; a traverse, by the plaintiff, of the fictitious title assigned to *him* in the plea, would seem necessarily fatal to his action: Since it would imply a *confession* of the defendant's title, as alleged in the plea. But the plaintiff is at liberty to contest the alleged title of the *defendant*, in the same manner in which he might contest any other matter, pleaded specially in bar, in the usual way (*z*).

§ 83. If the defendant, when intending to give *colour* to the plaintiff, assigns to him a title, *sufficient* for the maintenance of the action; the plea is ne-

(*x*) 2 Chitt. Pl. 555—6.
(*y*) 1 Chitt. Pl. 501.
(*z*) 3 Black. Com. 310. Lawes' Pl. 150.

CHAP. VI. PART II.

cessarily ill (*a*): Since it is, in effect, a *confession* of the plaintiff's right of action.

§ 84. There is no use in pleading title specially, and giving colour, except where the defendant wishes — instead of submitting his defence to the jury, under the general issue — to have the question of title presented distinctly upon *the face of the pleadings;* to the end that it may be the more formally and deliberately judged of by the Court; and that he may, with the more ease and certainty, take advantage of any error in law, that may intervene.

§ 85. 3. According to various authorities, a special plea amounting to a denial of the declaration, and *without* giving colour, may in some cases be allowed, at the *discretion* of the court (*b*). The cases, in which such a plea is held to be thus allowable, are those in which the matter pleaded is such as may 'breed a scruple, in the *lay gents*' — or, in more familiar language, such as is likely to perplex a jury, and therefore unfit to be determined by them.

Manner of excepting to.

§ 86. In regard to the *manner* of excepting to a special plea amounting to the general issue, when not thus allowable, there is some apparent contrariety of opinion in the books. According to one

(*a*) Com. Dig. *Pleader,* 3 M. 40. Cro. Jac. 122.

(*b*) Hob. 127. 1 Leon. 178. Com. Dig. *Pleader,* E. 14. Bac. Abr. *Pleas,* &c, G. 3. *Trespass,* I. 2. 2 Mod. 274.

class of authorities, such a plea is *demurrable* (c). But according to other opinions equally respectable, it is held that the fault in question is not a proper cause of *demurrer;* and that the only proper mode of taking exception to the plea is by a *motion* to the court for an order, that the *general issue*, or a *nil dicit*, be entered (d): And that if the order is made, the defendant must enter the general issue, or the plaintiff may take judgment, as by *nil dicit* (e).

§ 87. The question, whether this latter course, or that of demurring, is the proper mode of excepting to such a plea, appears manifestly to depend upon the correctness or incorrectness of the rule, (before stated), asserting a *discretion* in the court, in regard to the allowance of it. If such a discretion can legally be exercised by the court, (and it has been actually exercised, by high and repeated authority); the proper mode of objecting to the plea must be by *motion*. For questions raised by a demurrer are *stricti juris*, and admit of no discretion.

§ 88. The objection to a plea of this kind has, however, been taken, and the question decided, in each of the above modes. And perhaps the most

(c) 10 Co. 95. a. Cro. Car. 157. Cro. Eliz. 147. Bac. Abr. *Pleas*, &c, G. 3. N. 6. *Trespass*, I. 3. (2.) Com. Dig. *Pleader*, E. 14.—*Vid.* 4 B. & C. 547. 4 Bing. 470.

(d) Hob. 127. 1 Leon. 178. Cro. Jac. 165. Bro. Ab. *Traverse*, pl. 14. 2 Mod. 274. Com. Dig. *Pleader*, E. 14. Bac. Abr. *Pleas*, &c, G. 3. *Trespass*, I. 2. (2.) 2 Day, 431. Esp. Dig. 413.

(e) Bac. Abr. *Tresp.* I. 2. (2.) Cro. Jac. 165.

CHAP. VI. PART II.

satisfactory view of the subject will be found to be, that the proper mode of objecting to the plea is, in the first instance, by *motion* — and upon this supposition, if the plaintiff should *demur*, instead of *moving* the court, the defendant would not be bound to join in the demurrer; but might still refer the question to the *discretion* of the court: But that if, on the plaintiff's demurring, the defendant *accepts* the demurrer, by *joining* in it, and thus *waves* his right to appeal to the discretion of the court; the question may be decided under the *demurrer*. This supposition, if correct, may serve to explain how it happens, that two such dissimilar and apparently inconsistent modes of excepting to pleas of this kind, have been pursued; since according to this view of the subject, each of those modes may, under different circumstances, be correct (*f*).

§ 89. Not only *special* pleas, amounting to the general issue, but also pleas which allege *no new* matter, and which expressly and merely *deny* the declaration, but which vary, in their form and terms, from the general issue, are in general not allowable. The reason for disallowing pleas of this kind is not, however, that they tend to inconvenient *prolixity*, or that they refer matters of fact to *the court* — (for they are not, like pleas of the former class, liable to either of those objections); but that they lead to *innovation and confusion*, in the established modes of pleading, and tend, not only to destroy the settled

(*f*) *Vid.* 10 Co. 95. a. Bac. Abr. *Pleas*, &c, N. 6. Yelv. 174. b. *note.*

distinctions between the different species of pleas, but also to the introduction of *new* pleas, unknown to the law.

§ 90. If therefore to a declaration, alleging the beating of J. S. the plaintiff's servant, by reason whereof he lost *the service of J. S.*, the defendant pleads that the plaintiff *did not lose the* service of J. S., the plea is ill (*g*). For the loss of service being the *gist* of the action; the plea is, essentially, the *general issue*, in an argumentative and improper form. So also, where in trespass for entering the plaintiff's garden, the defendant pleaded that the plaintiff *had no such garden*—and where, in trespass for depasturing the plaintiff's herbage, the defendant pleaded, that he *did not* depasture the plaintiff's herbage—the pleas were, respectively, held to be ill, for the same reason (*h*).

Liberum tenementum—or the common bar.

§ 91. Although, as has before been shown, (*ante*, § 77), a special plea, alleging the *possessory title* to be in the defendant, and not giving colour, is ill, as amounting to the general issue, in trespass *quare clausum fregit;* yet the plea of *liberum tenementum*, (that the *locus in quo* was the defendant's freehold), has, by a long series of authorities, ancient and modern, been sanctioned, as a good special plea in that action, though it never gives colour (*i*).

(*g*) Bac. Abr. *Tresp.* I. 2. (2.) Bro. Ab. *Trav.* pl. 378.

(*h*) 10 H. 6. 16. Doct. Pl. 42.

(*i*) 1 Saund. 299. b. (n. 6.) Com. Dig. *Pleader*, 3 M. 40. 41. Willes, 218. Lawes' Pl. 128. 2 Chitt. Pl. 551–3. 2 Black. R. 1089. 2 Salk. 453. 1 Ld Ray. 333. 7 T. R. 335.

CHAP. VI. PART II.

§ 92. For the purpose of explaining why this latter plea does not amount to the general issue, it must be observed that every trespass upon property is an invasion of another's *possession;* and that the action of trespass, which is called a *possessory* action, is so called, because it is founded upon a *possessory title.* Every plea, therefore, which denies *such* a title in the plaintiff, whatever may be its form, is in effect *the general issue.* But the plea of *liberum tenementum*, or (as it is frequently called) '*the common bar*', is perfectly consistent with the existence of a *possessory title* in the plaintiff: Since a *freehold*, in one person, may co-exist with an actual and rightful *possession* of the same subject, in another. The freehold, for example, may be in A., while B. is in rightful possession, under a subsisting term for years, or otherwise; or the latter may, without any derivative title, be in the defendant's actual and quiet possession, which of itself confers a possessory title against all persons, except him, who has *the right* of possession. And as the plea in question does not deny such a title in the plaintiff, it does not amount to the general issue.

§ 93. But although these considerations do, indeed, show that the plea of *liberum tenementum* does not amount to the general issue; they also seem to show that, on strict principles, the plea is *defective in substance*—as some highly respectable opinions hold it to be (*k*): Inasmuch as it impliedly admits

(*k*) *Vid.* Willes, 222. 1 Saund. 299. c. (n. 6.)

a *possessory title*, and consequently a right of action, in the plaintiff. Indeed, it is difficult to understand how the matter of this plea could ever have been supposed to be a strict and full bar to the action. And it appears to have been sanctioned, not so much on account of its own inherent sufficiency, as from a kind of *necessity* — that is to say, from its being the only means of protecting the defendant against a *disadvantage*, to which he would otherwise be exposed, from the ancient mode of declaring in trespass *quare clausum fregit*. For formerly, the almost universal mode of describing the plaintiff's close, in this action, (a mode, which still may be, and sometimes is pursued (*l*), was merely to mention it as the plaintiff's 'close at A.', or his 'close lying in the parish of A.' without giving its name or abuttals, or any other designation. The consequence was, that the defendant could not discover from the declaration, in *what particular* close within the parish named, the plaintiff intended to prove the alleged trespass; and consequently, could not know, with certainty, how to frame his defence. He was, therefore, allowed to plead that the close, mentioned in the declaration, was 'his close, soil and freehold' (*m*) without giving it any name, or further description. For the description of the close, in the declaration, being *general;* that in the plea was allowed to be equally so: And hence the plea was called the *common* (i. e. *general*) bar; the *main object*

(*l*) 2 Chitt. Pl. 385–6. 387. (*note* n.) 2 Black. R. 1089. 1 Saund. 299. b. c. (n. 6.)

(*m*) 2 Chitt. Pl. 551–2. Com. Dig. *Pleader*, 3 M. 34.

CHAP. VI. PART II.

of which was, and still is, (though it may be useful for certain other purposes) (*n*), to drive the plaintiff to a *new assignment* of the trespass, and thus to compel him to *particularize* his close — so that the defendant may know how to adapt his defence to the actual ground of complaint: An object easily attained, in most cases. For if the plaintiff *traverses* the plea; the defendant, by proving a freehold in himself, in *any close* within the parish or vill named in the declaration, supports his plea, and defeats the action. And if the plaintiff makes a *new assignment*, which is in nature of a new declaration; the defendant may, in his rejoinder, plead to it, as to an original declaration.

Alleging facts, which would prove the general issue.

§ 94. A special plea, alleging facts which would, in *evidence*, *maintain* the general issue, does not, in all cases, and necessarily, *amount* to the general issue. For no plea — whether it admits or denies that there was once *a right of action* — can properly be said to amount to the general issue, unless it goes in *denial of the declaration*.

§ 95. Thus in assumpsit — *payment*, *release*, *accord*, &c, all which admit that the alleged cause of action once existed — as also, *infancy*, *coverture*, *duress*, *usury*, &c, which deny that it ever existed, may respectively be pleaded specially; although each of these defences would, in evidence, maintain the

Ante, § 47.

(*n*) 2 Chitt. Pl. 551. (n. s.) 8 T. R. 404.

general issue (*o*). For they all *admit* the truth of the declaration.

And this right in the defendant, either to *plead* special matters of defence, or to give them in evidence under the *general issue*, exists, to a great extent, as has been before shown (*ante*, §§ 54. 55), in actions of *trespass on the case, ex delicto* (*p*).

Must contain issuable matter.

§ 96. Every special plea must contain *issuable* matter (*q*); for the plain reason, that it would not otherwise be *triable*. The same rule extends to all special pleading, in all its stages. If therefore, in debt or assumpsit, the defendant pleads only that he was *ready*, or *willing*, to pay according to his contract; the plea is ill — because the fact averred is not *issuable*. Such a plea would indeed be ill for another reason, viz. that the fact of mere readiness, or willingness, is *immaterial;* since it is neither a *performance* nor a *discharge* of the contract. Its not being *issuable* is, however, a sufficient objection to it.

§ 97. On the same principle, every special plea, in which matter of fact and matter of law are so *blended*, that they cannot be separated, is ill (*r*).

(*o*) 1 Ld Ray. 88-9. 566. 1 Salk. 394. 3 Ib. 273. 5 Mod. 18. Com. Dig. *Pleader*, E. 14. Chitt. on Bills, 197-8. Lawes' Pl. 112. Tidd, 591. 599. Sayer, 270.

(*p*) 3 Burr. 1353. 1 Chitt. Pl. 486-7. 1 Black. R. 388. 1 Wils. 45. 8 East, 308. 2 Phil. Ev. 108.

(*q*) Lawes' Pl. 137-8. 2 Wils. 74.

(*r*) 9 Co. 25. a. Lawes' Pl. 138. 2 Mod. 55.

CHAP. VI. PART II.

If therefore, to trespass for false imprisonment, the defendant pleads that he arrested the plaintiff, *by lawful authority*, without showing what the authority was; the plea is bad, as not being issuable. For a traverse of the plea would put in issue all matters of *law*, as well as of fact, which might conduce to show the defendant's authority: Whereas matter of *law* is never issuable. The plea, in such a case, ought to state the defendant's authority *specially*—not only that its legal sufficiency may be judged of by the court, from the record; but also that the plaintiff may be enabled to traverse, distinctly, the matter of fact alleged in it. So also where the defendant, being bound by a condition, to produce to the plaintiff a *sufficient discharge* of a certain demand, pleaded that he had produced 'a sufficient discharge', without stating *its tenor or contents*, the plea was held ill, on the principles above stated (*s*).

Must answer the whole gravamen.

§ 98. A plea in bar, pleaded to the *whole* declaration, must contain a sufficient answer in law to the *whole* gravamen, or cause of action: Otherwise it is ill for the whole (*t*); and the plaintiff is entitled to recover for the *whole*. Thus, if in trespass for assault, battery and *mayhem*, the defendant pleads to the whole, matter which is in law a justification of the *assault and battery only;* the plea is

(*s*) 9 Co. 25. a.

(*t*) Co. Litt. 303. a. 1 Saund. 28. (n. 2). 2 Ib. 50. 127. 210. b. c. (n. 1). Yelv. 225. Com. Dig. *Pleader*, E. 1. Lawes' Pl. 135. 171. Cro. Eliz. 268. 331. Cro. Jac. 27. 5 T. R. 553. 1 Lev. 48.

ill *in toto*, and the plaintiff is entitled to damages, as well for the *assault and battery*, as for the *mayhem*. For an *entire* plea, going to the *whole* declaration, is *indivisible* in its effect; and cannot operate as a bar to any *part* of the cause of action, unless it constitutes in law a bar to the *whole*.

§ 99. Thus also, if to an action of trespass, the defendant pleads a justification, (as a license), on any day *different* from that laid in the declaration; he must traverse the commission of the trespass on any *other* day, either before or after that mentioned in his plea, and before the commencement of the suit (*u*): Otherwise the defence will not be *co-extensive* with the declaration; or in other words, will not cover the *whole time*, within which the plaintiff is at liberty to prove the trespass complained of. For the day in the declaration being immaterial; the plaintiff has a right to prove the trespass on *any* day before the date of the writ. But the justification, if true, applies only to *the particular* day laid in the plea—and without the traverse, would therefore imply an admission, that the trespass complained of was committed on any *other* day than that. Upon the same principle, if the defendant in trespass pleads a *release* on a particular day; he should traverse his guilt, as to all *subsequent* time, before the commencement of the suit: Or if he pleads *title*, acquired by himself—as by a feoff-

(*u*) Hob. 104. Bac. Abr. *Pleas*, &c, H. 4. 1 Saund. 14. 298. (n. 2). 2 Ib. 5. a. (n. 3). 1 T. R. 636. 1 Chitt. Pl. 534.—*Post.* ch. 7, § 45.

ment—on a particular day; he should traverse, as to all *previous* time (v): Otherwise, the plea will not cover *all* the time covered by the declaration. *Vid. ante*, ch. 3 (13).

§ 100. The general principle above stated, that an *entire* plea is indivisible, extends to all the subsequent pleadings; and therefore an entire replication, if bad for *part* of the plea—or an entire rejoinder, if bad for part of the replication, is so for the *whole* (w).

§ 101. Upon the same principle, if two co-defendants *join* in a plea, which is in law a sufficient justification for *one* of them only; it is bad as to *both* of them (x). If therefore an arrest is made under *irregular* process, (which though irregular, justifies the *officer* executing it, but not the *party* who prayed it out)—and in an action for false imprisonment, against both of them, they *join* in a plea, justifying the arrest by virtue of the process;

(v) Hob. 104. Bac. Abr. *Pleas*, &c. H. 4.
(w) 1 Saund. 28. (n. 2). 2 Ib. 127. 1 T. R. 40.
(x) Stra. 509. 993. 1184. 1 Wils. 17. 3 T. R. 377. Cas. Temp. Hardw. 62. 69. 3 Mass. R. 312.

---

(13) In cases like these two last, however, the simpler and better, and at this time the more usual, mode of pleading is, to divide the defence into *two* pleas, by pleading as to all time, *except* the day or time covered by the justification, or other matter of avoidance, *not guilty*, concluding to the country; and as to *that* day or time, by pleading the matter of justification, &c, *specially*, with a verification. (2 Chitt. Pl. 519. 520. n. y).

judgment must go against *both.* For the plea, which is *joint,* being ill *quoad* one of them, is consequently ill for both. The officer should have pleaded *separately.*

§ 102. But though the defence must, in all cases, answer the *whole* declaration, or alleged cause of action; it is not necessary that the whole be answered by *one* plea: It is necessary only, that the *whole* matter of defence pleaded, cover the *whole complaint.* The defendant may, therefore, plead several different matters of defence, in several *different* pleas, to as many *different parts* of the declaration, or alleged cause of action. And if all the pleas, taken together, form a sufficient answer to the whole matter of complaint; the defence is complete.

§ 103. Thus, in trespass for cutting down *ten* of the plaintiff's timber-trees, the defendant may plead, as to all the trees except *one*—*not guilty;* and as to the remaining one, any matter of *avoidance*—as a license, or other justification; or a *release,* a former recovery, &c. So also in debt, or assumpsit, for 1000 dollars, the defendant may plead as to 500 dollars, (parcel of the 1000), *non assumpsit;* and as to the residue, *release, payment, tender,* &c: or he may plead several *special* pleas to different parts of the demand—as *payment* of part, and *tender* of the residue (*y*): Or finally, he may

(*y*) Co. Litt. 304. a. Lawes' Pl. 107. Bac. Abr. *Pleas,* &c, K. 1. N. 1.

CHAP. VI. PART II.

plead to part of the declaration, and *demur* to the residue (*z*). Thus, if in covenant broken, the declaration alleges two breaches, one of which is well assigned, and the other ill; the defendant may *plead* to the former assignment, and *demur* to the latter.

§ 104. Every plea to the action is taken, as extending to the *whole* declaration or gravamen, unless *expressly* limited to a *part* of it, by beginning *as* an answer to a part only. And as to the *mode of taking advantage* of a plea, which does not answer the whole ground of the complaint, the three following rules are to be observed: —

When answering only part of the gravamen, how to except to it.

1. Where matter, pleaded as an answer to the *whole*, is in law a good answer to *a part only*, the proper mode of excepting to it is by *demurrer* (*a*) — as in the case before mentioned, where to assault, battery and *mayhem*, the defendant pleads to the *whole*, what is an answer in law to the *assault* and *battery only*. So also, if in an action against a bailee, for goods delivered to him 'to keep and carry,' he pleads to the *whole* declaration, that he was discharged from *keeping* them, without answering his obligation to *carry;* the plea is *demurrable* (*b*). For in these cases, the ground of objection to the plea is, not that it is *irregular and in-*

(*z*) Bac. Abr. *Pleas*, &c, N. 1.

(*a*) 1 Saund. 28. (n. 3). 1 Salk. 179. 1 Stra. 303. Lawes' Pl. 135—6.

(*b*) Iid.

admissible; but merely that it is *insufficient* in law. And such is the proper course for the plaintiff, whenever a plea, purporting to be an answer to the *whole* declaration, (as it does of course, unless expressly limited, as mentioned above), is in law a sufficient answer to *part* of it only.

§ 105. 2. But if the plea *purports* to answer only a *part* of the declaration, and is in law a sufficient answer to that part only, the other part being left unanswered — (as if, in an action like that stated above, against a bailee, for goods delivered to him to be *kept and carried,* he pleads, *as to his undertaking to keep,* that he was discharged thereof, without answering, in any way, the other part of his undertaking); the plea is void, and of course considered as *no* plea. The plaintiff therefore should not, in such a case, *demur;* but should sign judgment, as by *nil dicit,* that is, as for *want of a plea* (c). For such a plea, being considered in law as *no* plea, is a *discontinuance,* on the defendant's part. And therefore, if the plaintiff *accepts it* as a plea, by demurring to it, he *discontinues the whole* action.

§ 106. To explain the reason of this rule, it must be observed that the court has no right, in any case, to determine any one *part* of an entire cause of action, leaving the rest undecided. The *whole* must be, in some way, determined: Otherwise a

(c) Com. Dig. *Pleader,* E. 1. 1 Saund. 28. (n. 3.) Gilb. H. C. P. 158. 1 Salk. 179. 180. 1 Stra. 302. 2 Ld Ray. 841. 7 Mod. 124. 4 Co. 62. a. 1 Selw. N. P. 5. (n. 7.) Lawes' Pl. 135-6.

single right of action might require several suits. If then, the defendant makes answer to only *a part* of the plaintiff's complaint; the answer is regarded as *no plea*; because it does not enable the court to determine the whole. It is therefore tantamount to a *nil dicit*, and *discontinues the whole defence*. It results then, that if the plaintiff, who has a right to treat such an answer as a nullity, *accepts it* as a plea, by demurring or pleading to it; and thus, in effect, prays judgment for only *a part* of his cause of action; he *discontinues* his whole *action*.

§ 107. 3. And if the defendant pleads, to a *part* of the cause of action, matter which would be in law a sufficient answer to *the whole, if pleaded to the whole;* the rule is the same — and the plaintiff must not *demur*, but take his judgment, as in the preceding case, and for the same reason (*d*). For though the matter pleaded be sufficient to bar the *whole* action; yet, not being *pleaded* to the whole, it cannot be applied as an answer to the whole. If therefore, in trespass for cutting *ten* of the plaintiff's growing trees, the defendant pleads *as to all the trees, except one*, a release of *all* trespasses — or if in the case, mentioned above, of a bailment of goods to be kept and carried, the defendant pleads, as to his undertaking *to keep*, a release of *all demands;* the plaintiff must sign judgment, as by *nil dicit*. Such appear to be the established distinctions, under this head.

(*d*) 1 Stra. 302-3. 1 Ld Ray. 231. 1 Saund. 28. (n 3.) 4 Co. 62. a.

§ 108. Yet where a plea, beginning as an answer to only *a part* of the plaintiff's demand, not only alleged matter, which in law would have been a bar to the whole, but, in the body of it, actually *answered* the whole — (as where in assumpsit on a note, payable by sixteen half-yearly instalments, the defendant pleaded *as to all of them, except the last,* that *none* of them had accrued within six years) — it was resolved that the plea was ill, on *special demurrer*, by reason of its *inconsistency*, in beginning as an answer to *part* of the demand, and actually *answering the whole* (*e*). For the court appear to have considered the *inconsistency* of the plea with itself, as rendering it *anomalous*, and as thus taking it out of the rule stated in the last section.

Matter of aggravation needs no answer.

§ 109. But no plea is ever required to answer, expressly, any part of the declaration which is not of *the gist* of the action. Hence, matter of *aggravation* — as the *alia enormia*, in a declaration in trespass — requires no express answer (*f*). Thus, where in trespass for assault and battery, the declaration, after alleging the assault and beating, adds, 'and other wrongs to the plaintiff then and there did', a plea, justifying the *assault and battery only*, is a sufficient answer to the whole complaint.

(*e*) 2 Bos. & P. 427.

(*f*) 1 Saund. 28. (n. 3.) 3 Wils. 20. 2 Ib. 313. 2 Campb. 175. 3 T. R. 297.

CHAP. VI. PART II.

What answers the gist of the action, covers all matters of aggravation.

§ 110. Thus also, in trespass for breaking and entering the plaintiff's house, and *expelling* him therefrom, or *destroying his goods*, a plea to the whole, and which in law justifies the *breaking and entering the house*, though silent as to the other alleged wrongs, is a good answer to the whole declaration: The breaking, &c, being the *gist* of the action; and the expulsion, &c, only matter of *aggravation* (*g*). For as the action is, in its title, and consequently in its character, trespass *quare domum fregit;* the breaking, &c, of the house constitutes the whole *gist* of the complaint. Yet if the plaintiff, in the case now supposed, relies upon the *expulsion*, or the injury to his *goods*, as a *distinct* ground of damages; he may, by a *new assignment* of it, in his replication, convert it into a substantive cause of action, and thus entitle himself to a recovery, notwithstanding the justification of the breaking of the house (*h*) (14).

(*g*) 1 T. R. 479. 636. 3 Ib. 292. 3 Wils. 20. 1 H. Black. 555. 3 N. Hamp. R. 511.
(*h*) Iid.

---

(14) A *novel* or *new* assignment consists in alleging, with all necessary particularity, in the replication, facts which the declaration has alleged in *general terms;* and in this way, the plaintiff may convert into a *substantive* cause of action, what appears, in the declaration, as matter of mere *aggravation* — as in the example given in the text, (2 Chitt. Pl. 653–7. Lawes' Pl. 165. 1 Saund. 299. a. b. (n. 6.) A new assignment being in the nature of a *declaration;* the defendant may plead to it, *de novo*, as to a common declaration, (3 East, 294. Lawes' Pl. 165. 1 Saund. 299. a. b. (n. 6.) A new assignment must, in general, conclude

§ 111. Every *justification* pleaded must, expressly or tacitly, *confess* the act which it is intended to justify (*i*). For it is absurd to plead in avoidance of a fact, which the plea does not *admit*. If therefore, to a declaration charging assault, battery and wounding, the defendant, *as to the assault and battery*, confesses, and justifies an act *not amounting to a battery*, with a *quæ est eadem transgressio;* the plea is ill, for the above reason; but ill only on *special* demurrer — as the fault is only formal (*k*). The plea, in such a case, should be the *general issue.*

§ 112. Anciently, if the defence to an action consisted of matter of *avoidance;* it was necessary for the defendant to state specially, in his plea, *all* the particular facts, which constituted the defence, however multifarious they might be (*l*). And this rule is, undoubtedly, conformable to the strict principles of pleading. For each fact, essential to the

(*i*) 1 Saund. 13. 14. (n. 3.) 28. (n. 1.) 1 Salk. 394. 3 T. R. 298. Carth. 380. Esp. Dig. 318.
(*k*) 1 Saund. 14. (n. 3.) 28. (n. 1.)
(*l*) Co. Litt. 303. 8 Co. 133. Bac. Abr. *Pleas*, &c, I. 3.

---

with an averment, that the wrongs, or causes of complaint, alleged in it, are *different* from those mentioned in the *plea*, (1 Saund. 299. (n. 6.) Lawes' Pl. 164–5. 240. 241): For otherwise a new assignment is unnecessary. And if the averment is untrue, the defendant may, for that cause, plead the *general issue* to the new assignment — as that issue involves a denial of the averment. (1 Saund. 299. c (n. 6.) Lawes' Pl. 241. — Post. ch. 8, §§ 75–77.

CHAP. VI. PART II.

defence, being matter of law, ought, in strictness, to be shown to the court by the plea. But from *necessity*, or at least for the avoiding of great *inconvenience*, this rule has been somewhat relaxed.

General pleading when allowed.

§ 113. And now, as in declarations (*ante*, ch. 4), so also in special pleas in bar, *general* pleading is sometimes allowed, for the purpose of avoiding great *prolixity:* It being now an established rule, that no greater particularity can be required in pleading, than the nature of the subject will *conveniently admit of.* When therefore, one is sued on an obligation, binding him affirmatively to the performance of an *indefinite* number of acts, the particular recital of which would render the pleadings inconveniently *prolix*, he may plead performance, in *general* terms; and thus leave it to the plaintiff to assign any particular breach or breaches, in the replication. And as the breach or breaches, thus assigned, must be *specific;* the matter in controversy will of course be presented with sufficient certainty (*m*).

§ 114. Thus, if a sheriff executes a bond, with condition that he shall return *all* writs delivered to him, &c; he may, in an action on this obligation, plead performance in *general* terms, by averring that he has returned '*all* writs delivered to him,' &c, (pursuing the words of the condition) — without

(*m*) Cro. Eliz. 749. 916. Co. Litt. 303. b. Bac. Abr. *Pleas*, &c, I. 3. 1 Saund. 117. (n. 1). 2 Ib. 410. (n. 3. 4). 1 T. R. 753. 1 Sid. 215. 334. Sayer, 317.

specifying any *particular* writ (*n*). So also, where the defendant was bound in an obligation to deliver to the plaintiff, upon request, all the fat and tallow of all beasts, which he, his servants, &c, should kill before such a day — a plea, that upon every request made to him, he delivered to the plaintiff *all* the fat and tallow of all beasts, which were killed by him, his servants, &c, before the said day, without specifying any particular act of delivery, was adjudged sufficient (*o*). So also, if the defendant is bound in an obligation, with condition that he should pay over to the plaintiff '*all* the monies which he should receive for the plaintiff,' within a certain time; it is a sufficient plea of performance, that he has paid over to the plaintiff '*all* the monies' so received, within that time (*p*). Again: When the obligation is still more general — as that the obligor shall perform *all the duties* of a certain office, during a certain time, it is sufficient on his part, to plead that he has performed 'all the duties' of the office, during that time (*q*). And in all such cases, it becomes incumbent on the *plaintiff* to assign specially, in his replication, the breach or breaches on which he founds his right of recovery.

§ 115. But this relaxation of the original rule before mentioned, (*ante*, § 113), extends only to cases, in which the acts required to be done, on the

(*n*) 1 T. R. 753.
(*o*) Cro. Eliz. 749.
(*p*) 2 Burr. 772. 1 Bos. & P. 640. 8 T. R. 459. 8 East, 85.
(*q*) 2 Saund. 403. 410. (n. 3).

part of the defendant, are in some degree *indefinite*, or at least *not precisely ascertained*, either in the obligation sued upon, or in any other instrument referred to in it — as in the examples just stated, of an obligation to return all writs, &c.

§ 116. If therefore, the condition of the obligation, on which the action is founded, requires the performance of acts, which, however numerous, are *specifically ascertained* in the instrument itself, or in any other instrument referred to in it; the defendant must plead specially the performance of *each* of the particular acts, so ascertained (*r*). For in no such case, can it be objected, that the defendant is *unable* to specify each particular act of performance; and generally such a specification will not make the plea more *multifarious* than the condition itself, which enumerates the acts to be done. And therefore, if the defendant is bound, by the condition of a bond, to pay *all* the legacies contained in a certain will; he must enumerate them all, and specially allege payment of each of them; concluding with an averment, that those thus mentioned in the plea are *all*, that are contained in the will. Or if the condition be, that he shall enfeoff the plaintiff of *all* the lands described in a certain deed; he must plead in a similar manner, concluding with a similar averment (*s*).

(*r*) 1 T. R. 753. Cro. Eliz. 749. 916. 1 Saund. 116. 117. (n. 1). 4 East, 344.

(*s*) 1 Bulstr. 43. 1 Saund. 117. (n. 1). 1 T. R. 753. Palm. 70. Keilw. 95. b. pl. 3.

§ 117. In cases of this last kind, however, if the defendant pleads performance, in *general terms*, (as by averring that he did well and truly perform and fulfil all and singular the conditions, &c); the plea is ill, only on *special* demurrer (*t*). For *performance*, in whatever manner alleged, being in *substance* a sufficient defence; the fault in the plea is only formal.

§ 118. But to *negative* conditions or stipulations — as to a bond, conditioned for the keeping of *negative covenants*, a general or other plea of '*performance*' is never proper (*u*). For 'performance,' being a term implying some *positive* act, does not properly express the keeping of a mere *negative* condition or covenant. If then any of the covenants or stipulations, mentioned in the condition of an obligation, or in a deed of covenant, are in the *negative;* the defendant should plead, as to these, (and usually in the words of the condition or covenant), that he *has not done* any of the acts covenanted against.

§ 119. Thus if a lessee, having covenanted, among other things, that he will not cut down any of the timber-trees on the demised premises, nor suffer any of the buildings thereon to be injured for want of repairs, gives a bond for the performance of the covenants in the lease; in debt on the bond,

(*t*) 1 Saund. 117. (n. 1). Bac. Abr. *Pleas*, &c, I. 3.

(*u*) Co. Litt. 303. b. Esp. Dig. 305. Bac. Abr. *Pleas*, &c, I. 3. Cro. Eliz. 691.

CHAP. VI. PART II.

his proper mode of pleading, as to these negative covenants, is, that he did *not* cut down any of the timber-trees, &c, nor suffer any of the buildings to be injured for want of repairs (*v*). And if the covenant were more *general*, viz. that he would not *commit any waste;* he should still not plead that he had *performed* the covenant; but that he had not, in any manner, committed any waste. Yet if the defendant, in either of these last cases, pleads *performance affirmatively*, and in general terms; the fault in the plea is but formal (*w*).

Actionem non.

§ 120. A special plea in bar, (after the formal introduction, technically called the 'defence'), begins regularly with *actionem non* — an averment that the plaintiff ought not to have, or maintain, his action — concluding with a *verification*, and praying judgment of *the action* (*x*). The rejoinder, and subsequent special pleading on the part of the defendant, begin and conclude in a similar manner.

Precludi non.

§ 121. A special replication begins with *precludi non*, i. e. that the plaintiff ought not to be barred, &c; and concludes with a verification, and a prayer of judgment, and his debt, damages, &c, to be adjudged to him (*y*). The surrejoinder, and the special pleading which follows it, on the part of the plaintiff, begin and conclude in a similar manner.

(*v*) 2 Saund. 409. 410.
(*w*) Bac. Abr. *Pleas*, &c, I. 3. & see 1 Saund. 117. (n. 1).
(*x*) 2 Chitt. Pl. 421–2.
(*y*) 2 Chitt. Pl. 593–4. 615. 616.

Of Pleas Puis Darrein Continuance.

§ 122. As the defendant is allowed, by the common law, to plead only *one* plea, of any one kind or class; so also, after having pleaded, within the time allowed for that purpose, any one matter of defence, he cannot, in general, and as a matter of right, retract it and substitute another (*z*). If it were otherwise, the defendant might protract the proceedings interminably, by repeatedly shifting his ground of defence.

§ 123. But to this general rule there is an exception, when *new* matter of defence arises, *after* he has once pleaded, and after the last *continuance* (or adjournment) of the cause (*a*). For it would be unreasonable to preclude him from pleading matter thus arising, and which it was not in his power to plead in the first instance. The new plea, which this exception to the general rule allows, is called a plea *puis darrein continuance — since (or after) the last continuance.* — It is here to be observed, that during the whole proceedings in a suit, from the time of the defendant's appearance, until its final determination, the cause is to be *continued*, (or as it is sometimes expressed, the *parties* must be 'continued' in court), from day to day, or from time to

(*z*) Lawes' Pl. 173. Bac. Abr. *Pleas*, &c, Q. 1 Chitt. Pl. 635. Doct. Pl. 297.

(*a*) Iid. 3 Black. Com. 316. 317. Gilb. H. C. P. 105.

time, by regular entries, to be made for that purpose. And when any new matter of defence arises, *between* two of these continuances or adjournments, it may be pleaded *puis darrein continuance*, *before* the next continuance, notwithstanding the pendency of a prior plea (*b*).

§ 124. Pleas of this kind may be either in *abatement*, or in *bar;* and may be pleaded, even after an issue joined, either in fact or in law, if the new matter has arisen *after* the issue was joined, and is pleaded *before* the next adjournment (*c*). Thus, if the plaintiff, being a feme sole, has married since the last continuance; her marriage may be pleaded, before the next continuance, to her disability, although the *regular* time for pleading such a plea has elapsed. So also, if the plaintiff has, since the last continuance, *released* the right of action; the defendant may, in the same manner, plead the release in bar, although he has previously pleaded, and issue has been joined upon a different matter of defence. But if he suffers another continuance to intervene, before he pleads such new matter; he *waves* it, and cannot afterwards plead it (*d*). Nor can he plead any such plea, after a demurrer determined, or verdict found — all pleading in the cause being then at an end (*dd*).

(*b*) Iid.

(*c*) Com. Dig. *Abatement*, I. 24. 1 Chitt. Pl. 637. 3 Black. Com. 316. 5 Peters, 232.

(*d*) Iid. Bac. Abr. *Pleas*, &c, Q. Lawes' Pl. 174.

(*dd*) 3 Black. Com. 317.

§ 125. It is said that there can be but *one* plea *puis darrein continuance*, in one and the same cause, lest the proceedings should be protracted *in infinitum*, or beyond any assignable limit (*e*). But matter of *abatement* may be pleaded, *puis darrein continuance*, though the defendant has previously pleaded in *bar* (*f*). For a plea in bar waves only such matters of abatement, *as existed at the time* of pleading in bar.

§ 126. A plea of this kind, *in abatement*, begins and concludes like a plea of the same kind, when pleaded in the first instance; but when pleaded *in bar*, it begins with saying that the plaintiff ought not *further* to maintain his action; and concludes by praying judgment, if the plaintiff ought *further* to maintain his action (*g*). In other respects, pleas of this kind are governed by the same rules, which regulate other pleas in general.

(*e*) Lawes' Pl. 174. Gilb. H. C. P. 105. 1 Chitt. Pl. 638.

(*f*) Gilb. H. C. P. 105. Andr. 328. 2 Stra. 1106. 1 Chitt. Pl. 636. 14 Mass. R. 295.

(*g*) Lawes' Pl. 174-5. Bull. N. P. 310. Cro. Eliz. 49. 5 Peters, 231-2. 1 Chitt. Pl. 637. *Vid.* 3 N. Hamp. R. 102.

CHAPTER VII.

OF TRAVERSE.

CHAP. VII.

Section 1. A *traverse*, in pleading, is a *denial*, on one side, of some matter of fact before alleged, on the other; and (regularly) tenders an issue in fact (*h*).

§ 2. A traverse may be taken to any part of the pleadings — as to the declaration, the plea, the replication, &c (*i*): Though when the whole substance of the *declaration* is to be denied, the proper form of denial is the *general issue;* which is a compendious traverse of the whole complaint.

§ 3. A traverse, concluding to *the country*, forms an issue in fact; so that nothing more is necessary, to prepare the matter in controversy for trial, than the addition of the *similiter* — by the addition of which the issue is *joined*. But a traverse, concluding with a *verification*, only *tenders* an issue, which remains to be formed by the adverse party's *re-*

(*h*) Bac. Abr. *Pleas*, &c, H. 1. Co. Litt. 282.
(*i*) Doct. Pl. 344. Bac. Abr. *Pleas*, &c, H. 1.

affirming the allegation traversed, and concluding to the country (*k*).

§ 4. A *technical* traverse is one which is preceded by *introductory affirmative* matter, called the *inducement* to the traverse (*l*); and may be *general* or *special*.

General traverse.

§ 5. A *general* traverse, of the technical kind, is one preceded by a *general* inducement, and denying, in *general* terms, *all* that is last before alleged on the opposite side — instead of pursuing *the words* of the allegations, which it denies. Of this sort of traverse, the replication *de injuriâ suâ propriâ, absque tali causâ*, in answer to a justification, is a familiar example (*m*).

Special traverse.

§ 6. A technical traverse, when *special*, begins, in most cases, with the words '*absque hoc*,' (*without this*); which words, in pleading, constitute a technical form of negation (*n*). A traverse, commencing with these words, is called *special;* because, when it thus commences, the inducement and the negation are, regularly, both *special* — the former consisting of new special matter, and the latter pursuing, in general, the *words* of the allegation traversed, or at least, those of them which are material.

(k) Bac. Abr. *Pleas*, &c, H. 1.
(l) Ib.
(m) Ib.
(n) Ib. Lawes' Pl. 116 to 120.

CHAP. VII.

§ 7. Thus, if to debt on bond the defendant pleads, that he executed the bond by duress; and the plaintiff replies, that the defendant executed it of his own free will, and for valuable consideration, *without this*, that he executed it by duress; the traverse is *special.* So also, if the defendant pleads title to land, in himself, by alleging that J. S. died seised in fee, and devised the land to him; and the plaintiff replies, that J. S. died seised in fee, *intestate*, and alleges title in himself, as heir to J. S. '*without this*,' that J. S. devised the land to the defendant; the traverse is *special* (*o*). Here the allegation of J. S.'s intestacy, &c, forms a *special* inducement; and the *absque hoc*, with what follows it, is a *special* denial of the alleged devise, i. e. a denial of it, in *the words* of the allegation.

§ 8. In some cases, however, other words of equivalent import — as the words *et non* — are used, instead of the words *absque hoc.* Thus, if the defendant pleads that J. S. was arrested, by virtue of a warrant returnable on the *first* day of such a certain month; the plaintiff may reply, that J. S. was arrested upon a warrant returnable on the *second* day of the same month, '*and not*' by virtue of the warrant specified in the plea (*p*).

Absque tali causâ.

§ 9. The traverse *de injuriâ*, &c, *absque tali causâ*, (that the defendant, '*of his own wrong*', and *without the cause* in his plea alleged, did commit the

(*o*) Lawes' Pl. 119. 120.
(*p*) 1 Saund. 20. 21. Lawes' Pl. 119. 120.

said trespasses,' &c), though of frequent occurrence, is confined to actions *ex delicto*, and used only in *replications*. This does not, like a special traverse, follow the *words* of the allegations traversed; but denies the *whole* matter of the plea, by a general and comprehensive *formula*, devised for the purpose of abridging the replication.

Thus, if to an action of assault and battery, the defendant pleads *son assault demesne*, (that the plaintiff made the first assault, &c); the plaintiff, instead of traversing *specially* all the material allegations in the plea, may deny the whole, by replying that the defendant, '*of his own wrong, and without the cause* in his said plea alleged,' committed the several trespasses, &c, and conclude to the country (*q*). In this traverse, not only the form of denial, but the inducement also, varies essentially from that of a *special* traverse: Since the inducement *de injuriâ*, &c, alleges no *new* matter; but simply *re-affirms*, in general terms, the wrongs complained of in the declaration.

§ 10. The late precedents have introduced, in certain cases, (as in replications to pleas of *usury*, or other *illegality*), a new species of general or abridged traverse, preceded by a *general* inducement, which denies the plea, in *general* terms, according to an established form, instead of traversing it *specially*, by following the precise terms of it, as

(*q*) 2 Chitt. Pl. 523. 641—2. Cro. Car. 164. Bac. Abr. *Pleas*, &c, H. 1.

CHAP. VII.

was formerly done. This traverse concludes to the country (*r*) (1).

Common traverse.

§ 11. There is also a species of traverse, differing from all those called *technical*, not only in form and phraseology, but also in this — that it is preceded by no inducement, special or general. This traverse is taken without an *absque hoc*, or any similar words, and is simply a direct denial of the adverse allegation, in *common* negative language, (for which reason, perhaps, it is usually called a *common* traverse), and always concludes to *the country*. And because it has no inducement, it is also sometimes called 'an issue,' as distinguished from a 'traverse,' technically so called (*s*). Thus if one party pleads title to land in himself, under a devise from J. S., alleging that J. S. died seised in *fee*, and devised the land to him; the other party may traverse the seisin in fee of J. S., either by averring that J. S. 'died seised in *tail*, (or *for life*) *absque hoc*, that he died seised in fee;' and concluding with an averment — or, by a direct negative, alleging,

(*r*) 2 T. R. 439. 3 Ib. 426. 1 Saund. 103. b. (n. 3).
(*s*) Lawes' Pl. 117. 1 Saund. 103. b. (n. 1). 2 Stra. 871.

(1) The usual form of this traverse is as follows, viz. that 'the said bond, promise, &c, was made, for a good and lawful consideration, *and not* in pursuance of, or upon, the said corrupt and unlawful agreement, or for the purpose, in the said plea of the said C. D. mentioned, in manner and form, &c, and this the said A. B. prays may be inquired of by the country.' (*Vid.* 2 T. R. 439. 3 Ib. 426. 2 Chitt. Pl. 616.)

(without an inducement), that J. S. 'did *not* die seised in fee,' &c, and concluding to *the country*. CHAP. VII.

§ 12. But a *common* traverse is not adapted to all cases, in which the allegations of a party are to be denied. For it is, many times, necessary, as will hereafter appear, that the denial of an adverse allegation be preceded by affirmative matter, by way of *inducement;* and when this is necessary, a *common* traverse, (which has no inducement), can never be proper. It can properly be used, only where *no inducement* is necessary (*t*); that is, where the party traversing has no occasion to allege any *new* matter.

§ 13. But whenever a *common* traverse is proper, it is generally the more eligible mode of traversing—not only because it is a more simple and direct form of negation; but also because it produces an issue *sooner*, by one stage in the pleadings, than a traverse with an *absque hoc* usually does. For a common traverse always concludes to *the country:* Whereas, a traverse with an *absque hoc* concludes, in most cases, with *an averment;* and the issue is then formed by the opposite party's reaffirming, in *the next succeeding stage* of the pleadings, what the traverse has denied (*u*).

Thus, if to a plea of title, stating that J. S. died seised in fee, and devised the land to the defendant, the plaintiff denies the seisin in fee of J. S. by a

(*t*) 1 Saund. 103. b. (n. 1).
(*u*) 1 Saund. 103. b. (n. 1). Bac. Abr. *Pleas*, &c, H. 1.

common traverse, viz. that he *did not* die seised in fee, &c, concluding to the country; the issue is formed by the *replication*. But if the plaintiff traverses *specially*, by replying that J. S. died seised in tail, *absque hoc* that he died seised in fee, concluding with an averment; the issue is not formed, till the defendant re-affirms, in the *rejoinder*, that J. S. died seised in fee, as alleged in the plea, and concludes to the country.

§ 14. Whenever a special traverse, and its inducement, are properly adapted to each other, and both go to the '*same* point' — i. e. the same matter of fact (as in all the preceding examples they do) — the traverse is only *an inference from*, or a *consequence of*, the inducement; so that, if the one be true, the other is necessarily so (2). It results, therefore, that in all such cases, the inducement itself necessarily *contradicts* the allegation traversed. But though the inducement is repugnant to the allegation to be denied; the superaddition of a formal traverse is nevertheless indispensable: Because the adverse allegation, and the inducement to the traverse, being both in the *affirmative*, do not constitute *an issue*. (Vide ch. 6, §§ 1. 2. 3.)

§ 15. The truth of these remarks will be apparent, from a mere recurrence to the several exam-

---

(2) Examples of an inducement, and a traverse, going to *different* points, will be given hereafter, (Vid. 'traverse *after* a traverse'; post, § 45.)

ples, already given, of *special* traverses. One of these examples, however, may suffice; as the explanation to be given of it will apply equally to all the others: In the instance before mentioned, (ante, § 11), of an allegation in the plea, that 'J. S. died seised in fee', and a replication, that he 'died seised in tail, *without this*, that he died seised in fee', it is observable, in the first place, that the inducement and the traverse both go to the *same point*, i. e. to the single question, whether he died seised of a fee-simple, or not. It is very obvious also, that the traverse is a *mere inference* from the inducement; and that if the latter be true, the former must be so: And finally, that the inducement is as utterly *repugnant* to the allegation in the plea, (though not so, in *direct* terms), as is the traverse itself. In brief, the replication is merely tantamount to saying that 'J. S. died seised in tail, and *therefore* did not die seised in fee'. None of these observations, however, are applicable to cases, in which the inducement and the traverse go to *different* points.

Manner of concluding.

§ 16. As to the manner of *concluding* traverses, there is some discrepancy in the precedents; but the following appear to be the true distinctions:

1. A *common* traverse always concludes to the *country* (v). For, as it is preceded by no *inducement*, there can be no possible use in keeping the

(v) 1 Saund. 103. b. (n. 1.) Bac. Abr. *Pleas*, &c, H. 1. 2 Stra. 871. 7 Johns. R. 283.

pleadings longer open: Since the traverse, being connected with no *new* matter of any kind, leaves nothing to be *answered* by the adverse party. If, however, the traverse be immaterial, or otherwise ill taken; it may, like any other traverse thus faulty, be demurred to.

§ 17. 2. A *general* technical traverse, having *a general* inducement, (as in the instance of the replication *de injuriâ, &c, absque tali causâ*), concludes in the same manner (*w*). For in this case, the inducement, (which is but a reaffirmance, in general terms, of what has been before alleged in the declaration), contains, properly speaking, no *new* matter; and consequently, neither requires nor admits of any kind of *answer*. And it may be added, that as every such traverse denies *the whole* of what is last alleged in the adverse pleading; it cannot be *immaterial*, and consequently must be *accepted* by the opposite party, unless it be faulty in form — and if so, it may be demurred to. It is obvious, therefore, that in this case, as in the last, there can be no possible reason for keeping the pleadings any longer open to an answer.

§ 18. 3. When a traverse is taken with an *absque hoc*, and is preceded by a special inducement, containing new matter, it was formerly held by some, that the conclusion must, in *all* cases, be

(*w*) 2 Chitt. Pl. 523. 641. 642. Bac. Abr. *Pleas*, &c, H. 1. 1 Saund. 103. b. (n. 1.) 2 Black. R. 1165. 1 Bos. & P. 76.

with an averment (*x*) — in order to afford the adverse party an opportunity, to answer, (at his own peril, indeed), the *new* matter contained in the inducement.

§ 19. 4. But the modern authorities, more studious of brevity in pleading, than the ancient, have qualified this last rule ; and it appears now to be established, as a general rule, that where a traverse, even with an *absque hoc*, and preceded by a special inducement, denies the *whole substance* of what is alleged on the other side, it must conclude to *the country* (*y*) : Though, where it denies only a *part* of the matter, alleged by the adverse party, it must still, generally, conclude with an averment (*yy*).

§ 20. The reason of this distinction appears to be, on the one hand, that in the former case, the party, whose pleading is traversed, cannot object to the traverse as being *immaterial*, or as not comprehending the whole matter in controversy ; since, by the supposition, it embraces *all* the substantive matter alleged on his own part. No reason therefore can exist, (so far as regards the *substance* of the traverse), why he should refuse to join in it, and be permitted to answer over. But when, on the other hand, a special traverse embraces only *part* of the

(*x*) Co. Litt. 126. a. 1 Saund. 103. a. (n. 1.) 2 Stra. 871.

(*y*) 1 Salk. 4. 7 Mod. 105. Doug. 94. 428. 2 T. R. 441. 443. 2 Stra. 871. 1 Saund. 103. a. b. (n. 1.) Sayer, 234. 2 Johns. R. 428.

(*yy*) Iid.

CHAP. VII.

substance of the adverse pleading, the reason for concluding it with an averment is, that such a traverse *may be immaterial;* and that if it be so, it *may* be proper for him to whom it is tendered to answer *the inducement.* For which latter reason, a traverse, denying only a *part* of what is alleged on the other side, must (regularly) leave the pleadings open — in order to give the adverse party an opportunity to plead to the inducement, if he should judge it safe and proper so to plead.

§ 21. This view of the subject may be illustrated by the following example: In an action of waste, the declaration alleges that the defendant, (the lessee), felled, *and sold* the plaintiff's trees; and the defendant, confessing that he felled them, pleads, by way of justification, that he bestowed them in repairs, *absque hoc* that he sold them — thus traversing only a part, and an *immaterial* part, of the declaration. And as this traverse is clearly immaterial; the plaintiff is not bound to join in it, but has a right to reply that the defendant left the trees to decay, &c, *absque hoc* that he bestowed them in repairs — thus traversing *the inducement* to the defendant's traverse (*z*). But this the plaintiff could have no opportunity to do, if the defendant's traverse concluded to *the country:* And therefore, according to the general distinction above stated, the defendant's traverse ought to conclude with an *averment.* Such seems to be the principle or *reason* of the rule,

(*z*) Hob. 104.

that a special traverse with an *absque hoc*, embracing only *part* of what is alleged on the other side, must, in general, conclude with an averment.

A special traverse may, sometimes, conclude either way.

§ 22. But the rule, that a special traverse of only a part of what is alleged on the other side, must conclude with an averment, is by no means universal. For it seems now agreed, that 'in many cases' falling within the terms of the rule, the conclusion may be *either way* (*a*) (3). In *what* particular cases, however, such a traverse may conclude in '*either way*,' the books do not precisely show (*b*). In the case of *Baynham* v. *Mathews* (*c*), which was an action on a promissory note, the defendant pleaded usury, and the plaintiff replied that the note was given for a just debt, *absque hoc*, that it was corruptly agreed, &c, concluding to *the country*. And there being *two* material facts alleged in the plea, (viz. 1st, an usurious agreement; and 2d, that the note was given in consideration of that agreement), and *one* of them only being traversed; the court held, on special demurrer, that the traverse

(*a*) 1 Saund. 103. a. b. 2 T. R. 439. 443. 2 Wils. 113. Lawes' Pl. 121. 1 Chitt. Pl. 615. 616.
(*b*) 2 Stra. 871. 1 Burr. 317.
(*c*) 2 Stra. 871.

---

(3) It can be only by the sanction of *precedent*, (founded originally upon some mistake), that the pleader is allowed, in any instance whatever, to conclude a traverse *either* way, at his own election. On principle, the admission that *one* of the two modes of concluding any given traverse is proper, would seem to imply that the other is, by necessary consequence, improper.

CHAP. VII.

should have concluded with an *averment.* But in the subsequent case of *Hedges* v. *Sandon* (*d*), *Buller* and *Grose*, Js., in commenting on the case of *Baynham* v. *Mathews*, both expressed a decided opinion, that the traverse, in that case, might properly have concluded *either* way.

§ 23. It seems now, therefore, that although a plea of usury, to an action on a written security, regularly alleges *two* material facts, as above stated; yet *a special* traverse, denying the corrupt agreement only, *may* conclude to the country: Since the negation of that fact is a decisive answer in law to the whole defence. Such a conclusion, however, in such a case, is confessedly opposed to the rule which originally prevailed; and there is no doubt, that such a traverse *may still* conclude with an *averment.* And even in the more modern precedents, the latter, it seems, is the more usual mode of concluding such traverses (*e*). It may be added, that in cases, where a doubt still exists as to the proper manner of concluding such a traverse, this latter form is probably the safer; since, by all the opinions, it is a proper form — though, as some hold, not the only proper one.

§ 24. But where one of several facts, alleged by either party, constitutes the *whole substance* of his pleading — all the others being *immaterial* — the rule now appears to be, clearly, that a special traverse

(*d*) 2 T. R. 439. 443—4.
(*e*) 1 Saund. 103. b. (n. 1). 1 Chitt. Pl. 616.

of that fact alone may conclude to *the country;* and the Court of King's Bench (*f*) have held, that it *must* so conclude. The case, here referred to, was debt on bond: Plea, that the defendant executed the bond through force and restraint of imprisonment: Replication, that the defendant executed it of his own free will, *absque hoc,* that he executed it through force, &c, and concluding with *an averment.* On special demurrer, showing for cause, that the conclusion was ill, the court held that it was so; and that the conclusion should have been to *the country;* because — the imprisonment being immaterial — the duress was the *whole substance* of the plea.

A wrong conclusion vitiates the traverse.

§ 25. Whether, by the common law, the wrong conclusion of a traverse is a fault in *substance,* or in *form* only, the opinions are not all agreed. According to most of the authorities, it is matter of *substance,* and fatal on *general* demurrer (*g*). As, however, the conclusion of a traverse neither affirms nor denies any *fact* in controversy, and shows nothing material to the cause, on either side — but is simply a *technical form* of closing the pleadings, or keeping them open; this rule may, perhaps, on original principles, be questionable.

Absque tali causâ, when a proper form of traversing.

§ 26. The general replication, *de injuria,* &c, *absque tali causâ,* is adapted to the denial of matter

(*f*) Sayer, 234 — and (with some *circumstantial* differences) in Williams' *note,* 1 Saund. 103. a.

(*g*) 1 Vent. 240. T. Ray. 94. 1 Saund. 103. b. (n. 1). 3 Mod. 203. Cro. Car. 164.

CHAP. VII.

of *excuse* or *justification;* and where the excuse or justification consists, exclusively, of mere matter of *fact*, as distinguished from matter of *record*, *title*, *authority*, &c, this replication is the most appropriate mode of traversing it (*h*).

§ 27. But as this replication always denies the *whole* of the plea, to which it is an answer (*i*); it follows, that when the plea contains, among other things, matter of *record*, *right*, *title*, or *authority*, (all of which involve matter of *law*), the general traverse, *absque tali causâ*, is improper (*k*). For this general traverse, which must conclude to *the country* (*l*), is not only *inapposite* to the denial of such matters of law, but would refer to the jury matter both of *law and fact*, *blended* in one issue, instead of separating the one from the other, as the principles of pleading require, (ch. 6, § 97). And it would moreover, for the last reason, be faulty, as being *double* (*m*).

§ 28. It results then, that to the plea of *son assault demesne*, the traverse, *absque tali causâ*, is a good answer: Since the plea consists of matter of

(*h*) Lawes' Pl. 151—156. 8 Co. 67. Com. Dig. *Pleader*, F. 20. 21. Yelv. 158. n.

(*i*) 2 Saund. 295. (n. 1). 8 Co. 67. a.

(*k*) Iid. 1 Chitt. Pl. 578—9. 581—3. 8 Co. 67—8. Com. Dig. *Pleader*, F. 20. 21. 22. 1 Bos. & P. 79. 80. Willes, 103. n. a. 5 Johns. R. 112.

(*l*) Cro. Car. 164.

(*m*) 8 Co. 67. b. Bull. N. P. 93.

mere fact (*n*). And the same rule applies to all justifications, consisting *exclusively* of such matter.

When improper.

§ 29. But when the justification involves matter of *law*, (as where in an action for assault, battery and false imprisonment, the defendant justifies, under a *capias* directed to the sheriff, and a *warrant* from the sheriff to himself), this general traverse of the justification would be ill, as including matter of *record and authority*, viz. the *capias* and the *warrant* (*o*). But the plaintiff, in a case like this, may traverse, *separately*, any one material point in the plea; which point may consist either of the record or authority — or of the matter of *mere fact*, pleaded in connexion with it. He may, for example, traverse the *warrant*, by replying that the defendant, *de injuriâ*, &c, *absque tali warranto*, made the said assault, &c — or he may traverse the *capias*, by replying *nul tiel record:* Or on the other hand, he may admit the capias and warrant, and traverse the matter of *mere fact* alleged in the plea, by alleging that the defendant 'of his own wrong, and without *the residue* of the cause, in the said plea alleged', made the said assault, &c (*p*).

§ 30. But when matter of record, title, &c, is alleged, not as *the ground* of the justification, but

(*n*) 2 Chitt. Pl. 642. Com. Dig. *Pleader*, F. 18. 3 M. 15. Lawes' Pl. 155.

(*o*) 8 Co. 67. a. 2 Saund. 295. (n. 1.) 1 Bos. & P. 77. Com. Dig. *Pleader*, F. 20. 12 Mod. 580. Lawes' Pl. 154. 1 Chitt. Pl. 582.

(*p*) Iid. 3 Lev. 243. 2 Chitt. Pl. 644-5.

CHAP. VII.

only as inducement, the general replication, *de injuriâ*, &c, *absque tali causâ*, is good. If therefore, in assault and battery, the defendant alleges that he was seised of an estate in a certain close — that he had cut the corn, growing upon it — that the plaintiff came to take away the corn, and that the defendant, in defence of his corn, did the acts complained of; the plaintiff may traverse the plea, in the above general form (*q*). For in this case, the justification is not founded upon the defendant's *title;* but upon the alleged *aggression* of the plaintiff. The title pleaded is, therefore, but *inducement*, and being immaterial, the defendant is not bound to prove it strictly: Proof of his mere *possession* being, on this point, sufficient.

The superaddition of a technical, to a common, traverse, is ill.

§ 31. We have before seen, that one principal object of the science of pleading is to bring the parties to an *issue*, of some kind, as soon as the state of the facts, alleged in each case, will permit. When therefore an allegation, on one side, is directly denied on the other, by a *common* negative, the *superaddition* of a technical traverse is unnecessary and improper, and therefore a good cause of demurrer (*r*). Thus, if to a plea of usury, the plaintiff replies that it was *not* corruptly agreed, &c, as the defendant has alleged, *absque hoc* that it *was* corruptly agreed, &c; the replication is ill. For the

(*q*) Yelv. 157. Lawes' Pl. 156. 2 Saund. 295. b. (n. 1.) Cro. Jac. 224. Latch, 221.

(*r*) Yelv. 38. Cro. Eliz. 755. Bac. Abr. *Pleas*, &c, H. 1. 2 Saund. 188.

first negative forms a complete issue upon the plea, and should therefore conclude to the country. The *absque hoc* is unnecessary, and would *postpone* the issue, until the rejoinder is given.

CHAP. VII.

Traverse, when necessary.

§ 32. It is also a general rule, that when either party alleges new matter, *inconsistent* with a preceding traversable allegation of the adverse party, but which does not form an *issue* upon it, the new matter must conclude with a *traverse* (*s*). For in such a case, it is apparent, from the inconsistency of the adverse allegations, that the controversy is ripe for an issue. If therefore the last pleader were allowed to conclude without a traverse, the other party might, with equal propriety, do the same; and the issue might thus be postponed indefinitely. If therefore a defendant pleads that his co-defendant is *dead;* and the plaintiff replies that he is *alive;* the replication must add '*absque hoc* that he is dead.' For the two *affirmative* allegations, though repugnant to each other, do not form an issue. Thus also, if the defendant pleads that the bond, on which, &c, was given by duress; and the replication alleges that he executed it of his *free will;* there must be superadded a *formal traverse* of the duress, by an *absque hoc*, or *et non* (4).

(*s*) Hob. 103. 1 Saund. 22. & n. 2. 207. (n. 4.) 209. (n. 8.) Com. Dig. *Pleader,* G. 2. 1 Wils. 253. Lawes' Pl. 117-8. 150. 3 Black. Com. 310. Bac. Abr. *Pleas,* &c, H. 1.

---

(4) The omission of a traverse, when necessary, has been held to be matter of *substance*, at common law. (2 Mod. 60. Bac.

CHAP. VII.

When not proper.

§ 33. But to the above general rule, there is an exception, whenever, in answer to a *negative* plea, it is necessary for the plaintiff to set out new affirmative matter *specially*, in order *to make out* his case in full, upon the face of the pleadings. In such a case, the plaintiff cannot conclude with a traverse of the plea; although his new matter is absolutely inconsistent with it. For if he should thus conclude, the real ground of his demand could not appear from the pleadings (*t*). Thus, in debt on an arbitration-bond, if the defendant pleads, '*no award*', and the plaintiff replies that the arbitrators 'did make their award'; he cannot conclude this allegation with a traverse, tendering an issue on the plea — though the allegation is directly repugnant to it; but must proceed to set out the award, and assign a breach — concluding with an averment. For in a case like this (the declaration being *general*) the true cause of action never appears, until the *replication* discloses it. If therefore the plaintiff should conclude the general averment of an award made, with a traverse; the real cause of action, (which is some breach of the award), could never appear from the pleadings. To a plea of *non damnificatus* also, it is, for the same reason, not sufficient for the plaintiff to reply, that he '*has been damnified.*' The replica-

(*t*) Hob. 233. 1 Salk. 138. Lawes' Pl. 150. 6 East, 556-7. Carth. 116. 1 Saund. 103. (n. 1.) 2 Bos. & P. 362.

Abr. *Pleas*, &c, H. 2.) *Sed quære.* Vid. 1 Leon. 43-4.) But now, under the statute 4 & 5 *Ann.* c. 16, it is but matter of *form*.

tion must show *what particular damage* has accrued (*u*), and conclude with an averment.

Not proper, after matter of confession and avoidance.

§ 34. But when a party merely *confesses and avoids* his adversary's allegations, by new matter of his own, a traverse of those allegations would be improper and absurd; since it would be repugnant to the pleader's own confession (*v*). Ex. gr. The defendant pleads a *release;* and the plaintiff replies, that it was given by *duress:* Here a traverse of the release itself would be preposterous — as it would contradict the plaintiff's allegation of duress, which *admits* the release. Thus also, if the defendant pleads *infancy*, and the plaintiff replies *necessaries*, or a *promise after full age;* a traverse of the allegation of infancy would, for the same same reason, be ill. In cases like these, the matter of avoidance should conclude with a verification, and without a traverse (*w*).

Inducement to, sometimes necessary, to exclude a negative pregnant.

§ 35. It is said, in several books (*x*), principally, it would seem, on the authority of a remark of *Hobart* (*y*) (5), that a special traverse, without a pro-

(*u*) Bac. Abr. *Pleas*, &c, L. 2 Saund. 80. 1 Sid. 444.

(*v*) Com. Dig. *Pleader*, G. 3. Bac. Abr. *Pleas*, &c, H. 1. 1 Brownl. 148. 197. Sav. 2. Winch, 38. Cro. Car. 384. Yelv. 151. 1 Saund. 22. (n. 2.) 209. (n. 8.) 13 Mass. R. 520.

(*w*) Iid. 1 Wils. 253. 3 Black. Com. 309.

(*x*) Com. Dig. *Pleader*, G. 20. Lawes' Pl. 118.

(*y*) Hob. 321.

(5) Lord *Hobart*, however, lays down no such *general* rule. His remark is confined to the particular traverse, then in ques-

CHAP. VII.

per inducement, will be a *negative pregnant.* But the proposition, thus unqualified, appears to be much too general, and is likely to occasion misapprehension. Undoubtedly a *special* traverse must have an inducement, (and of course, a proper one); for an inducement enters into the definition of such a traverse; and a traverse, without an inducement, cannot be a *special* one. But that a traverse, in any form, having no inducement, is *therefore a negative pregnant,* is by no means universally, or perhaps, generally true. It is indeed certain, that in various instances, (as in that to which Ld *Hobart's* remark, in the above reference, applied), a traverse, without an inducement, would be a negative pregnant, when, with a proper inducement, limiting its extent and application, it would not be so: But it is equally certain, that in many, perhaps in most cases, the absence of an inducement does not at all affect the sufficiency of the traverse; and that an inducement is often used in pleading, when wholly unnecessary.

§ 36. These remarks may be illustrated by the following examples:—If in assault and battery, the defendant pleads *molliter manus imposuit,* in virtue of a lawful authority to arrest the plaintiff, and the plaintiff replies *non molliter manus imposuit,* without an inducement; the replication is a *negative pregnant.* For it is consistent with the supposition, and

tion, and which was a negative pregnant, from the want of a proper inducement.

therefore admits, by implication, that the defendant *did not* lay his hands upon the plaintiff at all. The plaintiff should therefore reply *an outrageous*, (or *excessive*) battery, *absque hoc*, *molliter manus*, &c (*z*).

§ 37. Again, if in an action of assault and battery, brought by a child or servant, the defendant pleads *moderatè castigavit*, in virtue of his authority as parent or master; and the plaintiff replies, *non moderatè castigavit;* the replication is a *negative pregnant*. For it is open to the implication that the defendant *did not* chastise him at all (*a*). The replication should, therefore, begin with an inducement, like that in the last example, and conclude with an *absque hoc*, that the defendant moderately chastised the plaintiff. For in both these cases, as in all others of the same kind, the inducement, taken in connexion with the traverse, so explains and limits its extent and meaning, as to exclude the objectionable implication or admission. There are numerous other instances, in which a proper inducement to a traverse is necessary, for the purpose of excluding a *negative pregnant* (*b*).

Inducement, not necessary, in all cases.

§ 38. But, as has been already observed, there are also very many cases, in which a traverse needs no inducement, for this, or any other purpose (*c*). Such is always the case, where a *common* traverse

(*z*) Com. Dig. *Pleader*, 3 M. 16. Skin. 387.
(*a*) 2 Keb. 623. 1 Vent. 70.
(*b*) Bac. Abr. *Pleas*, &c, I. 6. Com. Dig. *Pleader*, R. 5.
(*c*) 1 Saund. 103. b. (n. 1).

CHAP. VII.

is a proper form of denial; and this form is often proper, in cases, in which the precedents usually employ an inducement. Thus, if a defendant pleads that his co-defendant is dead; there can be no doubt that the plaintiff may safely reply, that he *is not* dead—instead of alleging that he is alive, *absque hoc*, that he is dead. For it is clear that the traverse, in the form first stated, contains no implication, which can render it a *negative pregnant*. To a plea of usury, also, alleging a corrupt agreement, in the usual form, a replication that it *was not* corruptly agreed, &c, (instead of the usual inducement of a 'good and lawful consideration' with an *absque hoc*, &c) is doubtless good, and for the same reason (*d*).

§ 39. But without accumulating examples of the same kind, it may suffice to add, that whenever a traverse is to be tendered, the pleader has only to determine for himself, whether, without an inducement, it would be a *negative pregnant*, or not, (a point easily decided, in most cases); and then to traverse, with or without it, as his judgment may direct.

An affirmative implication, not aiding the adverse party, does not vitiate.

§ 40. Whenever a traverse, or negative allegation of any kind, involves an affirmative implication, which *does not maintain the pleading of the adverse party*, the implication does not injure the traverse (*e*). Thus, if a plea of usury alleges a corrupt

(*d*) 2 Stra. 871. 1 Saund. 103. b. (n. 1).

(*e*) Com. Dig. *Pleader*, R. 6. Lawes' Pl. 114.

agreement for the payment of *ten* per cent for forbearance; and the plaintiff replies, by a common traverse, that it *was not* corruptly agreed that he should pay *ten* per cent; the traverse, it is conceived, is clearly good — though it impliedly admits a reservation of *nine*, or any other per cent, not amounting to *ten*. For the admission *does not maintain the plea*, which must be proved *precisely*, to defeat the action. And it is very obvious, that no implication, on one side, which does not *aid* the other, can injure the pleading of either party.

An 'absque hoc' must be followed by an affirmative.

§ 41. 'An issue, joined upon an *absque hoc*, &c, ought to have *an affirmative* after it' (*f*): In other words, no other than an *affirmative* allegation can be properly traversed with an *absque hoc*. For if a *negative* be thus denied, the traverse will consist of *two negatives;* and though these amount, in *English*, to an affirmative; yet such a mode of expressing an affirmative tends to confusion and perplexity, and is therefore, in point of form, not allowable in pleading. *Ex. gr.* If the defendant pleads that the plaintiff did not deliver such a certain writing; a replication, '*absque hoc* that he did not deliver,' &c, is the same thing, in effect, as saying 'he did *not not* deliver.' A *negative* allegation, then, can be properly traversed, only by an *affirmative* (6).

(*f*) Co. Litt. 126. a. Bac. Abr. *Pleas*, &c, H. 1. 1 Chitt. Pl. 587.

---

(6) It may be added, that when negative matter is to be contradicted by an affirmative, the latter generally advances such *new*

CHAP. VII.

Traverse upon a traverse, generally not allowed.

§ 42. It is a general rule, that a traverse, well tendered on one side, must be *accepted* on the other (*g*). And hence it follows, as a general rule, that there cannot be a *traverse upon a traverse*, if the first traverse is *material* (*h*) (7). The meaning of this rule is, that when one party has tendered *a material* traverse, the other cannot leave it, and tender another traverse of his own, to *the same point*, upon the inducement to the first traverse, but must *join* in that first tendered: Otherwise the parties might alternately tender traverses to each other, in unlimited succession, without coming to an issue. *Ex. gr.* The defendant pleads title, under a devise from J. S. alleging that he died seised *in fee:* The plaintiff replies, that 'J. S. died seised *in tail, absque hoc*, that he died seised in fee', with a verification: The defendant cannot now rejoin that J. S. died seised in fee, *absque hoc* that he died seised in tail; but must join in the plaintiff's traverse, by re-affirming that J. S. died seised in fee, as alleged in the plea, and conclude to the *country*. For both traverses

(*g*) Gilb. H. C. P. 66. Hob. 104. Bac. Abr. *Pleas*, &c, H. 4.

(*h*) Hob. 104. Bac. Abr. *Pleas*, &c, H. 4. 1 H. Black. 403. 1 Anst. 231. 1 Saund. 22. (n. 2.) Co. Litt. 282. 1 Salk. 222. 1 Ld Ray. 121. Com. Dig. *Pleader*, G. 17. Vaugh. 62.

---

matter, as must be left open, to be answered by the adverse party, (2 Lev. 5. 1 Vent. 121. 2 Burr. 772)—in which case, the following up of the new matter with a traverse, would be manifestly inadmissible.

(7) A traverse *upon* a traverse is one going to the *same point* (or subject-matter) as is embraced in a preceding traverse, on the other side.

would go to the *same point*, viz. whether or not J. S. *died seised in fee* — the only material point in controversy, and to the determination of which the first traverse is precisely adapted. If the defendant, then, might traverse the plaintiff's *inducement*, (the alleged seisin in *tail*); the plaintiff might, on the same principle, traverse that of the defendant, as at first, with a *verification*; and if this might be once done by either party, it might be repeated on both sides, to any indefinite extent, without producing an issue.

Traverse upon a traverse, when allowed.

§ 43. But the above general rule does not extend to cases, in which the traverse first tendered is *immaterial*. In such a case, there may be a *traverse upon a traverse* — i. e. the traverse first tendered may be passed over, and the *inducement* to it, if material, may be traversed; although both traverses go to *the same point* (*i*). Thus, in an action of waste for felling timber-trees, the plaintiff declares, that the defendant, (the lessee), felled and *sold* them: The defendant, confessing that he felled them, justifies that act, by pleading that he bestowed them in *repairing* the demised buildings, *absque hoc*, that he *sold* them. Now the plaintiff may refuse to join in the traverse tendered upon the *sale* of the trees — because that point is *immaterial*; and may himself traverse the *inducement* to the defend-

(*i*) Hob. 104, & Williams' *note* (1). Co. Litt. 282. b. 1 Saund. 20. 22. (n. 2.) 1 Ld Ray. 125. Bac. Abr. *Pleas*, &c, H. 4. 1 H. Black. 376. 406. Com. Dig. *Pleader*, G. 19. Vaugh. 62. 1 Anst. 231.

CHAP. VII.

ant's traverse, viz. the alleged *repairing;* for this is the only material point in the plea. Both the traverses here go to the *same point*, viz. the use or disposition made of the trees, when felled; upon which point the justification depends. Instead of answering the plea at all, however, the plaintiff might specially *demur* to it, for the *immateriality* of the defendant's traverse (*k*).

§ 44. And there is one class of cases, in which there may be a traverse *upon* a traverse, although the first traverse includes what is *material.* The cases, here referred to, are those in which *false* pleading, on the part of the defendant, might otherwise oust the plaintiff of *some right or liberty*, which the law allows him (*l*). *Ex. gr.* To an action of assault and battery and false imprisonment, laid in the county of *A.*, the defendant pleads a local justification, in the county of *B.*, viz. that he was sheriff of the latter county, and arrested the plaintiff *there*, under a *capias*, (or other lawful authority), *absque hoc*, that he is guilty in the county of *A.*, &c. Now as the defendant's alleged authority, which is the inducement to the traverse, may be *false;* the plaintiff, instead of joining in the traverse, may traverse that *authority.* For, assuming that the alleged trespass was actually committed in the county of *B.*— still, (the action being transitory), the plaintiff has by law a right to sue and recover for it, in any other

(*k*) Hob. 104. Cro. Jac. 221. 1 Saund. 21. (n. 1.) 22. (n. 2.) Yelv. 151.

(*l*) Poph. 101. Mo. 350. Com. Dig. *Pleader*, G. 18. Bac. Abr. *Pleas*, &c, H. 4. Hob. 104, *marg.* Cro. Eliz. 99. 418.

county. But if he were obliged to join in the defendant's traverse, by re-affirming that the defendant committed the trespasses in the county of *A.*; the plaintiff would necessarily fail on that issue — although he has, by the supposition, a right by law to recover in *that* county. And thus the plaintiff would, by the *falsity* of the defendant's justification, be deprived of the liberty, which the law allows him, of laying his action in what county he pleases, in a transitory action. On the other hand, if the defendant's justification be *true;* the traverse taken upon it can subject him to no disadvantage: Since by proving it true, he must prevail, upon the issue. The object of the rule, in cases like the above, is to prevent the defendant, in a transitory action, from *ousting the plaintiff's venue, by false pleading.*

Traverse after a traverse, allowable.

§ 45. A traverse *after* a traverse — i. e. one going to a *different* point or subject-matter, from that embraced in a preceding traverse, on the opposite side — is allowed, even though that first tendered be *material* (*m*). Thus if in trespass, the defendant pleads a justification on a particular day, with a traverse that he is guilty on any other day; the plaintiff, instead of joining in the traverse, by alleging a trespass within the time embraced in it — may pass by the defendant's traverse, and traverse the matter of *justification;* in which case, the traverse in the replication will be a traverse *after* a traverse;

Ante, ch. 6, § 99.

(*m*) Hob. 104. Bac. Abr. *Pleas,* &c, H. 4. Co. Litt. 282. b. 1 Saund. 21. 22-3. Com. Dig. *Pleader,* G. 18.

since it does not embrace the *same point*, as is embraced in the first traverse. For the plaintiff's traverse applies only to the trespass *justified*, which is a supposed trespass, on the particular day laid in the justification: Whereas the traverse in the plea extends only to a trespass on any *different* day. The reason, for allowing the plaintiff to traverse, in this manner, is, that the day, mentioned in the justification, may have been the day of the trespass complained of; and yet the justification may be false: Upon which supposition, if the plaintiff were not permitted to deny the justification, he would necessarily be defeated of a recovery — though having a complete right of action: For, by the same supposition, he would not be able to prove the trespass on a *different* day.

§ 46. When the right of recovery, as alleged in the declaration, is in its nature *divisible*, so that the plaintiff is by law entitled to recover for *as much as he can prove title to*, (though it should be less than he declares for), the defendant cannot make that part of his plea, which is in answer to a *part* of the plaintiff's demand, *the inducement to a traverse of the residue* (*n*). *Ex. gr.* in an action for obstructing three of the plaintiff's lights, the defendant cannot justify as to *one* of them, with an *absque hoc*, that he obstructed *three*. For the plaintiff, in the case supposed, is by law entitled to recover for the obstruction

(*n*) 1 Saund. 267—9. Com. Dig. *Pleader*, G. 20. Lawes' Pl. 118. Yelv. 225. 1 Bulstr. 116. *Vid.* 8 Taunt. 190. 9 Pick. 66. Steph. Pl. 259.

of *two*, or of *one* only, if his proof goes no further. Hence, even assuming that the justification pleaded is *true*, and also that only *two* lights were obstructed; yet the plea is ill. For if the plaintiff should join in the traverse, by re-affirming the obstruction of *three* lights, he would fail, on the trial, unless he could prove *three* lights obstructed—which, upon the state of facts now supposed, he could *not* do. And thus his action would be defeated, though he is, by the supposition, legally entitled to recover for the obstruction of *one* light. In all cases like this, if the traverse were good, (upon which supposition, the plaintiff must join in it), it would oblige him to prove the *whole gravamen* alleged, in order to maintain his action; although the law confessedly entitles him to recover, on proof of *any part* of it. In the case here supposed, then, the defendant ought to plead, as to the part not justified, i. e. two of the lights, *not guilty;* and as to the remaining one, to plead specially his matter of avoidance.

Must be on a point material.

§ 47. A traverse can properly be tendered, only on a point *material* (o)—for the obvious reason, that what is *immaterial* cannot decide the controversy. Hence matter of mere *inducement* or *aggravation* cannot, regularly, be traversed. Hence also, if a traverse includes *time* or *place*, when not material; it is ill (*p*).

(*o*) Com. Dig. *Pleader*, E. 34. G. 12. 14. Bac. Abr. *Pleas*, &c, H. 1. 6 Co. 24. a. Lawes' Pl. 118. 2 Saund. 5. 28. 1 Ib. 23. (n. 5).

(*p*) Com. Dig. *Pleader*, G. 12. 14. R. 7. 8. 9. 2 Saund. 318. 12 Mod. 507.

CHAP. VII.

And issuable.

§ 48. So also a traverse can properly be tendered only on an *issuable* point (*q*). For what is not issuable cannot be put in issue; and therefore matter of *law* cannot be traversed (*r*): Matter of *fact*, only, being traversable. Upon this principle, the *prout ei bene licuit*, (*'as by law he well might'*) in a plea of justification, is not traversable: As where the defendant pleads *son assault demesne*, and confesses his forcibly defending himself, *as he lawfully might*, &c. For these words are but a *conclusion of law* from the facts stated (*s*).

And on a single point.

§ 49. Every traverse must be confined to a *single point*, i. e. a *single ground* of demand, or defence: Otherwise it will be objectionable, as being *double* (*t*). The meaning of the rule is, that when the pleading, on one side, consists of several *distinct* and material points, all of which are necessary to its legal sufficiency, the adverse party is allowed to traverse only *one* of them. For in every such case, a denial of *one* of them is, in law, a sufficient answer to the whole; and he may traverse which of them he pleases (*u*).

(*q*) Com. Dig. *Pleader*, E. 34. Bac. Abr. *Pleas*, &c, H. 1.

(*r*) Iid. Com. Dig. *Pleader*, G. 12. 14. 1 Saund. 23. (n. 5). 298. (n. 3). 11 Co. 10. 2 Black. Rep. 776. 3 Wils. 234. 2 Keb. 607.

(*s*) Iid.

(*t*) Bac. Abr. *Pleas*, &c, H. 1. 5. 8 Co. 67. Co. Litt. 126. a. 1 Burr. 316. 321. 3 Lev. 40. 1 Bos. & P. 80. Lawes' Pl. 48. 152. Bull. N. P. 93.

(*u*) 1 Saund. 22. (n. 2). 6 Co. 24. b. 1 Wils. 338. *Vid. Duplicity, post.* ch. 8.

§ 50. If therefore, in trespass for false imprisonment, the defendant justifies under a *capias* directed to the sheriff, and a warrant from the sheriff to himself, the plaintiff may traverse either the *capias*, or the warrant, but should not traverse *both*. For the denial of either of them is a sufficient answer to the plea; since the *capias*, without the warrant, or the warrant, without the capias, would be no justification: And a traverse of both would, in effect, tender *two* issues instead of one, upon one and the same plea. Upon the same principle, if the defendant pleads title in a stranger, and justifies as servant to the latter, and by his command; the plaintiff may traverse the *title*, or the *command;* but should not traverse *both* (*v*).

§ 51. But it is not indispensable, that the 'single point,' mentioned in the above rule, consist of a single *fact:* Since two or more distinct facts may be, and often are, necessary to constitute one complete *point* or *ground* of complaint, or defence; and in such a case, *all* the particular facts, which go to that one point, may be traversed (*w*). Ex. gr. To an action of trespass, for breaking and entering the plaintiff's close, and depasturing it with beasts, &c, the defendant justified the depasturing, &c, under a prescriptive right of common in the *locus in quo*, and alleged, according to the established form of pleading in such a case, that 'the cattle were *his own* cattle, and that they were *levant and couchant* upon

(*v*) 8 Co. 67. b.

(*w*) Bac. Abr. *Pleas*, &c, H. 1. 1 Burr. 320. Lawes' Pl. 153.

CHAP. VII.

the premises, and were commonable cattle,' (i. e. of the *species* of cattle, called commonable): The plaintiff traversed the *whole* of the last allegation, in the terms of it—thus including in the traverse the *three* distinct facts, that the cattle were the *defendant's own* cattle—that they were *levant and couchant*—and that they were *commonable;* and on a special demurrer to this replication, for duplicity, the traverse was held good (*x*).

§ 52. Of this case it may be observed, that the defence, to which the traverse applied, consisted of *three* distinct points:—1. The existence of a prescriptive *right of common*—2. the defendant's *title* to share in that right, as tenant of the manor, or lordship—3. that the particular beasts in question *were entitled to common.* The replication applied to the last point only, viz. that the beasts were *entitled to common.* But to entitle them to common, in the defendant's right, they must have been, as alleged in the plea, his *own* cattle—and also *levant and couchant* on his tenement—and *commonable* cattle. These *three* last facts, therefore, the plaintiff precisely traversed; and the court held that the traverse was not *double*—inasmuch as it embraced only the *simple point*, that the cattle were *entitled to common.*

Must be only on matter alleged, or implied in what is alleged.

§ 53. In general, nothing but what is *expressly alleged*, or *necessarily implied* in what is thus alleged,

(*x*) 1 Burr. 316—322.

can be the subject of a traverse (*y*). For a traverse is in its nature a denial, on one side, of something before *alleged*, on the other. It would, indeed, be plainly absurd for either party to tender *an issue* upon matter, which the other had not actually, or virtually, pleaded. Still, a traverse may be taken upon matter which, though not *in terms* alleged, is *necessarily implied* in what is so alleged (*z*). Thus, if the defendant justifies under J. S., alleging that he *was seised* of the close in question; the plaintiff may reply that he himself was seised of one moiety of the close, *absque hoc* that J. S. was *sole* seised (*a*). For though the plea does not expressly aver that J. S. was *solely* seised; yet the general unqualified averment, that he was seised '*of the close*', must be understood to mean a seisin of the *whole*, or a *sole* seisin.

Exception to the last rule.

§ 54. But there is one case, in which it is necessary to include, in a traverse, what is neither expressly nor impliedly alleged on the other side: viz. when to debt on an obligation, payable '*on* or *before*' a certain day, (as the *tenth* day of May), the defendant pleads payment, on a day *before* that named in the condition, (as the *first* day of the same month): In which case, if the plaintiff would deny the plea, he must reply that the defendant did not

(*y*) Com. Dig. *Pleader*, G. 8. 13. 1 Ld Ray. 63. 1 Saund. 206. 312. d. (n. 4.) 2 Ib. 10. (n. 14.) 1 Salk. 298. Carth. 99. Bac. Abr. *Pleas*, &c, H. 1. 5.

(*z*) Iid.

(*a*) 6 Mod. 158. 2 Salk. 629. Com. Dig. *Pleader*, G. 13.

CHAP. VII.

Vide ch. 10, § 36, n. 4.

pay on the *first* of May, nor at any time *before the tenth*, nor *on the* tenth (*b*). For a traverse of payment on the *first* of May, without more, would not show an *absolute breach* of the condition of the bond, (which the replication must always show, when the defendant pleads *performance* of the condition), and consequently would not show a right of recovery. For such a traverse would be consistent with the supposed fact of payment on the *tenth*, or on any previous day, except the first; and payment, on either day, would be a strict performance of the condition. And now, since the statute 4 & 5 *Ann.* ch. 16, § 12, has made payment *after* the day a good defence, the traverse, it seems, should cover *all* time subsequent to the day named in the condition, and before the commencement of the suit (*c*).

When joining in a traverse, is a denial of the inducement.

§ 55. It has already been seen (*ante*, §§ 14. 15.), that when a traverse and its inducement both go to the *same point*, and are properly adapted to each other, the traverse is but an *inference* from the inducement; and hence it follows, that in every such case, *joining* in the traverse necessarily involves a *denial* of the matter alleged in the inducement. Thus, if the defendant pleads that J. S. died seised in fee, and the plaintiff replies that he died seised *in tail, absque hoc* that he died seised *in fee;* a rejoinder, re-affirming that he died seised *in fee*, is

(*b*) Sav. 96. 1 Black. Rep. 210. Com. R. 148. Esp. Dig. 225. 2 Burr. 944.

(*c*) 2 Burr. 944.

self-evidently a denial of the *inducement* to the traverse.

When it is an admission of the inducement.

§ 56. On the other hand, when the inducement and the traverse go to *different* points, (as in the case of a traverse *after* a traverse, (ante, § 45), joining in the traverse, first tendered, *admits* the truth of the inducement. Thus, if the defendant in trespass pleads a justification, (as a license), laid on some particular day, different from that laid in the declaration, and traverses that he is guilty on *any other* day; a replication, joining in the traverse, by alleging a trespass on *another* day than that laid in the plea, is an implied *admission* of the license, or other matter of justification averred in the inducement: It being a general principle, heretofore stated, that each party impliedly admits all such traversable allegations on the other side, as he *does not* traverse, (*ante*, ch. 3, § 166). And in the example now given, the plaintiff, instead of joining in the traverse, *might* have traversed *the inducement.* It may also be observed, that in the case just supposed, (as in every similar case), if the replication is true, and supported in proof; the plaintiff can suffer no *disadvantage*, from his admission of the inducement, even though the latter should be *untrue;* because, even upon this supposition, he must prevail, on *the issue* tendered by the defendant.

Protestation, nature and use of.

§ 57. If however the party, joining in such a traverse, wishes to prevent his implied admission of the inducement from operating against him, as an

CHAP. VII. *estoppel* in any *future* controversy; he may attain that end, by a *protestation*, or, (as it is often called) a *protestando;* and in general, any allegation or inference, which stands impliedly admitted by the *pleadings*, may, to the same effect, be denied or excluded, in the same manner (*d*).

§ 58. A *protestation*, which, according to Sir Edward Coke's definition, is 'the exclusion of a conclusion', has no other effect, than that of excluding or preventing some adverse allegation, or inference, (which stands confessed by the pleadings), from *estopping* the party protesting, in any *other* suit between the same parties, or their *privies* (*e*). For it is a general principle, in the law of evidence, that any fact, admitted by the *pleadings* in a suit, will, if not thus excluded, be forever *conclusive*, (between the same parties, and those in privity with them), in any other suit, in which the same fact may come in question.

§ 59. Thus, if the defendant pleads in bar a collateral satisfaction — as a pipe of wine — delivered to the plaintiff, and by him accepted, in full satisfaction; and the plaintiff, wishing to put the *acceptance only* in issue, is nevertheless unwilling to let the fact of *delivery* stand, as an *estoppel* to him

(*d*) 3 Black. Com. 311. Bac. Abr. *Pleas*, &c, II. 1. 4. Co. Litt. 124. b. 126. Plowd. 276. b. 2 Saund. 103. a. b. (n. 1.) Litt. § 192-3.

(*e*) Iid. 2 Saund. 103, a. (n. 1.) Lawes' Pl. 141. 143. Com. Dig. *Pleader*, N.

in any other case ; he may deny the delivery, by a *protestation*, and then, 'for replication', traverse the acceptance (*f*). And in general, when on one side, *two* material facts are pleaded, of which the opposite party can traverse but one, without making his pleading double, he may exclude the other, to the intent above explained, by a *protestation* (*g*).

Is no part of the pleadings.

§ 60. A protestation is, strictly, no part of *the pleadings*, and is distinguished from them in its form, by always commencing with the word, 'protesting,' or in Latin, '*protestando*' (*h*). It has therefore no effect whatever, in *the principal case*, the legal merits of which are, upon the face of the record, precisely the same as if the protestation were omitted. Indeed all traversable facts, which are *denied* under a protestation, are, for the purpose of deciding the principal cause, *admitted* (*i*). Thus, in the case last stated, the delivery of the wine, which the protestation *denies*, stands upon the face of the record, (so far as regards *that* case), *as confessed.*

Requires no answer.

§ 61. From these principles it follows, that a protestation requires *no answer;* and that the facts, denied or excluded by it, require *no proof* (*k*). Hence it also follows, that a protestation, which is *idle* or *superfluous*, or even *repugnant to the pleading*,

(*f*) 2 Chitt. Pl. 602. 644-5. 1 Lill. Ent. 105. 106.
(*g*) 2 Chitt. Pl. 602.
(*h*) Lawes' Pl. 141. 2 Chitt. Pl. 602. 2 T. R. 441.
(*i*) Bac. Abr. *Pleas*, &c, H. 4. Lawes' Pl. 141-3.
(*k*) Com. Dig. *Pleader*, N. Bac. Abr. *Pleas*, &c, H. 4. Lawes' Pl. 143.

CHAP. VII.

with which it is connected, does not injure the pleading, even on special demurrer (*l*); since the protestation forms no part of the pleading. Such a protestation is, however, of no avail, and cannot, therefore, exclude an *estoppel* (*m*).

§ 62. And it seems, that in general, a protestation does not avail the party protesting, if the issue be found *against* him (*n*): The reason of which may perhaps be, that as his *pleading* is found to be false; the protestation is, therefore, presumed to be so. This rule, however, appears to apply only to those cases, in which the facts protested against might have been directly *traversed* (*o*). When the issue is found *in favour* of the party protesting, the protestation has its full intended effect, as above explained (*p*). It is also observable, that a protestation is the only mode of denying such facts, as cannot be put *in issue* (*q*).

The inducement must consist of issuable matter.

§ 63. The inducement to a traverse must consist of *issuable* matter — whether the inducement and traverse go to one and the same point, or to different points (*r*). The correctness of this rule has been

(*l*) Com. Dig. *Pleader*, N. Plowd. 276. b. Lawes' Pl. 142.

(*m*) Iid.

(*n*) Co. Litt. 124. b. 126. a. Com. Dig. *Pleader*, N. 2 Saund. 103. a. b. (n. 1). Lawes' Pl. 142.

(*o*) 2 Saund. 103. a. b. (n. 1).

(*p*) 2 Saund. 103. c. (n. 1).

(*q*) Plowd. 276. b. Lawes' Pl. 141.

(*r*) Bac. Abr. *Pleas*, &c, H. 1. Com. Dig. *Pleader*, G. 20. Cro. Car. 336. 3 Salk. 353. 2 Leon. 32.

questioned, as it regards cases, in which the inducement and traverse both go to *the same* point (*s*). For as the party, to whom such a traverse is tendered, must (regularly) join in it, (if material), and cannot traverse the inducement (6); why, it may be asked, is it necessary that the inducement should consist of *issuable* matter? It will appear, however, upon examination, that the rule is founded upon sound principle. For

Reasons of the last rule.

§ 64. 1. When the inducement and the traverse go to *the same* point, they cannot, in the nature of the thing, be properly *adapted to each other*, unless the traverse follows, as a *necessary inference*, from the inducement (*ante*, § 14); so that if either of them is true, the other must necessarily be so. Indeed, the inducement and the traverse, when thus adapted to each other, (as they must be, in order to be secure against a demurrer), assert substantially the *same thing*, though in different forms — the one being in the *affirmative*, and the other in the *negative*. It is clear, therefore, when they are thus adapted to each other, that if the *traverse* consists of issuable matter, as it confessedly must; the *inducement* will, and must of necessity, consist of similar matter, or rather of *the same* matter, differently expressed.

(*s*) Bac. Abr. *Pleas*, &c, H. 1. *in notis*.

---

(6) Because a traverse of the inducement would be a traverse *upon* a traverse (*ante*, § 42).

CHAP. VII.

§ 65. This exposition of the rule may be sufficiently illustrated, by a single and very simple example:—If a defendant pleads that his co-defendant is dead, and the plaintiff replies that he is alive, *absque hoc* that he is dead; the inducement, (that he is alive), asserts in substance the *same* fact, as does the traverse: That 'he is *alive*,' and that 'he is *not dead*,' being in effect the same proposition, expressed in different terms; and a denial of either of these assertions is a denial of the other. It is manifest then, that if the *traverse*, in this case, consists of issuable matter; so, necessarily, does the inducement. A similar explanation will be found applicable to every other instance, in which the inducement and traverse go to the *same* point, if they are adapted to each other; and if not, the pleading is, for that cause, demurrable (*t*).

§ 66. 2. When the inducement and traverse go to *different* points, (of which, it is believed, no instance occurs, except in the defendant's plea), the rule, requiring the inducement to consist of *issuable* matter, is founded on equally clear, though different, reasons from those mentioned above. In cases of this kind, the inducement is, itself, traversable; as it forms a *substantive and distinct ground of defence*, not embraced in the traverse, and is indispensably necessary, to render the defence *complete*, or *co-extensive* with the declaration. And it is manifest, that whatever constitutes the defendant's *answer* to any material part of the complaint, must itself be

(*t*) Cro. Car. 266. 336. Com. Dig. *Pleader*, G. 20.

material, and capable of being put *in issue*. Thus, if in trespass, the defendant justifies for a *single day*, with a traverse that he is guilty on any other day; it is obviously necessary that the matter of justification, which constitutes the inducement to the traverse, be, itself, *material* and *issuable;* since the defence would otherwise be defective in substance, as not answering the *whole gravamen*, (*ante*, ch. 6, §§ 98. 99). The rule, then, that the inducement to a traverse must consist of *issuable* matter—whether it goes to the same point as the traverse, or to a different point—appears to be fully supported by the sound principles of pleading.

Uses of the inducement.

§ 67. It has been supposed by some (*u*), that an *inducement* to a traverse is but an arbitrary form, answering no useful purpose, and therefore always unnecessary. And it is doubtless true, that where the inducement and traverse go to the *same* point, (in which case the inducement cannot, in general, be itself traversed, or otherwise answered), an inducement, in many cases, answers no necessary purpose (*ante*, § 38). But on the other hand, it is certain that in many cases, an inducement is at least useful, and in some, absolutely necessary.

§ 68. Thus, 1. Where the inducement and traverse both go to the *same* point, the former must, in fair and liberal practice, be deemed *useful*, in disclosing the *particular grounds or facts*, on which the

(*u*) 1 Swift's Dig. 629.

traverse is founded, and by which it is to be maintained in proof. 2. In many cases of this kind, an inducement is indispensably *necessary*, to avoid a *negative pregnant*, which the traverse would otherwise be, (*ante*, §§ 35. 36.) 3. Where the inducement and traverse go to *different* points, the inducement, as has just been shown, is a *substantive and indispensable part of the defence*. It may also be suggested, that an inducement, by way of *protestation* (which is, indeed, no part of the *pleadings*), may often be necessary, for the purpose of excluding an *estoppel*, (ante, §§ 58. 59.)

CHAPTER VIII.

PART I.—OF DUPLICITY.

CHAP. VIII. PART I.

Duplicity, nature of.

SECTION 1. *Duplicity*, or *double* pleading, consists in alleging, *for one single* purpose or object, *two or more distinct grounds* of complaint, or defence, when one of them would be as effectual in law, as both or all. This, by the principles of the common law, is a fault in all pleading; because it produces useless *prolixity*, and always tends to confusion, and to the *multiplication of issues* (*a*). Duplicity in *the declaration* has been heretofore described, (ch. 4, § 99); and it now remains to treat of the same fault in the subsequent pleadings.

Is a fault in all pleading.

§ 2. The rule forbidding double pleading 'extends', says Lord *Coke*, 'to pleas *perpetual*, or *peremptory*, and not to pleas *dilatory*; for in their time and place, a man may use divers of them' (*b*). But by this, is not meant that any dilatory plea may be *double*, or in other words, that it may consist of *distinct* matters, or answers 'to one and the same

(*a*) Co. Litt. 304, a. Finch's Law, 393. 3 Black. Com. 311. Bac. Abr. *Pleas*, &c, K. 1.

(*b*) Co. Litt. 304, a.

CHAP. VIII. PART I.

thing' ; but merely, that as there are *several kinds*, or *classes*, of dilatory pleas, having *distinct* offices and effects ; a defendant may use 'divers of them' *successively*, (each being in itself *single*), in their proper order, (*vid.* ch. 5, § 45). And Lord Coke thus distinguishes dilatory pleas, from pleas *perpetual*, or *to the action ;* because the latter are pleas, all having *one and the same* effect—that of *perpetually barring* the action. And as any *one* of these latter pleas, if good, is as effectual, for this purpose, as any number of them ; the common law allows but *one* of them 'to one and the same thing'—i. e. to the *whole*, or to one and the same *part*, of the declaration, or demand.

In the pleadings, which follow the declaration.

§ 3. As to duplicity in the pleadings which follow the declaration, the rule of the common law is, that every plea must be *simple*, *entire*, *connected*, and confined to a SINGLE POINT, i. e. a single ground of complaint, or defence (*c*). And this rule extends as well to *traverses*, or matter of *denial*, (ch. 7, § 49), as to the allegation of new matter (*d*) ; and as well to the *replication*, and all the later stages of the pleadings, as to the defendant's *plea* (*e*).

§ 4. According to the general description already given of duplicity, a double plea is one, which

(*c*) 3 Black. Com. 311.

(*d*) Bac. Abr. *Pleas*, &c, H. 1. 5. Co. Litt. 126, a. 1 Stra. 317. Bull. N. P. 93. 1 Burr. 316. 321.

(*e*) Cas. Temp. Hardw. 290. Com. Dig. *Pleader*, F. 16. Fort. 335. 1 Stra. 317.

consists of several *distinct and independent* matters, alleged to the same point, (i. e. to the *whole*, or to one and the same part, of the demand, or defence), and *requiring different answers* (*f*). Thus, if the defendant pleads to the same trespass, a *justification* and a *release* — or to the same debt, *duress* and *payment* — or pleads, in one and the same suit, *two* causes of disability in the plaintiff — as two different *outlawries*, or *outlawry* and *alienage;* the plea is ill for duplicity (*g*).

§ 5. But the giving of different answers, (each being in itself single), to *different parts* of the declaration, or writ, does not constitute duplicity: Since the different matters, so pleaded, are not alleged to *one and the same* point, or thing (*h*). Ex. gr. The defendant may, at the same time, as to part of the declaration, plead the *general issue*, and matter of *avoidance* to the residue — or one matter of *abatement* to one part of the writ, and another, to another part (*i*): or he may, in the same manner, plead in *abatement*, as to *one* part of the demand, and in *bar*, as to another (*k*) — ex. gr. in debt on two bonds, he may plead a *nonjoinder*, or other matter of abate-

(*f*) Co. Litt. 303, b. 304, a. Bac. Abr. *Pleas*, &c, K. 1.
(*g*) Com. Dig. *Abatement*, C. & I. 3. 4. Tidd, 589. Lawes' Pl, 108. (Vide ch. 5, §§ 4. 5.)
(*h*) Co. Litt 304, a. Bac. Abr. *Pleas*, &c, K. 1. N. 1. Lawes' Pl. 107.
(*i*) Com. Dig. *Abatement*, I. 5. Lawes' Pl. 107-8. *Ante*, ch. 5, § 6.
(*k*) 2 Bos. & P. 420. Lawes' Pl. 108. *Vid.* 10 Mod. 285-6.

CHAP. VIII. PART I.

ment, as to one of them, and *non est factum*, or a special plea in bar, as to the other, (*vid.* ch. 5, § 7.)

Co-defendants may plead different pleas.

§ 6. And where there are *several* defendants in the same suit, *each* of them may, regularly, plead for himself a single matter of defence to the *whole*, or different matters to *different parts*, of the writ or declaration (*l*). In other words, each of the defendants may plead for himself, as if he were a *sole* defendant. For otherwise, any one of them might, through obstinacy or ignorance, or even by collusion with the plaintiff, reduce the others to the alternative of joining in a false or frivolous plea, or of foregoing all defence whatever.

Exception to the last rule.

§ 7. But this rule does not hold, where in an action on *contract*, against several co-defendants, who are charged as joint contractors, they all plead *the same* defence to the action — as where, for example, they all plead the general issue, or *the same* matter of avoidance. In this case, they cannot *sever* in pleading; but must plead jointly (*m*). Thus, in assumpsit against two or more, if they all plead *non assumpsit*, or any other *common* defence; they must do it in one and the same plea, and cannot plead it, *each for himself*, or severally (*n*). For in an action *on contract*, against several, where they all rely on the same matter of defence, there can be no neces-

(*l*) Hob. 70. 250. Stra. 509. 610. 1140. 2 Ld Ray. 1372. Co. Litt. 303, a. Lawes' Pl. 132. 2 M. & S. 26.

(*m*) 6 Mass. R. 444.

(*n*) Ib.

sity for their severing in pleading: Any matter of defence, which is good for any *one* of them, being necessarily good for *all;* because, a *joint* contract being alleged — a *joint liability* must be established, or there will be a *variance* between the evidence and the declaration, and consequently there can be *no* recovery. And therefore, if they all agree as to the kind of answer to be given to the action; they are respectively as safe in pleading it *jointly*, as they could be in alleging the same matter of defence *severally:* Whereas in an action *ex delicto*, against several, the same matter of defence, which may be good for one of them, may be ill for the others; and therefore they are allowed to plead the *same thing*, (the general issue, for example) *severally;* and if they plead thus, one may be convicted and another acquitted: Torts, though charged as joint, being *several* as well as joint (*o*) (1).

§ 8. And even, in an action *on contract*, against several, if they choose *different* defences, they may plead severally, i. e. each a *separate* plea, for himself (*p*). For such a case is not within the reason of the above exception (§ 7). Thus, in assumpsit against two, one may plead *non assumpsit*, and the

(*o*) 1 Saund. 207. a. b. (n. 2).
(*p*) 3 Esp. Rep. 76. 5 Ib. 47. 2 M. & S. 444.

---

(1) If however, several defendants, charged jointly in tort, *join* in a plea, which is ill for *either* of them, it is so for *all* of them (*ante*, ch. 6, § 101). For an entire plea cannot be *severed*, in its effect; and the defendants might have pleaded the same matter, *severally*.

CHAP. VIII. PART I.

other matter of *avoidance* — as *infancy*. For each defendant must be at liberty to choose the ground of his own defence: Otherwise, several defendants, charged as joint contractors, might all be unjustly subjected, by the refusal of any one of them to unite with the others in a proper plea.

The plea, &c, need not be confined to a single fact.

§ 9. The 'single point,' to which each plea, replication, &c, is required to be confined, need not, as of course, consist of a *single fact* (2). For several connected facts may be, and frequently are necessary, to constitute a single complete ground of demand, or defence (*q*). Thus, in pleading an *award* of arbitrators, the defendant may, and must, allege the *submission*, with a statement of the substance of it, and the *making* of the award by the arbitrators, together with a statement of the terms, or substance of it: All these facts being necessary to the establishment of the *single* defence of a decision of the controversy, by an award of arbitrators (*r*). And a single traverse either of the submission, or of the award, will be a sufficient answer to the whole plea.

§ 10. Thus also, in an action for *malicious prosecution* — in false imprisonment against a sheriff, for

(*q*) Bac. Abr. *Pleas*, &c, K. 2. 2 Black. Rep. 1028. 1 Burr. 320–1. 3 Salk. 142. 3 M. & S. 180. 2 Johns. R. 433. 462.
(*r*) 2 Chit. Pl. 437–8.

---

(2) This rule, as applied to a *traverse*, has been already explained, ch. 7, § 51.

an arrest made on suspicion of felony — the defendant may plead in bar all such circumstantial facts (however numerous), as conduce to show *reasonable grounds* of suspicion, as the cause of the prosecution, or arrest. For all such facts go to constitute the single defence of *probable cause* (*s*); and the replication, *de injuriâ, &c, absque tali causâ*, answers the whole plea — so that different facts pleaded do not require *different* answers, and consequently do not conduce to *multiply issues*.

§ 11. But if the defendant, in the case last supposed, relies for his justification, upon any criminal *act* of the plaintiff — as, when he justifies the arrest, on the ground of a felony *actually committed* by the plaintiff; he can allege in his plea only *one* such act, without making his defence *double:* Because one actual felony is as complete a justification as several would be.

§ 12. When however the fact, relied on as the *gist* of the defence, is but *the consequence* of another fact — or when one of them is a necessary or proper *inducement* to the other, *both* may be pleaded, without making the plea double (*u*). And therefore an executor, when sued for a debt due from his testator, may plead that he has 'fully administered, and so has nothing in his hands.' For the allegation of

(*s*) Cro. Eliz. 134. 871. 900. Bridgm. 61. 2 Hawk. P. C. ch. 12. § 8—16.

(*u*) Plowd. 140. a. Poph. 186. Mo. 25. Com. Dig. *Pleader*, E. 2. March, 74. Latch, 149. 1 Burr. 320.

CHAP. VIII. PART I.

'fully administered,' serves merely to show *how and why* the defendant has nothing in his hands. So also, to an action by a woman, the defendant may plead that after the cause of action accrued, she *took husband*, and that the husband afterwards *released* the action. For it would be of no avail to plead *the release*, without showing *the marriage*. Neither of these pleas, it may be observed, requires more than a *single* answer.

§ 13. In debt on bond, the assignment of more than *one* breach of the condition, in the replication, is by the common law, *duplicity* (*v*): Because, at common law, *one* breach incurs the forfeiture of the whole penalty; and nothing more could ensue in the plaintiff's favour, from any *number* of breaches. Besides, they would all go to *one and the same* point, viz. the forfeiture of the entire penalty.

§ 14. But in *covenant broken*, the plaintiff may, by the common law, assign as many breaches as he may think proper (*w*). For in this action, the plaintiff can recover only the damages *actually incurred*, from a breach or breaches of the covenant; and can legally prove no other breaches than those alleged.

§ 15. And now, since the statute 8 & 9 W. 3, c. 11, § 8, by which courts of *law* are enabled to

(*v*) Com. Dig. *Pleader*, C. 33. Comb. 297. 3 Salk. 108. 2 Wils. 267. Lawes' Pl. 25–7.

(*w*) Com. Dig. *Pleader*, C. 33. Cro. Car. 176. Bac. Abr. *Covenant*, I.

relieve against penalties, in bonds for the performance of covenants, or agreements in indentures, deeds, &c, the plaintiff, in all actions on *penal bonds*, falling within that statute, may, by express provision in the act, assign *as many breaches* as he pleases; and ought for his own sake, to assign as many as there are (*x*): Because in all cases within the statute, the plaintiff can recover for such breaches only as are *assigned;* and thus the same rule of damages, and of pleading, is now, in England, established in these cases, as by the common law prevails in actions of *covenant broken.* The same rule exists in the state of *Connecticut*, in *all* actions, in general, on penal obligations.

Surplusage does not make a plea double.

§ 16. Mere *surplusage*, pleaded in connexion with what is material, never renders a plea double (*y*) not only because *utile per inutile non vitiatur;* but more particularly, because matter of surplusage requires no *answer*, and consequently does not tend to *multiply issues.* If therefore the defendant pleads *payment*, and also a previous and subsequent *readiness* to pay; the plea is not double: For the alleged readiness to pay is not issuable.

§ 17. But any thing in itself material, though *ill pleaded*, will, if pleaded in connexion with other

(*x*) Bac. Abr. *Covenant*, I. 2 Black. Rep. 1016. 1111. 2 Burr. 820. 2 Wils. 377. Cowp. 357. 2 Chitt. Pl. 153. 8 T. R. 126. 6 East, 550. 613. 1 Saund. 58. (n. 1). 2 Mass. R. 542.

(*y*) 1 Keb. 661. 1 Sid. 175. Doct. Pl. 138. Bac. Abr. *Pleas*, &c, K. 2.

CHAP. VIII. PART I.

issuable matter, render the pleading double (*z*). And therefore, where in trespass for assault and battery, the defendant *justified*, by alleging a *molliter manus imposuit* for the due correction of the plaintiff as his servant, and also averred that the plaintiff had *released* the cause of complaint, but without averring that the release was *by deed;* it was resolved, that the latter averment made the plea double (*a*): Because the alleged release, though *ill pleaded*, in not being alleged to be *by deed*, was nevertheless *issuable*. And it was held, in the same case, that any matter which, if *well* pleaded, would make a pleading double, would have the same effect, though *ill* pleaded : Since such matter cannot be regarded as *surplusage*, nor the plea, which alleges it, as *void*. (3)

§ 18. As instances frequently occur, however, in which there exist *two* or more distinct grounds of defence, to one and the same demand ; it is obvious, that the common law rule, confining the defendant to a *single* plea consisting of a *single* matter of defence, must sometimes have operated unjustly against him : Inasmuch as any misapprehension on his part,

(*z*) Bac. Abr. *Pleas*, &c, K. 2.
(*a*) Ib. 1 Keb. 661. 1 Sid. 175.

---

(3) By a *void* plea, is to be understood one, of which the adverse party is not bound to take notice in any way, and which he may therefore entirely pass over, by signing judgment as *for want* of a plea.

or on that of his counsel, in regard to the law, or the facts of the case, or as to the eventual state of the proof, might sometimes induce him to choose an unavailing defence, in preference to another, which would have been successful. And thus he may have been subjected to a recovery, when the right of the controversy, both in law and in fact, was on his side. These considerations occasioned the enactment of the statute 4 *Ann.* c. 16, § 4, which provides that 'it shall be lawful, for any defendant, or tenant, in any action or suit, or for any plaintiff in replevin, in any court of record, with leave of the court, to plead *as many several* matters thereto as he shall think necessary for his defence' (*b*) (4).

Two or more pleas allowed by statute 4 *Anne.*

§ 19. Under this statute, the defendant, in any English court of record, may, with leave of the court, plead as many different pleas in bar, (each being in itself *single*), as he may think proper (*c*). But though this statute allows the defendant to plead several distinct and substantive matters of defence, (in *several distinct pleas*), to the *whole*, or *one and the same part* of the plaintiff's demand; yet it does not authorize him to allege more than *one*

(*b*) Bac. Abr. *Pleas*, &c, K. 3.
(*c*) 3 Black. Com. 308. Lawes' Pl. 27-8.

(4) There is a similar statute in the state of Connecticut, and probably in most of the states in the American Union.

CHAP. VIII. PART I.

ground of defence, in *one plea.* *Each* plea must still be *single*, as by the rule of the common law (*d*).

§ 20. Whenever the defendant pleads, in pursuance of this statute, more than one plea in bar, to one and the same demand, or thing, all of them, except the first, should (regularly) purport to be pleaded, *with leave of the court* — as in the following form, viz. 'and for a further plea in this behalf, the said C. D. by leave of the court here for this purpose first had and obtained, according to the form of the statute in such case made and provided, says' &c (*e*). This, or some similar form, seems necessary by the terms of the statute; which makes it lawful for the defendant, only 'with *leave* of the court,' to plead more than one plea. — The omission of this formula, however, is held to be an *irregularity only*, and not error, nor cause for demurrer. (*ee*).

§ 21. This statute extends only to pleas *to the declaration*, and does not embrace *replications*, *rejoinders*, or any of the subsequent pleadings (*f*). For in these later stages of the pleadings, the privilege of making several answers to the same thing, can seldom be necessary or useful. As to these pleadings, therefore, the common law rule against duplicity still remains in full force. And therefore the

(*d*) Lawes' Pl. 131. 1 Chitt. Pl. 512. 513.

(*e*) Lawes' Pl. 132. 2 Chitt. Pl. 421–2. Com. Dig. *Pleader*, E. 2. Story's Pl. 72, 76.

(*ee*) Andr. 109. 1 Wils. 219. 3 N. Hamp. R. 523.

(*f*) Bac. Abr. *Pleas*, &c, K. 2. Com. Dig. *Pleader*, E. 2.

plaintiff cannot, under this statute, *reply* two several matters to one *plea*, nor the defendant *rejoin* different matters to one replication (*g*).

§ 22. The plaintiff is at liberty, however, to reply *separately*, to each of the defendant's pleas — so that he may still plead as many replications, (each being itself single), as there are separate *pleas* admitting of answers. For, according to the first principles of pleading, each party must have a right to answer, in some form, all that is alleged against him (*h*).

§ 23. The statute is also limited, in construction, to such pleas of the defendant as go to *the action*, and does not extend to *dilatory* pleas (*i*). For though the terms of the statute do not exclude pleas of the latter class; yet as these are not favoured by the law; the court will not, in its discretion, give the defendant leave to plead two of them to the *same thing*.

§ 24. If any *one* of several pleas pleaded together, under this statute, is determined in the defendant's favour; it is a good bar to the action, or at least to so much of the plaintiff's demand, as the plea extends to; although all the others should be determined in favour of the *plaintiff*. For *one* good defence is as available, as far as it extends, as two

(*g*) Iid.
(*h*) 1 Saund. 337. b. (n. 2.)
(*i*) 1 Sell. Pract. 275. Steph. Pl. 295.

or more would be. If therefore, any one of the pleas, pleaded to any *one* count in the declaration, prevails, either on an issue in fact or in law; it is an effectual bar as to *that count;* and if any one plea to *the whole* declaration thus prevails, it bars the whole action (*k*).

§ 25. When several pleas in bar are pleaded, in virtue of this statute, to one and the same thing or demand, *each* of them is treated, and operates, as if it were pleaded alone: It being an established rule, that one of them 'cannot,' in the language of Lord Ch. J. *Willes*, 'be taken in to *help*, or *destroy* another;' but that 'every plea must stand or fall, *by itself*' (*l*). And the opinion of Mr J. *Buller* is expressed in terms almost literally the same (*ll*). No one of them, therefore, can have the effect of *dispensing with the proof* of what is denied by another (*m*). Hence if the defendant pleads, first the *general issue*, and then pleads specially matter in *avoidance*, which impliedly *confesses* the declaration —(as if he pleads first, *non est factum*, and adds a special plea of *usury*, *duress*, *infancy*, *payment*, &c; or pleads all these, in successive special pleas — or pleads first, *not guilty*, and then special matter of *justification* or *discharge*); the matter of avoidance

(*k*) 2 Burr. 753. 1 Saund. 80. (n. 1.)

(*l*) Willes, 380.

(*ll*) 1 T. R. 125—*Acc.* 5 Serg. & R. 411, per Duncan, J.

(*m*) 2 East, 426. 5 Ib. 463. 2 Johns. R. 437. 2 Phil. Ev. 97. n. a. 1 Stark. Ev. 296. n. 389. n. 1 Chitt. Pl. 543. 5 Taunt. 233. 2 N. Hamp. R. 89.

thus pleaded, though *inconsistent* with the general issue, does not supersede the necessity of the plaintiff's proving his *declaration* (5) For a contrary rule would defeat the very object of the statute — which manifestly is, to enable the defendant, not only to *plead*, but on the trial, to *rely upon*, as many different defences, as he may choose to put upon the record. But if a plea in avoidance were held to destroy the effect of the general issue; it is manifest that the statute, allowing the defendant to plead *both* pleas, would be altogether nugatory. And the effect would plainly be the same, if one of two inconsistent pleas in *avoidance* (as *payment*, and *accord and satisfaction*, both pleaded to the whole demand), were held to *disprove the other*. Indeed, it appears clear, that the *benefit* or *privilege* intended to be conferred upon the defendant, by this statute, must be lost to him, unless his several pleas are treated, and allowed to operate, as *entirely independent of each other*.

---

(5) See a contrary opinion, 15 Mass. R. 48, where, in an action of slander, the defendant pleaded (in virtue of a statute, similar to that of 4 *Ann.*) the *general issue*, and also a *special justification*: In which case it was resolved, that the admission contained in the special plea, that the words charged were uttered by the defendant, was sufficient proof of that fact; and that the plaintiff was, consequently, not bound *to prove* the uttering of the words. And in the very ingenious argument of the learned judge, who delivered the opinion of the court, the same rule is held to extend to every case, in which the *general issue*, and a special plea *in avoidance*, are pleaded to one and the same demand. But this opinion appears to be opposed, not only to the spirit of the statute, but to the general practice under it.

CHAP. VIII. PART I.

What different pleas are allowed under the statute of Anne.

§ 26. Many questions have heretofore arisen, as to *what* several defences in bar may be pleaded together, under this statute, to one and the same demand; and a copious catalogue of such pleas as may, and of such as may not, be thus pleaded together, is presented in *Comyns' Digest*, *Pleader*, E. 2. For an opinion was formerly entertained, that *mere inconsistency* between two given pleas was a decisive objection to their being pleaded together, under the statute. But if such a rule should prevail, the statute would, in a great measure, be practically repealed. For the *general issue*, which is almost universally the first of the several pleas pleaded together under the statute, is, on strict common-law principles, inconsistent with almost *every special* matter of defence whatever (6): Since the general issue *denies*, while a plea in avoidance *admits*, the truth of the declaration. At this day, however, it appears to be generally understood as a sound rule, in the construction of the statute, that *mere inconsistency*, between two or more pleas in bar, is no objection to their being pleaded together (*n*):

(*n*) 1 Chitt. Pl. 540–542. 2 Ib. 431, n. d. 4 T. R. 194. 13 East, 255. 2 Phill. Ev. 97, n. a. Com. Dig. *Pleader*, E. 2. 1 Sell. Pract. 299. 5 Taunt. 340. 3 Bing. 635. 3 Pick. 388.

---

(6) This proposition, as applied to actions *on the case*, and especially the action of *assumpsit*, must be understood with some modification. In these *equitable* actions, which were unknown to the ancient common law, the general issue is deemed consistent with, and comprehends many matters of *mere avoidance*. (*Vid.* ch. 6, §§ 46 to 54.)

A rule, which would appear to follow of course from one before laid down, viz. that each of several pleas, thus pleaded together, is to be considered as *independent* of all the others, and to operate as if pleaded *alone*.

§ 27. And it seems now, that when the several matters of defence, proposed to be pleaded, all require the same mode of trial, (as by jury), the defendant may plead, with the *general issue*, *any* special plea, except that of *tender* (*o*). The reason, why *tender* cannot be pleaded with the general issue, is not, however, merely or chiefly, that it is *inconsistent* with that issue (for so, generally, are all special pleas in bar); but that the former admits the debt or damages demanded to be still *due*, and in its effect goes only in bar of the *costs*, and the nominal damages of detention — while the general issue and other pleas in bar, in general, deny any existing liability or legal duty on the part of the defendant. Actions on *penal statutes* are, by the express words of the statute of *Anne*, excluded from its operation (*p*). And it is held, that the statute does not extend to actions at the suit of the king (*pp*).

§ 28. Neither at common law, nor under the statute of *Anne*, can a party *plead, and demur*, to

(*o*) 4 T. R. 194. 5 Ib. 97. 1 Chitt. Pl. 541. Steph. Pl. 293.

(*p*) 2 Stra. 1044. 4 T. R. 701. 1 Chitt. Pl. 541. 2 Wils. 21. Barnes, 365. Cas. Temp. Hardw. 262.

(*pp*) Parker's Rep. 1. Forrest's Rep. 57; where it is said that the case in Com. R. 422, is misreported.

the same matter or thing (*q*) — not at common law, by reason of the *incongruity* between the plea and the demurrer; not under the statute, because that only enables the defendant to *plead* several matters, &c: Whereas a demurrer merely assigns a reason for *not* pleading, and is not considered as a *plea*.

§ 29. But double pleading, (or duplicity), when not warranted by the statute, is only a fault in *form;* and therefore, under the statute 27 Eliz. c. 5, (7), no advantage can be taken of it, except by *special demurrer* (*r*). For the ground of objection to such pleading is, not that it is *deficient in substance;* but that it contains *more* than is necessary.

§ 30. But though, where two distinct and sufficient matters, not warranted by the statute to be pleaded together, are pleaded to the same point, by one party, the other may demur for that cause; yet if, instead of demurring, he *pleads over;* he must answer *both* of them: Otherwise, the part unanswered will remain decisive against him (*s*). And in such a case, an answer, (in itself single), to *each* matter, does not constitute *duplicity:* For the two answers are not to *one and the same* point, but to

(*q*) Bac. Abr. *Pleas*, &c, K. 1. N. 1.

(*r*) Bac. Abr. *Pleas*, &c, K. 1. 2 Lill. Ab. 397. 1 Saund. 337, b. (n. 3.) Com. R. 115. Com. Dig. *Pleader*, E. 2. 1 Wils. 219. 1 Bos. & P. 415. 416. Lawes' Pl. 132–5. 6 Mass. R. 337–8. 2 N. Hamp. R. 180. 308.

(*s*) 1 Vent. 272. Bac. Abr. *Pleas*, &c, K. 1.

---

(7) For this statute, see *Demurrer*, ch. 9.

two *different* points. If, for example, to a plea of *infancy*, in assumpsit, the plaintiff replies *necessaries*, and also a *promise* after full age; the defendant, if he does not demur for the duplicity, must give a substantive, single answer to the allegation of necessaries, and another, to that of the subsequent promise. For if the rejoinder should answer but *one* of these allegations; the other, remaining unanswered, would destroy the plea in bar.

§ 31. The rule, requiring a demurrer, for duplicity, to be special, does not extend to declarations, in which there is a *misjoinder of causes of action* — or in other words, to cases, in which the plaintiff joins, in different counts in one declaration, different and incongruous causes of action, as substantive and *distinct* grounds of recovery: As, where he thus joins *contract and tort*, or *case and trespass*. Such a misjoinder has been heretofore shown to be an incurable fault, and consequently ill, on *general* demurrer or (with the exception mentioned, *ante*, c. 4, § 97), on motion in *arrest of judgment*, after verdict, or on writ of error (*t*).

(*t*) 1 Salk. 10. Bac. Abr. *Pleas*, &c, B. 3. 1 T. R. 274. 1 H. Black. 108. 2 Bos. & P. 424. 7 Barn. & Cresw. 444. 12 Johns. R. 349. 11 Mass. R. 59. 60. 1 M. & S. 360.

CHAP. VIII. PART II.

Part II. — *Of Profert and Oyer.*

Profert of deeds, when necessary.

§ 32. It is a general rule of the common law, that when a party declares on, or otherwise pleads, *a deed* (as a bond, covenant, &c), and *makes title* under it (i. e. founds his demand or defence upon it), he must make a *profert* of it in his pleading, by averring that he 'brings here into court the said writing obligatory', (or other deed) (*u*).

§ 33. The practical use of a *profert*, in pleading, appears to be, that it enables the court to *inspect* the instrument pleaded (8), (the construction and legal effect of which are matter of *law*); and entitle the adverse party to *oyer* of it (*v*).

Oyer, what.

§ 34. Craving *oyer* of a writing, according to the original signification of that term, is demanding to *hear it read* (*w*); which prayer, or request, it is the province of the court, to grant or not, as the party praying it may, or may not, be entitled to it.

(*u*) Com. Dig. *Pleader*, O. 1. 10 Co. 92, a. b. 1 Brownl. 221. Yelv. 201. 3 Black. Com. *App.* XXII. Lawes' Pl. 96-7.
(*v*) 10 Co. 92, b. 1 Chitt. Pl. 414. 1 Archb. Pr. 164.
(*w*) 3 Black. Com. 299. *App.* No. III, § 6. Lawes' Pl. 96.

---

(8) When profert is made, the deed is supposed to be *in court*, and to remain there, to the end of the term, unless the cause is sooner determined; and if so, until it is determined. 2 Salk. 497. 3 Ib. 119. Bac. Abr. *Pleas*, &c, I. 12. (2).

§ 35. But in the modern practice, a right to *oyer* entitles the party demanding it, to a *copy* (at his own expense), of the instrument pleaded against him; to the end, that he may have an opportunity to recite it upon the record, and thus avail himself, (upon *the face of the record*), of any thing in the writing, which may aid him, in meeting the allegations of his adversary (*x*). Thus to debt on bond, the defendant having obtained *oyer* of it, and recited the condition, is enabled to avail himself of the latter, by pleading, or demurring, as his case may require (9).

§ 36. The ground on which *oyer* is awarded, in any case, is, that the party, whom the law entitles to it, is presumed to be unable, *without it*, to give a proper answer to the title made under the instrument, pleaded by the adverse party. And therefore, when he, who is entitled to *oyer*, demands it, he is not bound to answer, in any way, until it is given; but if he does plead, without demanding it, he waves his claim to it (*y*).

(*x*) Bac. Abr. *Pleas*, &c, I. 12. (1. 2.) Hob. 217. Show. P. C. 221.

(*y*) Bac. Abr. *Pleas*, &c, I. 12. (2) *in marg*. 2 Lill. Ab. 336.

---

(9) In the present practice, application to *the court*, for an order of *oyer*, is seldom, or never made, except in cases, where the *right* to it, on the part of him, who demands it, is questioned. In other cases the copy is usually given voluntarily, by the attorney of him, who pleads the deed, to the attorney of the adverse party, on the latter's private request, without the intervention of the court. (1 Tidd, 518. 2 T. R. 40. Steph. Pl. 87.)

CHAP. VIII. PART II.

§ 37. And in the English practice, if he, who is bound to give *oyer*, does not give it, within *two days* from the day of the demand, (*excluding that day*); the adverse party may *sign judgment* against him (*z*): Otherwise, the party, bound to give *oyer*, might, by neglecting it, delay the proceedings indefinitely. As however the right to *oyer* on one side, results from the *profert* made on the other; the first proper inquiry, under the present head, is, in what cases it is necessary, for him who pleads an instrument, to make a *profert* of it, in his pleading?

§ 38. It has already been stated (§ 32), that he, who pleads *a deed, and makes title* under it, must plead it with a *profert*. For the deed being, in every such case, *the foundation* of the pleader's suit, or defence, is therefore a matter, which the adverse party should have an opportunity to answer, directly upon the *record;* which, however, he cannot do, without having obtained *oyer* (*a*).

Of what instruments profert must be made.

§ 39. As a general rule, *profert* is required of no other instruments than deeds: These being the only private writings, which, by the original principles of the common law, are considered as *instruments*, on which an action or defence can be *directly* founded. And consequently, he who pleads a writing, *not under seal*—as a bill of exchange, promis-

(*z*) 2 T. R. 40. Com. Dig. *Pleader*, P. 1. Barnes, 245.

(*a*) 1 Keb. 513. Hutt. 33. 1 Saund. 317. (n. 2.) Bac. Abr. *Pleas*, &c, I. 12. (2.) 2 Ld Ray. 1135. 2 Black. R. 1108. 1 Stra. 227. 2 Saund. 60. (n. 3.) 366. (n. 1.) 409. 410.

sory note, or other *unsealed* written agreement — is not bound to make *profert* of it (*b*). For written contracts not under seal, are regarded by the common law, not as *instruments*, on which actions are founded; but merely as *simple* contracts, or, (more precisely), as *evidence of parol contracts* (*c*). Of such instruments, therefore, *oyer* is not demandable.

§ 40. Yet, as it has been customary, under the practical extension of the law-merchant, in modern times, to count upon bills of exchange and promissory notes, *as instruments;* it has become a practice, for the court, on the prayer of the defendant, to order *a copy* of such instrument, when declared upon, to be delivered to him, before he is obliged to plead (*d*). In this practice, however, the defendant, it seems, cannot *found his plea* upon a recital of the copy on the *record:* Since this can be done, only on *oyer* (*e*)*;* which is the technical, and only mode, in which the party, against whom an instrument is pleaded, can avail himself of any thing in it, *by plea.*

§ 41. Nor is *profert* necessary, of a *will*, or an *award*, though *under seal* (*f*). For neither of these

(*b*) 3 Lev. 205. Com. Dig. *Pleader*, O. 3. P. 1. 1 Sid. 386. Bac. Abr. *Pleas*, &c, I. 12. (2.) Chitt. on Bills, 185.

(*c*) 7 T. R. 351. n. 7 Bro. P. C. 550. 1 Salk. 215. 2 Black. Com. 465–6. Rob. on Fr. Conv. 99. 1 Pow. on Cont. 332–3. 341. Chitt. on Bills, 9.

(*d*) Tidd, 532. *Vide* Com. Dig. *Pleader*, P. 1. 1 Salk. 215.

(*e*) 1 Keb. 513. Hutt. 33. Bac. Abr. *Pleas*, &c, I. 12. (2.)

(*f*) Com. Dig. *Pleader*, O. 3. *Arbitrament*, I. Sty. 459. 3 Caines' R. 256.

instruments is *a deed;* and a seal neither constitutes an essential part, nor changes the legal character, of either of them.

§ 42. Of *records*, properly so called, *profert* is not required to be made (*g*). For records are *public* property, deposited and kept for public use, in public offices, designated for that purpose; and are, therefore, not removable for the convenience of individuals, nor subject to their control.

§ 43. But the general rule, that *profert* need be made of no other instruments than deeds, is subject to an exception, in actions brought by *executors, or administrators*, as such — in which cases, *profert* must be made of the *letters testamentary*, or *letters of administration*, by virtue of which the plaintiff asserts his right to bring the suit (*h*): These letters, though not strictly *deeds*, being writings to which a seal is essential, and on which the plaintiff *founds his title* to prosecute the action.

§ 44. A party may sometimes, *in evidence*, make title under a deed, without *pleading it;* and whenever he may, and does, take this course, no *profert* need, or can, be made of it (10).

(*g*) Co. Litt. 225. Tidd, 529. Bull. N. P. 252. 1 T. R. 150. Lawes' Pl. 97. 8 Wheat. 691.

(*h*) Com. Dig. *Pleader*, O. 3. Hob. 38. 1 Roll. Ab. 78. 1 Stra. 412. *Vid.* 11 Mass. R. 314.

---

(10) In what cases, a party may thus make title, is explained, ch. 4, §§ 43. 44.

§ 45. But where any interest or right, acquired by deed, *could not pass* by the common law, without deed, (as where a party claims, by deed, a thing lying only in *grant* — *ex. gr.* an *incorporeal* heredita-ment), he must plead the deed (11); and if he *founds* his action or defence upon it; he must also, by the first general rule (*ante*, § 32), make *profert* of it. The rule is the same, where one pleads a re-lease; because, by the common law, a seal is neces-sary to give effect to it (*i*). Hence also, in *covenant broken*, and in debt too, when founded on specialty, the instrument must be pleaded, and *profert* made of it (*k*). For in both cases, the action is *founded* on a deed.

§ 46. And even though the interest or right, asserted by the pleader, *might* pass without deed; yet if the deed *be pleaded*, (though unnecessarily), and title be made under it; *profert* of the deed must, regularly, be made (*l*). For in cases of this kind, the same reasons exist for requiring *profert*, as if the interest could *not* have passed without deed, viz. that the adverse party may have an op-portunity to answer, *upon the record*, the instrument, under which title is made against him, *upon the re-cord:* Since the deed, in the case here supposed, is

(*i*) 6 Co. 38. a. b. 43. b. Bac. Abr. *Pleas*, &c, I. 12. (1). 1 Bulstr. 119. 2 Salk. 519. Cro. Car. 143. 2 Wils. 376. Cro. Eliz. 571. 2 Stra. 814.

(*k*) Cro. Eliz. 571. 1 Saund. 276. (n. 1).

(*l*) Bac. Abr. *Pleas*, &c, I. 12. (1). Lawes' Pl. 97. 2 Mod. 64.

(11) Vid. ch. 4, § 41.

CHAP. VIII. PART II.

not *mere evidence* of the title of him who pleads it; but the *foundation* or *gist* of his pleading. Thus, in the case of a lease assigned by deed, if he, who alleges the assignment, pleads also *the deed* (though unnecessarily); and founds his action or defence upon it; he must plead it with *profert* — though he was under *no* necessity of *pleading* the deed. (*Vid.* ch. 4, § 43).

When profert of a deed is unnecessary.

§ 47. But where one pleads a deed of any kind, *without making title under it*, he is not bound to make *profert* of it: As where a deed is pleaded, merely as *inducement* to the action or defence (*m*). And therefore, in an action for *disturbance of a right of way*, (which lies *in grant*), if the plaintiff pleads the deed, under which he claims the right; he is not bound to make *profert* of it (*n*). For the *gist* of the action is the *tort* complained of; and the right of way only *inducement*, to which it is neither necessary nor proper for the defendant to plead; although he may contest it, in *evidence*.

Exceptions to the general rule, laid down, *ante*, § 32.

§ 48. And the general rule, first laid down, (§ 32) that he who pleads a deed, and makes title under it, must make *profert* of it, is subject to several exceptions — all of which, however, are founded on the pleader's actual, or presumed *inability to produce*

(*m*) 6 Co. 38. a. b. 10 Ib. 92. 1 Saund. 276. (n. 1). Bac. Abr. *Pleas*, &c, I. 12. (1). 8 T. R. 573. 1 Chitt. Pl. 476—7. 2 Ib. 174. n. (z).

(*n*) Iid. 2 Lill. Ab. 394. Palm. 387. Cro. Jac. 673.

the instrument (12). For the rule, requiring *profert* of a deed, in any case, presupposes or presumes, that the pleader has the *possession* or *control* of it (*o*). Hence, 1. a *stranger* to a deed may, in general, plead it, and make title under it, *without profert*. Thus if a grant, by deed, is made to *A.*, to *the use of B.*; the latter may plead the deed, without profert; though he deduces his own title from it: Because he is supposed not to have the control of it (*p*).

§ 49. Thus also, and for the same reason, one who claims title, accruing by *operation of law*, under a deed to another, may plead the deed, without *profert*: As where, in a writ of *dower*, the demandant pleads a grant to her deceased husband, of the subject in which she demands dower (*q*).

Profert, required of tenant by the curtesy, of a deed to his wife.

§ 50. Yet a tenant *by the curtesy*, who pleads a deed, to which his deceased wife was party, and makes title under it, must make *profert* of it; though he comes in by *operation of law*: Because he

(*o*) 10 Co. 93—4. Bac. Abr. *Pleas*, &c, I. 12. (1). Carth. 316. Cro. Car. 441. 1 Ves. 389. Com. Dig. *Pleader*, O. 8.

(*p*) Com. Dig. *Pleader*, O. 8. Cro. Jac. 217. Carth. 316. Cro. Car. 441.

(*q*) Co. Litt. 225. Bac. Abr. *Pleas*, &c, I. 12. (1). 5 Co. 75. Com. Dig. *Pleader*, O. 8.

(12) When he, who makes title under a deed, in pleading, is *party* or *privy* to it, he is presumed to have the control of it, until the contrary is shown. But a *stranger* to it is, in general, presumed unable to produce it.

CHAP. VIII. PART II.

is presumed to *have possession* of her muniments of title, and may retain them, during his life (*r*).

Of a servant.

§ 51. So also, where a *servant* justifies, under a deed to his *master*, without alleging any right or interest in himself, he must make *profert* of the deed (*s*). For the master's title is the *gist* of the defence; and the servant standing in, and voluntarily assuming, his *master's place*, and in the character of his *representative*, must plead the deed, as the master himself would be required to do, if *he* were defendant.

§ 52. 2. That the deed pleaded is in the hands of the *adverse party*, or has been *destroyed* by him, dispenses with the necessity of making *profert* of it, when profert would otherwise have been necessary (*t*). The reason is the same, as under the first general exception, above stated (§ 48).

§ 53. 3. It also appears, now, and for the same reason, to be established, that when a deed has been *lost* or *destroyed*, by time or casualty, it may be pleaded, and title made under it, without *profert* (*u*): Though it was formerly supposed, that the only re-

(*r*) Co. Litt. 226. a. Bac. Abr. *Pleas*, &c, I. 12. (1). 10 Co. 94. Com. Dig. *Pleader*, O. 9.

(*s*) 10 Co. 92. a. Com. Dig. *Pleader*, O. 5. Co. Litt. 226. a. Cro. Jac. 292. Bac. Abr. *Pleas*, &c, I. 12. (1).

(*t*) 5 Co. 75. a. 1 Saund. 9. a. (n. 1). 3 T. R. 151. 153. 2 H. Black. 259. 1 Chitt. Pl. 349. 2 Ib. 154. n. (k).

(*u*) 1 Saund. 9. a. (n. 1). 2 H. Black. 259. Peake Ev. 97. 307 (2d ed).

lief against such an accident was in *equity* (*v*). And even of late, this exception to the general rule, in a court of law, has been recognized with apparent reluctance (*w*).

The special facts, which dispense with profert, must be alleged.

§ 54. It follows from the preceding principles, that when a party, who is presumed to have *the controL* of a deed, pleads and makes title under it, he must make *profert* of it, unless the *profert* is dispensed with, in virtue of one of the two last exceptions; and in either of these two cases, he must — in order to justify the omission of a profert — allege, in his pleading, the *special facts*, which bring the case within the exception: As that the deed is in the hands of the adverse party, or lost, or destroyed, &c. For if he omits to make *profert*, and assigns no sufficient cause of the omission; his pleading is demurrable. And if he unadvisedly makes *profert*, in such a case; he enables the adverse party to demand *oyer*, and to sign judgment against him, for not giving it (*x*): Because, having *pleaded* that he brings the deed into court, he cannot, while that allegation remains, *retract* or *deny* it, by proving what might have dispensed with it. Yet, under the law of amendments, the court will, on motion, in the last case, allow the pleader of the deed to *amend* his pleading, by *striking out the profert*, and stating

(*v*) 1 Ves. 389. 1 Atk. 61. 6 Ves. jun. 812. 813. 9 Ib. 464. 1 Madd. Ch. 25. 1 Ridgway's Rep. 361.

(*w*) 10 East, 55.

(*x*) 1 Wils. 16. 2 Stra. 1186. 1 Mod. 266. 4 East, 586. 1 Saund. 9. a. (n. 1). *Ante*, § 37.

CHAP. VIII. PART II.

the special facts, which dispense with it (*y*); with an averment, that by reason of those facts, he cannot produce it.

Must be made by privies to the original party.

§ 55. Whenever an *original party* to a deed would, according to the preceding distinctions, have been bound to make *profert* of it, in pleading it, those in *privity* with him must plead it, in the same manner (13). Thus if an *heir*, as such, pleads and makes title under a deed to his ancestor; he must regularly make *profert* of it. And the rule is the same, when an *executor* or *administrator* sues upon a specialty, given to his *testator* or *intestate* (*z*): It being presumed that privies possess, or can command, deeds given to those with whom they are in privity.

§ 56. When *profert* of a deed is required by law, and is actually made, the adverse party, as has been heretofore stated, is entitled to *oyer* of the deed; but if *profert* is made, *unnecessarily*, and the pleader does *not make title* under the deed, (as where it is pleaded only as *inducement*); oyer of it is not demandable (*a*). The *profert*, in such a case, is *sur-*

(*y*) 1 Saund. 9. a. (n. 1). 1 Wils. 16. 8 T. R. 153. n. *Vid.* 1 Stark. R. 74. (60).

(*z*) Co. Litt. 267. 317. 10 Co. 92. 94. Bac. Abr. *Pleas*, &c. I. 12. (1). Com. Dig. *Pleader*, O. 4.

(*a*) Tidd, 529. 2 Salk. 497. Lawes' Pl. 96. 97. Doug. 476-7. 8 Wheat. 695.

---

(13) For the different sorts of *privity*, see Co. Litt. 352. Gilb. Ev. 81. Bull. N. P. 232. 3 Co. 23.

plusage. For the deed, being but *inducement*, cannot be the proper subject of any answer or notice, in *the pleading* of the adverse party.

§ 57. He who is entitled to, and obtains, *oyer* of a deed, is not bound to take any notice of it in his pleading (*b*): The object of granting it being merely to *enable* him to do so, at his pleasure. He *may*, however, after reciting the instrument, *verbatim*, on the record, avail himself of any advantage, which any part of it, not set out by his adversary, may afford him. The mode, in which such advantage may be taken, may be either by pleading, or demurring, as the case may require (ante, § 35). Thus, to debt on bond, the defendant, after reciting the condition, on *oyer*, may plead performance, or tender of performance, of the condition ; or any illegality in the contract, not appearing on the face of the instrument; or any other extrinsic fact, which may defeat a recovery on the bond. (*c*)

§ 58. Or if the instrument sued upon, or upon which the defence is founded, is, upon *the face of it*, *void*, either from illegality, or otherwise ; or is, from any other cause, *insufficient*, *upon the face of it*, to maintain the demand or defence founded upon it ; or if there is any material *variance* between the instrument, as recited on *oyer*, and the description of

(*b*) Lawes' Pl. 98. 2 Stra. 1241. 1 Wils. 97. Com. Dig. *Pleader*, P. 1.

(*c*) 3 Black. Com. 299. 300. Bac. Abr. *Pleas*, &c I. 12. (2). Lawes' Pl. 98. 99. 6 Mod. 28.

CHAP. VIII. PART II.

it in the pleading of him, who has made *profert* of it; the adverse party may *demur* to the pleading in which the *profert* is made (*d*). For in the two first cases, the voidness or insufficiency of the instrument, and in the last, the variance, will, from the recital, appear upon *the record*; and the deed, as recited, is considered as parcel of *the pleading* of him, who pleads it; and consequently, has the same effect, as if it had been set out, *verbatim, in his own pleading* (*e*).

Effect of a false recital, on oyer.

§ 59. But if the party, who has obtained *oyer* of a deed, and who professedly sets it out upon the record, recites it *falsely*, or omits to recite *the whole* of it; he who pleaded it, may relieve himself of the effect of the misrecital, in either of two ways. Thus, 1. he may *sign judgment*, as for want of a plea. For he, who undertakes to set out his adversary's deed, on *oyer*, is permitted to do so, only on the implied *condition*, that he recite it *truly*, and *in full*. And his failure, in either of these particulars, being a *breach* of this condition, has the same effect, as the failure of a party *to plead* in his proper turn. Or, 2. the pleader of the deed may, instead of signing judgment, pray that his deed may be *enrolled* upon the record, by a proper officer of the court; and on its being truly enrolled, may *demur*—

(*d*) Hob. 217. 1 Saund. 317. 2 Ib. 366. (n. 1.) Com. Dig. *Pleader*, P. 1. Bac. Abr. *Pleas*, &c. I. 12. (2.) 2 Wils. 342. Lawes' Pl. 99.

(*e*) Ibid.

as the misrecital, or omission, will, on the enrolment, appear *upon the record* (*f*).

Wrongful refusal of is error.

§ 60. On profert made, the awarding of *oyer*, when it is not of right demandable, is *not error;* but denying it to a party, legally entitled to it, is (*g*). For the ordering of *oyer* is supposed to have been of *no prejudice* to the party giving it; but the refusal of it is presumed to have been *injurious* to him who demanded it; as he is supposed to have been unable to plead, advantageously, without it.

§ 61. But in order to take advantage of the error, in the latter case, the party praying *oyer*, must either enter his prayer *upon the record*, to the intent that the error may be there apparent; or file a *bill of exceptions*, by which the same end may be attained (*h*). The former, however, appears to be the more usual course.

§ 62. And when a prayer of *oyer* is entered upon the record, it is in nature of a *plea;* to which the opposite party may *counterplead or demur*, as the case may appear to require; and on which the court will give judgment, awarding or refusing *oyer*, as upon an interlocutory plea (*i*).

(*f*) 4 T. R. 370. 1 Saund. 9. b. (n. 1.) 316. 317. Carth. 301. Com. Dig. *Pleader*, P. 1. Stra. 227. 1241. Lawes' Pl. 100. 101. 1 Wils. 97. 1 Chit. Pl. 418. 2 Ib. 461. n. (m). (n).

(*g*) 2 Salk. 498. 2 Lill. Ab. 338. 1 Saund. 9. b. (n. 1). 1 Chitt. Pl. 417. Lawes' Pl. 99. 2 Mass. R. 494.

(*h*) Bac. Abr. *Bill of Exceptions*. 2 Inst. 427.

(*i*) 2 Salk. 498. 1 Saund. 9. b. (n. 1.) Lawes' Pl. 99. 2 Ld Ray. 969.

CHAP. VIII. PART II.

Omission of profert, when necessary, effect of.

§ 63. If *profert* of an instrument, when required by the rules of pleading, be omitted; the omission, according to the preponderance of authority, is, by the common law, matter of *substance*, and fatal on *general* demurrer (*k*): Inasmuch as it deprives the adverse party of the benefit of *oyer*, without which he is supposed to be unable to plead advantageously. But by the statute 16 and 17 Car. 2, c. 8, the omission is cured by *verdict;* and by that of 4 & 5 Ann. c. 16, it is aided, except on *special* demurrer (*l*).

§ 64. In the state of Connecticut, it has long been an established rule, that a *profert*, in pleading, is in no case necessary, even in point of form: But that, whenever a party is, by the rules of the common law, entitled to *oyer*, on *profert* made, he is, in that state, entitled to it, *without profert* (*m*). The general *practice* of the profession in the state, however, is to make *profert* of instruments pleaded, whenever the rules of the English common law require it.

(*k*). Com. Dig. *Pleader*, O. 17. 10 Co. 94. Cro. Jac. 292. 409. 412. Hob. 83. Cro. Eliz. 551. 3 Bulstr. 223 — *Dub.* 1 Leon. 300. 310. *Cont.* 2 Salk. 497.

(*l*) Com. Dig. *Pleader*, E. 29. O. 17. Bac. Abr. *Pleas*, &c, I. 12. (1.)

(*m*) 1 Root, 566.

Part III.—*Of Departure.*

§ 65. *Departure* in pleading is the dereliction of an antecedent ground of complaint, or defence, for another, *distinct from*, and *not fortifying*, the former (*n*).

§ 66. This is a fault in all pleading. For, as has been heretofore explained, (ch. 2, §§ 27, 28, 29,) each succeeding stage of the pleadings, on each side, must fortify, or go in support of, what has been previously pleaded on the same side (*o*). Thus, the replication must support the *declaration;* the rejoinder, the *plea in bar*, &c. For otherwise, the parties might, at pleasure, *change* one cause of action, or one ground of defence, for another, entirely foreign to the first. Thus, if to debt or assumpsit, the defendant pleads *infancy*, and to a replication of *necessaries* rejoins *duress*, *payment*, *release*, *usury*, &c; the rejoinder is a *departure*, and a good cause of demurrer — though either of the matters alleged in it, would have been a good bar, if *first* pleaded as such.

§ 67. In assumpsit, brought by an executor, on an alleged promise to his *testator*, if the defendant pleads the statute of *limitations;* a replication al-

(*n*) 3 Black. Com. 310. Co. Litt. 303. b. 304. a. Finch's Law, 50. 391. Lawes' Pl. 162. Bull. N. P. 17.

(*o*) Iid. 2 H. Black. 280. 1 Stra. 422. Reg. Pl. 112.

leging a promise, within six years, *to the plaintiff himself*, is a departure (*p*): The promise *replied*, not going in support of that *counted upon*. To justify a recovery, on the second promise, it should have been *declared on*.

§ 68. If the defendant pleads in bar a *feoffment in fee-simple*, and in his rejoinder varies his title, or the mode of acquiring it — as by alleging a conveyance by *lease and release*, or a gift *in tail;* the rejoinder is a departure (*q*) : Since it substitutes a *new* ground of defence, for that first pleaded.

§ 69. Thus also, when the matter, first alleged as the ground of action or defence, is pleaded as at *common* law, any subsequent pleading by the same party, supporting it by a *particular custom*, is a *departure* (*r*). Ex. gr. If in covenant broken, against an apprentice, upon his indenture of apprenticeship, the plaintiff declares in common form, (i. e. *as at common law*), and the defendant pleads *infancy;* a replication of the *custom of London* (under which an infant may bind himself, as apprentice), is a *departure;* inasmuch as it abandons the legal foundation of the suit, as laid in the declaration, for an-

(*p*) Willes, 27. 1 Salk. 28. 3 East, 409. 3 B. & A. 631–2. 3 Har. & McHen. 152. 5 Binn. 573. 4 McCord, 93. 1 Hen. & Munf. 563. & *vid.* 1 B. & C. 248.— *Cont.* 8 Mass. R. 133. 9 Pick. 493. 3 N. Hamp. R. 467.

(*q*) Co. Litt. 304. Bac. Abr. *Pleas*, &c, L.

(*r*) Finch's Law, 392. Bac. Abr. *Pleas*, &c, L. 1 Keb. 376. 469. 512. 1 Lev. 81.

other, distinct from, and independent of it. The plaintiff should have declared upon the custom.

§ 70. Again, a declaration or plea, asserting a right at *common* law, is not fortified by the subsequent allegation of a right created by *statute*. If therefore, to an action of trespass, laid in common form, for taking the plaintiff's cattle, the defendant justifies the taking of them *damage feasant*, by distress; and the plaintiff replies, that the defendant *drove them out of the county*, (which is not actionable by the common law, though made so by the *statute* 52. H. 3, and 1 & 2 Ph. & M. c. 12); the replication is a *departure* (*s*); for the same reason, as in the last case. The plaintiff, in this case, should have *founded* his action upon the statutes.

§ 71. But if the plaintiff declares upon a statute, and the defendant pleads that it is repealed; a replication, that it has been *revived* by a subsequent act, is no departure (*t*). Here the replication fortifies the ground taken in the declaration. For the reviving act gives renewed effect to the *first*, on which the action is founded.

§ 72. If, in covenant broken, the defendant pleads performance in general terms, and the plaintiff replies non-performance of a particular act; a rejoinder, that the defendant was *ready* to perform, and *tendered performance*, and that the plaintiff *pre-*

(*s*) Bac. Abr. *Pleas*, &c, L. 3 Lev. 48. Finch's Law, 392–3.
(*t*) 1 Lev. 81. Bac. Abr. *ub. sup.*—*vid.* Yelv. 14. 15.

CHAP. VIII. PART III.

vented it, is a departure from the plea (*u*): *Performance*, and *tender and refusal*, being distinct and inconsistent grounds of defence. The matter rejoined should have been pleaded in the first instance.

Varying, in an immaterial point from a previous pleading, is no departure.

§ 73. But varying in an *immaterial* point, from what has been before alleged on the same side, is *no departure*: As a departure consists in changing the original *ground* or *foundation* of the action, or defence. Thus, in assumpsit on a parol promise, if the promise is laid *more than six years* before the commencement of the suit, and the defendant pleads the statute of *limitations*; the plaintiff may reply a promise *within* six years (*v*). For as the day, laid in the declaration, is *immaterial*; the replication, in stating a different day, cannot be considered as presenting a *new ground* of action.

§ 74. So too, when the promise is laid, as in the last case, and the *place* laid in the declaration is immaterial, a replication, (in answer to a plea of the statute of limitations) of a *different* place, in order to bring the case within the saving in favour of persons 'beyond the seas,' is, for the same reason, *no departure* (*w*).

(*u*) Co. Litt. 304. a. Bac. Abr. *Pleas*, &c, L. 1 Sid. 10. *Vid.* 14 Mass. R. 103.

(*v*) 2 Saund. 5 b. (n. 3.) 1 Ib. 299. (n. 6.) 1 Salk. 222. 223. Cro. Car. 245. 333. 1 Lev. 110. 143. 1 Stra. 21. 1 Keb. 566. 578. 10 Mod. 348. 16 East, 420. 9 Pick. 494.

(*w*) 1 Lev. 143. 10 Mod. 349.

Novel assignment is no departure.

§ 75. When the *gravamen*, or cause of action, is stated *generally* in the declaration, and the defendant pleads an evasive plea (14), a more particular statement of the cause of action, by way of *new assignment*, in the replication, is no departure (*x*). For a new assignment, when properly made, does not substitute a *new* cause of action, for that alleged in the declaration; but merely states the original one with more *particularity*, in order to repel the effect of the plea — or, (as may sometimes be necessary to the same end) assigns, as a *substantive* ground of damages, what the declaration has alleged only as *aggravation*.

§ 76. Thus if, to an action of any kind, the defendant pleads in bar a *former recovery*, for the same cause, when in fact it was for a *different cause of the same kind;* the plaintiff may, by a new assignment, state more particularly the *specific* cause of action, on which his complaint is founded, and show that it is a *different* one from that to which the plea applies (*y*).

(*x*) 3 Black. Com. 311. Bull. N. P. 17. Lawes' Pl. 164-5. 3. Wils. 20. 2 Saund. 5. a. b. (n. 3.) Willes, 218.
(*y*) Iid. 2 Chitt. Pl. 653. n. (e.) 9 Wentw. 10.

---

(14) Any plea, which makes a new assignment necessary, is called *an evasive plea* — i. e. as I understand it, a special plea, which, though *apparently* avoiding the *whole gravamen*, or ground of complaint, as laid, generally, in the declaration, does still not avoid the *particular* ground or cause, on which the plaintiff actually founds his right of recovery; as in the examples, which follow in the text. (See also ch. 6, § 110, and note 14).

CHAP. VIII. PART III.

§ 77. Thus also, if to an action against a sheriff, for an *escape*, he pleads recaption on fresh suit, before action brought, (which is a good defence for a *negligent*, though not so for a *voluntary* escape); the plaintiff may, by way of new assignment, reply a *voluntary* escape; and it will be *no departure*. It fortifies the declaration. (*z*).

§ 78. By the common law, departure is a good cause of *general* demurrer (*a*). Some, however, have supposed that under the statute 4 & 5 *Ann.* c. 16, it is aided, except on *special* demurrer (*b*). But this opinion seems clearly opposed to the authorities, last before cited; and on principle, the fault appears to be matter of *substance:* Inasmuch as it is an entire abandonment of the ground of action, or defence, first taken by the pleader, and for which he has, by law, no right to substitute any other. And see 2 Saund. 84, d. (n. 1), where Mr Serjeant *Williams retracts* the opinion, that the fault is but formal; though he had previously advanced that opinion in 1 Saund. 117, (n. 3.)

§ 79. Yet a *verdict*, in favour of him who makes a departure, cures the fault, if the matter, pleaded by way of departure, is a sufficient answer, *in sub-*

(*z*) 1 Vent. 211. 217. 2 T. R. 126. Bac. Abr. *Escape*, H.

(*a*) Com. Dig. *Pleader*, F. 10. 2 Wils. 96. 1 Ib. 122. Willes, 638. 4 T. R. 504. 2 Saund. 84. d. (n. 1.) 1 Ib. 117. 1 Salk. 221–2. T. Ray. 22. 94. 1 Stra. 422. 10 Johns. R. 262. 16 Mass. R. 1. 2 N. Hamp. R. 180. 308.

(*b*) Com. Dig. *Pleader*, F. O. 1 Saund. 117. (n. 3.) 1 Chitt. Pl. 623. n. (e.)

stance, to what is before pleaded by the adverse party; i. e. if it would have been sufficient, provided he had pleaded it, in the *first* instance (*c*). For after such a finding, it will necessarily appear, from the *whole* record taken together, that he is, in law, entitled to judgment. *Ex. gr.* The defendant, in assumpsit, pleads *infancy;* the plaintiff replies *necessaries;* and defendant rejoins a *release:* Now, if issue is taken upon the rejoinder, and a verdict found for the defendant, he must have judgment. For by the finding, it appears conclusively upon the record, that there is no right of action: Whereas, upon a *demurrer* to the rejoinder, this result could not thus appear. For the release being *ill pleaded;* a demurrer would not confess it. (*Vid. Demurrer*, ch. IX, § 4.)

(*c*) 1 Lill. Ab. 444. T. Ray. 86. 2 Saund. 84. Ib. 84. d. (n. 1.) 1 Keb. 566. 1 Lev. 110. Tidd, 689. 1 Chitt. Pl. 623.

CHAPTER IX.

OF DEMURRER.

Part I. — *Of Demurrer to the Pleadings.*

CHAP. IX. PART I.

Section 1. To *demur*, is to *rest*, or *pause;* and the party who demurs in law, to, (or upon), his adversary's pleadings, *rests*, or *pauses*, upon it, as requiring *no answer*, by reason of its supposed legal insufficiency (*d*).

§ 2. A demurrer, as has before been shown, (ch. 2, § 43), is, in strictness, *no plea* (*e*) *;* since it neither asserts nor denies any matter of *fact*, but merely advances a *legal* proposition, viz. that the pleading, demurred to, is *insufficient in law*, to maintain the case shown by the adverse party. It may be taken by either party, and to *any part* of the pleadings, until issue joined (*f*).

§ 3. A demurrer, though frequently called 'an issue' in law (*g*), may, with more propriety, be said

(*d*) Reg. Pl. 125. 3 Black. Com. 314.

(*e*) 3 Wils. 292. Bac. Abr. *Pleas*, &c, N. 1.

(*f*) Co. Litt. 72. a. Reg. Pl. 126. Bac. Abr. *Pleas*, &c, N. 1. Com. Dig. *Pleader*, Q. 6. 1 Lill. Ab. 435.

(*g*) 3 Black. Com. 314, 315. Co. Litt. 71-2.

to *tender* such an issue. For the issue is not formed, until there is a *joinder* in demurrer; which affirms the legal *sufficiency* of the allegations demurred to, in contradiction of the demurrer, which affirms their legal *insufficiency* (*h*).

CHAP. IX. PART I.

What facts it confesses.

§ 4. As the office of a demurrer is to deny, not the *truth*, but only the *legal sufficiency*, of the allegations demurred to; it therefore *admits* all such facts, alleged by the adverse party, as are *well pleaded* (*i*); and refers the question of law, arising upon them, to the court.

§ 5. But a demurrer regularly admits no other facts, than those which are *well pleaded*; and by the *common* law, which does not distinguish between the offices of a demurrer, assigning a special cause, and one assigning none, a demurrer of either kind confesses no other allegations, in general, than such as are sufficient, both in *substance* and *form* (*k*). For facts, insufficient *in substance*, cannot affect the right of the cause; and *material* facts, if *ill pleaded*, and demurred to, even generally, are, by the common law, as unavailing, as if they were altogether *immaterial*.

(*h*) 2 Chitt. Pl. 678. 682. 3 Black. Com. App. No. III, § 6, p. xxiv.

(*i*) 1 East, 636. Bac. Abr. *Pleas*, &c, N. 1. 3. Co. Litt. 71. b. 1 Saund. 338. (n. 3.) Hob. 233. Com. Dig. *Pleader*, Q. 5. 6. 1 Lill. Ab. 437-8.

(*k*) Hob. 233. Lawes' Pl. 167. 3 Salk. 122. 1 Chitt. Pl. 640. Com. Dig. *Pleader*, Q. 5. Bac. Abr. *Pleas*, &c, N. 3.

CHAP. IX. PART I.

§ 6. The rule, that a demurrer does not confess facts *ill pleaded*, means only, that it does not confess them, to the intent of *concluding* the party demurring, by way of *estoppel*, in any other suit, or of affecting the *determination* of the principal case.

§ 7. The pleading of a party may be ill, either in not alleging sufficient *matter*, or in alleging what is sufficient, in an informal or improper *manner* (*l*). And in neither case, is the matter, which is pleaded, confessed, according to the rule of the *common* law, even by a general demurrer. For by the common law, advantage might, in general, be taken of defects in *form*, by a demurrer of the same kind, as would reach defects in *substance* (*m*): Though now, in consequence of statute-enactments, there exists an important difference, as regards the manner of demurring, between *formal* and *substantial* faults in pleading.

Kinds of.

§ 8. To explain this difference, it must be observed, that demurrers are of two kinds—*general*, and *special*: The latter being called 'special', because they assign some *special cause* of demurrer; while the former assign none (*n*). But at *common* law, the distinction, between the one and the other, consisted in the mere *form* of demurring; since the office and effect of both, as has been before sug-

(*l*) Hob. 164. Bac. Abr. *Pleas*, &c. *Introd.*

(*m*) Lawes' Pl. 167-8. Com. Dig. *Pleader*, Q. 5.

(*n*) Co. Litt. 72. a. Bac. Abr. *Pleas*, &c, N. 5. Lawes' Pl. 167. 168. 2 Bulstr. 267.

gested, were the same: Faults, in mere *form*, being reached, at common law, as well by a *general*, as by a *special* demurrer (1).

Ante, ch. 6, § 35. Different uses of general and special demurrers, under the stat. 27 Eliz. & 4 Anne.

§ 9. But by the statute 27 Eliz. c. 5, § 1, on demurrer to the pleadings, on either side, (other than *dilatory* pleas), all defects and imperfections, merely *formal*, except such as are expressly and specially '*set down*', *and assigned* for cause of demurrer, *are aided*, and may, by the court, be *amended* (o). By the operation of this statute, all merely *formal* defects in pleading, except in *dilatory* pleas, are aided, on general demurrer.

§ 10. But doubts having arisen, upon the construction of this statute, whether certain particular defects in pleading were to be deemed formal, or substantial; the statute 4 & 5 *Ann.* c. 16, was enacted, partly in explanation, and partly in extension, of the healing operation of the former act — and also expressly specifying a variety of particular

(o) Bac. Abr. *Pleas*, &c, N. 6. Lawes' Pl. 167-8-9. Com. Dig. *Pleader*, Q. 7.

---

(1) To this proposition there appears to have been a single exception, and but one, viz. in the case of a demurrer for *duplicity*; for taking advantage of which, the demurrer, it seems, must, by the *common* law, have been *special*, (3 Salk. 122. Comb. 297. Bac. Abr. *Pleas*, &c, N. 6.) The reason of this exception may, perhaps, have been the *peculiarity* of this particular fault; which consists neither in want of substance, nor in the absence of technical form, in the pleader's averments; but in the statement of *superfluous* matter — of *more* substance than is necessary.

CHAP. IX. PART I.

defects, which, though before deemed *substantial*, are, by this latter act, virtually converted into matters of *form*, and thus aided on general demurrer (*p*) (2). The statute of *Elizabeth*, then, requires demurrers to be special, for formal defects, *in general;* and that of *Anne*, after re-enacting the same *general* provision, extends, or applies it to certain *particular* defects, expressly named in the act.

§ 11. These statutes, however, relate to pleadings in *civil* actions only — being confined, in their terms, to proceedings in any '*action or suit;*' and the former contains an express *proviso*, that it shall not extend to *criminal* proceedings (*q*). Formal defects, in *indictments* and other *criminal* prosecutions, remain, therefore, proper subjects of *general* demurrer, as at common law. The statute of *Anne* also contains a *proviso*, that it shall not extend to *actions on penal statutes*, which are strictly civil suits. But this last *proviso* is repealed by the statute 4 Geo. 2, c. 26, § 4 (*r*).

(*p*) Bac. Abr. *Pleas*, &c, N. 6. 1 Lill. Ab. 439. 440. 1 Chitt. Pl. 641-3.

(*q*) Bac. Abr. *Pleas*, &c, N. 6. Com. Dig. *Pleader*, Q. 7.

(*r*) Willes, 601. Tidd, 822. 1 Chitt. Pl. 642.

(2) The defects *specifically enumerated*, and cured, by this latter statute, are *immaterial traverses* — the omission of *profert* of deeds, &c, — or of the words *vi et armis*, and *contra pacem* — or of a verification *per recordum* — or of a *prout patet per recordum*. All these defects are therefore aided by this statute, on demurrer, unless specially assigned for cause of demurrer.

§ 12. There is also, in *civil* cases, as has before been suggested, one class of pleas, to which these statutes do not extend, viz. pleas *in abatement*, or rather, *dilatory* pleas, generally (*s*). For these pleas, not being *favoured* in the law, are held not to be within the spirit of these enactments; the object of which, as expressed in the title of the statute of *Elizabeth*, is for the '*furtherance of justice*' (*t*). In *dilatory* pleas, therefore, defects in *form* are still reached by *general* demurrer. The same rule holds, and for the same reason, of demurrers to *writs of error*, for duplicity, in assigning errors in fact, and in law, together (*u*).

§ 13. As the *general* enactments, above referred to, in these two statutes, are precisely similar, even to the letter; (those in the statute of *Anne* being only a *repetition* of the first section of that of *Elizabeth*); it will be sufficient — so far as regards the different natures and offices of general and special demurrers — to explain the provisions of the statute of *Elizabeth* only: That act being the original foundation of the important distinction, which now exists in the *English* law, between the uses and effects of the two kinds of demurrer.

§ 14. It has been observed, in a former chapter (ch. 3, § 1), that to all good pleading there are two

(*s*) Ld Ray. 337. 1015. 1 Salk. 194. Tidd, 885. 3 T. R. 186. 1 Chitt. Pl. 456. 2 Ib. 679. 2 M. & S. 485. 1 Mass. R. 501-2.

(*t*) Hob. 232.

(*u*) Sty. 69. Carth. 338-9. Bac. Abr. *Error*, K. 2.

CHAP. IX. PART I.

requisites:—1. That the *matter* pleaded be sufficient; and 2. that it be alleged, according to the *forms* of law (*v*). The omission of either of these requisites is, therefore, a good cause of demurrer. But as, under the above-mentioned statute of *Elizabeth*, defects of the *latter* kind can be reached only by *special* demurrer; it becomes necessary to distinguish, correctly, between the two kinds of demurrer.

§ 15. A *general* demurrer is one, not specially assigning any particular *cause* of demurrer, but simply asserting, in general terms, the legal insufficiency of the pleading, to which it applies: A *special* demurrer is one, which assigns, and points out specially, some particular *cause, or causes*, for demurring (*w*).

§ 16. But to constitute a *special* demurrer, within the statute of *Elizabeth*, some specific cause of demurrer must not only be assigned, but must be assigned and set out *specially* (*x*). The assignment of a cause, in general terms, does not answer the requisition of the statute; which is, that the cause be '*specially and particularly* set down.' Hence, a demurrer for *duplicity*, assigning for cause, merely that the pleading demurred to, 'is *double, and informal*,' is considered as a *general* demurrer, and will

(*v*) Hob. 164. Bac. Abr. *Pleas*, &c, *Introd.* Co. Litt. 303.

(*w*) Co. Litt. 72. a. Bac. Abr. *Pleas*, &c, N. 5. Lawes' Pl. 167.

(*x*) 1 Wils. 219. Bac. Abr. *Pleas*, &c, N. 5. 1 Show. 250. Comb. 297. 2 Ld Ray. 802.

not reach the fault mentioned. The demurrer, for such a cause, should point out, *specially* and *precisely, where, and in what particular*, the duplicity consists (*y*). And the same particularity is necessary, in all demurrers for faults in mere *form*. For the object proposed, in requiring a demurrer, in any case, to be special, is, that the *precise point*, in which the fault, in the pleading demurred to, consists, be designated as cause of demurrer.

Difference between form and substance.

§ 17. The difference between matter of form, and matter of substance, in general, under the statute of *Elizabeth*, as laid down by Lord *Hobart*, is, that *that*, 'without which *the right* doth sufficiently appear to the court, is *form*;' but that any defect, 'by reason whereof the *right appears not*,' is a defect in *substance* (*z*). But this description is too general, to be easily applied in particular instances.

§ 18. A distinction, somewhat more definite, is, that if the *matter* pleaded be in itself insufficient, without reference to the *manner* of pleading it, the defect is *substantial*; but, that if the only fault is in the form of alleging it, the defect is but *formal* (*a*). Thus, the omission of a *consideration*, in a declaration in assumpsit — or of the performance of a *condition precedent*, when such a condition exists — of a *conversion*, or *property* in the plaintiff, in trover — of

(*y*) Comb. 297. 1 Salk. 219. 1 Show. 230. Com. Dig. *Pleader*, Q. 9. Hob. 232. 2 Mass. R. 283-4.

(*z*) Hob. 233.

(*a*) Doug. 683.

CHAP. IX. PART I.

science in the defendant, in an action for mischief done by his dog—of *malice*, in an action for malicious prosecution, &c, are all defects in *substance*. On the other hand, *duplicity*—a *negative pregnant*—*argumentative* pleading—a special plea, *amounting to the general issue*—omission of *day*, when the time is immaterial—of a *place*, in transitory actions, &c, are only faults in form (*b*). For the defect, in the former class of examples, is in the *matter* pleaded; while the fault in the latter, is only in the *manner* of pleading.

Use of special demurrer.

§ 19. A special demurrer reaches no *other* faults in *form*, than those which are specially assigned for cause of demurrer (*c*). For as to all others, it is, in effect, a *general* demurrer; under which, no advantage can be taken of imperfections, merely *formal*.

§ 20. But under a special demurrer, advantage may be taken, as well of all *substantial* defects, though not assigned for cause, as of those formal faults, which are so assigned (*d*); and this, for the reason last before stated, viz. that as to faults, *not* so assigned, a special demurrer operates precisely like a *general* one.

§ 21. It has already been stated, that by the common law, a demurrer confesses no other facts,

(*b*) Bac. Abr. *Pleas*, &c, N. 5. 6. Com. Dig. *Pleader*, Q. 7. 10 Co. 95. a. 2 Stra. 694.

(*c*) Bac. Abr. *Pleas*, &c, N. 5. 10 Co. 88. Com. Dig. *Pleader*, Q. 8.

(*d*) Iid. 6 Greenleaf, 426.

alleged on the other side, than such as are, in *all* respects, well pleaded—that is, such as are sufficient, both in *matter* and *form*. And under the statute 27 *Eliz.* the rule, in regard to insufficient *matter*, is the same at as common law (*e*). But under this statute, a demurrer confesses not only all *sufficient matter, well pleaded*, as it does by the common law; but also, all *material* facts, *informally* pleaded, except such as are expressly and specially assigned for cause of demurrer (*f*).

§ 22. As under this statute, defects *in form* are aided, unless specially pointed out in a demurrer; it follows, that all such defects are now aided, by the adverse party's *pleading over*, instead of demurring specially. In this way, therefore, *formal* defects in the declaration are aided, by the defendant's pleading in bar, either by way of traverse, or in avoidance; in the same manner, those in the plea are cured by a *replication;* and the same rule applies to all the subsequent pleadings (*g*). But defects in *substance* are not thus aided (*h*). (2 *a*)

(*e*) Lawes' Pl. 168. Bac. Abr. *Pleas*, &c, N. 3. Com. Dig. *Pleader*, Q. 6, 2 Salk. 561.

(*f*) Bac. Abr. *Pleas*, &c, N. 6. Com. Dig. *Pleader*, Q. 7. Lawes' Pl. 167-8. Hob. 233.

(*g*) Bac. Abr. *Pleas*, &c, *Introd.* Com. Dig. *Pleader*, E. 37. 7 Co. 25, a. 8 Ib. 120. b. Co. Litt. 303. b. 2 Salk. 519. 14 Mass, R. 162.

(*h*) Iid.

(2 *a*) That is, by the adverse party's *merely pleading over*. But if he *expressly admits*, in his pleading, the matter of sub-

§ 23. From the principles already laid down, it is obvious that a demurrer *aids* no other pleading, than it *confesses* to be true. For what is not confessed by it, clearly cannot avail the adverse party, on the issue tendered by the demurrer; since the question of law, presented by the issue, can arise only upon facts *confessed* (*i*).

§ 24. And as it confesses not what is *ill pleaded*, it of course does not confess any averment, *contradicting* what before appears certain, on the record. Thus, if a party having admitted an allegation on the other side, afterwards makes an averment *inconsistent* with it, a demurrer does not confess the latter averment (*k*).

§ 25. On a similar principle, a demurrer, though general, never confesses an allegation, which, it appears upon the face of the pleadings, that he is *estopped* to make; as if, having pleaded or confessed a *record*, to which he is a party, he afterwards makes an averment, *contradicting* or *impugning* it. Thus, if to debt or *scire facias*, on judgment, the defendant pleads any thing in denial of the *original* right of action, on which the judgment was found-

(*i*) 2 H. Black. 205. 206.
(*k*) Com. Dig. *Pleader*, Q. 5. 6. 1 Sid. 10.

---

stance omitted by the other side, such omission is supplied and cured. (*Ante*, c. 3, § 192—and Com. R. 140. 10 Wheat. 287.)

ed (*l*) — or if, after a judgment *quod computet*, in an action of account, he pleads any matter, showing that he *ought not* to account (*m*); a demurrer does not confess the plea: Because the latter impugns the judgment. And the plea, in this case, is ill in *substance*. For it is not the *form* of the averment, but the making of it, in *any* form, that constitutes the fault. In such cases, however, the party, in whose favour the matter of the estoppel operates, may, instead of demurring, *reply* the matter specially, and in this way avail himself of it (*n*).

§ 26. Nor does a demurrer, of either kind, confess facts, however material, the pleading of which makes a *departure* (*o*).

§ 27. An averment of any thing, naturally or legally *impossible*, is not confessed by a demurrer (*p*). The averment being, upon the face of it, an absurdity.

§ 28. So also, allegations which are *impertinent*, or *immaterial*, are not confessed, by a demurrer (*q*). For what a party *cannot* contest, he does not confess, by leaving it unanswered.

(*l*) 1 Saund. 219. c. (n. 8.) Willes, 13. Lawes' Pl. 170. 3 T. R. 693. 1 Salk. 310. 6 Mod. 308.

(*m*) 3 Wils. 73. 101. 113. 114. Hetl. 114. Cro. Car. 116.

(*n*) Willes, 13. Lawes' Pl. 171.

(*o*) Com. Dig. *Pleader*, F. 10. 2 Wils. 96. 1 Ib. 122. Willes, 638. 2 Saund. 84. d. (n. 1.) T. Ray. 22. 94. — *Ante*, ch. 8, § 79.

(*p*) 1 Sid. 10. Com. Dig. *Pleader*, Q. 6. Lawes' Pl. 168.

(*q*) 2 Salk. 561. Lawes' Pl. 168. Bac. Abr. *Pleas*, &c, N. 3.

§ 29. Nor does a demurrer ever confess matter of *law* deduced, by either party, from the facts pleaded by him — as the *prout ei bene licuit*, in a plea of justification. For such matter is not a proper subject of a substantive averment, or of traverse, or avoidance, (*vid.* ch. 7, § 48); and consequently, not a subject of *admission* in the pleadings: It being exclusively the province of the *court*, to apply the law to the facts alleged (*r*).

§ 30. When an issue in *fact*, and an issue in *law*, are joined in the same cause, (as they may be, to *different parts* of the declaration, plea, &c), it is in the discretion of the court, which of the two issues shall be first determined (*s*). In practice, however, the more usual course is, to determine first the issue in law: Inasmuch as the jury can then, on the issue in fact, assess, at once, the whole damages on *both* issues, if both are determined in the plaintiff's favour — which could not be done, if the issue in fact were first determined.

§ 31. After an issue in fact joined, as by a conclusion to the country, on one side, and the *similiter* added, on the other, there can be no demurrer (*t*). For the issue joined puts an end to the altercations of the parties, on the record; and by joining in it,

(*r*) Hob. 56. *Vid.* Com. Dig. *Pleader*, Q. 5. 6.

(*s*) Co. Litt. 72. a. 125. b. Palm. 517. Bac. Abr. *Pleas*, &c, N. 1. 1 Saund. 80. (n. 1.)

(*t*) Com. Dig. *Pleader*, Q. 6. 1 Show. 213. Bac. Abr. *Pleas*, &c, N. 2.

the parties have placed the controversy upon a question of *fact* involved in the issue, and referred it to the jury.

Demurrer to a demurrer, not allowed.

§ 32. There cannot be a demurrer, on either side, *to* a demurrer, on the other (*u*); but the party, to whose pleading a demurrer is taken, must join in it. And though a demurrer be *informally* taken; (as by praying an *improper* judgment); the adverse party must still join in it. For being sufficient to present the *whole record* to the court, for its judgment; the court must render such a judgment upon it, as the state of the pleadings requires, without reference to the *manner*, in which judgment is prayed, or the *form*, in which the demurrer is expressed (*v*).

§ 33. If then, the party, to whom a demurrer is tendered, demurs *to* it, or refuses to join in it; he makes, in either case, a *discontinuance* of his action, or his defence, as the case may be (*w*): That is, if the plaintiff thus demurs, he discontinues his *action*: If the defendant does so, he discontinues his *defence*. For a refusal or omission, on one side, to join in a demurrer on the other, has the same effect as an omission to *plead*, when pleading is necessary. The omission, by either party, is therefore a virtual *abandonment* of his side of the case.

(*u*) Com. Dig. *Pleader*, Q. 3. Bac. Abr. *Pleas*, &c, N. 2. Lawes' Pl. 172. Comb. 306. 1 Ld Ray. 20. 1 Salk. 219.

(*v*) 3 Lev. 222.

(*w*) 1 Salk. 219. Bac. Abr. *Pleas*, &c, N. 2. Comb. 306. Com. Dig. *Pleader*, Q. 3.

CHAP. IX. PART I.

§ 34. But according to a *dictum* of Ld *Holt* (*x*), there is a single exception to the rule, that there cannot be a demurrer *to* a demurrer: viz. that where a demurrer to a plea in *abatement* is *not apposite*, the demurrer may itself be demurred to. But the reason of such an exception is certainly not obvious; and Ld *Holt's* opinion appears not to be recognized as law by the later authorities.

§ 35. A demurrer, and joinder in demurrer, both usually add a *verification*, before praying judgment (*y*): But a verification appears to be unnecessary (*z*); as no *proof* is assumed, by either of the parties.

A demurrer looks through the whole record.

§ 36. A demurrer, in whatever stage of the pleadings it is taken, reaches back, in its effect, through the *whole* record, and, in general, attaches ultimately upon the *first substantial* defect in the pleadings, on which ever side it may have occurred — defects *in substance* not being aided by the adverse party's mere pleading over, as formal defects are (*a*).

§ 37. Hence, though the parties join in demurrer, upon any one particular point, in any stage of

(*x*) Comb. 306.

(*y*) 2 Chitt. Pl. 679. 682.

(*z*) 1 Leon. 24. Lawes' Pl. 172.

(*a*) Hob. 56. & (n. 4) by Williams. 5 Co. 29. a. Com. Dig. *Pleader*, Q. 7. M. 1. 2. 2 Salk. 519. 1 Saund. 285. (n. 5). 1 Stra. 303. 2 Wils. 150. Bac. Abr. *Pleas*, &c, N. 3. 4 East, 502. *Vid.* ante, note to § 22.

the pleadings; judgment must, nevertheless, be given, upon *the whole* record, and regularly, against that party, in whose pleading the *first substantial* fault has occurred (*b*). Thus if the declaration is ill, in substance — the plea in bar frivolous — and demurrer joined, on the *plea;* judgment must be for the *defendant.* For though the issue in law is joined, immediately and in terms, on the *plea only*, and though that is worthless; yet a bad plea is sufficient for a *bad declaration.*

§ 38. Upon the same principle, if the declaration is good — the plea and replication *both ill in substance* — and demurrer joined on the replication; judgment must, regularly, be for the plaintiff (*c*). For the first substantial fault is on the *defendant's* part; and a bad replication is sufficient for a *bad plea.*

§ 39. But in the case last supposed, there is one exception to the general rule: viz. when the replication to an insufficient plea is not only *defective* in matter, but also shows that the plaintiff has *no cause of action.* In such a case, judgment, on demurrer to the *replication*, must be for the *defendant* — though his plea is radically insufficient (*d*). For, in every such case, it will necessarily appear, from *the whole record*, that the plaintiff is not entitled to judgment.

(*b*) Iid.
(*c*) Iid. Doug. 94—97.
(*d*) 8 Co. 120. b.

§ 40. Thus, when to a general declaration, on a penal bond, (as a bond, conditioned for the performance of covenants, &c), the defendant pleads an *insufficient* bar, and the replication assigns as a breach, what is in law *no* breach; judgment, on demurrer to the replication, must be for the *defendant;* though his plea is ill in substance (*e*). For, as in this, and all similar cases, the declaration counts only on the penal part of the bond; the real ground of the action does not appear, until a breach of the condition is assigned in the *replication;* which is, in effect, a *supplement to the declaration* — or *a specification* of the more general complaint presented in it. *In effect*, therefore, the first substantial fault in the pleadings is on the part of the plaintiff: For though, in the order of *pleading*, the plea precedes the replication; yet, in the order of *title*, the replication, in this class of cases, *precedes the plea.*

Judgment, on demurrer.

§ 41. The *judgment*, rendered upon a demurrer, regularly follows the *nature of the pleading* demurred to. Thus, as we have before seen, the judgment on demurrer to a plea in *abatement*, if for the defendant, is that the writ be *quashed* — and if for the plaintiff, that the defendant *answer over* (ch. 5, §§ 158. 159). And thus the form of the judgment corresponds to that of the *prayer* of judgment in the demurrer.

§ 42. In like manner, when a demurrer is joined on any of the pleadings *in chief* — as on the declara-

(*e*) Cro. Jac. 133. 220. 221. 3 Co. 52. 8 Ib. 120. b. 2 Bulstr 94. Palm. 287. 1 Brownl. 105. Yelv. 152. 2 Ld.Ray. 1080.

tion, plea in bar, or other pleading, which goes *to the action*, the judgment is *final*—i. e. if for the plaintiff, it is, *quod recuperet;* if for the defendant, it is, *quod eat sine die* (*f*): So that, on demurrer to any of the pleadings, which go to *the action*, the judgment, for either party, is the same as it would have been, on an issue *in fact*, joined upon the same pleading, and found in favour of the same party. If the defendant demurs to the *declaration*, but concludes in *abatement*, (as by praying judgment, that the *writ be quashed*); the plaintiff may join in the demurrer, as *in bar*, by praying judgment, that his debt, or damages, be adjudged to him; and if his declaration be good, he shall have judgment, *quod recuperet*. For by the demurrer, the declaration is *confessed* (*g*); and the defendant's having prayed judgment, as in *abatement*, cannot alter or impair the effect of that confession.

CHAP. IX. PART I.

§ 43. A judgment, rendered upon demurrer, is equally conclusive, (by way of *estoppel*), of the facts, confessed by the demurrer, as a verdict, finding the same facts, would have been (*h*): Since they are established, as well in the former case, as in the latter, by matter *of record*. And facts, thus established, can never afterwards be contested, between the same parties, or those in privity with them.

Conclusive, by way of estoppel.

(*f*) Bac. Abr. *Pleas*, &c, N. 4. 10 Co. 58.

(*g*) 3 Lev. 223. Com. Dig. *Pleader*, Q. 3. Lawes' Pl. 172.

(*h*) 6 Co. 7. Cro. Eliz. 668. 2 Black. R. 827. Peake Ev. 36. (2d ed). 1 Mod. 207. Bac. Abr. *Pleas*, &c, I. 13. 1 Freem. 198-9.

CHAP. IX. PART I.

§ 44. If therefore, on demurrer to the declaration, to the plea in bar, or to other pleading *in chief*, judgment is rendered for *the defendant;* the plaintiff can never afterwards maintain, against the same defendant or his privies, any *similar* or *concurrent* action, for the same cause; i. e. upon the *same grounds*, as were disclosed in the first declaration (*i*). For the judgment, upon such a demurrer, determines *the merits* of the cause; and a final judgment, deciding *the right* in controversy, must put an end to the dispute — or litigation would be endless.

§ 45. But if the plaintiff, on demurrer, fails in his first action, from the omission of an *essential allegation* in his declaration, which allegation is supplied in the second; the judgment in the first is no bar to the second; although both actions were brought to enforce the same right (*k*). For in this case, the *merits* of the cause, as disclosed in the second declaration, were not decided in the first.

§ 46. Upon the same principle, if the declaration is adjudged ill, on demurrer, because the action is *misconceived*, (as if *debt* or *assumpsit* is brought, where *account* is the only remedy; or if *trespass* is brought, where the only proper action is *trover*, or *detinue*); the judgment is no bar to a *proper* action, afterwards brought for the same cause (*l*).

(*i*) Iid.

(*k*) 1 Mod. 207. 1 Chitt. Pl. 195. Bac. Abr. *Pleas*, &c, I. 13.

(*l*) Cro. Eliz. 668. 2 Vent. 169. 170. T. Ray. 472. Polexf. 634. 2 Brownl. 83. 2 Black. Rep. 779. 827. 831. Cro. Car. 35. 1 Chitt. Pl. 195.

For in this case, as in the last, the *merits* of the cause could not be determined in the first action.

PART II. — *Of Demurrer to Evidence.*

§ 47. In some cases, when the pleadings terminate in an issue *in fact*, joined to the jury, the party (whether plaintiff or defendant), who takes the negative side of the issue, may withdraw the examination of the cause from the jury, to the court, by demurring to, (or upon), *the evidence*, exhibited by the adverse party, in support of the affirmative of the issue (*m*). By this proceeding, the issue *in fact*, closed to the jury, is exchanged for an issue *in law*; and on the determination of this latter issue, either way, judgment follows, as it would have done, on a *verdict* found for the same party, on the issue in fact.

§ 48. A demurrer of this kind, though called a demurrer *to evidence*, is essentially, as will appear in the sequel, a demurrer to *the facts shown in evidence*; and in this respect, it differs from the demurrer, already treated of, which is taken to the facts shown in the pleadings.

§ 49. The object of a demurrer to evidence is, to bring in question, on the record, the *relevancy* of

(*m*) Co. Litt. 72. 5 Co. 104. a. Cro. Eliz. 752. Aleyn, 18. T. Ray. 404. Bac. Abr. *Pleas*, &c, N. 7. Bull. N. P. 313. Reg. Pl. 129.

the evidence on one side, to the whole issue; and to make the question of its *relevancy* the sole point, on which the issue in fact is to be determined. For upon this demurrer, the issue *in fact* is determined, by the determination of the issue *in law:* So that a decision on the *demurrer*, in favour of either party, is, in effect, a finding of the issue *in fact* in favour of the same party.

The relevancy of evidence is matter of law; its credibility, of fact.

§ 50. It must here be premised, that the *relevancy* of evidence to any given issue (i. e. its *conduciveness* or *tendency* to prove or disprove the issue), is matter of *law*, to be determined by *the court:* But its relevancy being established — its *weight*, or the question *how far* it conduces to prove the issue, or fact in dispute, is matter of fact, to be determined by *the jury* (n): In other words — whether that, which is offered as evidence to any given point, *is* evidence to the point, is a question of *law;* whether, being evidence, it is, or is not, *sufficient to prove* the point, is a question of *fact.*

§ 51. Evidence is always *relevant* to any issue, which it conduces, *in any degree*, to prove. And as its *relevancy* is the only point, of which the court can judge, on the demurrer; it follows, that it can never be safe for a party to demur to evidence, which is clearly relevant to the *whole* issue (o), i. e. which clearly conduces, *in any degree*, to prove the whole affirmative side of the issue. But where the whole

(n) Doug. 375. 2 H. Black. 205.
(o) 2 H. Black. 205.

evidence, exhibited in support of the affirmative of the issue, is relevant to a *part* only of the issue, it may be safely demurred to ; because, in such a case, the evidence *could not* warrant a finding of the issue by the jury, in favour of the party exhibiting the evidence.

The demurrer must be to the whole evidence of the adverse party.

§ 52. As the question, raised by this demurrer, is, whether the evidence demurred to is sufficient in *law* to maintain the affirmative of the issue in *fact ;* it is manifest, that the demurrer should be taken to the *whole* evidence, exhibited by the adverse party (*p*) : Since the *whole* of it may be sufficient to maintain the issue, when a *part* of it would not be so. And as that party would have had the benefit of *all* the evidence, exhibited on his part, before the *jury*, from whom the issue is withdrawn by the demurrer ; he is clearly entitled to the opinion of the court, upon the *relevancy* of the whole of it, on the demurrer. If therefore any particular *part* of the evidence, offered in support of the issue, is objected to, as irrelevant, but admitted by the judge ; the party objecting cannot demur to that part *alone* (*q*) ; but should file his bill of exceptions, or move for a new trial.

§ 53. It appears manifest, from the nature and office of a demurrer of this kind, that it can be taken only to the evidence of that party, who takes *the burden of proof*, on the issue ; and this is, regu-

(*p*) 1 Salk. 284. Bull. N. P. 314.
(*q*) Iid.

CHAP. IX. PART II.

larly, the party who takes the *affirmative* of the issue. For it is not incumbent on the other party to *prove* his side of the question; since, as a general rule, the finding must, of course, be in his favour, unless the affirmative is proved against him.

§ 54. A demurrer to evidence, when accepted by the adverse party, or allowed by the court, puts an end to the trial of the question of *fact*, by the jury; and refers to the court the application of the *law* to the facts shown in evidence. The demurrer, therefore, when properly tendered, *admits* the facts thus shown; but denies their *sufficiency, in law*, to maintain the issue in favour of the adverse party (*r*).

§ 55. In the nature of the thing, therefore, *the fact*, or *facts*, which the evidence exhibited affirms, must be ascertained, before the question of law, intended to be raised by the demurrer, can arise (*s*). For, confessing simply the existence of *the evidence* offered, is not confessing the *fact*, intended to be proved by it; nor is a confession of *the truth* of the evidence, in all cases, and necessarily, a confession of the *fact* intended to be proved by it.

§ 56. And from this last consideration arises the necessity of requiring the party, demurring to evidence, to make, upon the record, certain *admissions*,

(*r*) Co. Litt. 72. 4 Co. 104. a. Bac. Abr. *Pleas*, &c, N. 7. 2 H. Black. 205–6.

(*s*) 2 H. Black. 205–6.

which will be hereafter stated and explained, and without which the opposite party cannot be required to join in demurrer; nor, if he does join, can the court pronounce any judgment upon it.

§ 57. Doubts, which no longer exist, were formerly entertained, as to *the kind* of evidence, which might properly be demurred to; but it is now well settled, that evidence of *any* kind, written or parol, direct or circumstantial, is a subject of demurrer: Though the manner of framing the demurrer, and of making the necessary admissions upon the record, is regulated by the nature of the evidence demurred to (*t*).

§ 58. When all the evidence, exhibited in support of the affirmative of the issue, *is written*, (as where, on the general issue, the plaintiff exhibits *a bond*, as evidence of the debt for which he sues, or a *deed of conveyance, or record*, as evidence of his title to land demanded), all the authorities, ancient and modern, agree that the defendant may demur to the evidence (*u*): There being, in such a case, no danger of a *variance*, in the statement of it. But how far *unwritten* evidence is liable to be demurred to, is a point not fully settled, in the older books (*v*).

(*t*) 2 H. Black. 206-9.

(*u*) 5 Co. 104. a. Cro. Eliz. 752. Com. Dig. *Pleader*, Q. 10. Co. Litt. 72. a. 3 Black. Com. 372. Bac. Abr. *Pleas*, &c, N. 7. Bull. N. P. 313.

(*v*) Co. Litt. 72. a. 5 Co. 104. a. 1 Lev. 87. 2 H. Black. 206 Bac. Abr. *Pleas*, &c, N. 7.

CHAP. IX. PART II.

§ 59. According to an opinion, formerly held by some, a party, exhibiting *parol* evidence in support of an issue, is never bound to join in a demurrer to it; because it is *uncertain* (*w*) — that is, because no *tenor* can be predicated of it; and therefore, there is danger of a *variance*, in stating it upon the record.

What admissions the party, demurring, must make, on the record.

§ 60. But there seems, now, to be no doubt that evidence of *any kind*, exhibited in support of an issue, may be demurred to, under the restrictions, or conditions, prescribed in the five following rules: So that if these conditions are complied with, by the party demurring; the opposite party must join in the demurrer, or *wave* the evidence.

§ 61. 1. Though all the evidence, exhibited in support of the issue, rests in *parol*; yet, if both parties *voluntarily join* in a demurrer to it, and if it is properly framed, and the necessary *admissions*, hereafter to be stated, are entered upon the record; the court must give judgment upon it (*x*).

§ 62. 2. When in support of the issue, a party exhibits evidence, written or parol, for the purpose of proving any *definite fact*, the opposite party may, by expressly admitting *the fact itself*, upon the record, demur, and oblige the party, exhibiting the evidence, to join in the demurrer, *or to wave* the

(*w*) Cro. Eliz. 752. Com. Dig. *Pleader*, Q. 10. Bac. Abr. *Pleas*, &c, N. 7.

(*x*) Cro. Eliz. 752. 2 H. Black. 206. Bac. Abr. *Pleas*, &c, N. 7.

evidence (*y*). For the fact being thus admitted; the question of law is distinctly presented to the court, upon the face of the record. Thus if, in *trover* against a bailee, or finder of goods, the only evidence exhibited, of a conversion, is such as goes to prove *mere negligence*, on the part of the defendant, in keeping the goods; the defendant, by admitting, upon the record, *the fact* of negligence in the keeping, may demur, and oblige the plaintiff to join, or wave the evidence. And the defendant, in this case, would be entirely safe in making this confession; because mere *negligence* never constitutes a conversion, in trover.

§ 63. 3. When *parol* evidence, exhibited in support of the issue, is *certain and direct*, the adverse party, by entering the evidence upon the record, together with an admission that it is *true*, may demur to it, and oblige the party exhibiting it, to join in the demurrer, or wave the evidence (*z*). For in this case, an admission of the truth of the *evidence*, (which by the supposition is *certain*, and *direct*), is an admission of the *fact* affirmed by it (3).

(*y*) Sty. 22. 34. Aleyn, 18. 2 H. Black. 207–8.

(*z*) Aleyn, 18. 2 H. Black. 207–8. Com. Dig. *Pleader*, Q. 10. 5 Co. 104. a. Co. Litt. 72. a. Bac. Abr. *Pleas*, &c, N. 7. Bull. N. P. 313.

---

(3) To understand this, and the two following rules, in the text, it is necessary to distinguish correctly between the several *kinds or qualities* of evidence, of which they are predicated. As I understand these distinctions, evidence is 'CERTAIN', and 'DI-

CHAP. IX. PART II.

§ 64. 4. If the evidence exhibited is 'LOOSE AND INDETERMINATE'; the adverse party cannot demur to it, without stating it upon the record, as *certain and determinate*, and admitting it, in *that* form, to *be true* (*a*). Thus, if a witness testifies, in support of the issue, that a fact is thus, *according to his present impression, recollection* or *belief;* the adverse party, to entitle himself to demur to it, must state the evidence upon the record, as 'certain', i. e. as affirming *absolutely*, that the fact is thus, and must admit the evidence, as thus stated, to be *true*. For in this case, confessing the testimony, *in the words* of the witness, to be true, would not amount to a confession of *the fact* testified about; but merely to an admission of the witness's *belief* of the fact: An admission, which, if allowed as sufficient,

(*a*) 2 H. Black. 207. 208. Aleyn, 18. Bac. Abr. *Pleas*, &c, N. 7. Bull. N. P. 313.

RECT', within the meaning of the rule, when it *explicitly, absolutely, and without qualification*, affirms the particular fact, intended to be proved by it: As, when a witness positively asserts a fact to be thus, or thus, without reservation. According to this explanation, evidence, which the rule terms 'certain', is contradistinguished from such, as is called '*loose, and indeterminate*'; by which appears to be meant evidence, affirming a fact, *doubtfully*, or with some *reservation:* As when a witness declares a fact to be thus, or thus, '*according to his best recollection, or belief*'. — 'CIRCUMSTANTIAL' evidence is that, which, by affirming some *collateral* matter of fact, conduces thereby to prove *another* (the principal) fact, *consequentially*, as an *inference*, or *conclusion* from the former. And in this sense '*circumstantial*' is distinguished from '*direct*', evidence; which is such, as in *express and direct* terms affirms the *principal* fact, or matter immediately in issue.

would refer *the weight* of the testimony to *the court.* And as the jury, from whom the demurrer withdraws the trial, *might*, from the testimony above supposed, have found *the fact* testified about; the party, exhibiting the testimony, is entitled to the full effect of such a finding. It follows, therefore, that unless the party, demurring to such evidence, makes the admission, required by this rule, the opposite party is not bound to join in the demurrer.

§ 65. 5. When the evidence, to which a demurrer is offered, is 'CIRCUMSTANTIAL', the party demurring must distinctly admit, upon the record, *every fact*, and *every conclusion*, in favour of the opposite party, which the evidence *conduces to prove* — in other words, every fact, which the jury *might* have inferred from it, in his favour (*b*): Otherwise, he is not bound to join in the demurrer; because, without such admission, *the weight*, as well as the *relevancy* of the evidence, would be referred to *the court.* For in this, as in the former case, merely confessing the evidence to be *true*, is not a confession of any *fact*, on which the proper question of law can arise: Since the truth of all circumstantial evidence, however strong it may be, is always consistent with the possible *non-existence* of the fact, which it conduces to prove. If however, the party demurring makes the admission, required by the rule; the other party must join in demurrer, or *wave* the evidence. But without such admission, the latter is not bound to join; and if he does, the

(*b*) Aleyn, 18. 2 H. Black. 187. 209. 3 Peters, 40.

CHAP. IX. PART II. court can pronounce no judgment upon the demurrer (*c*).

§ 66. This rule may be illustrated, by the following case: In an action by the holder, against the acceptors, of a bill of exchange, payable to a *fictitious payee, or order*, and which, after the acceptance, had been indorsed by the drawers, in the name of the *fictitious payee*, for valuable consideration, to the plaintiff — the latter exhibited evidence of a long course of dealing, in similar bills, between the drawers and acceptors — for the purpose of raising a *presumption*, from these circumstantial facts, that the defendants, at the time of accepting the bill, KNEW the payee to be *fictitious;* and of then urging as matter of law, that if this presumption was established, the defendants were bound by their acceptance. To this evidence the defendant demurred, without admitting, upon the record, their *knowledge*, at the time of accepting the bill, that the payee was fictitious; and the plaintiff joined in demurrer. But it was resolved, in the House of Lords, by the unanimous opinion of the Judges, that, because the defendant's *knowledge* of the payee's being a fictitious person, (which was the great point of fact in issue), was not *expressly admitted*, on the record; the point of law, intended to be raised by the demurrer, could not arise upon the record; and consequently, that *no* judgment could be given upon the demurrer (*d*).

(*c*) Sty. 34. 2 H. Black. 209.
(*d*) 2 H. Black. 187 to 209.

§ 67. Before this determination in the House of Lords, it had been resolved in B. R. (*e*), that on a demurrer to *circumstantial* evidence, 'every fact, which the jury could infer' from it, in favour of the party offering it, 'was to be *considered as admitted*,' without any *express* admission upon the record. But, to avoid any doubt that might arise, as to the extent of any such *implied* admission, the rule, as now definitively settled by the highest authority, is, as stated above, viz. that every such fact must be *expressly* admitted, upon the record.

If the necessary admissions are not made, no judgment can be given.

§ 68. From the principles already stated, it is apparent, that if the party, demurring to evidence of any kind, does not make, upon the record, the admissions required in the particular case, by the preceding rules; and the opposite party nevertheless joins in the demurrer; the court can give *no* judgment on the demurrer; but must award a *venire de novo* — that the issue in fact may be referred to another jury (*f*).

§ 69. As the only point in issue, on a demurrer to evidence, is, whether the evidence is sufficient, in law, to maintain *the issue in fact;* no exception can, on such a demurrer, be taken to any defect in *the pleadings;* as the demurrer does not extend to them (*g*).

(*e*) Doug. 119-134.

(*f*) Bull. N. P. 313. 2 H. Black. 209. Bac. Abr. *Pleas*, &c, N. 7.

(*g*) Bull. N. P. 313. Doug. 218-223.

§ 70. But after the demurrer is determined, advantage may be taken of such defects, on motion *in arrest of judgment*, as after verdict (*h*). The motion must, however, operate, I conceive, not as such a motion, made after a *general* verdict: For as the issue has not been found by the jury, no fact, not alleged, and not appearing in the evidence, as recited on the record, can be *presumed*, in favour of the party prevailing on the demurrer. The effect of such a motion, therefore, after a demurrer to evidence determined, must be the same, it would seem, as after a *special verdict;* from which nothing can be presumed, and by which no defect in the pleadings is aided, except such as would have been aided on *general demurrer*.

§ 71. The party, to whose evidence a demurrer is offered, may always demand the judgment of the court, whether he is bound to join in the demurrer. And if there is no *colourable* cause of demurrer, the court will not allow it — lest justice should be delayed, by frivolous exceptions (*i*). An offer to demur to evidence is, therefore, not *stricti juris*.

§ 72. The whole proceeding, in demurring to evidence — as the *statement* of the evidence, on the record, and the entering of the necessary *admissions*, required by the foregoing rules — is under the direction and control of *the judge*, at *Nisi Prius*, or

(*h*) Iid. 11 Wheat. 173.

(*i*) Aleyn, 18. Sty. 34. Bull. N. P. 313. 2 Rol. Rep. 119. 2 H. Black. 205. 208.

(if the trial be at bar), of the *court in bank;* and if no plausible cause of demurrer appears; it is the duty of the judge, or court, to disallow it (*k*).

§ 73. On a demurrer to evidence, properly framed, and joinder in demurrer, the usual course is, immediately to discharge the jury of the issue in fact; and if the plaintiff prevails, on the demurrer, the writ of inquiry of damages is executed afterwards. The jury may, however, before they are thus discharged, be required to assess the damages *provisionally* (*l*) ; And if the demurrer is determined in the *plaintiff's* favour ; he will have judgment for the damages, thus previously assessed.

§ 74. If a party, offering to demur to evidence, is wrongly overruled by the court; his remedy is by a *bill of exceptions*, and a writ of error, founded upon it (*m*). (4)

(*k*) 2 Rol. Rep. 119. 2 H. Black. 208–9.

(*l*) 1 Lill. Ab. 441. Bull. N. P. 314. Cro. Car. 143. 1 Ld Ray. 60. Plowd. 410. 2 H. Black. 200. 201.

(*m*) 9 Co. 13. b. Bac. Abr. *Bill of Exceptions.* Ib. *Pleas*, &c, N. 7. Cro. Car. 342.

---

(4) For the *form* of a demurrer to evidence, see Bull. N. P. 314. 2 H. Black. 198-200.

CHAPTER X.

OF ARREST OF JUDGMENT AND REPLEADER.

SECTION 1. To *arrest* judgment, is to *stay* or *prevent* it. This is done, on motion, entered upon the record (*a*).

§ 2. This proceeding most usually takes place, after an issue in fact tried, and *verdict* found; but the motion may also be made, after a *default*, or after a demurrer to evidence determined (*b*).

§ 3. The *principle* of this proceeding is, that as the judgment of the court, which is a conclusion of law from the facts ascertained upon the record, must be collected from the *whole* record (ch. 9, § 36); the party who does *not*, upon the whole record, appear entitled to judgment, cannot have it — even though a *verdict* has been found or a default suffered, or a *demurrer to evidence* determined, in his favour.

(*a*) 3 Black. Com. 387. 393. Ib. App. No. II, p. xi. Bac. Abr. *Pleas*, &c, M.

(*b*) 2 Burr. 900. Doug. 218. 223. 2 Stra. 1271. 9 Pick. 546. *Ante*, ch. 9, § 70.

For notwithstanding such verdict, default, &c, the whole record may disclose no right of action, or no legal defence, in his favour (*c*). And therefore, if a verdict is found for the plaintiff, upon a declaration *radically defective* — or for the defendant, on a plea in bar *totally void* of substance; judgment must, regularly, in either case, be arrested.

§ 4. The question, raised by a motion in arrest of judgment, is a question of *law*, arising from the face of the record: Judgments being arrested, only for *intrinsic* causes, i. e. such only as are *apparent* on the record (*d*).

§ 5. Anciently, judgments were constantly arrested, for defects or faults merely *formal*, in the pleadings, or other parts of the record; but, by the various *English* statutes of *amendments* and *jeofails*, which extend from the reign of *Edward the Third*, to that of *Anne* (*e*), this evil has been remedied. And as the law now is, judgments are, by these statutes, protected against arrest, for mere *formal* defects in general, and also for various others, which have been deemed *substantial*, but which are specifically enumerated in, and expressly cured by, some one or other of the same statutes.

(*c*) 8 Co. 120. b. 133. b. 1 Lutw. 608. 4 Burr. 2146. Wightw. 354.

(*d*) 3 Black. Com. 393.

(*e*) Bac. Abr. *Amendment*, &c, B.

CHAP. X.

§ 6. As to the *specific* defects and omissions, which are cured by the several statutes, above alluded to, it is unnecessary here to enter into any detail: As the several enactments, being in their nature positive, cannot be referred to any one general and uniform principle, and can be understood, only by a recurrence to the statutes themselves (*f*).

Causes of arrest of judgment, after verdict.

§ 7. But as *substantial defects, in general*, are not cured by any of these enactments; it remains to enquire, what defects and omissions are cured by verdict, or otherwise, *without* the aid of any statute, and upon *common-law* principles. For, independently of any statute-provision, many defects in pleading, which have been formerly deemed *substantial*, and which would be otherwise fatal, are aided by *verdict:* And the principal object of enquiry, under the head of *Arrest of Judgment*, is, *what* defects of this sort are, and what are not, cured by *verdict*, on *common-law* principles?

§ 8. *Formal* defects and errors in the record, being now harmless, except on special demurrer; it follows, that judgment can be arrested, for no other than substantial faults; and these may exist, either in the *pleadings*, or, where a verdict has been found, in the *verdict* (*g*). Thus, if the *declaration*, on which the plaintiff has obtained a verdict, is *totally defective* in substance, or *varies totally* from the *writ*, (as, if the one sounds in *debt*, and the other in *tort*);

(*f*) *Vid.* Bac. Abr. *ubi sup.*
(*g*) 3 Black. Com. 393. 1 Salk. 365.

judgment may be arrested on the *defendant's* motion: Or if — the declaration being good — the plea in bar, on which the defendant has obtained a verdict, is radically defective; judgment may be arrested, on the motion of the *plaintiff* (h). In both these cases, the defect, which sustains the motion, is in the *pleadings.*

Faults in the verdict.

§ 9. And if the pleadings are perfect, but the jury find a verdict *varying materially* from the issue, instead of finding the matter in issue itself, either way; judgment will be arrested, for the insufficiency of *the verdict* (i): Because the court cannot learn from it, for which party judgment ought to be given.

§ 10. In regard to the arresting of judgment, *after verdict*, it is a universal rule, that any defect in the record, which would render a judgment, in pursuance of the verdict, *erroneous*, is a sufficient ground for arresting the judgment (k). For no court should do so nugatory an act, as to render a judgment, which, when rendered, must be *erroneous.*

In pursuing this subject, it will be proper to treat of arrest of judgment,

I. For defects in *the pleadings;* and

II. For defects in the *verdict.*

(h) 3 Black. Com. 395. Cro. Eliz. 778. 2 Vent. 196.
(i) 3 Black. Com. 393.
(k) 1 Salk. 77. 2 Roll. Ab. 716. Com. Dig. *Pleader*, S. 47.

CHAP. X.

For faults in the pleadings.

§ 11. I. Under the first of these heads, it is an invariable rule, that *no* defect in the pleadings, which would not have been fatal to them, on *general demurrer*, can ever be a sufficient cause for arresting judgment (*l*). The principle of this rule is apparent, from the consideration, that all merely *formal* defects in pleading are aided, except on *special* demurrer, assigning them for cause; and consequently, that all defects, on either side, which would not have been fatal on *general* demurrer, are cured by the adverse party's pleading to *issue*, or by a *default* — in other words, by his omitting to demur *specially*.

§ 12. It is, however, by no means universally true, *è converso*, that every defect in the pleadings, which would have been fatal on general demurrer, is a sufficient ground for arresting judgment, after a *general verdict* (*m*) (1). For if the pleading of the party, for whom such a verdict has been found, is faulty, in omitting some particular fact or circumstance, without which he ought not to have judgment, *but which is, nevertheless, implied in, or inferrible from*, the finding of those facts, which *are* ex-

(*l*) 3 Black. Com. 394. Carth. 389.
(*m*) Iid. Doug. 683.

(1) By a *general* verdict is meant a verdict, found in *the terms* of *the issue*. A *special* verdict is one *not* following the terms of the issue, but finding certain *special facts*, and referring it to the court, as a question of law, whether those facts maintain the issue — a question, bearing a strong analogy to that which is raised by a *demurrer to evidence*, (*ante*, ch. 9, § 52.)

pressly alleged and found; the pleading is aided, (because the omission is supplied), by *the verdict:* In other words, the court, in such a case, must *presume* that the fact or circumstance omitted was *proved to the jury* (*n*).

§ 13. The criterion, by which to distinguish between such defects in a declaration, as are, and such as are not, cured by a general verdict for the plaintiff, is laid down by Lord *Mansfield*, in the case of *Rushton* v. *Aspinall*, to the following effect: Where the *statement* of the plaintiff's cause of action, and that only, is defective or inaccurate, the defect is cured by a general verdict in his favour; because — 'to entitle him to recover, all *circumstances* necessary, in form or substance, to complete the title so imperfectly stated, *must be proved* at the trial'; and it is, therefore, 'a fair presumption, that they were proved'. But where *no cause of action* is stated, the omission is not cured by verdict. For, as no right of recovery was necessary to be *proved*, or could have been legally proved, under such a declaration; there can be no ground for presuming that it was proved, at the trial (*o*). The same criterion extends, *mutatis mutandis*, to defects in

(*n*) Iid. Cro. Jac. 44. 1 Saund. 228. a. (n. 1.) T. Ray. 487. Carth. 304. 1 Salk. 365. Forrest's Rep. 54.

(*o*) Doug. 683. See Plowd. 202. 1 Saund. 228. c. (n. 1.) 3 Black. Com. 395. 1 Salk. 365. Bac. Abr. *Verdict*, X. Hob. 56. c. (n. 4.) *Williams*' ed. Carth. 130. 1 Lev. 308. Cro. Car. 497. 1 Mod. 292. Com. R. 116. 3 Wils. 274. 4 T. R. 472. 7 Ib. 523. 2 Burr. 1159. 2 Mass. R. 522.

CHAP. X. the defendant's *plea*, or in any other part of the pleadings.

§ 14. The ground or principle, on which any fact, not alleged, is to be *presumed*, in support of a general verdict, is, that as the verdict must be considered as *true*, and as founded on *legal evidence* exhibited at the trial; the Court, (which can judge only from the record), must *presume* in support of it, that any and every fact, (not alleged), *the proof of which was necessary to justify* the jury in finding as they have done, was *proved* to them, on the trial: In other words, the court must, in support of such a verdict, presume every thing to have been proved, *without* proof of which, the jury *could not have truly found* from the evidence, as they have found (*p*). And thus the verdict, by legal and necessary *intendment*, SUPPLIES facts, omitted in the pleadings. This explanation of the principle, on which omissions in the pleadings are aided by verdict, will be found to coincide, in its result, with the statement, given in the twelfth section, of what is to be presumed in support of a general verdict. But as this principle, though simple and rational in itself, has often presented nice and difficult questions, in its application to particular cases; a somewhat detailed illustration of it may be useful:

(*p*) Iid. 1 Vent. 109. 1 Saund. 228. (n. 1.) 2 Ib. 171. c. T. Ray. 487. 1 T. R. 145. 545. 7 Ib. 518. Bull. N. P. 320. 321. 1 Salk. 130. Cowp. 827.

§ 15. If, in an action of trespass, the declaration omits to lay the trespass on any particular *day* (an omission, which by the common law, is a good cause of general demurrer), but the defendant pleads to issue, and a general verdict is found against him; the declaration is cured by the verdict (*q*). For, as the court must presume that the trespass was duly *proved* to the jury; it must also follow, as a necessary presumption, that the wrong was proved to have been done on *some* particular day, and that *before* the commencement of the suit: Because proof of a trespass, *subsequent* to the issuing of the writ, would have been *legally inadmissible*. And thus, all that was necessary to be supplied in the declaration, viz. *some particular time*, when the trespass was committed—is, by legal intendment, supplied by *the verdict*.

§ 16. Thus also, if in trover for converting, or trespass for taking away, the plaintiff's goods, the declaration omits to allege their *value;* but the defendant pleads to issue, and the jury find a general verdict, with damages, for the plaintiff; the declaration, though it would have been ill, at common law, on general demurrer, is aided by the verdict (*r*). For it must be presumed, from the jury's having assessed the *damages*, that the value was in proof before them. And thus by intendment, as in the last

(*q*) 3 Black. Com. 394. Carth. 389. 2 Salk. 662. 5 Mod. 287. Bac. Abr. *Verdict*, X.

(*r*) 1 Sid. 39. Bac. Abr. *Trespass*, I. 2. (1). Esp. Dig. 407. 4 Burr. 2455. *arg.* *Vid.* 2 Johns. R. 421. *note.*

CHAP. X.

case, the *verdict ascertains* what the declaration had omitted.

§ 17. Upon the same principle, if a party pleads a grant of any thing, lying only *in grant*, (as an incorporeal hereditament), without alleging that the conveyance was *by deed*, and the opposite party, instead of demurring, as he might, for the omission of that allegation, traverses the grant, and the jury find it; the omission is aided by the verdict (*s*). For as the court is bound to presume a grant *proved* to the jury; and as nothing, except *a deed* would have been *legal evidence* of the grant; it must necessarily be presumed that *a deed* of grant was proved, on the trial.

§ 18. If a party pleads the *grant of a reversion*, without alleging the *attornment* of the tenant—which, by the common law, was necessary to the completion of the grantee's title—and on issue joined, the jury *find* the grant; the pleading is cured—though the omission would have been fatal, by the common law, on demurrer. And the result is the same, whether the finding is upon a special issue, taken on *the grant alone*, or upon the general issue. As where in debt for rent, by the grantee of a reversion, the declaration alleges *the grant*, but omits to state an *attornment*: Here, if the defendant pleads *nil debet*, and the jury find the issue for the

(*s*) Hutt. 54. 10 Mod. 301. Bac. Abr. *Verdict*, X. 2 Wils. 376. 1 Saund. 228. b. (n. 1).

plaintiff; the declaration is cured by the verdict (*t*). For, the jury having, under the direction of the judge, found *the grant;* the court must intend, that it was found upon evidence sufficient to prove a *complete* grant (2).

§ 19. Again: If, in debt on bond, the defendant pleads *nil debet*, and the plaintiff, instead of demurring, joins in the issue tendered by the plea, and the verdict is for the defendant; the plea is cured, and the defendant entitled to judgment (*u*). For, as the

(*t*) 2 Show. 233. 1 Saund. 228. a. b. (n. 1). Com. Dig. *Pleader*, C. 87. T. Ray. 487. Bac. Abr. *Verdict*, X. Lawes' Pl. 48.
(*u*) 2 Wils. 10.

(2) An example, several times given in the books, of the effect of a verdict, in aiding defective pleadings, is that of a *feoffment* pleaded, without an express allegation of *livery of seisin;* in which case, the *verdict*, it is said, cures the defect in the pleading (1 T. R. 145. 4 Ib. 472. 1 Saund. 228 b. (n. 1). But with submission, this example seems not to be an instance, in which the pleading is *aided by verdict*, or in which it requires any such aid. For, according to high and multiplied authority, ancient and modern, the allegation of a feoffment, *without* an averment of livery of seisin, is good, both in substance and form, on *demurrer* (Co. Litt. 303. b. Cro. Jac. 411. 8 Co. 82. b. Cro. Eliz. 401. Plowd. 149. Com. Dig. *Pleader*, E. 9. Bac. Abr. *Pleas*, &c, I. 7. Lawes' Pl. 48). For a feoffment, *ex vi termini*, *implies* livery of seisin; since the act of enfeoffing is the delivering of seisin. And therefore, alleging a *feoffment* is, in effect, alleging *livery of seisin* (see ch. 3, § 6): Whereas, in the above case of the grant of a reversion, the attornment is an act, *distinct* from that of the grant itself, and to be done by a different party. And as the former act is, therefore, not *implied* in the latter; the allegation of the one is *not*, by any implication, an allegation of the other (8 Co. 82. b).

plaintiff has, by joining issue on the plea, *waved the estoppel*, which, (if he had demurred), the deed would have furnished, in his favour, and has submitted to the jury the naked question of the defendant's being *indebted*, which the verdict has negatived; the inference must be, that it was *disproved* to the jury.

§ 20. On the other hand, facts not alleged, and which are *not implied in, or inferrible from*, those which are alleged and found, *cannot* be presumed to have been proved to the jury: In other words, no fact, not alleged, can be presumed in support of a verdict, unless proof of its existence must have been *involved in*, or is *inferrible from*, the proof of those which are alleged, and which the verdict has found (*v*): There being no foundation, furnished by the record, for any intendment or inference, that any other fact, not averred, was *proved* at the trial.

§ 21. If then, the declaration is totally defective *in substance* — as in the common instance given, of an action of slander for calling the plaintiff a *Jew* — a verdict for the plaintiff will not entitle him to judgment (*w*). For the words charged, being not *actionable*, the finding of the jury cannot make them so; and the defect in the declaration is not in the *statement* of the cause of action (for no manner of

(*v*) Doug. 683. 3 Black. Com. 394. 1 Saund. 228. a. b. c. (n. 1). 1 T. R. 145. 3 Burr. 1728. Cowp. 826. Bac. Abr. *Verdict*, X. 17 Johns. R. 456. 4 Pick. 341. 11 Mass. R. 308.

(*w*) 3 Black. Com. 394.

stating the words can make them actionable); but in the alleged *cause of action itself*. And nothing is *implied in*, or *inferrible from*, the finding, which can constitute a right of recovery.

§ 22. If the declaration omits to allege any substantive fact, which is essential to a right of action, and which is *not implied in*, or *inferrible from*, the finding of those which are alleged; a verdict for the plaintiff does *not* cure the defect (*x*). Thus in assumpsit, if the declaration alleges no *consideration*, and the jury find a verdict for the plaintiff: judgment must be arrested (*y*). For the fact, that the defendant promised, furnishes no legal intendment or inference, that the promise was founded upon any consideration.

§ 23. Thus also, in an action by a master, for a battery committed upon his servant, if the declaration omits to allege a *loss of service*, in consequence of the beating; a verdict for the plaintiff does not cure the omission (*z*). For it is very manifest, that proof of the alleged battery, and of all the other facts usually alleged in such a declaration, does not necessarily involve any proof of a *loss of service;* and therefore no legal intendment can *imply* the latter fact, from the finding of the jury.

(*x*) Bac. Abr. *Verdict*, X. Com. Dig. *Pleader*, C. 87.

(*y*) 1 Salk. 364. Com. Dig. *Pleader*, C. 87. 7 T. R. 351. (n. 1). 1 Vent. 27.

(*z*) Keilw. 71. b. 72. a. 10 Co. 130. Yelv. 90. (n. 1). 6 Mod. 127. Bac. Abr. *Verdict*, X.

§ 24. Again: If in an action, for an injury done by the defendant's *dog*, to the person or beast of the plaintiff, the declaration omits the *scienter* (an allegation of the defendant's previous *knowledge*, that his dog was addicted to similar mischief); a verdict of 'guilty' will not aid the declaration (*a*). For all the material facts alleged in the declaration, viz. the defendant's ownership of the mischievous animal — the latter's addictedness to similar mischief — and the damage done to the plaintiff — furnish no *legal* inference of the defendant's previous *science:* Since proof of any, or all, of the former facts, does not necessarily *involve* any evidence of the latter.

§ 25. So also, when the right of action depends upon the performance of a *condition precedent*, by the plaintiff, if the declaration omits to allege performance of it, or what is in law equivalent to performance; the omission is incurable by verdict (*b*), For in every case of this kind, performance of the condition, or what is equivalent to it, is of the *gist* of the action; and is, moreover, a *distinct*, *collateral* fact, which cannot be *inferred* or *presumed* from the other facts necessary to be alleged (3). Thus, if

(*a*) 2 Salk. 662. 3 Ib. 12. 13. Bac. Abr. *Verdict*, X. 1 Ld Ray. 109. Doug. 683. Esp. Dig. 601–2.

(*b*) 6 T. R. 710. 7 Ib. 125. 8 Ib. 366. 2 H. Black. 574. 582. n. 1 East, 203. 2 Saund. 352. (n. 3.) 3 Bulstr. 299. 2 Bos. & P. 447. Com. Dig. *Pleader*, C. 69.

---

(3) It is said, (1 Saund. 228. b. n. 1.) by Mr Serjeant *Williams* — an authority, not to be slightly questioned — that 'when

A. engages to pay to B. a sum of money, on a certain future day, on condition that B. shall, before that day, perform certain services for A.; it is clear, that unless B. performs the services, within the time named, he can have no right to recover the money; and it is equally clear, that the finding of the only other material facts in the case, viz. the making of the promise, and the non-payment of the money, neither raises, nor even conduces to raise, any legal presumption of the performance of the *services*.

§ 26. A *default* cures no defect in the declaration, which would not have been aided, on a *general*

---

a promise depends upon the performance of something, to be first done by him, to whom the promise is made, and in an action on such promise, the declaration does not aver performance by the plaintiff, or that he was ready to perform, and there is a verdict for the plaintiff; such omission *is cured by the verdict*, by the common law, but is a fatal objection, after a judgment by default.' But with great deference, the former of these propositions, although apparently countenanced by a general remark of Lord *Mansfield*, in the case referred to by the learned writer, (2 Burr. 900), appears inconsistent, not only with the whole current of authority; but also with the definite and well established principles, stated and explained in the text. Indeed the principle of the great and standard case, as it may properly be called, of *Rushton v. Aspinall*, before mentioned (§ 13) seems to stand in direct opposition to the rule laid down by Mr Serjeant *Williams*. In that case, which was an action against the *indorser* of a bill of exchange, the declaration, though complete in other respects, alleged neither a *demand* on the acceptor, nor *notice* to the defendant, of the dishonor of the bill. And after *a general verdict* for the plaintiff, judgment was arrested, by the court of King's Bench, who held *each* of

CHAP. X.

demurrer (c). For *no* fact can be presumed to have been proved, when *no trial* has been had, and no proof exhibited. And therefore a motion in arrest of judgment, for the insufficiency of the declaration, *after a default*, operates precisely as a general demurrer to the declaration would have operated.

§ 27. The same principle, which renders radical defects, in a *declaration*, incurable by verdict, extends to all stages of the pleadings, on either side. And therefore, if the defendant's *plea* discloses no legal defence; a verdict in his favour will not make the plea good. And judgment may be arrested, (the declaration being sufficient) on the *plaintiff's* motion (*d*).

For faults in the issue.

§ 28. It often happens, that when the pleadings are otherwise perfect, judgment is arrested, after verdict, for some radical fault in the *issue*. In cases of this kind, in which the same principle governs,

(c) 2 Burr. 900. 1 Saund. 228. a. b. c. (n. 1.) 2 Stra. 1271. 1 Wils. 171. 10 East, 364.
(d) 3 Black. Com. 395.

---

the omissions, above mentioned, fatal. The precise principle of this determination was, that as against the *indorser* of a bill, whose liability is only secondary and conditional, such demand and notice are *conditions precedent*; the performance of which, or either of which, cannot be presumed, from the finding of the facts alleged in the declaration; because proof of all the latter facts does not, and cannot, *involve* proof of such performance. *Vid.* 2 New Rep. 239. 240.

as in all the foregoing examples, the general rule is, that if the issue is *immaterial, so that the court cannot discover, from the finding upon it, for which party judgment ought to be given,* the judgment must be arrested (*e*). Thus, if in an action against husband and wife, for a wrong committed by *her* alone, they plead that *they* are not guilty, and the verdict is for them; the judgment must be arrested (*f*). For the verdict determines nothing, from which the court can discover how judgment ought to be given; since the matter, put in issue, is not that, which the declaration charges: The complaint being, not that the *defendants* are guilty of the wrong; but only that the *wife* is so; and the verdict does not show whether *she* is, or is not guilty, but only that *both* defendants are not so. Thus also, if in assumpsit against an executor, on a promise, alleged to have been made by his *testator*, the defendant pleads that *he* did not promise; a verdict in his favour, on this plea, cannot avail him; and judgment will be arrested, (if the declaration be sufficient) on the *plaintiff's* motion (*g*).

§ 29. Whenever, then, one of the parties, *passing by what is material* in the adverse pleading, tenders an issue upon a point which is *not so*, and obtains a verdict, the judgment must, regularly, be ar-

(*e*) Com. Dig. *Pleader*, R. 18. 2 Saund. 319. a. b. (n. 6.) 1 Ib. 228. a. b. (n. 1.) 1 Lev. 32. Carth. 371. Bac. Abr. *Pleas*, &c, M. 6 Mod. 1. 2 Salk. 579. Ld Ray. 707. 922.

(*f*) Cro. Jac. 5. Lawes' Pl. 176. Bac. Abr. *Pleas*, &c, M.

(*g*) 3 Black. Com. 395. 2 Vent. 196.

CHAP. X.

rested (*h*). Thus, if the declaration and plea in bar are both good, and the plaintiff traverses an *immaterial* part of the plea, and obtains a verdict; judgment must, according to the general rule, be arrested. And generally in such cases, (i. e. where the only fault is in *the issue*), the court, on arresting the judgment, will award a *repleader*, in order that a better issue may be framed (*i*) (4).

Repleader when awarded.

(*h*) 3 Black. Com. 395. 1 Saund. 228. a. b. (n. 1.) 2 Ib. 319. a. b. (n. 6.) Com. Dig. *Pleader*, R. 18. Bac. Abr. *Pleas*, &c, M. Cro. Jac. 434. 2 Burr. 944. 1 Ib. 302. 2 Stra. 994.

(*i*) Iid.

---

(4) As the plea in bar, in the case here supposed, is a sufficient answer to the declaration; and as the substance of the plea stands confessed, by not being traversed; the question can hardly fail to suggest itself— why should not the court, instead of awarding a *repleader*, give judgment directly for the defendant, who appears — though not from the *verdict*, yet from *the whole record* — entitled to it, the verdict notwithstanding ? For the verdict decides nothing against him; and the pleadings show, confessedly, sufficient matter in bar of the action. And the same question must naturally present itself, whenever a *repleader* is awarded, after verdict, for the immateriality of the issue. The true answer to this inquiry appears to be, that the awarding of a *repleader*, in such a case, was originally rather an act of *indulgence* to the party who tendered an improper issue, than a matter of *strict right:* An indulgence, grounded on the presumption, that the issue was misjoined through the *inadvertence and oversight* of the pleaders; and that a further opportunity to plead would probably result in a *material* issue, decisive of the merits of the cause. And this indulgence may have been deemed the more reasonable, inasmuch as the traverse, though faulty, is found to be *true;* and also as the party, to whom it was tendered, has, by joining in it, *concurred in occasioning a useless trial*, which he might have prevented, by demurring to the traverse.

§ 30. Such is the usual course, whenever the *verdict* does not show for whom judgment ought to be rendered; or in other words, when the matter of fact, found by it, is *immaterial*, or *not decisive* of the right in controversy (*k*); though in some cases of this kind, as will hereafter appear, a *repleader* is refused, and final judgment rendered, according to the legal merits of the case, as they appear from *the pleadings*, and without reference to the *verdict*.

§ 31. An issue, as has been stated in a former chapter, (ch. 6, § 34) is sometimes so framed, that a verdict upon it, on *one* side, is decisive of the merits of the cause, when a finding *the other* way would not be so. In such cases, the general rule of the common law is, that when the finding is thus *decisive* of the merits, it cures the issue; but that when it is not *thus* decisive, the judgment must be arrested, and a *repleader* awarded (*l*). But, by the statute 32 H. 8, c. 30, such issues are now. in general, as *negatives pregnant*, aided by a verdict *either* way. Yet an issue, *strictly* immaterial, (i. e. including *nothing material*, so that *no* verdict upon it, for either party, can decide the merits of the controversy), remains incurable, as at common law (*m*).

Repleader when refused.

§ 32. A repleader, for the immateriality of the issue, is never awarded, it seems, for that party who

(*k*) Gilb. H. C. P. 147. 1 Lev. 32. 2 Saund. 319. a. (n. 6.)

(*l*) 2 Saund. 317. 319. a. (n. 6.) Cro. Jac. 550. 2 Lev. 11.

(*m*) Carth. 371. 2 Mod. 137. 2 Saund. 319. a. (n. 6.) Cro. Jac. 434. 585. 1 Saund. 228. (n. 1.)

CHAP. X.

tendered the issue (*n*). And therefore, if the verdict is *against him;* judgment must also regularly go against him. For as the fault in the issue commenced on *his* part — his traverse being bad in law; and it being, moreover, found to be false in fact; it is deemed unreasonable to grant him the indulgence of a repleader. Yet, if the verdict were *for* the same party; a repleader would, regularly, be awarded, on the grounds stated in the foregoing sections, and in the last preceding note.

Issue on a negative pregnant.

§ 33. By the *common* law, the same diversity prevails, as to the awarding or refusal of a repleader, when the verdict is founded on an issue, including both what is *material*, and what is *not so* — in other words, when the traverse, on which the issue was joined, is a *negative pregnant;* in which case, if the verdict is *for* the party tendering the traverse, the judgment must, by the common law, be arrested, and a repleader awarded; though if the verdict were *against* him, judgment would pass against him (*o*).

§ 34. The reason of this diversity, in regard to the effect of the verdict, when the issue is joined on a *negative pregnant*, has been already suggested, (ch. 6, § 34): viz. that when a verdict is found on

(*n*) Doug. 396. 747. 749. Com. Dig. *Pleader*, R. 18. 1 Saund. 308. 2 Ib. 319. b. (n. 6.) Tidd, 824. 1 H. Black. 644. 1 Ld Ray. 170. 8 Mod. 174.

(*o*) Co. Litt. 126. a. 303. a. Gilb. H. C. P. 147. 2 Saund. 319. (n. 6.) 1 Burr. 302.

such an issue, and the *only* fault, in the pleading, is in the issue, the finding, if against the party tendering the issue, will generally, and I trust, universally, show that judgment ought to go against him; although a verdict *for* him would determine nothing material to the merits of the cause.

§ 35. Thus, as heretofore stated, (ch. 6, § 34), if to a plea, that the plaintiff has released the cause of action, *since the date of the writ*, he traverses that he has released 'since the date of the writ' — thus making *the time*, which is immaterial, parcel of the issue; a verdict for *the defendant* would be plainly decisive in his favour, and entitle him to judgment: Whereas, a finding for the *plaintiff* — the party who *tendered* the traverse — would as plainly be indecisive; as being consistent with the supposable fact of a release, *before* the date of the writ. For the verdict ascertains nothing more, than that the alleged release was not made *after* the date of the writ — leaving the question, whether there was any release given at any time, undetermined. And therefore, according to the principles of the common law, the judgment must, in the case last supposed, be arrested, and a *repleader* awarded; though under the before mentioned statute 32 H. 8, c. 30, the issue, in this case also, is now made good by the verdict, and the party, *tendering* the traverse, entitled to judgment.

§ 36. So also, if in debt or assumpsit, the defendant pleads a tender, on a certain day; and the

CHAP. X.

replication denies that such tender was made *on that day*, (a denial, which is a mere *negative pregnant*); a verdict for the *defendant* would entitle him to judgment; while a finding for the *plaintiff*, *who tendered the issue*, would not show for whom judgment ought to be given. And therefore in this, as in the last preceding case, the judgment must, according to the principles of the *common* law, be arrested, and a *repleader* awarded. And this diversity, between the effect of a verdict for, and one against, the party, tendering the issue on a *negative pregnant*, will be found to exist, in every example of such an issue, heretofore given in this treatise, and probably to *all* issues of the same kind (5).

(5) Though issues, joined on *negatives pregnant*, are regularly aided, under the before mentioned statute, 32 H. 8, c. 30, by a verdict *either* way, (*ante*, §§ 31. 35); yet this is not universally the case. In one instance at least, an issue of this kind, if found *for* the party tendering it, is *not* aided by the statute. The instance referred to, is that of debt on an obligation payable *on, or before*, a particular day (as the 30*th* of January), and a plea of payment before the day, as on the 10*th* of the same January: In which case, if the plaintiff replies only, that the defendant did not pay 'on the 10th of January', and the jury find for the *plaintiff*; the finding is immaterial, and a repleader must still be awarded — though a verdict for the *defendant* would have been decisive, and have entitled him to judgment, (2 Stra. 994. 3 Black. Com. 395. 2 Burr. 944. 1 Ib. 301–2. Com. R. 148). Now, though the issue, tendered in this case, appears clearly to be only a *negative pregnant*, it is nevertheless not cured, under the above statute, by a verdict for the plaintiff, for a reason, peculiar to this particular case, and which has been heretofore stated, ch. 7, § 54.

§ 37. The foregoing rules and examples, from the 28th section, inclusive, are intended to explain the object, and the effect, of motions in arrest of judgment, when the *only* substantial defect in the pleadings is in *the issue*, on which the verdict has been found. But the effect of such motions may be varied essentially from those stated in the foregoing sections, by radical defects in the pleadings, which *precede* the issue, and which would render a repleader, or arrest of judgment, *nugatory*. For courts ought never to award a repleader, or to arrest judgment, for faults in the issue, when it is apparent, that *no useful end* can be attained, by so doing (*p*).

§ 38. And therefore, if it is apparent to the court, from the whole record, that *no manner* of joining issue could avail the party against whom the verdict is found — or in other words, that *no issue, which could be tendered* upon the MATTER of his pleading, as it is alleged, or in any form, in which it could be alleged, would be a *material* issue; a repleader cannot legally be awarded, nor judgment arrested, at *his* instance, for any fault in the issue joined (*q*). Thus, if the declaration is good — the plea in bar *totally* void of substance — and issue joined on any part, or the whole of the plea, and verdict is for the *plaintiff;* he is entitled to judgment — the immateriality of the matter of the issue

(*p*) 1 Stra. 397. Com. Dig. *Pleader*, R. 18.

(*q*) 1 Burr. 301. Cowp. 510. Bac. Abr. *Pleas*, &c, M. Com. Dig. *Pleader*, R. 18. 1 Stra. 394. 397. 398. 1 Salk. 173. 4 Burr. 2143. 2146.

CHAP. X.

notwithstanding. For in such a case, it would be plainly nugatory to award a repleader; since *no possible* issue, tendered upon such a plea, or upon the *matter* of it, in whatever manner alleged, could decide the merits of the cause. And it would be as plainly improper, to arrest the judgment—inasmuch as the plaintiff appears, from the whole record, clearly entitled to it (*r*).

§ 39. If, in trespass, for example, the defendant pleads, as a justification, matter, which *however* stated, could not amount to a justification in law, and on a traverse of the plea, the verdict is for the *plaintiff;* the latter is immediately entitled to judgment (*s*). For, upon the grounds last mentioned, a *repleader* would be nugatory; and as the whole record shows a right of recovery, in the plaintiff; it would be unjust to arrest the judgment.

§ 40. If however, the matter of the plea, in the case last supposed, had been *substantially a good* justification in law, but so inaccurately alleged, as to render the traverse of it immaterial, and the verdict, as before supposed, for the *plaintiff;* judgment must have been arrested, and a repleader awarded (*t*): Because, in the case, as now stated, it would appear from the record, that a *good* issue might be formed, upon the matter of the plea, when *properly pleaded;* and when this is the case, the ends of jus-

(*r*) 1 Stra. 394. 397. 398. 1 Salk. 173. 2 Pick. 614.

(*s*) 1 Stra. 398. 1 Burr. 302.

(*t*) Iid.

tice require that an opportunity, for forming such an issue, should be afforded.

§ 41. It is, therefore, a general rule, that whenever the matter of the pleading, on which the issue has been joined, is sufficient *in substance*, but so incorrectly pleaded, as to render the issue and finding indecisive, and the verdict is *for* the party tendering the issue; the judgment must be arrested and a repleader awarded (*u*): It being deemed reasonable, that after verdict, such mere *inaccuracies* should be corrected.

§ 42. In conformity to this principle is the following case:—To debt on bond, the defendant pleaded usury—counting upon the statute of usury, 'made of the *sixth* of Feb.' 13 Eliz. (whereas the statute was actually passed on the *second* of Feb.) The plaintiff replied, that the obligation was not made for usury, &c, '*against the form of the statute, in manner and form aforesaid.*' This issue was found for the *defendant;* but, as statutes of usury are, in their nature, *public* acts; the court knew judicially, that no such statute existed, as that pleaded by the defendant; and therefore held the finding to be clearly incorrect, and nugatory. But as the ground of the defence, (usury), was in substance sufficient in law; the issue and finding were faulty, only in consequence of an *inaccuracy in the mode of pleading* that defence; the court refused to give

(*u*) Cro. Eliz. 245. 1 Burr. 302.

CHAP. X.

judgment for the plaintiff, as the case stood, and awarded a *repleader* (v). For it was apparent, that the matter of the defence *might* be so pleaded, as to form the subject of a *good* issue (6): Whereas, when the pleading, on which the issue is joined, contains *no substance*, or none which could, in any form of statement, avail the pleader, the awarding of a *repleader* would, as has been before shown (*ante*, § 38), be altogether useless: Since no manner of pleading the same matter could form the subject of a *material* issue; nor would it be possible, in such a case, to lay the foundation of *such* an issue, unless the pleader were allowed, on pleading anew, to abandon the whole matter, first pleaded by him, and to allege a new and distinct ground of demand, or defence — which can never be allowed, as it would be, in effect, allowing a *departure*.

§ 43. In some cases, the greatest defects *in the issue* are not a sufficient ground for arresting judgment, after verdict. For if there be a radical defect, in any of the *previous* stages of the pleadings, and if the *first* defect, of this kind, is on the part of *him who moves* in arrest of judgment; the motion cannot prevail: Since in every such case, it must be

(v) Iid.

(6) In this case, the verdict was, indeed, *against* the party tendering the issue; but as it was judicially known to the court, and appeared, necessarily, from the record, that the finding was legally *untrue;* the determination was the same, as if the verdict had been *for* him, who tendered the issue — the plaintiff.

apparent, from the whole record, that judgment ought to pass against him. Thus, if an immaterial issue is joined upon a *good replication*, and found for the *defendant;* still if the *declaration* is radically defective, the defendant is entitled to judgment. For it would be useless to arrest the judgment, at the plaintiff's instance; since he could, by no possibility, be entitled to judgment upon such a declaration (*w*).

§ 44. And although the particular *part* of the pleadings, on which the issue is joined, be *good*, and the issue and finding be on a material point; yet if there exists a radical fault, (and that the first), in the previous pleading of him, *for* whom the verdict is found; judgment must, regularly, upon the foregoing principles, be arrested (*x*). Thus, if to a declaration, *defective in substance*, the defendant pleads a substantial defence, (as a *release* of the action), and upon a traverse of the plea, the verdict is for the *plaintiff*; judgment must be arrested. For there appears, upon the whole record, to be no right of action.

§ 45. And whenever the merits of a motion in arrest of judgment depend upon the sufficiency of any of the *previous* pleadings, the governing principle appears to be, that judgment ought never to be given for, nor arrested in behalf of, that party, in whose pleading the *first* substantial defect is found.

(*w*) 1 Ld Ray. 170. Hob. 56. 199. 200. 8 Co. 120. b.
(*x*) Iid.

CHAP. X.

Judgment, veredicto non obstante.

§ 46. In some cases, where the party, who has obtained a verdict, is not entitled to judgment upon it, the court not only arrest judgment *in pursuance* of the verdict; but immediately render judgment in chief, *veredicto non obstante*—i. e. in favour of the party, *against whom* the verdict has been found. But this, it seems, is done only in *very clear cases*, where there can be no doubt, that the party, against whom the issue is found, is, upon the whole record, entitled to judgment (*y*). This is done, for example, where a plea in bar, *confessing* a good declaration, is clearly *frivolous*, or so *totally destitute* of substance, as to constitute no semblance of a legal defence: In which case, (the right of recovery being confessed), to withhold from the plaintiff a judgment in chief, would be a virtual denial of justice. The judgment, in such cases, however, is given as upon *confession*, (the right of action being, in law, *confessed* by the plea), without regard to *the verdict* (*z*); as the latter decides nothing, either way.

§ 47. The awarding of a repleader, when it ought to be refused, or the refusal of it, when it ought to be awarded, is *error* (*a*): As the mistake must be to the prejudice of one, or the other, of the parties.

(*y*) 6 Mod. 2. 1 Ld Ray. 641. 1 Stra. 394. Cro. Eliz. 214. 8 Taunt. 413. 1 Chit. Pl. 634. Yelv. 24. (n. 1). Hob. 56. (n. 4). *Williams'* ed. 3 B. & A. 710. 4 Ib. 564. 8 Mass. R. 261. 5 Pick. 187.

(*z*) Iid.

(*a*) 6 Mod. 2. 2 Saund. 319. b. (n. 6). 2 Salk. 579. 1 Day, 27. 152. 1 Chitt. Pl. 633.

CHAP. X.

§ 48. When judgment is arrested, for any insufficiency in the issue, or other part of the pleadings, no *costs* are allowed to either party (*b*) — not to the party, on whose motion the judgment has been arrested; because he might have taken advantage of the insufficiency of his adversary's pleading, in an earlier stage of the proceedings, by *demurring*, and thus have prevented the delay, and expense of a trial—not to him, *against* whom the motion has prevailed; because, having no merits, he cannot be entitled to recover any thing.

§ 49. A repleader can properly be awarded, only after an *issue in fact* (joined and tried) (*c*): The main object of awarding it, being, as we have seen (*ante*, § 29), to enable the parties to substitute a good *issue*, for a bad one. It seems, however, that before the statutes of *jeofails*, repleaders were awarded, as well before as after the trial of the issue; because, in general, defects in the issue could not at common law, be cured by verdict. But now a repleader is, regularly, not awarded, until the issue has been *tried* (*d*); because, under those statutes, a verdict may possibly *cure* the fault in the issue, and thus supersede the necessity of repleading; and this point the court will not, generally,

(*b*) 2 Salk. 579. 6 Mod. 2. Com. Dig. *Pleader*, R. 18. 2 Vent. 196. 1 T. R. 267. 1 Stra. 617. Cowp. 407. 1 Chitt. Pl. 639.

(*c*) 3 Salk. 306. 2 Saund. 319. b. (n. 6). 2 Salk. 579. Bac. Abr. *Pleas*, &c, M. 1. 3. Com. Dig. *Pleader*, R. 18. 6 Mod. 3. 102. Carth. 371.

(*d*) Iid.

CHAP. X.

decide by *anticipation;* but will await the finding of the jury.

§ 50. A repleader cannot be awarded, after a demurrer (*e*). For, by the demurrer, the parties have put themselves upon the judgment of the court: and as the demurrer reaches back, through the whole record; the issue in law, raised by it, cannot, in the nature of the thing, be *immaterial or indecisive,* as an issue in fact may be. And on similar grounds, a repleader cannot be awarded, after a *writ of error* (*f*).

§ 51. Again—no repleader can be awarded, after a *default, or discontinuance* (*g*); not only because there is, in such case, no *issue tried,* but also because the default, or discontinuance, is a *waiver* of all further pleading, as well as an abandonment of all that may have been before pleaded, by the party defaulted, or discontinuing.

§ 52. The regular course, on a repleader awarded, is, for the pleadings to recommence, at that stage, at which the *first* deviation from good plead-

(*e*) Poph. 42. Sav. 89. Latch, 148. 3 Salk. 306. 6 Mod. 102. 2 Saund. 319. b. (n. 6). Com. Dig. *Pleader,* R. 18. 5 Co. 52. Bac. Abr. *Pleas,* &c, M. 3. 2 Lev. 12. 1 Chitt. Pl. 634.——3 Lev. 20. 440. *cont.*

(*f*) Iid.

(*g*) Bac. Abr. *Pleas,* &c, M. 3. 6 Mod. 3. Com. Dig. *Pleader,* R. 18. 2 Salk. 579. Comb. 323. 2 Saund. 319. b. (n. 6). 1 Chitt. Pl. 633.

ing occurred — or rather, at the *first* fault, which *occasioned* the immateriality of the issue (*h*). CHAP. X.

§ 53. If therefore, the only substantial fault is in the *traverse*, which tendered the immaterial issue; the pleading is to commence *de novo*, from that point, by the tender of a new traverse (*i*). But if the pleading, on which the issue was first tendered, — whether it be the declaration, plea in bar, replication, or other part of the pleading — be, (although good in substance), so incorrectly framed, as to render the issue, tendered upon it, immaterial; the repleading must begin, at the *same* stage or part of the pleadings — in order that it may be so corrected, as to furnish the subject of a material issue (*k*).

§ 54. But though the *immediate object* of repleading is only to produce a good *issue;* yet, as the award of a repleader is in *general* terms — '*quod partes replacitent;*' either party, it seems, may avail himself of this general award, for the purpose of correcting all *mere inaccuracies*, in any part of his previous pleading — though not for the purpose of alleging any *new and distinct ground* of demand, or defence (*l*).

(*h*) 1 Ld Ray. 169. Com. Dig. *Pleader*, R. 18. 2 Saund. 319. b. (n. 6). 6 Mod. 2. 2 Salk. 579. T. Ray. 458. 1 Burr. 301. 302. 3 Black. Com. 395.

(*i*) Iid. 2 Vent. 196. 2 Stra. 994.

(*k*) Iid.

(*l*) 1 Ld Ray. 169. Com. Dig. *Pleader*, R. 18. 2 Salk. 579.

For faults in the verdict.

§ 55. II. Judgment is sometimes arrested, when the pleadings are good, for faults in the *verdict* (*m*). If the verdict *varies substantially* from the issue, (as if, instead of finding the matter in issue, either way, the jury find something *foreign* to it); judgment must be arrested — because the finding does not ascertain the matter of fact in issue, and cannot therefore show, for which party judgment ought to be given (*n*).

§ 56. The rule is the same, when the verdict finds only *part* of the matter in issue — omitting to find, either way, another *material* part (*o*). For it is the duty of the jury to ascertain, and that of the court to give judgment upon, *all* the material facts, put in issue by the pleadings. But a verdict, finding the whole *substance* of the issue is good — although it be silent, as to what is *immaterial* (*p*): Since the latter cannot affect the merits of the controversy.

§ 57. A verdict, finding the whole issue, or the substance of it, is not vitiated, by finding *more* (*q*). For the finding of what was not in issue, is but *surplusage;* and *utile per inutile non vitiatur.*

(*m*) Bac. Abr. *Verdict*, M.

(*n*) 2 Roll. Abr. 707. 719. Bac. Abr. *Verdict*, O. 2 Vent. 151.

(*o*) Cro. Eliz. 133. Andr. 156. Bac. Abr. *Verdict*, M. 3 Leon. 82. 2 Stra. 1089.

(*p*) Co. Litt. 227. a.

(*q*) Reg. Pl. 219. 6 Co. 46. Bac. Abr. *Verdict*, N. 6 Mass. R. 304.

§ 58. In general, where one count in a declaration is good, and another substantially ill, if the *jury*, upon a plea to the whole declaration, or upon a default, find a general verdict for the plaintiff, with *entire* damages, (i. e. without *discriminating* in the assessment of the damages, between the different counts); the defendant may arrest the judgment; or if judgment is given, in pursuance of the verdict, may reverse it by writ of error (*r*). For it is impossible for the court, judging, as it must, from the record alone, to discover, on which count the damages were assessed, or what proportion of them may have been assessed on the one, or the other; and the jury, as the law presumes, are as likely to have assessed them, on a bad count, as on a good one (7).

(*r*) 1 T. R. 151. 508. 532. 3 Ib. 435. 2 Saund. 171. b. (n. 1.) Bac. Abr. *Damages*, D. 3. Cro. Eliz. 329. Bull. N. P. 8. 2 H. Black. 318. Doug. 731. 1 Caines R. 347. 2 Mass. R. 53. 408. 5 Greenleaf, 446. 9 Pick. 547.

---

(7) In *Grant* v. *Astle*, (Doug. 730), Lord *Mansfield* expressed his disapprobation of this rule, as being 'inconvenient and ill-founded'; and the courts of several of the United States have rejected it, (2 Connect. R. 324. 338. 2 Bay, 204. 439. 1 Hen. & Munf. 361). Yet, no rule appears to be more clearly warranted, by the original principles of law, than this. For the judgment of the court, which is only an inference of law, from the facts ascertained upon the record, must always be formed from the *face of the record itself, and from that alone*. And as the jurors are, and must be, presumed to know nothing of the sufficiency or insufficiency of counts; the conclusion seems perfectly just, in legal theory, that the damages are as likely to have been assessed, in part, or in whole, upon a bad count, as upon a good one. In

CHAP. X.

§ 59. The above rule, however, applies only to *civil* actions. If therefore, an *indictment* contains several counts, of which one is good, and the others ill; the court, on a general verdict of 'guilty', will award the punishment, on the *good* counts only (*s*). But this rule is, in no degree, inconsistent with the principle of that which prevails, in civil suits. For, in criminal cases, no *damages* are assessed; nor is it the province of the jury to decide upon the *punishment*, incurred by the offence. This is to be determined, exclusively by the *court;* whose proper duty it is, to judge of the sufficiency of the several counts, and to give sentence against the prisoner, upon that, or those, only, which they find to be sufficient in law.

§ 60. In *civil* cases also, where the declaration contains a good and a bad count, and a general verdict is found for the plaintiff, with *entire* damages; if it appears, from the notes of the judge, before whom the trial was had, that *no* part of the evidence, exhibited to the jury, applied to the bad count; the verdict may be *amended*, by order of the court, so as to apply to the good count only: After

(*s*) 2 Burr. 985. Doug. 730. 1 Bos. & P. 186-7. 1 Salk. 384. 2 Ld Ray. 886. 1 Johns. R. 322.

---

regard to the alleged practical *inconvenience* of the rule, courts, not bound by it, are doubtless at liberty to judge for themselves; but material deviations from well established principles of the common law, are, in general — to say the least — of very questionable expediency.

which amendment, the court will give judgment, (in pursuance of the verdict), for the plaintiff, on that count only (*t*). For, as the verdict stands, after the amendment, and before judgment is given, it appears from the face of the record itself, that the damages were assessed only on the good count.

§ 61. If the jury assess damages *separately*, upon each of the counts, where some are good, and others ill; the court will arrest the judgment on the bad counts only; and give judgment for the plaintiff, for the damages assessed on those which are good (*u*): For in this case, the record will distinctly show, to *what part* of the damages assessed, the plaintiff is by law entitled, and to what part of them he has no legal claim; and the court are thus enabled to distinguish between them, in giving judgment.

§ 62. If, in a *special* verdict, the jury find only the *evidence* of a material fact, instead of the fact itself, or otherwise omit to find, upon such a fact, either way; no judgment can be rendered upon the finding, for either party: Since a matter of fact, essential to the determination of the cause, is left unascertained by the verdict (*v*). Thus, if in trover, on the general issue pleaded, the jury return a special verdict, finding the property in the goods to be

(*t*) Doug. 376. 1 Saund. 171. b. (n. 1.) 1 Bos. & P. 329. 7 Mass. R. 358. 2 Johns. Cas. 18. — *Vid.* 1 H. Black. 78. 6 Taunt. 67.

(*u*) 3 T. R. 433. 435. Stra. 189. 808. 4 Burr. 2022. *Vid.* 6 Taunt. 629.

(*v*) 10 Co. 56-7. 3 Burr. 1243. 1 East, 111. Esp Dig. 590.

in the plaintiff — the loss of them, by him — the finding of them, by the defendant — and the *refusal of the latter to restore them, on the plaintiff's demand* — without showing any fact, either amounting to a conversion, or disproving it; the court can render no judgment upon the verdict (*w*). For the *conversion*, which is the gist of the action, is neither found, nor denied, by it; the demand and refusal being only *prima facie evidence* of a conversion.

§ 63. In all the foregoing cases, in which judgment is arrested for defects in *the verdict*, a *venire de novo*, must be awarded — i. e. another jury must be summoned, to try the same issue (*x*); but no *repleader* is awarded in such a case — the fault being, not in the *pleading*, but in the *verdict*.

(*w*) Iid.

(*x*) Bac. Abr. *Verdict*, M. Doug. 377-8. 10 Co. 118. 119. 2 Stra. 1052-3. 6 T. R. 691.

THE END.

INDEX.

*** *The numerals stand for Chapters — the figures for Sections.*